The Twilight
of Britain

Social Policy and Social Theory Series

David Marsland, Series Editor

The Twilight of Britain

of Britain

Cultural Nationalism,
Multiculturalism,
and the Politics of
Toleration

G. Gordon Betts

 Transaction Publishers
New Brunswick (U.S.A.) and London (U.K.)

Library of Congress Catalog Number: 2001041591
ISBN: 0-7658-0065-9
Printed in the United States of America

Library of Congress Cataloging-in-Publication Data

Betts, G. Gordon, 1926-
    The twilight of Britain : cultural nationalism, multiculturalism, and the politics of toleration / G. Gordon Betts.
        p. cm.
    Includes bibliographical references and index.
    ISBN 0-7658-0065-9 (acid-free paper)
    1. Great Britain—Ethnic relations—History—20th century. 2. Great Britain—Politics and government—20th century. 3. Multiculturalism—Government policy—Great Britain. 4. Great Britain—Foreign relations—20th century. 5. Toleration—Government policy—Great Britain. 6. Nationalism—Social aspects—Great Britain. I. Title.

DA125.A1 B448 2001
305.8'00941'0904—dc21   2001041591

Contents

Acknowledgments

The origin of this book lies in a doctoral thesis I submitted in 1998–99 as a part-time mature student in the Department of Philosophy at the University of Kent at Canterbury. My time at Canterbury taught me that philosophy must not distance itself from the today's world, and should make its voice heard.

I wish to express special thanks to my supervisor, Laurence Chase, an expatriate from multicultural Los Angeles, who nurtured my interest in philosophy, encouraged me throughout the development of my thesis, and tolerated my views.

I should also like to express my appreciation of the efficient and friendly assistance with which I was provided by my editor Michael Paley and by the staff of the Kent County Libraries in accessing some of the less readily available books used in this study.

Grateful acknowledgment is made for permission to reprint the following copyright material:

Ahmed, A., "An Ambassador for Islam." Article first appeared in *CAM, University of Cambridge Alumni Magazine*, Issue No. X, Term X, 1995. Used by permission.

Alibhai-Brown, Y., *Who Do We Think We Are? Imagining the New Britain* (Allen Lane: The Penguin Press, 2000), pp. 1, 3–4, 103, 259, 271–272. Copyright 2000 by Yasmin Alibhai-Brown. Reproduced by permission of Penguin Books Ltd. and Yasmin Alibhai-Brown.

Ayer, A.J. and O'Grady, J., *A Dictionary of Philosophical Quotations* (Oxford: Blackwell Publishers, 1994). Used by permission of the publishers.

Beloff, M., *An Historian in the Twentieth Century* (New Haven, Yale University Press, 1992). Copyright 1992 by Yale University Press. Used by permission of the publisher.

Berger, B., "Multiculturalism and the Modern University" (*Partisan Review*, Vol. LX, No. 4, 1993). Used by permission of Brigitte Berger.

Bernstein, R., *Dictatorship of Virtue—Multiculturalism and the Battle for*

Excerpts from *The Culture of Contentment* by John Kenneth Galbraith. Copyright © 1992 by John Kenneth Galbraith. Reprinted by permission of Houghton Mifflin Company. All rights reserved (United States, Canada and Open Market). From *The Culture of Contentment* by J K Galbraith, published by Sinclair Stevenson. *Reprinted by permission of The Random House Group Ltd.* (British Commonwealth excluding Canada).

Excerpts from *The Good Society* by John Kenneth Galbraith. Copyright © 1996 by John Kenneth Galbraith. Reprinted by permission of Houghton Mifflin Company. All rights reserved (United States, Canada and Open Market). From *The Good Society* by J K Galbraith, published by Sinclair Stevenson. *Reprinted by permission of The Random House Group Ltd.* (British Commonwealth excluding Canada).

Ernst Gellner, *Thought and Change* (London: Weidenfeld and Nicolson, 1964. Used by permission of the publisher.

Reprinted by permission of the publisher from *We Are All Multiculturalists Now* by Nathan Glazer, Cambridge, Mass.: Harvard University Press, Copyright © 1997 by the President and Fellows of Harvard College.

Nathan Glazer, "The Universalization of Ethnicity" (*Encounter*, Cambridge, Mass.: Harvard University Press, 1975). Used by permission of the author.

Nathan Glazer, "The Ethnic Factor" (*Encounter*, Cambridge, Mass.: Harvard University Press, 1981). Used by permission of the author.

Nathan Glazer, "Limits of Loyalty" (*Nussbaum, M.C. For Love of Country—Debating the Limits of Patriotism*, Boston: Beacon Press, 1996). Used by permission of the author.

Gray, J., *Enlightenment's Wake* (London: Routledge, 1995). Used by permission of the publisher.

Gray, J,. "Toleration and the Currently Offensive Implication of the Loss of Judgement" (*The Loss of Virtue*, London: Social Affairs Unit, 1992). Used by permission.

Grosby, S., "The Verdict of History: the Inexpungeable Tie of Primordiality" (*Ethnic and Racial Studies*, Abingdon: Routledge Journals, Taylor & Francis Ltd, 1994), http://www.tandf.co.uk/journals. Used by permission of the publisher.

Denis Healey, *The Time of My Life* (London: Penguin Books Ltd., 1989), pp. 98–99, 115, 191, 223. Reproduced by permission of Penguin Books Ltd. (worldwide rights excluding USA and Canada). Reproduced from *The Time of My Life* by Denis Healey (Copyright © Denis Healey 1989) by permission of PFD on behalf of Lord Healey of Riddlesden (US and Canadian rights).

Honeyford, R., *The Commission for Racial Equality* (New Brunswick, NJ: Transaction Publishers, 1998). Used by permission.

From *The Clash of Civilizations and the Remaking of World Order* by

1997). Copyright © 1997 Nigel Nicolson. Reprinted by permission of Orion Publishing Group (worldwide rights excluding USA and Canada). Reprinted by permission of Penguin Putnam Inc. and the author (US and Canadian rights).

From *For Love of Country* by Martha C. Nussbaum, Copyright © 1996 by Martha C. Nussbaum and Joshua Cohen. Reprinted by permission of Beacon Press, Boston.

O'Hear, A., "Diana, Queen of Hearts," in *Faking It—The Sentimentalisation of Modern Society*, Anderson, D. and Mullen, P. (Eds.), London, Social Affairs Unit, 1998.

A Time to Declare © David Owen 1991, first published by Michael Joseph, 1991.

The Future of Multi-Ethnic Britain, by The Commission on the Future of Multi-Ethnic Britain, established by The Runnymede Trust, 2000, published by Profile Books. Used by permission.

Putnam, H., *Pragmatism* (Oxford: Blackwell Publishers, 1995). Used by permission of the publishers.

Joseph Raz, "Multiculturalism—A Liberal Perspective." This article was originally published in *Dissent* magazine, Winter 1994. To subscribe to *Dissent*: editors@dissentmagazine.org.

Joseph Raz, *The Morality of Freedom*, Oxford, Clarendon Press, 1986. Copyright Joseph Raz. Reprinted by permission.

Rex, J., *Race and Ethnicity* (Buckingham: Open University Press, 1986). Used by permission of the publisher.

Reproduced from Rex, J. (1991) 'The Political Sociology of a Multicultural Society' in *European Journal of Inter-cultural Studies*, vol. 2, no. 1, Trentham Books with permission.

From *Assimilation, American Style* by Peter D. Salins. Copyright © 1997 by Basic Books. Used by permission of the publisher.

From *The Disuniting of America: Reflections on a Multicultural Society* by Arthur M. Schlesinger, Jr. © 1992, 1991 by Arthur M. Schlesinger, Jr. Reprinted by permission of W.W. Norton & Company Ltd.

Excerpt from *The Cycles of American History* by Arthur M. Schlesinger, Jr. Copyright © 1986 by Arthur M. Schlesinger, Jr. Reprinted by permission of Houghton Mifflin Company. All rights reserved (US and its territories/Canadian rights). Reprinted by permission of Andre Deutsch Ltd (worldwide rights excluding Canada, USA, its dependencies, and the Phillipine Islands).

Schwartz, W.F., *Justice in Immigration* (New York: Cambridge University Press, 1995). Reprinted with the permission of Cambridge University Press.

Shaw, M.N., *International Law* (New York: Cambridge University Press, 1997). Reprinted with the permission of Cambridge University Press.

From David Sidorsky, "Multiculturalism and the University" in *Our Country, Our Culture* edited by Edith Kurzweil and William Phillips, Partisan Review Press, Boston, 1994). Used by permission of David Sidorsky.

Anthony D. Smith, *National Identity* (London: Penguin Books Ltd., 1991), p. 175. Reproduced by permission of Penguin Books Ltd. (worldwide rights excluding USA and Canada). *National Identity* (Reno, Nevada: University of Nevada Press, 1991). Used by permission of the publisher (US and Canadian rights).

Social Trends, No. 22, 30, 31/*Regional Trends*, No.35 (extract paraphrased) (Norwich: Controller H.M. Stationary Office). Crown copyright is reproduced with the permission of the Controller of Her Majesty's Stationary Office.

Spencer, I.R.G., *British Immigration Policy Since 1939* (London: Routledge, 1997). Used by permission of the publisher.

Lord Swann, *Education for All—The Report of the Committee of Inquiry into the Education of Children from Ethnic Minority Groups* (Norwich: Controller H.M. Stationery Office, 1985). Crown copyright is reproduced with the permission of the Controller of Her Majesty's Stationary Office.

Tamir, Yael; *Liberal Nationalism.* Copyright © 1993 by Princeton University Press. Reprinted by permission of Princeton University Press.

Reprinted from *Tolerance and Community* by Glenn Tinder, by permission of the University of Missouri Press. Copyright 1995 by the Curators of the University of Missouri.

Maurizio Viroli, *For Love of Country: An Essay on Patriotism and Nationalism* (1995; reissued 1997). Used by permission of Oxford University Press.

M. Walzer, "The New Tribalism." This article was originally published in *Dissent* magazine, Spring 1992. "Multiculturalism and Individualism." This article was originally published in *Dissent* magazine, Spring 1994. To subscribe to *Dissent*: editors@dissentmagazine.org.

Reprinted from *Social Forces*, Volume 55, February 1976. "Origins of Tolerance: Findings from a Replication of Stouffer's Communism, Conformity and Civil Liberties" by Williams, J.A, Nunn, C. et al. Copyright © The University of North Carolina Press.

The author apologises for any omissions. Every effort has been made to secure permissions to reprint quoted materials. Additional permissions may be added to future editions.

Preface

Dr. Betts' book provides a systematic and scholarly analysis of issues which, with very few exceptions, contemporary British social scientists either embarrassedly ignore or treat with liberalistic insouciance. I welcome its publication enthusiastically and commend it to readers without reservation.

For far too long cultural relativism, multiculturalism, and internationalism have escaped critical analysis. Subjected here to a rigorous conceptual examination and to a thorough practical investigation, they are exposed as incoherent and politically destructive—alien cuckoos in the nest of democracy.

The nation, nationalism, national sovereignty, national culture, and even patriotism have been routinely traduced as phenomena scarcely more deserving of intellectual support—or even serious analysis—than cannibalism, human sacrifice, or slavery. Dr. Betts' careful, patient, wide-ranging and closely evidenced analysis subverts these left-liberal pieties completely.

The national community, for the most part, is a necessary, positive and fundamentally important collective structure. Alongside the family, it remains the major source of human meaning and identity. Political movements that serve to defend national society and national culture, or to rescue them from localist and internationalist threats, are to be welcomed. Loyalty and patriotism are defensible as entirely rational sentiments.

Among the more particular issues on which *The Twilight of Britain* focuses, I would select the following as especially interesting and important:

- The imbricated relationship between race, culture, ethnicity and identity.
- The glib incoherence of the concept of "tolerance" in many of its current usages.
- The destructive threat to great nations and to freedom posed by European political union.
- The extravagantly fanciful claims made by internationalist cosmopolitans as expressed in particular by the United Nations.

- Routine misuse of the concept of "human rights."
- The dangers of uncontrolled migration.

Critics of Dr. Betts' defence of nation and national culture will no doubt claim that, by the criteria of their own shameless progressivism, his analysis is introverted and reactionary. In fact, there is not a trace of chauvinism or mere nostalgia anywhere in the book. It provides, on the contrary, a powerfully argued, dispassionate case for defending national states— the United Kingdom and the United States not least—as essential bastions of democracy and as crucial instruments of continued progress in human affairs.

Dr. Betts' irresistible arguments for indefinite postponement of national twilight reminds me of the journal of the *Anti-Jacobin*, which Prime Minister Pitt initiated as the cutting edge of intellectual resistance to Bonapartist imperialism in 1797, in particular these quietly ironical yet eloquently ringing words from the Prospectus of November 20:

> To that freedom from partiality and prejudice, of which we have spoken above, by the profession of which so many of our contemporaries recommend themselves, we make little pretension—at least in the sense in which those terms appear now too often to be used. We have not arrived (to our shame perhaps we avow it) at that wild and unshackled freedom of thought which rejects all habit, all wisdom of former times, all restraints of ancient usage, and of local attachment, and which judges upon each subject, whether of politicks or morals, as it arises, by lights entirely its own, without reference to recognized principle or established practice.
>
> We confess, whatever disgrace may attend such a confession, that we have not so far gotten the better of the influence of long habits and early education, not so far imbibed the spirit of liberal indifference, of diffused and comprehensive philanthropy, which distinguishes the candid character of the present age, but that we have our feelings, our preferences, and our affections attaching on particular places, manners and institutions, and even on particular portions of the human race.
>
> It may be thought a narrow and illiberal distinction—but we avow ourselves to be partial to the country in which we live, notwithstanding the daily panegyricks which we read and hear on the superior virtues and endowments of its rival and hostile neighbours. We are prejudiced in favor of her Establishments, civil and religious; though without claiming for either that ideal perfection which modern philosophy professes to discover in the other more luminous systems which are arising on all sides of us.

The threats posed today to British freedom—and to the maintenance of democracy throughout the great nations of the British diaspora—are at least as grave as those that Pitt successfully challenged, as grave, indeed, as those offered later by Nazism and Communism. Now, as then, the destructive power of these threats is rooted primarily in incoherent concepts, mischievous ideas and foolish theories. This book addresses them vigorously and rebuts them decisively. I, for one, am grateful for Dr. Betts' remarkable contribution to the defence of genuine democracy against its importunate and dangerously plausible enemies.

Professor D. Marsland
Brunel University
London

Abstract

This is a holistic and cross-disciplinary discussion in which the philosophical background of the issues of nationalism, culturalism, and toleration are contrasted with the contemporary evidence demonstrating the extent to which they are relevant to the world today, and to Britain in particular. A case is argued for the preservation of British cultural hegemony and sovereignty by resisting multiculturalism, regional devolution, and the political and immigration aspects of Europeanisation and its enlargement, together with global cosmopolitanism. This mode of cultural nationalism, which is both internally benign and externally irenic, is contrasted with pre-WW2 British fascism and the adverse experience of the aggressive German political nationalism leading up to WW2. The re-emergence of worldwide ethno-national conflicts and nationalism is seen as confirmation of the continuing need for a national identity, as well as an appeal to nationhood, kinship, patriotism and loyalty to a culturally homogenous nation-state. The effect of the failure of the United Nations and the international community to resolve ethno-national conflicts, along with the adverse influence of devolution and Europeanisation on the national identity, institutions, and sovereignty of the British nation-state, are discussed.

The potential threat of the toleration of separatist multiculturalism to the social cohesion and security of the British nation-state is outlined. Multiculturalism could become so extensive that Britain's traditional culture could lose its distinctive features. Multiculturalism is being reinforced by uncontrolled and unselective migration into Britain together with the misappropriation of the outmoded 1951 (Geneva) UN Convention on Refugees as amended by the 1967 (New York) Protocol, and the universal rights claimed by economic migrants and bogus refugees. The intractable problems already apparent in societies which either are or have inherited multiculturalism are used to reinforce the case made for managing cultural diversity in Britain by voluntary gradual assimilation and quota based and selective immigration. The political and social dilemmas inherent in a separatist multiculturalism and ghettoisation are discussed together with the issues of racism, freedom of religion and speech, education, equality, discrimination, and political correctness. The paradigm of the demise of the institution of the Anglican Church in its liberal tolerance and ambivalent response to secular and religious cultural pluralism is considered.

The influence of human nature and psychological distancing on the toleration of diversity are discussed. It is argued that toleration should not necessarily be seen as being a unilateral and moral virtue arising from praiseworthy motives. A case is made for toleration to be employed primarily in an instrumental role, namely, as an enabling process for negotiation based on reciprocity and mutual trust, to resolve the differing objectives and values arising from the potential conflicts in a culturally diverse society.

Abbreviations

AFL/CIO	American Federation of Labor-Congress of Industrial Organizations
BBC	British Broadcasting Corporation
BMA	British Medical Association
BNP	British National Party
BUF	British Union of Fascists
CARF	Campaign Against Racism and Fascism
C-E	Church of England
CFX	Ceefax (BBC1 Television)
CIA	Central Intelligence Agency
CPS	Crown Prosecution Service
CRE	Commission for Racial Equality
DE	Daily Express (newspaper or its supplements)
DM	Daily Mail (newspaper or its supplements)
DT	Daily Telegraph (newspaper or its supplements)
EC	European Commission
ECHR	The European Court of Human Rights
ECJ	European Court of Justice
EEC	European Economic Community
EOC	Equal Opportunities Commission

ESRC	The Economic and Social Research Council
EU	European Union
GB	Great Britain (England, Wales, and Scotland)
GDP	Gross Domestic Product
ICI	Imperial Chemical Industries
IMF	The International Monetary Fund
IND	Independent (newspaper)
INLA	Irish National Liberation Army
IRA	The Irish Republican Army
ISER	The Institute for Social and Economic Research
ITV	Independent Television
Kfor	Kosovo Force
KLA	Kosovo Liberation Army
MORI	Marketing Opinion and Research International
MoS	Mail on Sunday (newspaper or its supplements)
MP	Member of Parliament
MPS	Metropolitan Police Service
NATO	North Atlantic Treaty Organisation
NGO	Non-Government Organisation
NHS	National Health Service
NIMBY	Not In My Back Yard
NLA	National Liberation Army (Macedonia)
NOP	National Opinion Poll
OFSTED	The Office for Standards in Education
OSCE	Organisation for Security and Cooperation in Europe
PC	Politically Correct
PCA	Police Complaints Authority
PD	Positive Discrimination

PLO	The Palestine Liberation Organisation
PM	Prime Minister
RUC	Royal Ulster Constabulary
SDP	Social Democratic Party
Sfor	Stabilisation Force (Bosnia/Herzogovina)
SNP	Scottish National Party
SS	Shutzstaffel
STM	Sunday Times (newspaper or its supplements)
STMG	Sunday Times Magazine
TLS	Times Literary Supplement
TM	Times (newspaper or its supplements)
TMG	Times Magazine
TUC	Trade Union Congress
TXT	Teletext (ITV Television)
UK	The United Kingdom of Great Britain and Northern Ireland
UN	United Nations
UNESCO	UN Educational, Scientific and Cultural Organisation
UNHCR	United Nations High Commission on Refugees
US	The United States
USA	The United States of America
USSR	The Union of Soviet Socialist Republics
WASP	White Anglo-Saxon Protestant
WTO	World Trade Organisation
WW1	World War One (1914–18)
WW2	World War Two (1939–45)

1

Introduction and the Principal Propositions

The issues of a) the interrelationship between culture, race and ethnicity, immigration, nationalism, patriotism, globalism, and universal rights, and b) how the politics of toleration have a practical application on this interrelationship, are of topical interest. This is certainly evidenced by the abundance of media coverage of ethno-national conflicts, civil wars, and the concern about multiculturalism and immigration. The great issue of our time in Britain today is the continuing erosion of sovereignty and national identity brought about by the failure of immigration control, separatist multiculturalism, the devolution of Scotland, Wales, and Ulster, the escalation of political Europeanisation, and the United Nations. It has now become clear that the governments of the 1950s to mid–1970s were economical in disclosing to the British public the implications of uncontrolled immigration and Europeanisation on British sovereignty and national identity—which must surely add to the growing scepticism in Britain of the democratic process. In the lead up to the 2001 general election, these issues became, for the first time, priorities for all three political parties in their public campaigns. In this election, forty one percent of the total electorate of 44 million did not vote—the lowest turnout since the voting franchise of 1918—and the Labour party was elected by only twenty five percent of the electorate [TM 8 June 01]. The voter turnout in 2001 was twelve percent less than in 1997. These issues now portend the twilight of Britain, which need not be inevitable, if there is a pause for reflection about the defining phase through which Britain is passing, albeit during a period of economic prosperity. Since around the mid–1980s, something has been happening to the culture of British society, and not all of it good. Notwithstanding its current, and maybe cyclical, economic prosperity, those old enough to remember, and maybe some Anglophile observers as well, will have noted a change. There has been a decline in the respect of and

1

confidence in the monarchy, parliament, institutions of the state, and the public services and its servants, together with a diminution in national pride and sense of identity. These have been undermined by a debilitating and increasing concern about Europeanisation, devolution (including Ulster), and race relations.

David Owen, the former Labour Foreign Minister (1977–1979) and a founder and one time leader of the SDP (Social Democrat Party), said (1991:148) "I have always believed that politicians in France or Britain, preferably both, while supporting European unity, will also feel strongly about the need to maintain the sinews of nationhood. And that they will use the power of veto within the European Community treaties to halt any development which crosses the threshold to a federal Europe. It is a hard distinction to make but instinct, on which all political leadership in the last analysis rests, must guide these decisions." Also (797) "It is Britain's European destiny to resist tides of Euro-federalism, hopefully in combination with other nations. But, if necessary, we must do it alone, confidently insisting on retaining the essentials of nationhood within the Community." And (807) "To believe that political union with majority voting on foreign and security policy within the Community would result in a stronger and more coherent European response defies the lessons of the past and recent history." And (808) "The United States of America would not be balanced by a United States of Europe. Such a Europe would neither seek nor sustain a superpower status and if the United States of America were ever to retreat again into isolationism it would not provide a replacement."

Europeanisation and globalism are major topics in their own right. This discussion is confined to those issues that affect the national identity and institutions of Britain, such as immigration, border control, and defence. It has to be said, however, that giving up the national veto in favour of a qualified majority vote in the EU (European Union) on certain other issues, such as the environment, can be in the national interest. At Maastricht (1991) 30 vetoes were ceded; at Amsterdam (1997) 16; and at Nice (2000) 31 [TM 28 March 01]. To the dismay of the fourteen other EU member states, Ireland recently refused to ratify the Treaty of Nice and its proposed twelve—member EU enlargement [TM 9 June 01]. In a national referendum in which the turnout was only thirty three percent, fifty four percent opposed the Nice Treaty. Technically, the Treaty is now void, as it requires the unanimous approval by all the fifteen member states. Ireland is the only member state required by its constitution to hold a referendum; every other state requires only a parliamentary vote—which does not necessarily represent national opinion on such fundamental issues. Until recently Ireland has financially benefited from EU membership and is about to become a net contributor [DM 9 June 01].

There is today a clear trend towards nationalism and the formation of nation-states in many regions of the world. Nation-states have been, and will continue to be, a response to deeply held psycho-sociological needs, notwithstanding the arguments both against them and their concomitant cultural hegemony. Even if multiculturalism was not perceived as being undesirable and/or unworkable, its separatism imposes constraints on the ideal of the inclusive assimilation of migrants. Diversity and difference require an element of synergy and reciprocity of toleration, and it may be argued that unless and until a viable degree of homogeneity is achieved, they should be pragmatically managed within the nation-state by voluntary gradual assimilation. Toleration should not be perceived as referring to the genteel management of the inevitable decline of the liberal/democratic culture of the West—otherwise everyone is in danger of losing it. Appeals to toleration are never far from the political rhetoric of diversity—and without much attention paid to its implications. For instance, too much diversity can lead to separatism and alienation. Toleration has an important role to play, but practically and conceptually it is prudent to recognise its features and its limits.

The idea of multiculturalism should lead to a consideration of its political, sociological and ethical aspects. This discussion is not idealistic and recognises the complexity of human nature. It assesses the viability and consequences of multiculturalism taking into account the historical and contemporary evidence available to date. It is justifiable to be sceptical of abstract philosophical principles unless they contribute to practical outcomes. In particular, idealism can lead to the unworkable and irreversible. It is also proper to be cautious of arguments based on causality, especially mono-causality, such as relating the economic prosperity of a state to its homogeneity or heterogeneity, and ignoring other independent but influential factors.

Multiculturalism may be a well-intentioned response to the cultural diversities and differences that already exist in some states, or be seen as unavoidable in other still essentially homogeneous nation-states due to mass migration. It can be seen as a holistic approach to diversity and difference, but in its militant and aggressive form it seeks to *emphasise* difference, and has become a focus for political struggle. In the long run it could be assumed that multiculturalism will eventually become problem-free, but this will not occur unless fears of its outcome have been shown with time to be ill-founded or successfully managed. This study contends that in the meantime a cultural hegemony should be preserved and multiculturalism minimised wherever it does not yet exist to a significant degree. Unless and until there is a positive electoral mandate favouring an increasingly racially/ethnically diverse society, Britain should not promote it by liberal, quota-free, and unselective immigration. Immigration is not a uniquely cultural issue because it is also conjoined with economic and environmental concerns—particularly in a small and relatively densely populated island and urbanised nation-state like Britain. Multiculturalism is a confused ideology and a potential threat because, if unregulated, it could lead to major social dissent and political instability, which would prove adverse to the prosperity of the economy. Those who assertively promote it should recognise these potential outcomes. Pluralism relies on mutual and reciprocal toleration to endure. As the Home Office Minister Boateng observed, "The question is the extent to which we can make a success of it [a multiracial society]—I am not a black politician, I am a politician who is black; there is a difference and you have to make a choice." [BBC 2 7 Nov. 99/31 May 00]

The literature on multiculturalism and toleration is either realistic or philosophically idealistic, and a sharp division is often exhibited between them. Both categories are discussed here, but with an emphasis on the former. The Socratic tradition is that moral views should be in accordance with the way in which one is actually prepared to live, and should not be expressions of abstract opinions about how other people should live. John Stuart Mill, the eminent nineteenth-century British philosopher, and Immanuel Kant, the important eighteenth-century German philosopher, also favoured this approach. The way in which people live is contingent upon an ongoing interchange between utility, sentiment and values. It is incumbent to test principles and theories against real-life situations and to assess their validity, not only as to their immediate and direct expectations, but also to their indirect and long-term consequences. History and tradition are also important, not because they will necessarily be repeated, but because they provide a background, a context, and an interpretation with which to understand the thinking and actions of the past and their relevance or otherwise to the present.

The arguments for restricting immigration and pluralism are not new—in the United States they go back for about 150 years, and have been a governmental concern in Britain since the early 1950s. Bob Carter [1987:1–2] "argues that by 1955 the state had developed a clear policy towards Black immigration…it amounted to the construction of an ideological framework in which 'Black' people were seen to be threatening, alien and unassimilable and to the development of policies to discourage and control Black immigration…Black immigration raised the prospect of a permanent Black presence in British society. Concern about the deleterious effects of Black immigration on the 'racial character of the English people' was voiced as early as 1948." Spencer [1997:161] says that "British policy grouped them together as 'coloured' and resisted their entry. Perhaps there is a parallel between the 'racialised' outlook of those British governments and the attitudes and assumptions of academics and commentators who have persistently classified these communities as 'black.'" The term 'black' is now commonly used by most ethnics in Britain and by Spencer himself, although it is not necessarily the preferred term elsewhere. Spencer does not allow that government policy at that time and since might have reflected the views of the electorate. The official mindset by the 1950s [Spencer 1997:43] was that "the limit of 'acceptable' numbers appeared to be set by the perceived ability of British society to assimilate immigrants who were different in appearance and culture to indigenous people. British subjects from the white Commonwealth and immigrants from Ireland, by contrast, could enter in unlimited numbers. The assimilation of 'coloured' immigrants would be facilitated, it was believed, if concentrations of immigrants were avoided. This could be achieved by pursuing a policy of dispersal." This discussion contends that migrants of varying ethnic groups are likely to be more culturally different and potentially separatist. Given the pragmatism of a policy of assimilation and its relationship to numbers, this, and any prudential policy, could inevitably be condemned as 'racialised.' Unique rights of free movement and political enfranchisement between Britain and Ireland date back to its partition in 1923. Spencer does not indicate if he favours an "open door" policy and although his book was published as recently as 1997, no mention is made about economic migrants claiming asylum.

Asylum seekers have been frequent subjects of the media and warnings by immigration officials since at least 1994. Until recently, politicians have been unwilling to admit publicly any concern about this, but public anxiety is now gaining support across the political spectrum. Concern about refugees has risen to the extent that only health and education matter more [TM 15 Mar.00]. A MORI (Marketing Opinion and Research International) poll indicated that compared with the end of 1999, concern over immigration and race, particularly among pensioners and Londoners, has risen to its highest level since more than twenty years ago when they were rated fourteenth. Now almost one in five people say that these are the most important issues facing Britain [TM 20 April 00]. In Britain worries about race relations and immigration have risen from three percent in 1996 to nineteen percent now, and the European response reveals a similar pattern [M-RI 21 June 01]. This concern is sometimes ascribed to the conservatism of the older generation whose attitudes were formed in a mono-cultural era and supposedly is not held by the post-war generations. Tony Blair, the British Prime Minister, has said that his government is perceived as being "out of touch with gut British instincts on asylum etc." [TM 17 July 00] and "lacking in gut patriotic instincts" [TM 19 July 00]. Since Britain joined the then EEC (European Economic Community) in 1973, the issues of Europeanisation and race have been important, but today they are the *most* important issues, and governments have been uncertain how to react for fear of being labelled racist, xenophobic or both. Successive governments and the public have been rendered virtually impotent and silent for decades by the accusation that any restrictions on immigration must be racist. Anti-racists claim that immigration control is a euphemism for racism, but in so doing, are dismissive of all other considerations.

Apart from wealth, arguably the most important long-term divisions between the peoples of the world today are not likely to be political, but cultural and religious. Moral principles and values are ultimately culturally dependent. It may be argued that immigrants from other—and possibly intolerant—cultures should not expect to claim the rights and benefits accruing to a liberal democratic culture without a communality and reciprocity of toleration, which would otherwise degenerate into licence and abuse. The scale of migration today, coupled with the seductive ideology of pluralism and universal claim rights, gives this debate urgency. Multiculturalism should be challenged because it denies the realities of affection, security of, and loyalty to a traditional culture and to a territorial nation-state, for which it attempts to substitute a vague cosmopolitanism or pluralism—its adherents apparently indifferent to the political and social chaos that separatism could cause. The principal feature to which people relate is their national and cultural motherland. If these are threatened by separatism, and if no one else provides a response, then it is conceivable that the far right may do so.

It is necessary to consider the different forms of multiculturalism and nationalism in the world and how these have arisen, otherwise any analysis may produce only general principles having little value to the actuality of the particular political and social environment in which they have to operate. Stjepan Mestrovic [1994:9] observes that "good nationalism will always be locked in struggle with bad nationalism, the kind that leads to megalomania and oppression. The important point is that nationalism is inescapable, because without it no society could possibly be more than an aggregate of individuals who are perpetually hostile to each other. And if nationalism is inevitable, then it is ludicrous to pretend that it does not exist simply because one would be forced to choose between good and evil." Paul Hoskenos [1993:6], in his book which discusses ethnic hatreds in the former East European communist states, argues "in and of itself, nationalism does not preclude the creation of democratic institutions or the guarantee of basic rights. While all of the far Right movements in Eastern Europe are nationalist, not all nationalism is right wing. The free expression of identity and culture also has its place—and arguably a constructive one—in modern societies."

Professor John Gray [1995:1–2] argues that "because political philosophy in the Anglo-American mode remains for the most part, animated by the hopes of the Enlightenment, above all by the hope that human beings will shed their traditional allegiances and their local identities and unite in a universal civilization grounded in generic humanity and a rational morality, it cannot even begin to grapple with the political dilemmas of an age in which political life is dominated by renascent particularisms, militant religions and resurgent ethnicities. As a result, the main current in political philosophy, which remains wedded to the Enlightenment project in the particularly uncompelling form of a species of eviscerated Kantian liberalism, has condemned itself to political nullity and intellectual sterility."

It is not the intention of this discussion to argue the case for a polity which is intolerant of other cultures, simply because it might be assumed that a nation-state founded on a cultural hegemony must be wholly exclusive. People have a variety of motives that are complex and may range from self-interest to a categorical moral imperative, and their origin may be emotional as well as rational. Toleration is one such feature of human nature that has acquired the ethos of a virtue in Western culture and ought, therefore, to have wide limits. It is, however, the features and the limits of toleration that are critical—toleration has limits, licence has none. This discussion focuses on its instrumental role—namely the "work" which toleration can do—in accepting human nature as it is, rather than what it ought to be.

The issues involved are considered from a British perspective largely as they are reported from day to day in the media (principally the *Times* newspaper and its supplements) following the 2001 general election. This is open to the criticism that media reports are ethnocentric, incomplete, inaccurate, unfair, "cherry picked," derived from secondary sources, and open to differing interpretations and accounts. Additionally, it could be argued that there might be more than a single truth. It also has to be said that numerical data published in the press can vary between newspapers and are sometimes not internally consistent—but they are the best that are immediately available. The present British government has acquired a reputation for "spinning," and there is sometimes no way of determining the facts because there are conflicting accounts. The conclusions and recommendations of investigative committees and sociological research, surveys, and opinions polls are also open to criticism. The questions asked, the giving of pleasing answers, the makeup of the research teams and committees, and the preconceptions and affiliations of their members can influence and sometimes pre-determine the outcome.

The principal question to be addressed by this discussion is: what should be the response by the British nation-state to the influences currently eroding its sovereignty, if it is committed to preserving its cultural hegemony, given the validity of the following propositions?

1. The current trend towards the formation and re-emergence of nation-states, often arising from the break-up of larger multiracial/ethnic states, will continue in the foreseeable future. It is not axiomatic that economic globalism will necessarily be accompanied by cultural cosmopolitanism. Nationalism is here to stay and one should not condemn

all versions of it. This contrasts with an assessment of the situation by Professor Nathan Glazer in 1975 [11 and 12]: "The old hope of nationalism...for each Nation a state, for each State a nation has receded into the distance" and that "aside from the fact that each nation's ethnic purification leads to another's greater diversity, one senses that the effort at (ethnic) purity, for most states, is a lost cause." The nation-state based on cultural hegemony/nationalism appears to meet a basic and continuing human need. The fundamental reasons for its existence are its sovereignty and security, namely its survival if it should ever be at risk.

2. A nation-state and its nationhood is shaped by cultural history, religion, traditions, practices, and values, and the foundation of its citizenship remains essentially ethno-national. This is the focus of the social coherence of its people that manifests itself in a spirit of nationhood, kinship, loyalty, and patriotism together with pride in its heritage and heroes. A cultural hegemony, which is protective of its political sovereignty, does not have to be inward looking or isolationist in respect of its commerce and alliances, and can and should have a significant global influence, both politically and economically. Culture, race, ethnicity, and religion converge into a national identity, but these features are not exclusive of one another. Nor is a sense of national identity racist or xenophobic, but is a feature of human nature. The concept of cultural nationalism proposed by the Enlightenment German philosophers was that the nation-state and national identity were based on territory and a cultural hegemony. If so, it follows that multiculturalism does not lend itself to nationhood, and its likely outcome will not be one of "celebrating diversity," but a non-assimilated society accentuated by sectarian separatism. Unrestricted diversity could end up with nothing worth celebrating.

3. The territorially aggressive German, Italian, and Japanese nationalism leading up to WW2 (World War Two, 1939–45), should not be used as a de facto or deterministic argument against all forms of nationalism. Contrary to a prevalent perception of nationalism and the stigma it acquired from totalitarianism, there is a benign and irenic form based on the liberal democratic polity of the West, which although culturally protectionist, is not territorially aggressive. Aggressive and virulent nationalism arises from a special combination of circumstances leading to a totalitarian state, dependent upon support from its legislature and institutions, its media, its army, and its secret police. As long as a traditionally liberal democratic nation-state is not subsumed into the ideology of extremist political or religious demagogues, no extraterritorial threat should be posed thereby.

4. There are strong pressures on the nation-states of the West to adopt, or to acquire by default, increasing degrees of multiculturalism by uncontrolled and unselective immigration. This pressure arises from: the disparate relative growth between the developed and the developing regions of the world in their populations and living standards; the socially and economically disruptive effect of ethno-national conflicts and civil wars; the relatively cheap and easy facilities for migration; the impact of technology on the global dissemination of information; and an ethos of universalised claim rights embodied in the outmoded 1951 UN (United Nations) (Geneva) Convention on Refugees as amended by the 1967 (New York) Protocol, which have in the last decade been misappropriated by economic migrants presenting themselves as asylum seekers.

5. The rhetoric that "diversity and difference" is good and beneficial should be treated with scepticism, as this qualitative and abstract claim contradicts the evidence currently available. Too much diversity and difference can be divisive, and can readily lend itself to the "racialization" of competing claims. In the extreme this could lead to virtual anarchy. Although there is no universal formulaic "best way," the experience of multiculturalism elsewhere in the world should be studied with reference to its particular origins and circumstances, including whether it has been inherited, and/or electively adopted or acquired by default. Without diversity, a society is less amenable to change, but all change is not good if the effects are unpredictable, undesirable, and irreversible. Although the work ethic and aspirations of some immigrants may contribute to the economic vitality of a society, this is not the only or the principal outcome to be evaluated. It is contended that Britain, which is still largely mono-ethnic, should resist multiculturalism, as have the newly emerged post-Cold War hegemonic nation-states. An indigenous society is justified in protecting its way of life by adopting a policy which preserves its cultural hegemony and sovereignty, and which recognises and protects its prior obligations towards its nationals.

6. Advocates of multiculturalism might claim that such diversity has worked in the New World migrant societies of the United States, Canada, and Australia where it has been inherited and/or has been an elective government policy. There is evidence to challenge this claim and its eventual outcome is in doubt. Separatist multiculturalism can have an adverse and irrevocable influence, including the erosion of the traditional values, including loyalty to the state, and to its political and social coherence. A nation-state that tolerates wide limits of multicultural separatism is unlikely to maintain its coherence. This

can present a potential threat both to its internal stability and to its security in a national emergency. It is further argued that separatist multiculturalism is an untenable and confused ideology. It emphasises the racial/cultural differences between ethnic groups, which is contrary to the ideal of an integrated, shared culture which it purports to achieve, in such a way as to generalise it beyond usefulness and to degenerate into racism. Those who advocate unrestrained multiculturalism, and who sometimes accompany their rhetoric with accusations of xenophobia and racism, should recognise its potentially adverse prognosis.

7. The culture of Britain is not changeless, having evolved into loosely knit subcultures of limited social pluralism with a diversity of political and religious beliefs, class, status, wealth, education, and lifestyles. Non-Western cultures may embody religious and moral values and practices manifestly different from, and unacceptable to, Britain and other Western societies. The governments of these basically liberal democratic nation-states endeavour to remain morally neutral and treat their citizens as being free, rational, and equal in law, allowing individual choice to evolve without coercion. Governments and their institutions have substantial resources and should not use these to obscure, permit, promote, or attempt to impose the ideology of multiculturalism in response to pressure groups supporting liberal immigration. Legislation and practices relating to universal rights, equality, and discrimination should be pragmatic and reciprocal, but should also ensure that they do not harm indigenous citizens to whom there exists a primary responsibility.

8. Although probably not its philosophical intention, multiculturalism could be manipulated from being a permissive liberal social theory to a politicised ideology based on racial/ethnic separatism, which overrides the objections to it on the grounds of moral relativism and rights. Racial/cultural ghettoisation can translate into political separatism. Separatist multiculturalists may have a latent agenda, the ultimate aim of which is political power, but which is initially presented to mainstream society under the moral guise of liberal universalism, anti-discrimination, minority rights, and freedom of religion and education. It is easier, in a society with a liberal tradition, such as Britain, to sell a moral crusade than a political agenda. Restrictions on the freedom of objecting to the issues involved imposed by single-minded political correctness, or by the misuse of religious freedom, or by adopting a moral high ground, distorts reality, and can become an intellectual tyranny.

9. The principal means by which acquired multiculturalism and potential

ethno-national conflicts can be avoided, at least in those states which are still principally mono-cultural, is by a controlled, quota-based and selective policy of immigration together with the promotion of gradual voluntary assimilation. The claim that immigration, together with the other nativist objections, poses a potential threat to an indigenous society, reoccurs in history and is not new, and at least in the past, has proved to be largely unfounded. Today, however, there exists a major step-change in the potential scale of global migration which is markedly different than heretofore, arising from increasing economic migration and sham refugees from Asia, Africa, and Eastern and Central Europe. This concern can be mitigated by the superficial appeal of the claim that migration and multiculturalism should be facilitated or even welcomed, because it is inevitable and/or because it is economically beneficial or socially desirable. The British press, in 1994, was drawing attention to the Immigration Service, which reported the increasing scale and abuse by asylum seekers of immigration regulations. Official statistics were understating the size of the problem, but in 2000 the government belatedly acknowledged that there did exist a crisis with concomitant social tensions, which were becoming increasingly apparent.

10. The time is long since past, if it ever existed with any justification, that Britain should tolerate the accusation, together with the implied moral guilt, about its former imperial and colonial past, or be apologetic about its national history and heroes. This and other guilt-laden victimisation arguments should be firmly rejected whenever they are used to foster a passive acquiescence and acceptance of multiculturalism, liberal immigration and cosmopolitanism. The proportion of all ethnics in Britain at the time of the 1991 census was officially about six percent, but is now probably more due to the upsurge of uncontrolled immigration and disappeared asylum seekers. The mantras that "Britain is now a multicultural society" and that "we are all ethnics" with the inference that this is now an established quantitative fact, should not deter the objections to it. This assertion would have as much validity as claiming that Britain is a nation of Buddhists, cyclists, or alcoholics. Moreover, Britain is not a multicultural society to the extent suggested by its racial/ethnic demography, because some of its racial/ethnic immigrant groups have, over time, and to varying degrees, assimilated to a significant degree into the indigenous society and culture.

11. The UN and European Conventions of Human Rights and the Status of Refugees are being seriously abused by increasing numbers of economic refugees claiming political asylum and rights in the West.

These Conventions provide an easy way for the normally strictly controlled immigration requirements of visas to be circumvented. The number, cost, and culture clash of sham refugees present a threat to the cultural hegemonies of the nation-states of the West. It is contended that since the immediate post-WW2 Cold War—with messianism, the sometimes double standard idealism of the United States, and the experience of half a century—some aspects of these Conventions, together with the adverse influence of the UN on national sovereignty, are now seriously outmoded. The UN has become largely ineffective in respect to the validity and universality of the conflict prevention and resolution role for which it was principally set up, and its partisan approach to the "conforming" nation-states of the West undermines their sovereignty. The concept of the unified British state and its national identity is also being undermined by regional devolution, increasing political Europeanisation, and cosmopolitan idealism, and unless resisted, will portend—not as it is sometimes claimed, a renewal, but—the twilight of Britain.

12. Universal human rights crusades and ethical foreign policies are viewed by some non-Western states and cultures as modern versions of cultural imperialism. In these regions, the ideal of moral universalism has never been fully recognised nor reciprocated. Universalism in respect to the validity of certain societal and unqualified claim rights needs to be rethought in the light of the changed conditions of today. Universalised claim rights can serve to undermine the national sovereignty and social coherence in the nation-states of the West and can lead to "acquired" multiculturalism. Outmoded aspects of the UN Conventions should be reviewed to reclaim the natural rights of the conforming nation-states, whose obligations for societal claim rights should be limited to their own citizens.

13. Toleration is a complex and paradoxical concept. It should not be founded on the unquestioned notion that it is a virtue, because it is capable of being abused. It has differing features and motives, not all of which are commendable, and which are influenced by human nature. Toleration should be viewed instrumentally, namely, as facilitating negotiation aimed at the reconciliation of differing objectives. The limits of toleration towards multiculturalism should reflect the political, social, and economic overall well-being of the citizens of the whole nation-state and not sectarian interests. The liberal toleration articulated by some leading politicians and church leaders can be contingent upon their proximity to, or distancing from, its outcome, and the extent and immediacy of the effect to which they perceive it presenting to their self-interest. There can be differing limits of tolera-

tion displayed on the one hand in lip-service and distanced support of short term liberal principles, and on the other, towards recognising and accepting their longer term and more permanent effects.

14. Toleration should be pragmatic in nature, and the limits negotiated between the mainstream culture and minorities should follow the principle that it should be reciprocal and commensurate between the tolerating party and the party being tolerated, rather than a virtue-laden unilateral obligation. Social development should be pragmatic—adopting those changes which can be tested and shown to work, and should rely on individual voluntarism rather than coercive legislation or "education led" social engineering that may have little effect on deeply held attitudes. This means that changes should be gradual, and preferably capable of being modified or abandoned, rather than the start of an irreversible and accelerating slippery slope, or serial concessions based on questionable precedents. For, if they are found to be unworkable, they may be met with a "you can't turn the clock back" rhetoric. If social cohesion is to be maintained, the stereotyping of "guilt-laden perpetrators" and "permanent victims" must be avoided. To eliminate on the one hand continuing claims of racial discrimination, and on the other hand the inevitable backlash, education and employment legislation and practice must be both publicly and transparently seen to be that of strict equality of opportunity for all citizens.

NOTES

Carter, B. Harris, C. et al. *The 1951–55 Conservative Government and the Racialisation of Black Immigration.* University of Warwick, Centre for Research into Ethnic Relations, 1987. 1–2.

Glazer. N. "The Universalisation of Ethnicity," *Encounter,* vol. 44. February 1975. 11, 12.

Gray, J. *Enlightenment's Wake.* London: Routledge, 1995. 1–2.

Hockenos, P. *Free to Hate.* London: Routledge, 1993. 6.

Mestrovic, S.G. *Balkanisation of the West.* London: Routledge, 1994. 9.

Owen, D. *Time to Declare.* London: Michael Joseph, 1991. 148.

Ibid. 797.

Ibid. 807–8.

Spencer, I.R.G. *British Immigration Policy Since 1939.* London: Routledge, 1997. 43.

Ibid. 161.

BBC 2. *Playing the Race Card.* 7 November 1999.

BBC 2. *Black Britain Special—Bernie Grant.* 31 May 2000.

2

Culture and the Appeal of Culturalism

Arguably the most important non-wealth distinction between peoples to-day is culture. Culture often subsumes race and religion, and to a lesser extent political ideology, wealth, class, and status—all of which may overlap culture. It is significant that the term culture is philologically related to the agricultural and horticultural processes of cultivating and nurturing. The complex social forces termed "culture" become metaphorically associated with the notion of cultivating persons socially, and from this psychological determinism there develops particular systems of beliefs, practices, and values. Human beings have a natural disposition towards their own culture and kind ("us") and are wary of others ("them"). Though seemingly politically incorrect, this liking for "sameness" is an innate natural trait.

The American sociologist Francis Fukuyama [1996:34–36] defines culture narrowly as an "inherited ethical habit. An ethical habit can consist of an idea or value . . . or it can consist of an actual social relationship . . . Traditional religions or ethical systems constitute the major institutionalized sources of culturally determined behaviour. Ethical systems create moral communities because their shared language of good and evil give their members a common moral life . . . To identify culture with habit rather than rational choice is not to say that cultures are irrational; they are simply arational with regard to means by which decisions are made. It can be that cultures actually embed a high degree of rationality." Culture might be seen as behaviour peculiar to human beings, which together with the material objects that they use, is an integral part of their behaviour. Like religion, it is not a universal entity and varies in different parts of the world. Some deny that any culture is real, namely, that it is simply a construct. Others take a reductionist view that at some basic level all cultures are the same; or that a culture is never static and changes to reflect the times; or that an eclectic culture will emerge to replace national and regional cultures. Even if a dominant culture and value system could be deconstructed, there might be nothing to replace it and an incoherent vacuum would ensue.

There are alternative views, including those of Grosby S. [1994:164–171], Eller, J. and Coughlan, R. [1993:183–202], and Trigg R. [1984:93–110], that discuss the relative influence of genetics, family, and sociological determinism on culture. But it would seem self-evident that patterns of behaviour are transferred between individuals and generations from their man-made environment in a broadly defined process of education, both formal and informal. This sociocultural system makes life reassuring and secure for those living in it. There tends to be a close correlation between the kind of habitat and the type of culture that influences the differences between them. Culture is evolutionary and is learned from being brought up within a framework; a large component of culture is below the level of conscious awareness; and cultural patterns structure both thought and perception. In the past, cultures were thought of in rationalistic ways as conscious creations. Nevertheless, existentialism holds that mankind has complete freedom to choose and is not the product of anything—though empirical evidence suggests otherwise. Communitarianism, on the other hand, holds that culture is constituted by social environment and not by individuals for whom group membership is a matter of free will.

Cultures comprise a political and social organisation, a language, religion, morality, values, attitudes, beliefs, traditions, taboos, prejudices, rituals, symbols, and ceremonies together with their art, literature, and music. Language, and sometimes religion and its morality, is the necessary, but not always the sufficient qualification for belonging. Mankind in different countries and different times has taken Christ, Mahomet, or Buddha as the exemplars of human morality. What is common to all moralities is its utility to a particular society by increasing the total of human happiness in that society. If there is no common morality but only individual beliefs, then a society tends towards individualistic permissiveness. Sociologists Jack Eller and Reed Coughlan [1993:183] say that "The notion of primordialism [meaning a priori, ineffable, and coercive] has been used to describe the origins and strength of ethnic attachments in the literature on ethnicity for the last three decades . . . (but) conclude that the term primordialism is unsociologocal, unanalytical and vacuous . . . [198] Every society has specific devices and mechanisms of cultural reproduction, including ethnic-identity and-attachment reproduction. These devices and mechanisms should be the goal of the analysis of ethnicity." Bernie Grant [1995:157] the black MP (Member of Parliament) for Tottenham, when asked if he felt more at home in Guyana, Britain, or Africa said, "I think that I feel most at home in Guyana. But that is probably because I haven't spent a long time in Africa . . . I think that I'd feel most at home [in Africa] because when you go there you fit into the place in a way that I don't even feel in Guyana." This is unsurprising bearing in mind that the population of Guyana is forty-three percent Afro-Guyanese and fifty-one percent Asian. According to Cristopher Berry [1986:71] "a culture, like a language, is not the product of an individual. Just as a language is neither invented nor its usage a matter of individual choice or caprice so the individual is similarly born into an on-going community. An individual's culture is not some separable external means to be exploited at will in order to attain independent goals but is, rather, the context within which the individual conceives of himself or herself as an individual. This context [language, religion, art, politics, customs] is irreducibly social." Denis Healey (1989:191), a one-time Cabinet Minister, found that "the Russians, like us, were human beings, although they were not human beings like us," or according to the fourth century Zuozhuan (one of China's basic philosophy texts), "if he is not of our race, he is sure to have a different mind." Fukuyama [1996:92–93] notes that "in Chinese Confucianism, there is no such thing as a universal moral obligation to all human beings as there is in the Christian religion. Obligations are graded and fall off in intensity the further one moves from the inner family circle." The peaceful coexistence of global nation-states having different cultures is made viable by a mutually recognised sovereignty, and a reciprocal but arm's-length toleration. The defence and preservation of an inherited culture indicates a resistance to change, but can be interpreted as, or attributed to, racism, discrimination, and/or the means by which the dominant majority preserves its power. If immigrants of different race or ethnicity assimilate, then the visibility of their differences becomes less significant to the mainstream. If they maintain their cultural separatism, it is accentuated.

Cultures encompass different perceptions and values of humanity and preferred ways of living together. Their influence can be powerful, denying personal satisfactions on the one hand, whilst fulfilling desires on the other. All sociocultural systems have a means of regulation and control and core mode beliefs and values in order to function and to continue. This is a method by which the relationship between the individual to the well being of his or her society as a whole is governed, such as rights and duties and what is permitted and tolerated and what is not. People form perceptions of the society around them from which they derive their attitudes, beliefs, and values. The attitudes of young people towards these cultural norms are formed or handed down by their parents and home background, together with education in school and in university; peer group pressure; the economic, political, cultural, and social environment; and the media, particularly television. Cultural affinity and a stable society are reinforced by its political, religious and cultural institutions. The predominant difference between peoples is not necessarily their political tradition or ideology: there may be major and irreconcilable cultural differences including religion.

A basic human need that is reflected in attitudes, particularly as people get older, is the desire for security coupled with moral conservatism. It is usually the society and culture in which they have been brought up that is seen as providing this continuity of stability, and which affects their attitudes towards the separatism of "Others." Frequently, emotions are involved, which serve to reinforce the developing of perceptions. This comfortable framework of reference provides a sense of psychological security. The individual may be reluctant to abandon those attitudes and behaviours that enhance this security. He or she may retain a sense of security and set limits on the toleration of "others," by selecting those arguments that support his perceptions.

This discussion does not address the social anthropology of culture. Suffice it to say that it is a characteristic possessed by man alone. The anthropologist Ruth Benedict [1935:5] in the 1930s studied the cultural behaviour of primitive civilisations and the absence of cosmopolitanism and concluded that "primitive man never looked out over the world and saw 'mankind' as a group and felt his common cause with his species . . . the first and important distinction was between his own human group and those beyond the pale. His own group, and all its ways of behaving, was unique." Sociologists attempt to distinguish between race and culture, but it is insufficient to simply characterise race as phenotypical, and ethnicity as cultural difference. A difference in race is usually more visible than a difference in culture, but in popular usage the two terms subsume one another and are often used interchangeably. It is difficult to disentangle the notion of race from that of culture, although Professor Antony Flew [1986:3] observes that "the truth is, of course, that 'race' and 'culture' are just about as far as could be from constituting convertible terms." The ideology of multiculturalism is confused, because in the absence of assimilation, the concept of an identifiable national culture no longer exists. If it is to include anything and everything both in its scope and in its composition, it will generalise itself beyond usefulness. Being all things to all people can result in it meaning nothing to anyone. Similarly, when all clothing is fashionable, there is no fashion.

This raises the question "what counts as a culture?" The concept of a culture is similar to that of a nation, being a cluster of characteristics rather than a fixed menu, and is difficult to define. There are two associated versions. Firstly, it is the whole way of life of a society—its language, religion, history, morality, values, laws, customs, traditions, and beliefs—and it may or may not include an inherited political system. However, if an individual is asked to describe his culture, the description will be selective and may differ from that of other individuals. Secondly, and not part of this discussion, is its aesthetic or "high" culture—its art, literature, and other manifestations of its intellectual and artistic achievements viewed collectively. Nazism officially promoted a puritanical aesthetic culture that coexisted with its aggressive nationalism and totalitarianism. From 1933, with the setting up of the Reich Culture Chamber, all aspects of artistic life, including the artists themselves with the partial exception of music, were totally subordinated to Nazi doctrine, whose *diktats* had the force of legislation. The Germans thought British aesthetic culture sufficiently important to target the architectural heritage of its defenceless cathedral cities to reduce morale with the "Baedeker" 1942 air raids. The extremist Taleban in Afghanistan are destroying all ancient relics and Buddhist statues to erase the last traces of the country's 2000 year old Pre-Islamic cultural heritage [TM 6 Mar.01]. In this discussion, culture refers specifically to the ethnicity and/or religion associated with a group's race, history, and/or domicile. Culture may overlay class, status, and/or gender, but it does not include sociological subcultural diversities such as homosexuality or feminism. Nor does the term culture as used herein refer to other sociological divisions, namely the differences between the cultures of the working and professional classes, persons of high and low aesthetic tastes, and urban and country dwellers.

The term "British" culture is used although people increasingly describe themselves as English, Welsh, or Scottish. According to figures from a 1998 study [Social Trends 2000:22], Britain (strictly speaking, Great Britain) is comprised of England (49.495 million), Scotland (5.120 million), and Wales (2.933 million). The United Kingdom (of Great Britain and Northern Ireland) is comprised of a total of 59.237 million and includes Ulster (1.689 million), which is the United Kingdom's only land frontier. This provides a haven for cross border terrorists and a lucrative business for smugglers. The umbrella terms "British" and "Britishness" at one time probably related to a geographical entity, but have become equated with "English," which is not surprising in view of the relative populations (83.5 percent English) and the shared nature of the cultures. Historian Professor Norman Davies, [1999: 1039] in his book *The Isles—A History,* claims largely on constitutional/institutional grounds that "the United Kingdom is not, and never has been, a nation-state . . . It is essentially a dynastic conglomerate, which could never equalise the functions of its four constituent parts and which, as a result, could never fully harmonize the identities of the national communities within its borders." A response to this argument is that for the vast majority of people, it never seemed necessary to do so. Recently, historians and anthropologists have begun to cast doubt on a genuinely Celtic identity. The SNP's definition of being Scottish as simply being someone who lives in Scotland lacks conviction. In the 1997 Scotland referendum, about 62 percent voted, of whom 74.3 percent were in favour of a Scottish parliament. It has 35 SNP members out of a total of 129, and is elected every 4 years. In the 1997 Wales referendum, about 50 percent voted, of whom 50.3 percent were in favour of a Welsh Assembly. It has 16 Plaid Cymru members out of a total of 60, and is elected every 4 years. [Whitaker's 2000:559/65]. The 1991 census revealed that [TM 12 Sept.00] nearly three quarters of a million Scottish-born people and more than half a million Welsh-born people were living in England. Of the people born in England, 20 percent were living in Wales, and nearly 8 percent were living in Scotland. The Scottish-born people living in England equates to about 15 percent of the population of Scotland [TM 12 Feb.00]. Particularly in the case of Wales, the "immigration" from outside the region weakens the appeal of Welsh nationalism. Northern Ireland had a devolved parliament at Stormont, set up under the 1920 Government of Ireland Act, but this was suspended in 1972 by direct rule from Westminster, and reinstated by the Good Friday Agreement.

Immigrants tend to regard themselves as British, which seems more inclusive and less ethnic than English. Since Scottish and Welsh devolution, the BBC have advised their staff that the words "British" and "English" are not interchangeable. In her book about British cultures entitled *Studying British Cultures: An Introduction*, Susan Bassnett [1997] includes chapters on the Scottish, Welsh, Irish and Afro-Caribbean cultures, and nothing about the English culture. Two theories have been advanced to explain the lack of an English identity. The English, though, have been confident enough of their identity that they have not needed to emphasise it—or more probably they have been denied a distinct identity because it has been subsumed into their Britishness. Devolution institutionalised the notion that Britain was not one nation and that there were differences between nations in the British Isles simply based on where one happened to be living. The English, who were thereby excluded, are now seeing a need for the first time to establish their own separate identity. Some devolution enthusiasts would like to go further and see England itself divided into self-governing regions. It is unlikely that, given the diversity of the nation-states and cultures within the present EU, that the construct of a European "identity" (i.e. a citizen of the United States of Europe) will ever attain any credibility, loyalty, or sense of common allegiance from British citizens. This would almost certainly be the case when this "identity" is further diluted by the proposed expansion of the EU. One thing is certain: the EU will do nothing to encourage or maintain the national identity of its member states.

The concept of a culture is highly subjective and personal—as when George Orwell described what for him were the elements of the British way of life [1962:11–13]. There has been a recent upsurge in interest in books and television documentaries about English identity variously describing what "Englishness" means. The British broadcaster Jeremy Paxman's [1998] book, *The English,* sold over 166,000 copies and was in the ten top general paperbacks for twenty weeks [STM 23 July 00]. Television programmes have investigated the demise of English culture and "crisis" in English identity, either real or imagined, from what it was thirty or more years ago. Of the explanations advanced, it is incredible that the effect of substantial immigration since the 1960s has not always been highlighted. Nevertheless, a survey [STM 19 March 00] of 1000 British schoolchildren indicated that youngsters do not think of their nationality as either British (only 24 percent) or European (only 1 percent) and are increasingly defining themselves as English (66 percent) as a reaction to rising Scottish and Welsh nationalism. They also regarded their nationality (75 percent) as important. The plans to expand the EU from fifteen to twenty seven/twenty eight member states with a population of more than 500 million will no doubt dilute the appeal of the concept of a European national identity even more. Regional devolution may well lead to Scotland and Wales being attracted to the EU and Brussels as a centre, rather than to London, for the status of separate nations and for economic assistance. This could signal the twilight of Britain with the United Kingdom no longer united. The Scottish parliament has begun to describe itself as a "government" [TM 18 Jan.01]. All university student tuition fees have been abolished in Scotland, teachers pay has been increased above the English/Welsh level, and there is a commitment by its First Minister to provide free health care for the elderly, irrespective of income. None of these are available in the rest of Britain, they marginalise the heretofore egalitarian policy of the national government, and put into question the higher national treasury grant per head of population for Scotland.

Maybe those minorities who believe that a United States of Europe made up of already diverse nation-states will be able to give more recognition to their differences should note that the Celts, for example, are already separated into five distinct types: Bretons, Irish, Cornish, Welsh and Scots—small dots in a big entity. Blair, in attempting to attract the patriotic vote to the Labour party and to downplay calls for the regional devolution of England, claimed that Scottish and Welsh devolution had helped to hold the Union together rather than undermine it. He identified "British" values as "creativity, tolerance, openness, and adaptability, with strong communities and families" [TM. 29 March.00]. Some other nations might not see these characteristics as being exclusively British. He has also pronounced that "Britain is, and should be, a multicultural society" [TM. 19 April.00]. Why it "should be" is not apparent. Although shared values are necessary, the notion of a national identity must have the basis of citizenship and allegiance.

A diffusion and porosity of cultural values can take place between societies, particularly if they are not dissimilar, for example, between the United States and Britain—the "special relationship." Nevertheless, Vera Lynn [1989:168] notes that almost sixty years ago, the first American troops arriving in Britain in 1942 were given the booklet *A Short Guide to Britain* outlining the cultural differences between the United States and Britain. Even where cultures are dissimilar as in the days of British India, the indigenous Indian culture adopted some of the features of their British Others. In Western society, there have been gradual shifts in moral values with time particularly in sexual relationships. Attitudes have been influenced by developments in medicine and genetics and increasingly by the limits on resources. A major cultural change was the anti-authoritarianism secessionism brought about in the late 1960s/early 70s by Vietnam and generational student unrest. Within a culture there will be disagreements about particular issues. Some moralists believe that there are firm value judgements between right and wrong applying to society, which should be instilled by parents and teachers. Liberal individualists tend not to distinguish between good and bad morality, such as opposing abortion and euthanasia, because to them individual choice is paramount and no one has an overriding authority. Rights give rise to irreconcilable and incommensurable values—abortion, for example has two irreconcilable arguments based on different perspectives—the right to life, or the right to choose.

There are significant differences between the beliefs, practices, and values of different cultures. With some, their acceptance or rejection is fundamental and arises from deeply held beliefs or principles, whereas with others it is their prioritisation, such as obligations to a group versus the autonomy and respect for persons. What may be considered to be moral and/or religious in one culture may be immoral or morally neutral and/or secular in another. Cultural practices that the West regard as unacceptable or objectionable when manifest in the public domain include: infanticide of female babies; selling girls into marriage by dowry and forced marriages; attitudes towards womens' and basic human rights; purdah/concubines; forced prostitution; matriarchy; polygamy; ritual male and female circumcision; ritual child prostitution; ritual animal/child sacrifice; stoning to death for adultery; obligatory public prayer; the caste system; child labour; child abduction; domestic and industrial slavery; religious fatwas; capital/corporal punishment; death for apostasy and adultery; public executions; cruelty to animals; ritual animal slaughter; serial abortion/contraception/adulterous pregnancy; degradation and torture featured on television game shows; attitudes toward losing face/apologising, suicide, homosexuality, gambling, alcohol and drug abuse; attitudes to fatherhood and to the work/welfare ethic. What is potentially more serious is the culture prevalent in some societies of authoritarianism, lawlessness and religious fundamentalism, and the threat to the political traditions and attitudes to parliamentary and liberal democracy of the West and respect for the law. It is not incidentally within the remit of this discussion to debate the contentious issue of what type of polity qualifies as a "true" democracy, albeit that it is the least worst system of government. Both in politics and in business, the spread of bribery and corruption seriously undermines the credibility of democratic political and institutional processes, and the result of voter cynicism adversely affects international commercial stability. Some cultures see hypocrisy and failings in the culture of the West with its loss of those traditional values that were once commonly shared. Moreover some of its modernistic liberal beliefs, practices, and customs are unacceptable and offensive to them—they can see the 1960s individualistic "revolution" as an ethos of self-interest, or the hedonistic "me" society. They see alcohol and drug abuse, gambling and teenage pregnancies as features of the decadence of the British individualistic culture. It is not possible to give a convincing account of why one culture is thought to be superior to others—its value is in the mind of its adherent. What is easier to identify is which facets of other cultures are subjectively disliked or positively objected to.

Maybe it is not stretching a cultural analogy too far in recalling that business diversification was fashionable in the 1970s and 1980s—a business being part of a corporate society. Most of these conglomerates have abandoned this diversity and now extol the virtues of concentrating on their "core skills and culture"—business diversification is reversible, cultural diversity is not. Business organisations talk about their internal culture or their corporate ethos, and sometimes mergers fail because of culture clash. Professional institutions have their own protective culture of self-regulation and lack of transparency. When British Rail was privatised its corporate safety culture was eroded and this was officially acknowledged as contributing to the Southall rail disaster of 1997.

The police and the armed forces have a conformist culture with a particular identity and values because they share a unique common risk. This culture is to some extent blocked off from the general public. If the sense of pride in belonging to these institutions is undermined by unfounded criticism then society as a whole suffers and this will become evident by falling recruitment. The military, especially their front line troops, aims to instil a homogeneous culture and a uniform identity by means of physically and psychologically rigorous training by which the divisiveness of race, ethnicity, culture, class, and self-interest is sublimated into unquestioning trust. Overseas employees of multinationals are advised of differing cultural attitudes to corporate paternalism, relationships between employer and employees, deference to authority, local customs and practices, group as opposed to individual achievement and risk taking, familial nepotism as opposed to meritocracy, and the ethics of work and business. Behaviour, and in particular the nuances of language, can have different implications to different cultures—the same words do not convey the same message. The prominent British businessman John Harvey-Jones, one time Chairman of ICI (Imperial Chemical Industries) noted [1988:117] that in spite of economic globalisation "in reality national differences are becoming more accentuated . . . most of us feel that in learning to speak another language we automatically gain with it a deeper understanding of the people. Nothing could be further from the truth" [119]. Studies by Geert Hofstede [1989:80] made on the impact of national cultural differences on how organisations function concluded that "it is important even for international organisations to have a dominant national culture to fall back on . . . organisations without a home culture, in which the key decision-makers can come from any country [such as UNESCO [UN Educational, Scientific and Cultural Organisation] find it very difficult to function effectively because of this lack."

According to the British philosopher Bryan Magee [1990:239], Nietzsche took the view that "different moralities are right for different people. [If so] nothing could more flatly contradict the standard notion among philosophers—derived most immediately from Kant—that a morality must be universalisable if it is to be seriously defensible." The culture/morality clash was exemplified by the accusation of cultural imperialism by the Home Affairs Minister of Singapore to criticisms of the flogging of an American graffiti offender. Primitive peoples such as the Australian and Canadian aborigines can become trapped between their tribal culture and contemporary society—which may lead to a loss of their identity and be marked by alcoholism, domestic violence and suicide. Stigmatisation can differ in different cultures: in some Brazilian and African cultures—in contrast to the West—epilepsy is a qualification for the prestigious role of witch doctor or medium. Religious freedom is a major difference between the Islamic and Western cultures, on which it appears that there can be no reconciliation or compromise.

Economic globalisation or foreign economic domination may be seen as the leading edge of a Western hegemony or post-colonial imperialism, as was perceived by the anti-globalist Noam Chomsky. It can be seen as eroding the sovereignty of nation-states in the developing world and shifting power away from their political institutions to trans-national corporations. Although foreign investment may be seen as a resurgence of colonialism or neo-capitalist liberalism or global coercive corporate power, the paradox is that the developing world will remain as such without it. Another assumption is that since modern technologies are largely the products of Western culture, mastering their use by Others also requires the adoption of Western patterns of thinking and behaviour. However it does not necessarily follow that these countries will adopt a Western style liberal democratic political system. It is also sometimes asserted that an indigenous Westernised elite favours abolishing the local cultural traditions if they conflict with the efficient pursuit of their socioeconomic developmental objectives. However, a different, more culture-conscious elite of intellectuals, possibly politically motivated, may resist all attempts to abandon their indigenous culture or allow it to weaken their social life, including the effect on it from mass tourism. Fearing degenerative change, they may resist cultural intrusion, and a new cultural nationalism could emerge in reaction against a deepening dependency on, and subordination to, the capitalist/consumerist West. When a culture is on the verge of extinction it can become especially romanticised. There is also a debate about the developing ex-colonial multiracial/cultural countries and their newfound nationalism. This questions whether or not industrialisation is an integrative ideological force that facilitates the establishment of a viable cohesive nation-state and accelerates its economic development.

The seductive appeal of Western capitalism, consumerism, materialism, and industrialisation has sometimes overcome political or theological ideologies—most recently communism. As in 1923 Turkey under Kemal Ataturk, the new ruler of 1925 Iran embarked on a policy of secularization and an attack on the Islamic culture, continued by his son the Shah until he was deposed in 1979. Although he was a strong nationalist, he failed to impose a Western ethos onto his people and Iran reverted to a fundamentalist Islamic culture under Khomeini. Since then there have been similar challenges by fundamentalists with varying degrees of success to the secular governments in Turkey, Lebanon, Pakistan, Tunisia, Egypt and Algeria (Islamic), in Israel (by ultra-Orthodox Jews), and in India (by Hindus). This suggests that even after a period of fifty years, whenever a cultural change or cultural schizophrenia has brought about a loss of identity and the moral certainties of the past, the traditional identity and culture will be re-asserted.

Another hypothesis, by Ronald Dworkin [1993:72], states that "We think it a shame when any distinctive form of human culture, especially a complex and interesting one, dies and languishes . . . [74] Something is sacred or inviolable when its deliberate destruction would dishonour what ought to be honoured . . . [the flag-reverent patriot] values the flag as sacred rather than incrementally valuable, and its sacred character is a matter of association . . . [78] we are horrified at the idea of the deliberate destruction of a work of art not just because we lose the art but because destroying it seems to demean a creative process, we consider very important. Similarly, we honour and protect cultures, which are also, more abstractly, forms of art, because they are communal products of the kinds of enterprise we treat as important . . . [79] [to destroy them] is a shame, an intrinsically bad thing to do."

However, for David Bromwich [1995:89], the very concept of [liberal] culturalism seems to be "a lie"—namely that which says that "Culturalism is a thesis which says that there is a universal human need to belong to a culture—to belong, that is, to a self-conscious group with a known history, a group that by preserving and transmitting its customs, memories, and common practices, confers the primary pigment of individual identity on the persons it comprehends . . . It brings a characterization of the [social] critic as someone who owes his first loyalty to a community in which his thought, being, and social identity have matured." He questions whether the liberal philosophers Michael Walzer, Charles Taylor and Joseph Raz are truly liberal multiculturalists because they do not affirm the pre-eminence of the non-cultural liberal perspective. Another view of culture is that it is the living law of a community. Professor Northrop of Yale University [Magee 1997:136] distinguished between the positive law enacted by governments and enforced by the administrative apparatus, and what he called the "living law" of a community, namely its inherited culture . . . "It was what more than anything else gave a community its unique identity . . . there was a rich mix of established procedure, custom, habit, mutual expectation, assumption, common language, family structure, folk memory, popular art, rituals, possibly a religion and so on . . . If the positive law came too persistently into conflict with the living law [namely its inherited culture] the result would be serious social disruption and upheaval."

When exposed to political and economic strains and crises, cultures usually exhibit an instinctive reflex of self-protection. They may adopt a partial but selective cultural withdrawal from the global community, as have some of the oil-rich Middle Eastern states. They ban, or at least resist the influence of, Others and the extent of cultural diversity by controls on immigration, citizenship, and religion. Some may attempt to face up to the challenge and adapt to multiculturalism only to find that their integrity, and perhaps their very identity, are eroding. Some states that have mass tourism strive to maintain their national identity in spite of tourism's supposedly trans-cultural influence. It would be ingenuous to assume that tourism results in any substantial degree of cross-culturization other than consumerism—nor is it generally attractive to the tourists themselves. Nevertheless, residential mobility can have, to a varying degree, an eroding effect on a culture.

UNESCO, according to Ervin Laszlo [1993: ix-x] recognises that "cultural differences have become battle lines for open conflict. . . . for if culture is part of the problem, it is also our key to the solution. For it is through education, that vital element of culture, that we can begin to combat the rise of intolerance." This raises the question—are these battle lines also latent within the confines of a multicultural society, and to what extent, and which other cultures, are porous or impervious to that of the indigenous society? Moreover can other cultures genuinely assimilate and can an indigenous culture genuinely tolerate, a major and relatively rapid cultural change?

Sissela Bok [1995:1] takes a limited cosmopolitan view that cultural diversity and respect for common values are not mutually exclusive, nor do they diminish one another. She suggests that "we look for a limited set of values so down-to-earth and so commonplace as to be most easily recognised across societal and other boundaries." There is indeed basic cultural commonality within Europe: many share traditions and have common reference points, some of which are also common to the cultures of other racial/ethnic groups and can facilitate trans-cultural cooperation, usually if they serve a common self-interest. This is analogous to the acceptance of racial/ethnic groups into the broad church of a foreign religion such as Catholicism by "modifying" it to meet local traditions. John Beattie [1992:272] states that "social anthropologists are not committed to the view that every culture is 'just as good' as every other culture. But more perhaps, than most people, anthropologists are aware of the dangers of 'holistic' cultural comparisons; different aspects of cultures, different institutions, may usefully be compared, but not whole cultures . . . Some day, perhaps, a single 'admass' culture will be universal, but happily that time is not yet." Nevertheless there are important values that are highly specific to a particular culture, such as a love of animals and respect for democracy. However, other values compete or are irreconcilable, hence the scope for communality or compromise with fundamentalist cultures is limited because of their absolutist religious ethos.

In cases of a major generational change such as in Germany and Japan from an aggressive to a superficially benign and irenic nationalism, no certain answer can be given to the credibility of such a cultural change and what might cause it to revert. After their war crimes, can these formerly aggressive nationalistic cultures have genuinely and permanently re-invented themselves as benign and peaceful nation-states. Their history suggests that certain conditions are necessary. Firstly, the absence of a tradition, or the enforced breakdown, or the voluntary abandonment, often by a heretofore politically neutral indifferent society, of a representative democracy into a totalitarian state. Secondly, continuing severe economic hardship, giving rise to high unemployment and a deteriorating standard of living. Thirdly, a national sense of injustice or humiliation arising from some actual or imagined settlement or restriction imposed by Others. Fourthly, the real or imagined threat of an enemy from without or from within, such as the Jewish world communist conspiracy in Nazi Germany or communism in the Un-American activities era. Fifthly, a convincing and populist ideology that is exploited by a charismatic leader and which also has an appeal to business and other vested influential interests.

NOTES

Beattie, J. *Other Cultures*. London: Routledge and Kegan Paul, 1992. 272.
Benedict, R. *Patterns of Culture*. London: Routledge and Kegan Paul, 1935. 5.
Berry, C J. *Human Nature*. London: Macmillan Education, 1986. 71.
Bok, S. *Common Values*. Columbia: University of Missouri Press, 1995. 1.
Bromwich, D. "Culturalism—The Euthanasia Of Liberalism." In *Dissent*. Winter, 1995. 89–102.
Davies, N. *The Isles—A History* . London: Macmillan, 1999. 1039.

Dworkin, R. *Life's Dominion.'* London: Harper Collins. 1993 72–9.

Eller, J.D. and Coughlan, R.M. "The Poverty of Primordialism: The Demystification of Ethnic Attachments." In *Ethnic and Racial Studies.* Routledge Journals. vol. 16. no. 2. April 1993. 183–202.

Flew, A. "Three Concepts of Racism" In *The Salisbury Review.* October, 1986. 3.

Fukuyama, F. *Trust—The Social Virtues and the Creation of Prosperity.* London: Penguin Books, 1996. 34–6.

Ibid. 996. 92–3.

Grant, B. In *In the Psychiatrist's Chair* II. Clare, A. London: Heinemann, 1995. 157.

Grosby, S. "The Verdict of History: The Inexpungeable Tie of Primordiality – A Response to Eller and Coughlan." In *Ethnic and Racial Studies.* Routledge Journals. vol. 17. no. 1. 1994. 164–171.

Healey, D. *The Time of My Life.* London, Michael Joseph, 1989. 191.

Harvey-Jones, J. *Making It Happen.* London: William Collins, 1988. 117 and 119.

Hofstede, G. In *Writers on Organizations.* Pugh, D.S. and Hickson, D.J. (Eds.) London: Penguin Books, 1989. 80.

Howe, D. Channel 4. *White Tribe.* 13/20/27 January, 2000.

Laszlo, E. (Ed.) *The Multicultural Planet—The Report of a Unesco International Expert Group.* Oxford: One World Publications, 1993. ix-x.

Lynn, V. *We'll Meet Again.* London: Sidgwick and Jackson, 1989. 168.

Magee, B. *Confessions of a Philosopher.* London: Weidenfeld and Nicholson, 1997. 136.

Magee, B. *The Great Philosophers.* Oxford, Oxford University Press. 1987. 239.

Marr, A. BBC 2. *The Day Britain Died.* 31 January/February 1/2, 2000.

Orwell, G. *The Lion and the Unicorn.* London: Martin Secker and Warburg, 1962. 11–3.

Paxman, J. *The English—A Portrait of People.* London, M. Joseph, 1998.

Stationery Office. *Whitaker's Almanack.* London. 2000. 559 and 565.

Trigg, R. "The Sociobiological View of Man." In *Objectivity and Cultural Divergence.* (Ed.) Brown, S.C. Cambridge: Cambridge University Press, 1984. 93–110.

Wittgenstein, L. *Philosophical Investigations* 1. para. 71.

3

The Convergence of Race, Culture, Ethnicity, Class, and Identity

No precise and universally applicable distinction can be made between race, culture and ethnicity. Their boundaries can be indistinct and discussion of any one of these topics cannot be ring-fenced. All three are powerful psychological concepts providing a focus of identity. Race, culture, ethnicity, and class are employed to explain or to justify differences in society, notably in educational or employment under-performance. Some writers on race relations differentiate between racism and racialism, but the distinction is lost in their everyday use. Ian Spencer [1997: xv], writing about immigration, says that he avoids using the terms "race" or "racially." Races do not exist and persistent use of the term as a category supports the contrary impression. Nevertheless race relates to a group that is defined by common descent and is an involuntary and designated phenotype category having distinctly visible physical characteristics. A characteristic of race is inbreeding usually arising from a shared culture and/or territory.

Ethnicity relates to a social group defined primarily by descent, that consciously shares the same characteristics, which may include race, language, religion, and territory, and is affiliated to a common culture. Different races often, but not always, share aspects of the same culture. The trend of present day genetic research is to minimise the genetic variation between races which lends emphasis on the importance of cultural diversity. Where race ends and ethnicity begins is not clear-cut, but ethnicity is commonly regarded as a subdivision of race. At present, it is rare for the media in Britain to avoid referring to race and culture, but talking about cultural differences can be labelled "legitimised racism." Race can sometimes conveniently symbolise less visible cultural and social differences. African-Caribbeans and African-Americans are racially distinct from whites, but their culture is similar, due to centuries of Anglo-Saxon influence. Economic class and social status, which are related to wealth, education, profession, and family background, also influence identity and can overcome a handicap to an individual's social identity and equality of opportunity, which might otherwise be ascribed to race, culture, or ethnicity. The dilemma of identity is illustrated by the black MP Bernie Grant [1995:129], whose upbringing was in a multiethnic Irish Jesuit school in British Guyana, with a Protestant father and a Catholic mother and who came to Britain in 1963 at age nineteen joined by his parents and four siblings. After being a hardline Trotskyite in his youth, he joined the Labour party in 1975 and in 1987 became an MP. After two marriages and three sons, his marriage to a white woman upset some black people and compromised Grant's identity as a spokesperson for his black community. He risked being accused of a desire to be white by proxy and of unconsciously distrusting his own blackness.

The Race Relations Act 1976 avoids defining race by a broad reference to one or more of the following: colour, race, nationality or ethnic or national origins. Muslims consider themselves to be a multiracial, multilinguistic religious global community rather than a specific ethnic, racial, or even national group. To complicate matters, and under the Act's and parts of the Public Order Act 1986 case law, Jews, Sikhs and Ulster Protestants and Catholics (but not Muslims) even though they may be aetheist or non-observant, are recognised as ethnic groups, because an ethnic group can be wider than a religious group. Muslims are at present unprotected by race legislation on discrimination and incitement to racial hatred which has now been proposed. A survey of British Jews by Stephen Miller, Marlena Schmool and Antony Lerman [1996:3] concluded that "unlike other religious groups, in the Jewish community levels of ritual observance are far more closely related to ethnic identity than to strength of belief. For most Jews, religious observance is a means of identifying with the Jewish community, rather than an expression of religious faith." This suggests that some ethno-national conflicts, as in Ulster, can be essentially cultural/racial, but with the importance of the religious component of the cultural difference over-emphasised.

Avtar Brah [1993:11], who has been active in black, antiracist and feminist struggles, claims that differences in culture (pseudoculturalism) are exaggerated so as to justify the exclusion of Others: "cultural racism may be silent or even deny any notion of biological superiority or inferiority, but what characterises it specifically as racism is the subtext of innate difference that implicitly or explicitly serves to denote a group as a 'race.' In other words racism constructs 'racial' difference." This implies that culture is a word of convenient ambiguity and that culture equals race—however a multiracial society does not necessarily have to be multicultural, nor must a multicultural society necessarily be multiracial. Stephen Howe [1995:33] goes further in saying that "one shorthand way of seeing what's wrong with these books [about multiculturalism] would be to go through them, mentally substituting the word 'race' wherever [their authors write] 'culture,' 'ethnic group,' 'nationality' and so on. How many of their claims would still seem acceptable to liberals then?" Presumably this book would also be subject to this criticism.

Anti-racists maintain that race is a social construct created and reproduced through economic, political, and ideological institutions. If so, this renders this construct amenable to deconstruction. Multiculturalists will assert that a British national identity based on a common ethnicity is an ideological construction. The notion of "pure races" is however a genetic myth. A genetic study has shown that Jews and Arabs are closely related going back over four thousand years. American blacks are an admixture, estimated to be twenty-five to thirty percent white genes, and the English are a mixture of Angles, Saxons, Normans and Danes, but this does not mean that DNA research will not confirm that different races do not have different gene pools and are not of "common descent." On the other hand, genetics can provide authenticity for racial separatism and to claims for special territorial rights. The eminent British psychologist Hans Eysenck [1971:36] defines race as "populations that differ genetically and may be distinguished phenotypically [by appearance]. Races are not species; they are able to inter-breed . . . but this does not mean that different populations do not have different gene pools." There are thirty-four classifications of race based on morphological (appearance) characteristics, but if sub-populations are included there could be literally thousands [Eysenck 1971:37]. This makes the term "race" in anti-racist legislation difficult to define. Most Europeans identify Asians by their appearance, although in the Asian Indian sub-continent there are distinct communities speaking many languages, formed into five main groups in which many more are considered to be major. Moreover, what is simply categorised as "Indian" or "Asian" can be ethnically Kashmiri, Pathan, Punjabi, Tamil, Gujurati, Bengali, and religiously Hindu, Muslim, Sikh or Jain. Race relations have evolved from the rhetoric of being simply a matter of "the colour of someone's skin," but recent high profile racial discrimination litigation has had the effect, principally in the media, of labelling all ethnic minorities as "black." This can in fact vary from a deep black to a light tan to Jewish or Irish white. Mixed marriages are sometimes referred to as a "whitening" or "lactification." A truly colour blind society would probably necessitate complete assimilation and government policy would not recognise race or ethnicity.

National origin relates to the nationality received at birth, but it can be changed by naturalisation and acquiring citizenship. Nationhood and national identity are reinforced if the individual's national origin, race, ethnicity, and domicile are all essentially incorporated within a nation-state—criteria unlikely to be satisfied by multiculturalism. There has been, at universities, a resurgence of cultural studies of the European regions that reinforce cultural identities. The fading of cultural difference creates a politics of nostalgia. Language is actively used to foster a sense of national identity and is expressed principally in cultural terms. There is a Welsh language television station, and Ireland's Gaelic television channel has programmes designed to revive the Irish language in school children—spoken by only four percent of a population of 3.6 million. A nationalist Sinn Fein member addresses the Ulster Assembly in Gaelic. Protestants campaigning for recognition as Ulster-Scots, as a counter to Gaelic, have opened the Institute of Ulster-Scot Studies at the University of Ulster in Londonderry for the study of the Ulster-Scots language, heritage and culture [TM 8 Jan. 01]. The British government approved £6 million to promote Gaelic and its traditions in Scotland and to promote links between Scotland and Ireland [TM 17 Dec. 97]. English and Gaelic road signs are to be erected in Scotland [STM 1 April 01]. The French government promotes linguistic diversity in the EU as the best weapon against the English language monopoly and to preserve the Gaelic culture. The Brussels EU bureaucracy can be seen as an appendage of Paris and the French political elite. Nevertheless, French has lost the battle against English on the Internet and elsewhere [TM 30 Jan. 99]. The Japanese government has taken steps after more than fifty years to instil a sense of national identity and patriotism in the nation's children, for the first time giving legal status to the national flag and anthem despite their disturbing associations with the prewar era.

A response to the question "what counts as a nation-state?" is that it is a society having a common ethno-national origin, sharing the same culture and heritage, and having autonomous political self-determination within a given national territory. It may be significant that the multicultural United States may call a state a nation whereas to most Europeans, nation refers to an ethno-national group, and a state refers to the political organisation granting citizenship. The characteristics of a nation are not, and never have been, fixed: they evolve over time.

Professor Anthony Appiah [1997:30] who is an American-Ghanian, doubts whether "the turn-of-the-century wave of immigrants has assimilated, become American. But, from another perspective, we might say that they became white." He sees the replacement of cultural identity with that of a social identity—that is membership of one or other of diverse groups being central to with whom one identifies. "The identities that demand recognition are extremely multifarious." They include earlier cultures, or correspond to old races, religions, territorial regions, old ethnicities, or social categories. "The new talk of 'identity' offers the promise of forms of recognition and of solidarity that could make up for the loss of the rich old kitchen comforts of ethnicity." There is another interpretation—in recent years full assimilation in the United States has not occurred, and dissatisfaction with the resulting de facto multiculturalism has led to a new and more potentially divisive cultural/ racial diversity. Assimilation, or "going native," is clearly very difficult for all races and cultures, and ghettoisation and discrimination emphasise this. In the past "melting pot" assimilation took place over two or three generations whereas today separatist multiculturalism and ease of travel and communication provides an alternative. A similar proposition is that national identity based on racial/ethnic origins either has, or should be, replaced by commonly held civic values of citizenship and loyalties, namely, the citizen-nation. Talk of civic values raises the question of whose values?—which in turn opens up the issue of cultural nationalism.

In today's politically correct and sensitive climate it is more acceptable to talk about culture or ethnicity rather than race. The euphemism *ethnocentrism* is sometimes used to avoid the negative and pejorative connotations of racism together with the broader concept of culturalism. Whereas cultural hegemonists are not all racists, all racists are cultural hegemonists. If a racial group perceives that it has not been fully accepted into the mainstream society, it may reject the mainstream culture which surrounds it, and create a new identity such as the black Muslims, or reassert their identity with mottos such as "black is beautiful." The boundaries between race and culture insofar as they affect people's actions and pronouncements are impossible to assess because the underlying motives are not transparent. When whites move away from areas of multiracial housing or schools, is the real motive because they believe that property values, or the quality of the education, will decline, and/or because they do not want themselves or their children to socialise with Others?

The treatment of Turks and Kurds in Germany and Algerians in France may underlie a reason why some young blacks in Britain are apprehensive about a Europeanisation in which they would provide a new stereotype and visible minority—as did the East European gypsies. A poll showed that forty percent of French people admit to holding racist or xenophobic views— maybe twice the rate in Britain or Germany. The British radical author Paul Foot [1965:229], writing in the early days of non-white immigration, was surprised that there was "less sign of 'quiescence' after fifteen years of Commonwealth immigration than there was after fifteen years of Irish or Jewish immigration." He concluded that "All the signs point gloomily towards increased antagonism." An obvious explanation could be that the Jews and Irish were less numerous and less visible than the non-whites and had been in Britain for much longer than fifteen years. African-Caribbeans, with their diffuse island regional identity, have a problem claiming a distinctive national identity, which particularly the older immigrants compensate for to some extent by adherence to a common Pentecostal religion. Return to the Caribbean may now be of more interest to the younger generation of professionally trained British blacks than it was to the older generation. The younger, professionally trained middle class face less competition there, together with the emotional pull of their roots. Conversely, other migrants, such as those having originally an Indian, then a Ugandan, then a British background who feel unsure of their identity in Britain, may look forward to a regional European identity that may help to dilute most other identities.

Anti-racists claim that almost every problem which affects a black or Asian person such as poverty or lack of success, or "under-representation," is identified a priori as racial discrimination. This adversely affects the toleration by poor young whites who cannot claim the victimisation of race. It is true that the latest wave of economic immigrants has always been made the scapegoats for some social problems that existed before they came, but that is not the same thing as saying that they may not have contributed to them. If minorities fully assimilate and become less differentiated in respect of their ethnicity, class, status, gender, education and wealth, then the assumption that any failure in their political and social aspirations can be explained solely by race or ethnicity becomes less valid.

"Marrying out," or mixed race marriages, can be seen as cultural treachery leading to a hybrid race. Marrying out is less likely in non-migrating and separatist communities. There is a concern by Jewish and Muslim parents in particular, that mixed marriages will result in their religion and culture dying out. There is a paradox inasmuch that the liberal toleration of individualism by the indigenous majority may result in older Muslims feeling that their youth and traditions are threatened. The last national census in 1991 [Peach:1996], which probably significantly understates the present position, showed that forty percent of men of Caribbean origin who are married or in steady relationships live with white women compared to twenty percent black women with white men—the figures for Indians are seven percent and four percent respectively, probably due to religious taboos. A study by Warwick University [TM 19 July 98] indicated that black men are twelve times more likely to have a family with a white wife than a black woman with a white man. The ISER (The Institute for Social and Economic Research) has published an analysis of multicultural family formation in Britain (Berthoud. 2000). It comments [2] that "One extreme position is to argue that minorities' behaviour should be judged exclusively according to the conventions of their own societies, in their country of origin. That overlooks the essential fact that the minorities' current social structures are no longer in their countries of origin, but are located in multicultural Britain . . . [12] Most commentators seem to welcome the increase in the number of mixed relationships, as an indicator of reducing cultural, social and economic barriers between ethnic groups. Perhaps it is a sign of declining racism within the white community . . . [13] From the point of view of Caribbeans as a community though, the trend may lead either to the decline, or the increasing isolation, of black-ness as an independent identity." Britain's rate of interracial relationship is ten times above the European average [STM 9 April 00]. Nine out of ten black men in a domestic relationship at the age of twenty are with non-black women. The successful British black high profile role models who married whites—the broadcasters Trevor Macdonald, Darcus Howe, the comedian Lenny Henry, the academic Stuart Hall, the boxer Frank Bruno, and the MP Bernie Grant are sometimes resented by black women who feel that they are a "dying breed." The reservations sometimes displayed by whites, particu-larly parents, towards mixed race couples, are no more than that displayed by blacks, Jews, and Muslims to marrying out. Bernie Grant said [1995:147] that his mixed race relationship "has caused some difficulty and he knows that there are some groups and black people who avoid me like the plague . . . they'd say that I'm not wholly a black person because I've got a white partner." Opposition to marrying out is not confined to blacks and whites. In Westernised South Korea, 1500 American soldiers marry each year, but the Korean par-ents object to the "marrying out" and the irreconcilable culture clash results in eight out of ten divorces [BBC 2 17 June 2000].

The identity crisis caused by mixed race children is exemplified by talk of being a "third race," or by a Children's Society advertisement for foster-parents that said "her mother is black-Caribbean and her father is white. A new family will need to reflect her racial origins and help her develop a positive sense of identity." The question is—which identity? The 1990 Children's Act works against assimilation—it restricts adoption to where a child's culture, religion, and race needs will be understood. The compelling need for an identity is evidenced at the personal level by the insistence of some adopted children to discover their "real" or natural parentage. This is part of the continuing debate between the government and social services as to whether children raised by loving transracial parents are likely to have an identity crisis. According to the British Agencies of Fostering and Adoption [TM 19 Feb. 00], of the children waiting for adoption, ten percent are black and seventeen percent are of mixed race. About eighty-nine percent of adopt-ers are white. It is unlikely that a white couple would be allowed to adopt any of them, and a lack of black adoptive parents condemns thousands of chil-dren, particularly black children, to years in institutional care. A survey of thirty local authorities showed that black children wait half as long again as whites and that there are twice as many ethnic minority children in care as white children. Nevertheless, the adoption agencies have been averse to the "melting pot" approach of the 1960s and 1970s to transracial adoption and insist that this is not due to ageism, education, or racism. The black separatist Nation of Islam asserts that transracially adopted/fostered children tend to be "educated against themselves." Others argue that that it is no more certain that a transracial placement will succeed than a same-race adoption will fail—family background is the key. None of this addresses the dilemma as to where should one place a mixed race child.

Intolerance and prejudice can exist between minority ethnic groups, particularly if they perceive a threat to their group interest, such as between Asian Pacifics and blacks, Africans and African-Caribbeans, Sikhs and Muslims, Hindus and Muslims, Muslims and Christians, and blacks and whites with Asians. A 1997 survey by the Institute of Public Policy Research and NOP (National Opinion Poll) was conducted on inter-ethnic prejudice in Britain—many Jewish and Asian peoples show negative attitudes to African-Caribbeans—but the main target of prejudice is thought to be Pakistanis [Howe14 Feb. 97]. The effect of the relative proportion of non-whites to the white indigenous population and the difference between accepting a visitor and a permanent resident is illustrated by the acceptance of black troops who were temporarily in Britain. During pre-WW2 it was estimated that the non-white population of Britain was perhaps eight thousand, which by D-Day had grown to 130 thousand—one in every thirteen GI's [Reynolds 1996:103 and 303].

Asians and Asian-Pacifics have largely self-prospered in the United States in spite of initial poverty and discrimination. Some now out-perform whites .in educational achievement and income, but this is not generally so with blacks disadvantaged by three decades of discrimination. This has led to the view that blacks pose the principal race problem in the United States. Spencer Holland, a black American educational psychologist [DM 14 Sept. 95], studied school boys both in Washington and in the London borough of Hackney. His theory is that black youths under-achieve, because they spend the whole of their lives without a male role model in their families or in their communities. Many black men do not marry and the mother brings up the children on her own, and their teachers are almost exclusively women. He brought into the classroom male volunteers of any colour who could be listened to with respect. By the age of ten, eighty-five percent of the boys were at the standard level of attainment or above, compared with eighty-five percent elsewhere who were below. In black culture many children are brought up by a lone parent—amongst American blacks who live in a ghettoised environment it is currently greater than seventy percent. *Social Trends* [2001:43–4] reported that in Spring 2000, of the families with dependent children in GB (Great Britain: England, Wales, and Scotland), nearly half (forty-nine percent) of those headed by a black person were lone parent families, compared with one in thirteen headed by Asians (eight percent Indian, fifteen percent Pakistani/Bangladeshi), and about one in five (twenty-one percent) headed by whites. These figures reflect the African-Caribbean culture of unmarried couples having children. It has to be said that in Britain, the long-term relationship of marriage together with parenting has become eroded in recent years [STMG 1 July 01]. Indian and Pakistani/ Bangladeshi households tended to be larger than those from other ethnic groups, at 3.5 and 4.6 persons per household respectively. *Social Trends* [43] observes that "Such households may contain three generations with grandparents living with a married couple and their children. Even once age structure has been taken into account, the South Asian population still have the largest households." Although the general ethnic/radial category of "Asians" is widely used, it should be remembered that Pakistanis and Bangladeshis originate from poorer areas of the Indian sub-continent, have poorer educational and other qualifications, and have not been in Britain as long as Indians who, when they arrived, were generally better off. Deprivation is not exclusively a racial problem—it also applies to the under-class elsewhere. Young people need to see a clear purpose and benefit in becoming like a role model, and their performance is closely related to the strength of the family unit. Where this culture is strong and its successful role models are in evidence, the group tends to succeed. Ray Honeyford [1992:194] offers the cultural hypothesis that Asian-Pacifics and Asians have a stronger family structure. "Racism had little to do with black educational failure, the causes of which were located in West Indian family structure and values." A generation of young blacks may possibly never know their father. Lord Scarman [1981:105], in his report on the 1981 Brixton riot, also drew attention to the need for pre-school provision "among West Indian children partly as a result of family breakdown."

NOTES

Anon. *Catholic Children's Society Newsletter.* Winter 1994–95.
Appiah, K.A. "The Multiculturalist Misunderstanding." In *The New York Review.* 9 October 1997. 30.
Berthoud, R. *Family Formation in Multicultural Britain—Three Patterns of Diversity.* Colchester. ISER. 2000 2.
Ibid. 12 and 13.
Brah, A. "Re-Framing Europe." In *Feminist Review.* no.45, Autumn 1993. 11
Eysenck, H.J. *Race, Intelligence and Education.* London:Temple Smith, 1971. 37.
Foot, P. *Immigration and British Politics.* Harmondsworth, Middx: Penguin Books, 1965. 229.
Grant, B. *In the Psychiatrist's Chair II.* Clare, A. London:Heinemann, 1995. 129.
Ibid. 1995. 147.
Home Office Research Report. "The Attitudes of Ethnic Minorities." 1984.
Honeyford, R. *Race And Politics in Britain.* Saggar, S. Hemel Hempstead: Harvester Wheatsheaf, 1992. 194.
Howe, D. *New Statesman and Society.* February 14 1997.
Howe, S. *New Statesman and Society.* Book Reviews. 18 August. 1995. 33.
Miller, S. Schmool et al. *Social and Political Attitudes of British Jews; Some Key Findings of the J.P.R. Survey.* London: Institute forJewish Policy Research, 1996. 3.

Peach, C. (Ed.). *Ethnicity in the 1991 Census*. vol. 2. London, Stationery Office, 1996.
Reynolds, D. *Rich Relations—The American Occupation of Britain 1942–45*. London: Harper Collins. 1996. 103 and 303.
Scarman, Lord. *The Brixton Disorders 10–12 April1981*. Stationery Office, London, 1981, 105.
Spencer, I.R.G. *British Immigration Policy Since 1939*. London: Routledge, 1997. xv.
BBC 2. *Seoul Mates*. 17 June 2000.
Channel 4. *The Colour of Love*. February 17 2000.
Channel 4. *Audrey and Mark's Story*. 1994.

4

Relativism:
Cultural, Moral, and Political

Cultural relativism is the recognition and acceptance of other cultures, without grading them as higher or lower, superior or inferior than one another. Eurocentrism, for example, implies the superiority of the European culture. Multiculturalism implies that an indigenous society is at fault, not just if it fails to value any or all other cultures as being of equal worth globally, but of equal worth within its own territory. It supposes that cultural differences are acceptable and reducible, and cultural values are commensurable. The cultural nationalist, on the other hand, prefers to live within his own culture and its way of "living together" and not with that of Others. This is not necessarily judgmental of their relative values—he might prefer tea rather than coffee, whilst acknowledging that others prefer coffee, and not be obliged to provide a rationale or accept blame for this preference.

Cultural relativism avoids having a belief in the pre-eminence of a particular culture. It can lead to its attrition and may remove any preference over other cultures. With cultural relativism there is no universal norm and any judgmental comparison between cultures is questionable. Critics of multiculturalism, whilst accepting cultural relativism on the global dimension, would not necessarily assert that their inherited culture was the best. They might instinctively say that it was the "best for them," or that which they best "understood," or were "used to," or with which they felt "most comfortable" or "secure." Other than religious evangelism and diplomatic human rights "mission statements," there is not today much global missionary spirit or cultural imperialism—there is more cultural protectionism.

Relativism says that there are no absolutes, and that all cultural norms, moral principles, and values, whatever their origin, are simply a matter of individual taste. Supposedly people are able to co-exist amicably within a pluralist and separatist society, independently and relatively uninfluenced by one another. Arthur Melzer [1991:11], however, sees dangers in relativism: "two new mutant strains of intolerance have evolved today that are resistant to 'multiculturalism' precisely because they grow not from ignorance of diversity, but somehow from diversity itself . . . [first], students today believe as a matter of course that 'everyone is different' . . . [as a result] they have less of the crusading, idealistic, dogmatic type of intolerance, but more of the visceral, nihilistic, self-indulgent kind . . . There is also a second new strain of intolerance that tends to arise precisely in a multicultural society. When people experience the debilitating effects of diversity—the loss of certainty, strong belief, and universal principles—they often counteract them by actively closing their minds . . . [and] tend to mutate into dogmatisms, hardened against outside influence . . . Let us start by recognising that human beings do not want to be tolerant." David Steel, a former leader of Liberal Democrat party, indulged in vacuous political rhetoric [1985:146] when he said that "The paradox of modern Britain is that we need more diversity and more unity . . . If we could accept the challenge of pluralism . . . we would find it easier to recapture what unites us as a nation." The diversity in Britain is now apparent, its unity less so, which suggests that diversity undermines unity.

A basic premise of this discussion is that non-Western cultures are, broadly speaking, incompatible with, and if they are imported and remain separatist, may pose a threat to, the national identity which the majority have inherited, become accustomed to, and do not wish to have undermined. This is not to argue that a monocultural hegemony should remain unchangeable, or that it remains unaffected over time by internal and external influences—but that it should change at its own pace and in its own way, namely by a pragmatic process of social gradualism. It should not have imposed on it or acquire without its express consent, different cultures, races, and religions by a socially engineered policy of multiculturalism or unrestricted immigration. Nor does this imply a sceptical belief that all aspects of other cultures lack their own validity, provided that they are exercised within their own territorial and social milieu.

A pluralist and separatist multicultural state requires a high degree of acceptance of moral relativism for its social cohesion and stability, otherwise its factions cannot co-exist peacefully. Mary Midgeley [1991:76–7] characterises the compromise of "simple, confident relativism" as saying that the "customs and moral beliefs [of Others] are valid within the cultures to which they belong, but they have no validity outside them." On the other hand, the relativism may be "negative, sceptical or fatalistic" and "nobody can say anything valid about moral questions in cultures other than their own. It has no view about whether people can do this 'difficult' thing inside their own culture." In both cases the majority must surrender the pre-eminence of its culture either consciously or by default. Once the common enemy has been defeated, sub-conflicts would probably begin. There would no longer be a majority—only sectarian minorities, probably competing for power and disinclined to accept a unifying cultural identity.

Cultural relativism is manifest in political correctness. It requires that there should be no discrimination between cultures, and that no value judgement can be free of opinionated prejudices. Relativism would see this as reflecting differing perceptions of values and rights, with each culture being treated on its own merits. Ultimately there would no longer be any framework of rules in a society influencing behaviour or any common moral standards, even though most know intuitively right from wrong. Adoption of this personalised and customised perspective would lead to the loss of moral certitudes, moral relativism, and loss of a national identity. Some of the present-day politicised ethno-national conflicts, some of which have led to the re-emergence of nation-states, resulted from different cultures having deeply held moral and religious beliefs and values, created and developed since time immemorial and reflecting their particular history and needs.

Western society has been subjected to the psychological "provocation" of the manifestations of non-Western cultures which increasingly surround them— mosques, minarets, temples, idols, language, rituals, dress. This may reflect the West's present day liberal moral ambivalence and secularism, and suggest a loss of conviction, with Christianity seen as a "colonial faith" which has lost its coherence. In Victorian society, the Christian Protestant culture was associated with being British, and enabled most people to feel comfortable with a set of deontological rules and a moral framework to guide their lives, which to some extent were supervised by the Church. Nowadays abstract and absolute deontological principles tend to be accepted only if individual and societal experience shows them to be valid in practice. However, cultural relativism, together with limitless toleration and the absence of moral stigma, can lead to the feeling of being lost in a moral vacuum, particularly by the older generation. Moreover, relativism undermines precise thinking that not only leads to blandness, but also to a loss of definition and coherence.

Religious pluralism is an important feature within the broader context of multiculturalism. The authority and moral leadership of the established Anglican Church has been largely replaced by an unformulated spirituality without observance, or a secular utilitarian humanism, or as Archbishop George Carey declared [DM 28 Oct. 00] "a tacit aetheism now prevails." Nevertheless, there continues to be recognised the importance to European culture of humanist Christian values and virtues, irrespective of whether these are directly ascribed to the Christian religion or to a God. The prominent playwright John Mortimer, of the humanist Atheists For Christ Society [MoS 16 April 95], echoed an appeal for a moral hegemony and attacked puritanical political correctness: "What is beyond argument is that they [the Gospels] provide a system of ethics to which we must return if we are to avoid social disaster." The Anglican Church, in the recent past, has condoned moral and religious relativism coupled with pleas for toleration. But the Senior Chaplain of Eton College observed "the Archbishop of Canterbury should take lessons from the Moslems on how to promote [the Christian] faith, [and condemned its] bending over backwards to appease other faiths and fashionable causes" [DM 13 Jan. 95]. Carey has belatedly begun to attack "liberal tolerant" moral and cultural relativism and "privatised morality," and urged that Britain should rediscover moral objectivism [DM 6 July 96]. He said "when morality becomes a matter of individual opinion, traditional sources of authority become irrelevant and we lose the objective of absolute standards of right and wrong. I long for our country to recover its idealism—its vision for truth, honesty, goodness, fairness and love, which can be regenerated only by nurturing the spiritual truths which lie at the heart of our society . . . we have lost a sense of shared values. People do their own thing, lost in a jungle of moral relativism where what is good and right is no more than a matter of individual opinion. This I believe, is the backdrop to the weakening of social cohesion and the increase of anti-social, hurtful behaviour . . . Britain was in danger of squandering the inheritance of faith and values that underpinned the ethics of our civilisation" [DM 16 Mar. 96].

These comments raise the question as to whether the Anglican Church's calls for toleration and the welcoming of diversity and difference in cultures and religions in Britain can do other than encourage cultural relativism, which may lead to moral relativism, the erosion of moral certainties and apathy towards all morality. A Church of England report, "The Search for Faith and Witness of the Church" [TM 11 Nov. 96], examined post-modern life—it did not "argue for a theocracy, but believed society must acknowledge that its basic moral and spiritual vision was inspired by the Judaeo-Christian tradition." It cited a "need for a common language about ultimate values and beliefs," and that "the more people move away from belonging to institutions, the less they have something to anchor their faith. People pick up all kinds of things. This drifting of belief is causing fragmentation. We can see this personal and social fragmentation all around us." Multiculturalism necessitates at least a subliminal belief and acceptance of cultural relativism by the mainstream society in which toleration becomes an obligatory response. Once a society has become multicultural, any attempt by political or religious leaders to resurrect the traditional mores of the inherited culture will meet with limited success, because there is no longer a shared morality.

Some argue that it is virtues and not values that are the foundation of a moral society. Virtues remain relatively fixed and absolute and originate from the theocratic tradition of the society. Values are variable because individuals have a differing menu of values and their prioritisation. Some might think that the American system of life imprisonment, which means exactly that, is contrary to a basic human right—but others would claim that it is a necessary utilitarian response to a violent society. If British animal rights campaigners tried to persuade the Spanish not to patronise bull fights, this would be seen as "busybodying" outside of their own country, as well as being ineffective. Relativism would mean that bull fighting would have to be permitted in Britain. This type of conflict led to the French actress Brigitte Bardot being convicted of racism when she objected to Muslim ritual public animal slaughter [TM 10 Oct. 97]. This was made illegal in 1997 in France, but is officially condoned using British sheep [TM 29 March 99]. In Britain more than 60,000 sheep and cows are slaughtered in abattoirs over the three day Islamic festival [TM 6 March 00].

NOTES

Melzer, A.M. "Tolerance 101." In *The New Republic.* 1 July, 1991. 11.
Midgeley, M. *Can We Make Moral Judgements?* Bristol: The Bristol Press, 1991. 76–7.
Steel, D. *Partners In One Nation—A New Vision of Britain 2000.* London: The Bodley Head. 1985. 146.

5

Multiculturalism and the Politics of Identity

Multiculturalism can become a feature of the politics of polarisation and difference, but one that may be presented in terms of the moral imperatives of equality and rights. A philosophical question is: what, if anything, should elevate the toleration of multiculturalism from being a political and sociological issue into a moral obligation? Multiculturalism is a general term that can mean different things to different people who understandably have a preference which particular version they envisage. A culturally pluralist society could co-exist stably, provided that the toleration is both received and offered by all its component groups, not just by the mainstream society. If this reciprocity is withheld whilst more toleration and rights are demanded, then public practices and political influence of minority cultures should not be automatically acquiesced to by the state.

The term *multiculturalism* is a neologism that did not appear in the American press until about 1989. Politicians and most writers on the subject do not define it or assume that everyone knows what it means. It is an umbrella term that covers different types of cultural pluralism—a multicultural society is one made up of diverse ethno-national cultures. The exact form it takes differs from country to country depending on the origin, history, and nature of its particular cultural pluralism. The term *multicultural* as used in this discussion refers to significant sectarian cultural diversity and difference arising from race, ethnicity, and/or religion. There is no single global model of a multicultural society, and it is unlikely that any particular experience can be translated, at least in its entirety, to other situations in the world, so generalisations have to be considered with this in mind. Michael Walzer [1992:168 and 170] observes on the "'new tribalism'. . . . what form this accommodation [of minorities] might take is not a matter to be determined in any a priori way . . . arrangements of these sorts should always be allowed, but they can't be imposed . . . there is no single correct outcome . . . these won't be unitary structures: nor will they be identical [171] . . . our common humanity will never make us members of a single universal tribe. The crucial commonality of the human race is particularism."

Unlike Britain and the rest of Western Europe, the New World countries of America, Canada, and Australia, with vast under-populated land masses, had the incentive to populate or perish, and a cultural history extending back in time for only about two to three hundred years. Multiculturalism can be inherited from the history of the region, such as in North America, New Zealand, South Africa, Australia, Israel, Yugoslavia, and Ulster. These have sizeable groups of American-Indians, Maoris, Bantus, Hispanics, Aborigines, French-Canadians, Palestinians, Basque Spaniards, Balkan Muslims, and Irish Catholics who have been domiciled in these regions for centuries and/or were the original inhabitants. Oddly enough, the only occasion when the rights of an indigenous people become an issue is when they are a minority and not the majority. Some states have inherited their multiculturalism almost from their inception, followed by sizeable immigration by Others. Non-racial multiculturalism is evident in Israel and in some Muslim states, where there is an ongoing conflict between Western secularism and religious fundamentalism in forging a national identity. In such cases the problem is how to best manage or limit cultural pluralism, and not whether it can avoided. Multiculturalism and multiracialism, globally, between nation-states, is and always has been, a fact of human existence—its acceptance within a nation-state is not as self-evident.

Multinational (or multiracial or multiethnic) states such as the former USSR and Yugoslavia, including most of the Central/Eastern European and Central Asian states and the newly independent African states, inherited their multiculturalism together with an imperial political ideology. These are or were political "states" rather than "nation-states," their diversity arising from the political incorporation of territorially concentrated cultures and national minorities. This arose from a history of population movements and/or the drawing or redrawing of post-conflict boundaries which attempted to subsume ethnic and cultural divisions by compounding them into larger states, hoping for the assimilation of ethnic differences. Some of these have not achieved the post-colonial and post-Cold War nationalist aspirations of their majority ethnic/cultural group, but with others, and because of their lack of a convincing national identity and sovereignty, their ethno-national divisions have re-erupted after remaining dormant for long periods. Such is the history of the Balkans from the early nineteenth century and Ulster in the twentieth century: both powder kegs of ethnic strife. This experience gives rise to the issue as to whether or not Britain and the West should discourage its own multiculturalism acquired by liberal immigration and endeavour to maintain their essentially monocultural hegemonies. The obvious way to manage this, but the one which most writers on this issue avoid (no doubt conscious of its political incorrectness) is by firmly controlling immigration by a strictly enforced quota based and selective policy.

Fukuyama [1996:269–70] opposes multiculturalism and argues that the United States effectively remains a monocultural society: "Americans in the 1990s have become preoccupied—pro or con—with the issue of 'multiculturalism.' The proponents of multicultural studies have argued that the United States is a diverse society and that Americans need to recognise and better understand the positive contributions of many cultures, particularly those outside Europe, that make it up. Multicultural proponents argue that either the United States never had a single culture beyond its universalistic political and legal system, or else that the dominant European culture of generations past was oppressive and should not be a model to which all Americans must conform. No one, of course, can object to the idea of seriously studying other cultures, and in a liberal society it is clearly necessary to learn to tolerate differences among people. It is quite another thing, however, to argue that either the United States never had a dominant culture of its own or that as a matter of principle it ought not to have a dominant culture to which diverse groups can assimilate . . . Diversity surely can bring real economic benefits, but past a certain point it erects new barriers to communication and cooperation with potentially devastating economic and political consequences. Nor is it the case that the United States was always a highly diverse place, knit only by a common Constitution and legal system. Beyond the United States' universalisitic political-legal system, there has always been a central cultural tradition that gave coherence to American social institutions and permitted the rise of the United States as a dominant global economic power. That culture, originally the attribute of a particular religious and ethnic group, later became deracinated from those ethnoreligious roots and became a broadly accessible identity for all Americans."

Spencer [1997:1] says that "The idea that Britain has for long been a multiracial society is one that has been widely aired and is now widely believed, fostered principally by liberally minded people associated with spreading and reinforcing the multicultural approach to education and race relations." John Rex asserts [1991:7] that "the idea that we now do have a multicultural society, and that this is not only inevitable but desirable, is widely accepted. Unfortunately it is not at all clear what exactly the term means. Although it purports to being a sociological description, sociologists have done little to clarify the kinds of structure to which it refers." He identifies the difficulties with its resolution and recognises that it will be a continuing process of conflict and compromise. Professor Joseph Raz [1994:67] also recognises that "multiculturalism is a problem today and for the foreseeable future—a problem for politics and the ethics of politics."

Multiculturalists may attempt to discredit a cultural hegemony by reductionism, namely by using objective arguments to minimise its validity. Thus the appeal of an inherited cultural/national identity can be summarily dismissed as being merely the emotional outcome of an "imagined or transient community," an "elective affinity" or a "collective hallucination," which cannot be intellectually valid or sustainable. Nevertheless, the empirical evidence leads to the rejection of this claim and its supposedly rational/reasoned basis as unconvincing, if it is counter-intuitive. The benefits of forsaking monoculturalism for acquired/elective multiculturalism remain unproven. The benefits, let alone the penalties, are never positively identified other than perhaps by trite statements about the choice of exotic foods and restaurants, or "it makes one realise that there are other people in the world"— an experience readily acquired by travel. Moreover, the evidence to date does not support the futurology that some common eclectic geoculture will develop, and that war will be abolished, and that people will become cosmopolitan "citizens of the world." Michael Ignatieff the philosopher [1994] characterises the cosmopolitan as "someone who's got a passport in his pocket" (or preferably two passports with dual nationality and maybe expatriate voting rights), and that it "is only possible because of the secure order of stable nation states." Internationalism or regionalism is only, if ever, likely to prevail over nationalism when individuals perceive their economic welfare and security being significantly enhanced thereby.

A tactic used by proponents of multiculturalism is to promote the belief that Britain not only is, but always has been, an immigrant society, and that there is no longer any such thing that can be defined as a distinctive British or English culture. They will assert that any claim to the existence of a British indigenous culture or Britishness is simply a prejudice, or that all Western societies have always been multicultural or multiracial, and label the British indigenous majority an ethnic group. Britain and Europe have indeed been qualitatively multiracial for at least a hundred years, but only to a minor degree. There is no pure British national identity—it being made up originally of migrant Saxons, Angles, Jutes, Danes, and Normans. These regional groups were racially similar and they conflated into a common culture that has existed for at least nine centuries. According to Dr. David Coleman, Reader in Demography, Oxford University [TM 30 Jan. 01], "No population can have 'pure' origins. But relative cultural homogeneity was regarded at home and abroad as a strength . . . Even without detailed data it seems clear that immigration from outside the British Isles has been a minor factor in the development of our population from the eleventh century up to WW2. It is correctly relegated to footnotes in the demographic reconstruction of the population of England, which is the most complete of any in the world. Surname and genetic data reinforce the general demographic picture . . . Occasional notable episodes of immigration, of Flemings, Poor Palatines, Huguenots, Ashkenazi Jews and many others, do not disturb this general conclusion. Migration is usually a two-way process. But from the seventeenth to the mid-twentieth century we have been a nation of emigrants, not immigrants." A similar criticism, namely that they are a "nation of immigrants" could equally be levelled against most nations of the world which claim a national identity if one goes back far enough in time. Although the scale, scope and nature of migration over the last millennium has radically widened and accelerated, and although some aspects of all world cultures have been influenced by migration and globalisation, the appeal of a unique identity remains as strong as ever.

Joseph Raz [1994:68 –9] identifies three stages of the "liberal response" to the progression into a multicultural society. There is initially toleration. This is eventually supplemented by the assertion of non-discriminatory minority rights. This is then followed by the political affirmation of multiculturalism. Another analysis of the stages through which the relationships between the mainstream and ethnic minorities can go is: initially curiosity; then economic welcome; then industrial and social antagonism; then legislative antagonism; then fair-play tendencies; then quiesence; followed by second generation difficulties. An idealised multicultural society can be abstractly characterised as one of "equal [cultural] dignity" or "equal respect," and more specifically as one in which its component groups co-exist and maintain their separate cultural identity, including their different value systems to whatever degree they choose, and which are unreservedly tolerated by the mainstream society (as long as one continues to exist) and by each other. In the absence of complete assimilation what is more likely to develop is one of the three versions of multiculturalism, the boundaries of which merge with changes in the demography and with the passage of time.

There is a category of partially assimilated and partially separatist "two domain" multiculturalism (sometimes termed "liberal" multiculturalism) in which the ethnic groups have incompatible national origins, values, beliefs, and customs and retain their cultural, intellectual and spiritual ties. They may not fully accept or be fully accepted by the mainstream society or by one another, but their racial and cultural diversity and differences are maintained privately and are tolerated by the mainstream society within acceptable limits. They maintain a separate and supposedly neutral set of common and noncompeting values with the mainstream society, whilst retaining effective autonomy over their private cultural determination and expressions. This category of political and economic socialisation requires an outward conformity—like being American/British in public and Jewish/Muslim in private, with the different groups living and sometimes working in virtually completely separate communities. They cooperate in, or may be indifferent albeit initially, to the democratic political process of social and economic decision making of the mainstream society, with whom they maintain a general consensus about objectives insofar as they relate to the common good. Two-domain assimilation alleviates inter-group conflict and tension and improves relationships because ethnic minorities have autonomy over their cultural space. It can be argued that this partial assimilation should be encouraged by the majority since it does not impinge on the public domain. This compromise largely insulates the public, political, and institutional aspects of the nation-state from cultural encroachment. Peter Salins [1997:56–7] expresses a concern about one type of "two-domain" multiculturalism, namely acculturation: "acculturation may or may not accompany assimilation. Usually, immigrants who assimilate—or at least their children—become acculturated as well, but not always and not completely . . . except for the need to speak English, acculturation, in the American historical context, may be meaningless because the base culture to which immigrant communities may be expected to relate is so fluid . . . because it is manifestly clear that people can be acculturated without being assimilated, there is a great deal to worry about. Indeed, in most of the world's hot spots of ethnic conflict, acculturation is not an issue, but assimilation is."

A second broad category of multiculturalism is one in which the ethnic groups are not assimilated and remain completely separatist (illiberal multiculturalism), retaining their distinct national identity and culture, and a loyalty which may transcend national borders. These separatist minority groups may harbour a different and intolerant political agenda that is not related to the common good, but is aimed at enhancing their separatism and increasing their political and economic influence. Even with the first category of partially assimilated and partially separatist multiculturalism, the mainstream society may have a latent concern that sooner or later, and given favourable conditions, extremist elements in one or more of the minority groups may revert to this second completely separatist and sectarian category.

A third category of multiculturalism, usually where the diverse groups approximate in size, is more highly politicised. This is called *incorporation* or *integration*—sometimes termed *plural multiculturalism*. There is a continuing dual (two-way) political/cultural transformation between both groups whereby the minority insists on a more complete incorporation into the polity, which the heretofore dominant majority allows. An example of this has been Ulster since the civil rights campaign of the late 1960s. There is a continuous political contestation whereby the government is the agent for this transformative incorporation, rather than the base from which "minority" exclusions can be managed. If the relative proportion and influence of an ethnic minority increases, there will be a tendency for it to demand incorporation. The Parekh Report [2000] has a vision of cultural incorporation being applied to Britain even though the quantity of all non-white cultures is less than ten percent. Supposedly the indigenous majority and the minority groups would jointly develop and accept a common culture made up of the "best" features of the diverse cultures. Since there are several culturally different ethnic groups this could be a recipe for unworkable chaos, with the mainstream group trying to hold the ring. It assumes that not only the mainstream society, but each and every minority group—some aspects of whose cultures are known to be mutually incompatible—could negotiate a cultural mix which would be generally accepted. In practice, what set out to be a cultural discourse could develop into a conflict for political influence with racist overtones. In theory, an *incorporatist* society could be culture blind and ideally multicultural, inasmuch that it accepted all cultural diversity and distinctions but with none predominating.

A weakness of social engineering, including that of promoting multiculturalism, is the assumption that other aspects of the social environment remain unchanged by it, whereas they react to it. Moreover, sociological-like economic prediction is susceptible to error because it is not unifactorial and human nature is involved. The individual may take risks; society should not. The use of historical precedents to support an argument can be selective, inaccurate and misleading and may have more to do with motives today than with the past. The eminent philosopher Karl Popper [1957:47] recognised the fallacy inherent in radical historicism (interpreting the past in order to predict the future), which implies that the course of history is predetermined. He saw the fallacy in social engineering towards a pre-determined utopian end: "the real outcome will always be different from the rational construction. It will always be the resultant of the momentary constellation of contesting forces. Furthermore, under no circumstances could the outcome of rational planning become a stable structure; for the balance of forces is bound to change. All social engineering, no matter how much it prides itself on its realism and on its scientific character, is doomed to remain a Utopian dream." He also warned [54] that "the historicist may even go further. He may add that the most resonable attitude to adopt is so to adjust one's system of values as to make it conform with the impending changes." Popper [1966:167], also favoured a piecemeal approach (gradualism), stated "what some people have in mind who speak of our 'social system,' and of the need to replace it by another 'system,' is very similar to a picture painted on a canvas which has to be wiped clean before one can paint a new one. But there are some great differences . . . in all matters, we can only learn by trial and error, by making mistakes and improvements . . . accordingly, it is not reasonable to assume that a complete reconstruction of our social world would lead at once to a workable system." Popper's thinking is relevant to multiculturalism and cosmopolitanism, namely, the assertion that diversity and difference must be good and/or are inevitable and workable and should be socially engineered, and this should not be resisted.

Integrative multiculturalism does have a conceptual appeal in spite of its problems, inasmuch that conceivably it could lead to a new cosmopolitan culture taking the best features from other cultures and eliminating a potential source of global conflict. With what process this cultural selection/rejection would take place and be generally accepted, though, is not clear. Unlike other ideologies such as in education, if the multicultural experiment does not work, there is no reversal, no going back. In 1996 the British Labour party, after thirty years of the dogma of mixed ability education, was able to reverse it to a meritocratic system. Irreversible social experiments should be treated with caution and introduced with a pragmatic gradualism. Account should be taken of the limited and particularised evidence on multiculturalism elsewhere in the world over the relatively short time span of about fifty years. Its consequences, both short-term and long term, should be evaluated, and its effects, both direct and indirect, monitored, so that problems, when they become apparent, are not aggravated.

Rex [1986:125] suggests that in Britain minorities "argue for multiculturalism. No one suggests, however, that this means a right of the groups as such to share in the control of government [as in Quebec or Belgium] or that the various languages concerned should become Civil Service languages. What is sought is equality of opportunity in these spheres together with a respect for their right to manage their own domestic and communal affairs in their own way. This is all that is usually claimed under the banner of multiculturalism." This is unsurprising in Britain where ethnic minorities account for only about ten percent of the population, but the situation might well be different if and when they account for, say, thirty percent.

He also believes [133] that "multiculturalism is only likely to be tolerated if it does not threaten the shared civic culture, including of course the idea of equality of opportunity . . . the reason why the term multiculturalism is often retained is that in an ideal multicultural society all cultures come to share a common core which prevents the derogation of anyone because of his cultural background. . . . the question has to be asked whether one could envisage a multicultural society in which all cultures were taken equally seriously. Is it simply because we only think about them as generalized community structures with definite and restricted functions that we tolerate the idea of multiculturalism at all?" Once again, in Britain, where all the various ethnic groups account for approximately ten percent of the population, how in practical terms could all these differing cultures (including the indigenous culture) be taken "equally seriously?"

Rex [134] contends that "multiculturalism is a feasible social and political ideal. The real difficulty is that what may gain support under this title will be a fraudulent alternative which dissociates multiculturalism from equality of opportunity and thereby opens the way to de facto differential incorporation." "Differential incorporation" as used here implies conceding only the right to be culturally different and separatist, but without allowing for equality of opportunity, as was the case with apartheid.

Rex [130] suspects that "racism can often lie behind opposition to multiculturalism . . . when arranged marriage is given prominence before all else in an account of a minority culture, and is seen only from a partial point of view, we may suspect that the critic is hostile to the minority culture and is using an argument about arranged marriage as a form of derogatory abuse." One may ask whether the same explanation would be advanced if the objection were to forced as opposed to arranged marriages. A High Court judge has made a landmark ruling that served notice on schools and social workers who are afraid that they might be accused of interfering with religious and cultural freedom. It stated that they must intervene to prevent young girls being abducted from Britain against their will into forced marriages, which, although they may be a way of preserving a culture, are prima facie legally void. Forced marriages in Britain are estimated to be at least one thousand a year and, in Bradford alone, up to two thousand girls are believed to have run away from home in recent years. It has been conjectured that the Home Office is considering charging the parents with abduction. Until now this cultural issue has been avoided, the government fearing that it might be accused of interfering with the cultural and religious freedoms of ethnic minorities. Might this be a case of political correctness gone wrong? Whilst accepting that the motives underlying the opposition to some cultural practices may be complex and include racism, it seems preposterous to suggest that intolerance of forced marriages and other features of Other cultures unacceptable to the mainstream society are not justifiable if they offend or are felt to be immoral. Another example, albeit minor, of outlawing a cultural practice was the Home Office Minister Paul Boateng pledging that the law on aggressive begging would be more strictly enforced if the police required it. "Romanian gypsies may claim that begging is part of their culture but it is not acceptable to British people"[TXT 12 March 00]. Up to twenty a week were being prosecuted for harassing the public, sometimes using babes in arms, and were warned by a London magistrate that they risked imprisonment [TM 9 March 00].

Rex does not discuss whether a multicultural society, to qualify as being ideal, should in any way be numerically limited and selective as to those cultures which are included, and those to be excluded. An ideal multicultural society must be relativist, otherwise its diverse culturalism may end up as intolerance or even racism. The viability of such total cultural relativism is contrary to the current evidence and with human nature. Elective or acquired multiculturalism can only take place with the tacit acquiescence or positive consent of the indigenous mainstream society who provide the necessary ongoing stability, but who may, when the critical mass stage is reached, positively react to it.

John Locke, the eminent English seventeenth-century philosopher, thought that a centralised and coherent government was essential to the survival of a stable society without which the political dimension would suffer. Without political and institutional stability, multiculturalism would negate the resolution of internal racial/ethnic conflicts hopefully by objective means, leading to a breakdown of law and order. Arguably people will ultimately prefer economic and political stability to an individualised marginal anarchy, as evidenced by the crime, moral corruption, and loss of stability after the break up of the post-Communist USSR. Some perceive that the eventual outcome of limitless toleration towards increasing cultural pluralism would be an *admass* society—a twenty-first century anarchy in which a non-dominant and liberal majority would be trying to manage minorities competing for political power. In a multicultural society, the cultural practices of Others may be performed publicly, but only insofar as the mainstream society continues to at least tolerate them. If not, this "right" may have to be surrendered or practised privately. It can become an issue of "whose culture?" and "what identity?" In his analysis of anti-semitism James Parkes [1963: xi] observes "There is a limit to the extent to which an established group can be expected to accept the transformation of its life by a minority, either an existing minority to which a new relationship has developed, or a new minority entering in. A determination to resist an innovation is not always 'prejudice.'"

The responsibilities of the nation-state include the promotion of the common good and the adjudication of disputes between parties. Its legislation reflects its historical development, its national culture, and morality, and provides a reference point for social behaviour. In a completely multicultural society, there would presumably be no unique and inherited system of jurisprudence and there would be pressure to change the legislation to accommodate the values of diverse Others. The former High Court judge, Lord Devlin, in his 1965 book *The Enforcement of Morals*, argued that a shared morality is essential to the very existence of a society, and that the infringement of a shared moral code is analogous to treason in that both, if allowed, would destroy the society in which they took place. He believed that deviations from the norms of morality, values, and system of law of a society endangers its existence. The former Cabinet Minister Lord Tebbitt [1993] also made the point that "to make a society, its members must have in common, laws, customs, standards, values, language, culture and religion." He contrasted with today, the way in which earlier immigrants had harmoniously assimilated into the cultural and religious mix of Britons. Given that a culture subsumes or constructs a morality, Devlin's and Tebbitt's remarks suggest that the indigenous culture should be supported by the state and other opinion-forming institutions, through its legislation, education, and the media. This gives rise to the belief that sees a potential threat of separatism as being ultimately political and subversively disloyal.

For groups in a multicultural society to co-exist harmoniously, they need an environment of economic prosperity, equal opportunity for all groups, and reciprocal toleration. Thus Gray [1995:23–4] observes that "it is in the area of multiculturalism that a policy of toleration is most needed, and ideas of radical equality and positive discrimination most unfortunate . . . [policies of group rights—such as affirmative action]. The nemesis of such policies—not far off in the United States—is a sort of reverse apartheid, in which people's opportunities and entitlements are decided by the morally arbitrary fact of ethnic origins rather than by their deserts or needs . . . [A] common culture need not encompass a shared religion and it certainly need not presuppose ethnic homogeneity, but it does demand widespread acceptance of certain norms and conventions of behaviour and, in our times, it typically expresses a shared sense of nationality." He suggests elsewhere [1992: 40] that the nemesis of the American policies of "reverse apartheid" is not far off.

A multicultural society has to resolve those issues on which there exists genuine and fundamental cultural divisions and loyalties such as the equality of women and the freedoms of speech and religion. The outcome of long-term multiculturalism, assuming that this would be peaceful, could be the "dumbing down" of all cultures to an incoherent concoction of "pick and mix" values individually selected from whatever was on offer. What would probably emerge would be an admass, undefinable culture, which would satisfy no one—a veritable Tower of Babel of different languages, religions, and moral values and rules, with their evaluative confusion and disparity, lacking coherence. The concept of multiculturalism is confused because it generalises culture in such a way as to render it meaningless. If anything qualifies including both novel and alien beliefs and practices, then a complete change in the concept has occurred—culture then equals anything and everything.

A Committee of Inquiry was set up by the government in 1979 to investigate the causes of under-achievement of schoolchildren of African-Caribbean origin. The first chairman was Lord Rampton, who produced an interim report in 1981, which did not satisfy multiculturalists. The committee was reconstituted under Lord Swann and its terms of reference were extended to eight other ethnic groups. Its membership underwent frequent resignations and appointments, which suggests that its proceedings were not without controversy. The factors considered included racism, language, nature, nurture and discrimination. This new committee reported in 1985. It identified [1985:20–1] as migrant myths, the "alternative" (regular visits "home"); the "return" (to their country of origin); and "belonging" (Britain as the "mother" country). It recommended (7–8) integration, stating that "some people when faced with our (Swann's) aim of a more genuinely pluralist society may challenge this as in some way seeking to undermine an ill-defined and nebulous concept of 'true Britishness.' . . . whilst we are not looking for the assimilation of the minority communities within an unchanged dominant way of life, we are perhaps looking for the 'assimilation' of all groups within a redefined concept of what it means to live in British society today . . . we are looking to recast the mould into a form which retains the fundamental principles of the original but within a broader pluralist conspectus—diversity within unity."

Swann was criticised as a secularist and relativist [Hiskett 1989: 24 and 27] and the report was seen as "blatant social engineering." On multicultural education Mervyn Hiskett [42–3] observed "mother-tongue teaching is among the greatest absurdities of multiculturalism. I [Hiskett] have counted twelve major Asian and African languages widely spoken among immigrant communities in the U.K. (United Kingdom of Great Britain and Northern Ireland). There are no doubt many more. These are in addition to such Eastern European languages such as Turkish, Greek, Armenian and so on. All of them candidates for mother-tongue teaching in state schools." This objection is essentially on practical grounds. Another prognosis was offered by the Social Affairs Unit, which noted the objections of Muslims to the Swann proposals, and that six of its committee members signed a dissenting report from the majority recommendation for non-denominational (multifaith) and undogmatic religious education, and supported the granting of separate denominational status to Muslim schools. Hiskett [4] believes this to be "the least worst solution." No mention of this objection was made in the report, which was itself largely ignored by the then government. A prominent British Muslim [DM 22 Feb. 96] condemned multifaith religious education as a "confusing mishmash." Multiculturalists argue that all cultures are worthy of respect and recognition, and that the state has a responsibility to protect and accommodate them. Whatever the response by the state may be to the diverse issues raised by multiculturalism, the outcome will probably be satisfying for some cultural groups and less so for others, including the majority culture, up to outright opposition.

Politicians, especially when they are in trouble, will go out of their way to court the ethnic vote. The unsuccessful Labour party 2000 mayoral candidate for London, targeted the black and Asian communities as his independent and successful rival was being demonised for helping a "racist" friend. Before the 1997 general election the Labour party realised that in twelve of its top sixty target seats, the Asian vote (about three percent of the constituency) could be decisive. Politicians of all persuasions with an eye on the ethnic vote in marginal constituencies will assert that Britain is now a multicultural society and appear disproportionately with members of ethnic groups in their photocalls. It is self-evident that most ethnics will lend their political support to multicultural and liberal immigration policies. Blair, whose "spin" has lost much of his credibility, has said that he "shares the belief that Britain is and should be a multicultural society"—although what sort of multicultural society he does not say. This is echoed by the monarchy, some Church leaders, and some populist politicians seeking to broaden their support, and is political evangelising by moving from being descriptive to being prescriptive. It implies that all cultural diversity and difference should be accepted, and presumably officially endorsed, and that a multicultural Britain is a fact, so that toleration is outmoded and any objections are either racist or pointless or both. This is reflected in a 1989 newspaper article reported by Walker Connor [1993:375]: "the pernicious doctrine of multiracialism has so debilitated the English that they have lost their voice and no longer think of themselves as the only possessors of England . . . the English have become the 'white section of the community.'"

William Galston [1991:141–3] voices concern about the adverse effect on social unity of "The civil rights movement [which] unleashed a torrent of new demands on the part of previously marginalized groups [which included race and ethnicity, national origin, and religion] . . . A central focus of social policy became the legitimation of difference . . . in liberal social philosophy, it produced a renewed emphasis on the task of forging a meaningful and usable political unity in the midst of (some would say, in the teeth of) ever increasing social diversity." He criticises Rawls' liberal theory of justice with fairness: "No political community can exist simply on the basis of diversity or of natural harmony; every community must rest on—indeed, is constituted by—some agreement on what is just . . . the grounds of agreement (Rawls) professes to find latent in our public culture would be rejected by many individuals and groups who form important elements in that culture." Such agreement is especially improbable in a separatist multicultural society.

Multiculturalism merits serious debate, but the sloganising mantra of its advocates is often mindless rhetoric that obscures what it implies and who it affects. Typically it states that "there are many ways to be (American)," or it "represents the true face of the United States," or "there is unity (or a cultural richness) in diversity and difference," or "we are all hybrids now," or we should "celebrate diversity." Recent book titles have been *We [Americans] are all Multiculturalists Now* [Glazer:1997] and *Windrush—the Irresistible Rise of Multicultural Britain.* The term multicultural has an attractive and almost aesthetic tone—less harsh than multiracial. Diversity has an aesthetic appeal and implies a choice which uniformity does not, occasionally trivialised by appealing to the wider gastronomic choice of ethnic restaurants. However, to others, "diversity and difference," at least insofar as it relates to cultures, suggests multiplicity, division and disorder. Integrationist multiculturalists claim that mutual benefits arise from cross-culturalisation between disparate groups. Ezra Mishan [1988:19] disagrees: "contrary to the elements of fantasy that occasionally captivate the race relations industry, is a multiracial Britain to be conceived as a free assemblage of diverse races committed to interfusing their diverse cultures into a richer whole guided by the initiatives of a benevolent bureaucracy." He argues that the "racial aspirations of the mass of the indigenous population do not, at their most liberal, extend beyond a vague hope that in the fullness of time new ethnic minorities may somehow become assimilated into a white British culture or, at least, comfortably grafted onto its main trunk." This was the aspiration of the American melting pot. The view of Professor Glenn Tinder [1995:229] is that "pluralism expresses an abiding mistrust of society. In setting society against itself, it provides individuals with platforms from which they can criticize and resist society. The ideal it poses is not harmonious order but fruitful conflict." The fact is that pluralistic diversity may provide nothing worth celebrating. Bangladeshi immigrants for example, may feel that they have no more affinity with African-Caribbeans or Albanian Muslims, than they have with the indigenous English, Scots or Welsh.

Flew [1993:284] questions the commonplace claim that "in a multiracial society—all (cultures) equally must be 'affirmed' and encouraged. . . . to maintain that anything is non-instrumentally valuable is indeed to make a value judgement which is, no doubt, an inherently contentious move. For it is to say that, regardless of consequences, but all other things being equal, whatever it is that is thus non—instrumentally valued ought to be preferred . . . for it is to say, only and precisely, that what is thus instrumentally valuable in fact just is an effective means of achieving a certain objective, and all this quite regardless of whether you or I or anyone else either does want or ought to want that particular objective." In Britain, no government has yet established, let alone permitted, a public debate as to whether or not it is the desire or the intention of its mainstream society that the country, under the mantra of diversity and difference, should progressively shed its national identity and become a collection of ethnic groups, each having its own cultural, religious, regional, and linguistic affiliation, looking to the 1998 Human Rights Act, or maybe finally to the ECHR (The European Court of Human Rights), to adjudicate between competing racial/ethnic claims.

In Western Europe, including Britain, the extent and influence of multiculturalism is still relatively modest. It has been acquired since the end of WW2 and the demise of the colonial empires and the USSR mainly through economic migrants and refugees, both legal and illegal, and their dependants and descendants. In Britain, prior to the mass migration of post-WW2, this was not felt to be, or indeed proved to be, of any concern, because the mainstream felt no threat to their culture or social coherence. The levels of racial/cultural pluralism were not perceived as being significant and did not and have still not reached those of California. A benevolent view of multiculturalism is that it is a humane response to mass migration, but it is in fact intolerant of anything which works against the notion of universal claim rights, and its political correctness has its own intolerance. Advocates of multiculturalism should ask themselves, "where, if anywhere, should it all end?" Is the objective—the ideal—for Western nation-states to be constituted of the world's major races, cultures, and religions, all in the correct global proportions so as not to discriminate racially? If not, what limits should there be to the magnitude and composition of immigration and to the rate of change towards cultural diversity and difference? On what basis would they justify these limits and would they accept some and reject other migrants, and what would be their defence against the accusation of prejudice and racism? The issue is not clear cut—namely, whether racial/cultural heterogeneity and diversity are unquestionably desirable, or whether racial/cultural homogeneity and uniformity are undeniably undesirable—in practice the issue is the relative scale of the heterogeneity or homogeneity.

Acquiescence to multiculturalism may be from a non-relativist cultural high ground, namely that the indigenous (Western) culture is seen to be more attractive to ethnic immigrants, whose cultures will become displaced by the time their third generation comes of age. This assimilation by the osmosis of trans-culturalism will eventually make them become "like us." Although the probability of this outcome is true to an extent mainly due intermarriage/ miscegenation and the influence of an increasingly individualistic and atomised consumerist society, it is neither universally so, nor can it be assumed to be so. The extent to which "appreciation" of the mainstream culture will lead to assimilation, if at all, will be determined by the attitudes developed by young Others. Any feeling or experience, both real and imaginary, of discrimination, will be counterproductive to assimilation. If liberal immigration is "imposed" on a society by a government, immigrants will not be generally welcomed. They will then feel no loyalty and will not assimilate and will retain their original identity. Nevertheless assimilation is important to the preservation of a cultural hegemony. Germany, Japan, and Israel, who seek to preserve their cultural homogeneity, grant citizenship on the basis of parentage/ blood. In Japan "foreigners" make up only about one percent of the population. In Britain the requirements for naturalisation as a citizen, with which goes voting rights, are modest: five years legal residence free from any restriction or breach of immigration laws; over eighteen years of age; not of unsound mind; good character; and a sufficient knowledge of English. Spouses of British citizens qualify after three years residence. Unlike the United States, no oath of allegiance is required (other than for British protected persons), and Britain allows dual nationality. Asylum seekers who have been in residence for more than five years, having been granted temporary leave to remain, followed by indefinite leave to remain, and provided that the other conditions are met, are eligible to apply for British citizenship.

Roy Hattersley, the former deputy leader of the Labour party, [DM 19 Sept. 95] and MP from 1964 to 1997 for a constituency in Birmingham which has a high Muslim/Sikh population, has mutually irreconcilable views on two-domain multiculturalism. He criticised the modern teaching of history in schools, which he says has obliterated national heroes, saying that national heroes "gave [him] an understanding of who [he] is, and what [he] came from. These days, that feeling is called 'a sense of national identity.' [He] thinks of it as the pride [he] feels in this nation's achievements. For a nation needs its heroes . . . [they] are making the saga of England come alive and rejoicing in both our heritage and our identity." But he then says "One of the characteristics which I most admire about Moslems and Sikhs who have come to Britain, is their fierce determination to safeguard their cultural and religious heritage. We should take the same pride in our own past and live together, not pretending that we are all the same, but glorying in our diversity." His City Council—Birmingham—renamed the traditional Christian Christmas "Winterval" and is proposing to abolish Easter to create a more multicultural atmosphere.

An indication of how immigration has affected the ethnic/racial mix of the United States from 1961 to 1990 can be approximately shown by computing the ratio of non-European to European migrants (counting Canadians as "Europeans"). These were (1961–70) 1.14; (1971–80) 3.76; and (1981–90) 7.61 (excluding Canadians 9.07) [Parker 1993:287]. Moreover, immigrants are not uniformly distributed throughout the country but tend to concentrate in established urban ghettoes. Official figures do not represent the full story, because of the high number of illegal immigrants in the U.S. (The United States). According to David Mauk and John Oakland [1997:72–80], the 1965 Act abolished national origin quotas and replaced them with hemispheric limits to annual immigration together with a system of preferences: 120,000 for the Western and 170,000 for the Eastern hemisphere including 20,000 from each Eastern nation, later extended to the Western nations. After the 1990 Act, the nominal ceiling on immigration was 700,000 per year through 1994. Of this total, 520,000 visas were for family reunification according to a kinship priority system, 140,000 for employment-based immigration, 40,000 for a 'transitional diversity' programme, and some others for a miscellany of 'transition' programmes. The allowable immigration level was scheduled to fall to 675,000 in 1995. The actual level of immigration will exceed these ceilings, however, because refugees are not counted against the ceiling [Sykes 1995:184]. A 1996 law imposed no new limits but tighter controls. According to Salins [1997:200], "Since the forty year era of restrictive immigration officially ended with the passage of the [Johnson] Immigration and Nationality Act amendments of 1965, nearly twenty million immigrants have legally entered the United States, and another three to five million immigrants have entered the country illegally or over stayed their visitor status." In the two decades before this new immigration policy, fifty-five percent of all immigrants came from Europe, twenty-two percent from Latin America and the Caribbean, and five percent from Asia. In the two decades afterwards, thirteen percent of all immigrants were European, forty-five percent were Latin or Caribbean, and thirty-seven percent were Asian. U.S. immigration regulations provide a six-year visa but carry no guarantee of a "green card" which permits permanent residence. The rhetoric [BBC 2 3 May 94] of the Head of the U.S. Immigration and Naturalization Service was less of a justification of this policy, but rather a statement of resignation and irreversibility. She said that "by and large immigrants bring human assets and energy that contributes—it's never been easy; it never was easy in the past and it is not easy now. We are in it, it is part of what we are . . . if you do not educate, you are creating an under-class that works against your interests as a democratic country, works against your social interests."

What is the demography of ethnicity in Britain? In the previous ten yearly national census of 1991, about 5.5 percent of the population overall was officially classed as ethnic, although today's figure must be higher. This is due to later migration, refugees, family chain migration, illegal immigration, and disproportionately higher birth rates. The 1991 census was the first to include a question on ethnicity. Of the then total population of 54.9 million, 94.5 percent were classed as white, and 90.5 percent of the total population were born in Britain. There was a total of just over three million ethnics made up of 27.9 percent Indian; 15.8 percent Pakistani; 5.4 percent Bangladeshi; 16.6 percent Afro-Caribbean; 7.0 percent Black African, and 11.8 percent Chinese and other Asian. It was later reported that the ethnics had been undercounted by about five percent. Another finding was that eighteen percent of Chinese men are in the professions, compared with seven percent of white men.

The next census in 2001 is expected to ask for the first time a question on religion, and for whites to state if they are Irish or Scottish, but not English or Welsh. The latest [1999–00] estimate [Social Trends 2001:32] gives a total ethnic non-white population of 3.8 million [6.7 percent] out of a total of 56.9

million. Migrants from the Republic of Ireland and Ulster (not included above) residing in Britain in 1991 were estimated as 837,000 or 1.5 percent [Owen,D. 1993:2]. It is estimated that by 2020 the non-white population (excluding Irish) will have increased to 5.86 million or 10.1 percent [Parekh 2000:375]. By 2020 the number of British Muslims is expected to be about two million. This is because of their youthful profile—about seventy percent are under the age of twenty-five and by the next century two thirds will have been born in Britain. In the 1991 census, 13.8 percent of the white population was aged five to fifteen, compared with 29.6 percent of the Pakistani, 32.2 percent of the Bangladeshi.

Advocates of multiculturalism suggest that the economic success of the United States is due to its "diversity and difference." The selection of this single factor from a complex multi-factorial system is questionable, if it is used to compare with the economic/cultural systems of other countries with different factors. Moreover, economic success is not the only or the principal criterion of a successful society. Nevertheless the economic benefit argument of immigration is often advanced, and can have a powerful influence on the electorate during periods of prosperity, because the long-term downside cost of uncontrolled and unselective immigration is not immediately apparent. The eminent economist Professor John Kenneth Galbraith [1996:96] sees benefits in immigration: "the national community is enriched by those of foreign culture and sophistication, and by the exchange of ideas and talents that a liberal immigration policy allows." This is however qualified [95] by "given the responsibility of the national state for its own working force, should migration be at least controlled in its favour?— the practical answer is yes." He advocates no limitation on those in "higher brackets of achieve-ment" and political refugees. This selectivity does not fit in easily with anti-racism and would require strictly controlled immigration. In practice, immi-gration in Western Europe and the United States is not strictly controllable—both in respect of its numbers and its selectivity—because of illegal immi-grants and refugees. The benefits which he envisages are those of the aca-demic, artistic, and professional worlds, reminiscent of the gifted German refugees such as Freud, Einstein, Peierls and Kissinger who arrived before the mass economic migration of post-WW2. However, their successful per-sonal careers have no great national economic impact. The question is whether a random sample of the same number of the indigenous population would contain a comparable proportion of gifted individuals as any other immigrant group from a developed country.

Ezra Mishan, one-time Professor Economics at the London School of Economics, says that the debate in favour of immigration is fuelled by popu-lar economic fallacies [2001 Jan/March 6–7]. He says that the theory that a general shortage of labour favours a policy of large-scale immigration is an economic fallacy, and acts to reduce the national real wage, or at least acts to curtail its rate of growth. The situation of a shortage of goods can be described as "too much money chasing too few goods" and is a symptom of actual or potential inflation, which has occurred in countries that have an ample supply of labour, such as India and China. If the response is importing labour, it will aggravate the inflation, because it would initially require an expansion of industrial capital together with that required for the social infrastructure. With regard to particular shortages of labour and skills, the solution is to offer better pay, conditions, and equipment to attract indigenous personnel. And this involves only a redistribution of real income. Professor Mishan demolishes other economic fallacies such as the need to offset the "ageing British population," and that particular immigrant groups make a disproportionate contribution to the British economy. Immigrants, as they themselves age, will simply require more immigrants.

Another economist also casts doubt on the economic benefit case for large-scale unselective immigration. Susan Vroman [1995:214–5] says that "If the United States were to allow immigrant flows of low-skilled workers that are far greater than the recent historical experience, native workers or permanent immigrants could well be harmed. They could either be displaced by less costly temporary workers or they might have their earnings eroded by competition with the temporary workers." This is why unions, and others who represent labour, lobby for a restrictive immigration policy. "A less restrictive immigration policy has an effect on the distribution of national income that may entail a redistribution from less well-off to better-off segments of the population." This would add to the social inequality of wealth that Galbraith describes in his book the *Culture of Contentment*. In Britain, as in the United States, over the last twenty years, the gap between the rich and poor continues to widen, which can fuel feelings of deprivation, discrimination and racism, particularly by the immigrant underclass. Vroman adds [217] 'We [Americans] do not focus on whether immigrants will change our culture, since ours is an immigrant culture. Many Europeans, on the other hand, are very concerned about the cultural effects of immigration."

It is unrepresentative to stereotype immigrants as being in general either beneficial or detrimental to a host country, but nonetheless two anti-terrorism acts were enacted in Britain in 1998 and 2000, and another was proposed in 2001, which took account of the realpolitik, and are intended to be "judge proof." Immigrants are not all Einsteins, and equally they are not all Jamaican "Yardie" drug dealing criminals who have targeted the black community in London and account for sixty-eight percent of shootings in London with twenty-six killings in 1999 [TM 11 March 00]. Nor are they all Eastern Europeans who employ children in pickpocket gangs or aggressive begging in Central London (which has doubled in the past year); or who have attacked village stores and rural sub-post-offices; or the fifteen-year-old girl who graduated from Oxford University in mathematics and then absconded from home (whose Pakistani parents had been convicted of fifty-four mortgage frauds amounting to £1.5 million) [STM 9 July 00]. There is also a moral dimension: an EU survey [TM 18 May 00] reported that criminal gangs smuggle about 500,000 women each year from Eastern Europe, Russia, and Turkey into Western Europe for the sex trade. The police say that in Britain at least 1,400 female illegal immigrants a year, together with some of the unescorted under-age asylum seekers disappear, mainly into prostitution. According to the MPS (Metropolitan Police Sevice) [STM 18 Feb. 01], more than seventy percent of women working in the Soho brothels are from the former Soviet Union and Eastern Europe. it appears that traffickers and brothel owners have made profits of at least £50 million.

NOTES

Connor, W. *Beyond Reason—The Nature of the Ethno-National Bond. Ethnic and Racial Studies*. vol. 16. no.3. July 1993. 375.

Devlin, P. *The Enforcement of Morals*. Oxford: Oxford University Press, 1965.

Flew, A. "Three Concepts of Racism." In *Atheistic Humanism*. Buffalo, New York: Prometheus Books. 1993. 284.

Fukuyama, F. *Trust—The Social Virtues and the Creation of Prosperity*. London: Penguin Books, 1996. 269–70.

Galbraith, J.K. *The Good Society*. London: Sinclair Stevenson, 1996. 95.

Ibid. 96.

Galston, W.A. *Liberal Purposes*. Cambridge: Cambridge University Press, 1991. 141–143.

Glazer, N. *We Are All Multiculturalists Now*. Cambridge, Mass: Harvard University Press, 1997.

Gray, J. *Enlightenment's Wake*. London: Routledge, 1995. 23–4.

_____"Toleration and the Currently Offensive Implication of Judgement." In *The Loss of Virtue*. London: Social Affairs Unit, 1992. 40

Hiskett, M. *Schooling for British Muslims—Integrated, Opted-Out or Denominational*. London: Social Affairs Unit, 1989. 4.

Ibid. 24–7.

Ibid. 42–3.

Ignatieff, M. *The Fate of Nations*. BBC Radio 4. 5 May 1994.

Lee, D. (Trans. and Intro.) *Plato—The Republic*. London: Penguin Books, 1987. 55.

Mauk, D. and Oakland, J. *American Civilization*. London: Routledge, 1997. 72–80.

Mishan, E.J. "What Future for a Multicultural Britain." In *The Salisbury Review*. Part 1. June, 1988. 19.

_____"Popular Economic Fallacies About Immigration." In *Right Now*. London. Issue 30. Jan/March., 2001. 6–7.

Owen, D. *National Ethnic Minority Data Archive*. Coventry: University of Warwick. 1993. 2.

Parekh, Lord. *The Future of Multi-Ethnic Britain*. London: Profile Books. 2000. 375.

Parker, G. (Ed.) *Atlas of the World 4th Ed.—The United States 1933-1993*. London: Times Books, 1993. 287.

Parkes, J. *Anti Semitism*. London: Valentine Mitchell, 1963. Xi.

Popper, K.R. *The Poverty of Historicism*. London: Routledge. 1957. 47.

Ibid. 54.

_____ *The Open Society and Its Enemies—Plato*. vol.l. London: Routledge, 1966. 167.

Raz, J. "Multiculturalism—A Liberal Perspective." In *Dissent*. Winter, 1994. 67.

Ibid. 68–9.

Rex, J. *Race and Ethnicity*. Buckingham: Open University Press, 1986. 125.

Ibid. 130.

Ibid. 133.

Ibid. 134.

Rex, J. 'The Political Sociology Of A Multi Cultural Society." In *European Journal of Inter-Cultural Studies*. vol. 2. no.1, 1991. 7.

Salins, P.D. *Assimilation, American Style*. New York: Basic Books.1997. 56–7.

Ibid. 200.

Spencer, I.R.G. *British Immigration Policy Since 1939*. London: Routledge, 1997. 1.

Swann, Lord. *Education for All—The Report of the Committee of Inquiry Into the Education of Children from Ethnic Minority Groups*. London: Stationery Office, 1985. 7–8.

Ibid. 20–1.

Sykes, A.O. "The Welfare Economics of Immigration." In *Justice in Immigration*. Schwartz, W.F. (Ed.) Cambridge, Cambridge University Press, 1995. 184.

Tebbit, N. *The Ridley Memorial Lecture*. London. 1993.

Tinder, G. *Toleration and Community*. Columbia, Missouri: University of Missouri Press, 1995. 229.

Vroman, S.B. "Some Caveats on the Welfare Economics of Immigration Law." In *Justice in Immigration*. Schwartz, W.F. (Ed.) Cambridge: Cambridge University Press, 1995. 214–5 and 217.

Walzer, M. "The New Tribalism." In *Dissent*. Spring. vol. 39. 1992. 168–170.

Ibid. 171.

BBC 2. *Windrush*—06/13/20 June1998.

BBC 2. *Social Unrest in California. Assignment*. 3 May 1994.

ITV. *Beware—Pickpockets About*. 8 May 2000.

BBC 2. *Black Britain*. 23 September 1998/Times 27 February 1999.

BBC 2. *Forced Marriages*. Newsnight. 12 July 1999.

ITV. Teletext 12 March 2000.

6

The Multicultural Threat

Diversity and difference covers many aspects of human life and behaviour other than the issue of culturalism—some aspects of which may be beneficial and welcomed. Provided that the diversity and difference are embodied in the secure traditional framework of communality of the indigenous society, it will be accepted, but if it is perceived as a threat, then it will not. Elective multiculturalism (i.e. a government policy), as opposed to one that has been acquired or inherited, presumes to positively welcome diversity and difference, and is prepared to socially engineer its society into cultural pluralism. It presumes that social relations can be constructed and changed by political action. Multiculturalism presages fundamentally different ways of living and major changes. Many aspects of cultural diversity and difference are of no clear benefit with little to be gained—only tolerated. If they breach the commonly acceptable limits of toleration, or begin to be articulated in the assertive language of entitlement to special and particularised rights, they can become unacceptable and lead to dissent. A Gallup opinion poll in 1982 in the United States compared public opinion (effectively a measure of toleration)' towards fifteen immigrant groups with Europeans. The English, Irish, Jews, Germans, Italians and Poles were in the top six categories [Mauk and Oakland 1997:77]. The English were the most favoured at sixty-six percent good/six percent bad; then blacks—forty-six percent good/sixteen percent bad; Chinese—forty-four percent good/nineteen percent bad; Vietnamese—twenty percent good/thirty-eight percent bad; Cubans—nine percent good/fifty nine percent bad. The Swann report [1985:36] concluded that [racism] "damages not only the groups seen and treated as in some way inferior or manipulable, but also the more powerful groups in that it feeds them with a totally false sense of superiority and thus distorts their understanding of themselves and the world around them. All members of a racist society suffer

67

from feelings of fears and insecurity." This comment would be equally valid if "racist" was replaced by "multicultural." An initial overt response of indifference by the mainstream society towards Others should not be misinterpreted. It may mask a covert intolerance, which will become apparent only when their limits of toleration have been reached followed by a backlash. As Melanie Philips the journalist points out, "To oppose the 'multicultural' agenda is to be accused of racism. But racism is fuelled by insecurity, and the more people fear that their cultural identity and ability to express it are threatened, the more racism will grow" [STM 6 May 01].

Minorities may believe that, because they must by definition be disadvantaged, they should have a more than proportional prominence and influence, which may find a particular resonance with cultures which are tolerant and sympathetic to the "underdog," or are susceptible to feelings of shame or accusations of guilt. It erodes the legitimate role of the state in denying some claims to rights. Even supposing that a monocultural society was sufficiently tolerant or acquiescent to "acquire" creeping multiculturalism, there would be no certainty that an assertive and militant ethnic group would not eventually seek to establish their hegemony, over a passive indigenous majority. The transition from a stable cultural hegemony to an ideal multicultural society requires an ordered and orderly society, unencumbered by unrestrained separatism and a fragile community. An editorial [STM 13 Feb. 00] observed "The truth is that Britain is no longer a tolerant society united by shared values and civilised attitudes. What were once conventional norms of behaviour are being overturned across the board." The erosion of cultural and moral values could lead to the deconstruction of British society as we know it, and can only be accelerated by increasing cultural diversity.

The downside of the potential consequences of multiculturalism need to be recognised, if the major and intractable ethno-national conflicts evident in the world today are not to be replayed on a national dimension. Multiculturalism lends itself to separatism, a loss of societal and cultural coherence, and undermines the national identity. Without a sense of a common identity a society becomes ungovernable. Cultural hegemonies do not remain rigid and unchangeable, nor will all the objections or adverse experience of multiculturalism necessarily be repeated elsewhere, but cultures change at their own pace and in their own way by cautious incremental pragmatism. In his book *The Dictatorship of Virtue-The Battle for America's Future*, Richard Bernstein [1994:4] observes that "we are threatened by a narrow orthodoxy—and the occasional outright atrocity—imposed, or committed, in the name of the very values that are supposed to define a pluralist society . . . multiculturalism [7], in short, cannot be taken at face value, and that is what makes it so tricky. Nobody wants to appear to be against multiculturalism. Hence, the irresistible temptation of the post–1960s, radical-left inhabitants of a political dreamland to use the term 'multiculturalism' as a defence against exposure or criticism and to bring into service a vocabulary to which multiculturalism has an almost salacious attraction, words like 'racist,' 'sexist' and 'homophobic.' To put matters bluntly, the multiculturalist rhetoric has us on the run, unable to respond for fear of being branded unicultural or racist, or (to get into the trendy academic lingo) complicit in the structures of hegemony imposed by the Eurocentric patriachy and its strategies of domination . . . the pattern of assimilation [9], so easily dismissed by champions of sweeping change, worked pretty well for millions of people and continues to work well for the many new arrivals who flock, legally or otherwise, to our shores every year. Now a certain racial militancy and small-group affiliation are encouraged by the multiculturalist missionaries on the grounds that these attitudes will help to break the vicious cycles of poverty and violence that are keeping millions of American citizens down." Bernstein cites the various ethno-national conflicts around the world and concludes [9] that these involve "not usually race, but an aggressive ethnicity demonstrating that human beings are just as likely to live in conditions of group animosity as in some harmonious ethnic salad. My [Bernstein's] own sense is that we are more likely to end up in a simmering sort of mutual dislike on the level of everyday unpleasantness than we are in full scale Balkan warfare. But that is bad enough." Leon Wieseltier [1994] in reviewing Bernstein's book sees it as "a study of panic . . . it reflects a fear of heterogeneity, which is classically an American fear," and suggests that "Many things are possible in America, but the singleness of identity is not one of them." And he makes the perplexing observation that "a multicultural society produces multicultural individuals."

Multiculturalism is a vision of society that distorts the historical reality of the world's cultural divisions, and it does not foresee its effects if translated to a nation-state. It is asking much of human beings that they should be expected to live with alien cultures as if they were of equal value to their own, and that they should make compromises to accommodate what may be totally differing beliefs and perceptions of value, like "cuckoos in the nest." Connor [1993:373] opines that "by and large, both statesmen and scholars have failed to comprehend the non-rational, emotional well-springs of ethno-nationalism and consequently, have tended to under-estimate its capacity for influencing group behaviour." One could reasonably relate this ethno-psychology to the relative proportion of Others, inasmuch that the higher the proportion, the more the threat to the sense of communality of the mainstream group. Tensions arise when the proportion and impact of a minority relative to the mainstream begins to induce intolerance. It begins to be felt that this minority has an influence which is perceived as being disproportionate—being "ruled by strangers" who are creating changes which they should resist, albeit belatedly. In Kenya and Fiji there exists a risk of conflict, as occurred in Uganda, where Indian migrants maintain their separatism from the indigenous majority from a position of economic superiority and influence. This recently led to a coup in Fiji (and later in the Solomons), where the fifty-one percent of indigenous Fijians narrowly constitute the majority of the population, which is forty-four percent Indian. The 1997 Constitution gave ethnic Indians an equal democratic right with indigenous Fijians, and a prime minister who was of Indian ancestry. There is a critical mass or tipping point or threshold limit of toleration at which mainstream society feels it is losing control and its intolerance becomes overt. This was found with Chicago mixed housing projects: "between ten to thirty percent would work alright. More than thirty percent would tip it over [into all black projects]" [Banton 1994:9]. This poses the question: is there a minimum proportion of the indigenous group which is necessary to maintain the cohesion in a multiracial/ethnic society?

Glazer [1975:17], writing about twenty-five years ago, observed that "since almost every ethnic group is disadvantaged in relationship to some other; and so, by appealing to class interest and ethnic interest together, the white European [and his descendants wherever they may be] can everywhere be marked as the enemy." This has been true with some American black activists. The title of Glazer's later book [1997:7], *We Are All Multiculturalists Now*, suggests an inevitable irreversibility, which for the United States may be true. He instances (as does Bernstein 1994:4) the "explosion" of the number of times multiculturalism has been referred to in the major newspapers—none in 1988, rising to a peak of 1500 in 1994—"it is no easy task to describe what one means by multiculturalism" [7]. Glazer [1997:147] thinks that "multiculturalism is the price America is paying for its inability or unwillingness to incorporate into its society African-Americans, in the same way and to the same degree it has incorporated so many groups. The anger and frustration at their continuing separation gave them the impetus for rejecting traditions which excluded them." He accepts [1997:21] that "the critics of multiculturalism have much wisdom on their side, and on many issues I [Glazer] join them . . . I [Glazer] believe the elements of the American system that hold us together, in particular the basic political rules that we have adhered to for so long, will permit us to escape the extremes of rancour and divisiveness that the critics of multiculturalism fear." On the other hand, Gray [1992:40] concludes that "the United States which at least in recent years has been founded on the belief that a common culture is not a necessary pre-condition of a liberal civil society, shows that the view that civil society can be secured solely by adherence to abstract rules is merely an illusion. Insofar as policy has been animated by it, the result has been further social division, including what amounts to low intensity civil war between the races. As things stand, the likelihood in the United States is of a slow slide into ungovernability, as the remaining patrimony of a common cultural inheritance is frittered away by the fragmenting forces of multiculturalism."

President Clinton, in his 1997 inaugural address, called racial hatred "America's constant curse. Prejudice and contempt have nearly destroyed us in the past. They plague us still." Clinton also warned that America was at risk of bringing back racial divisions and mounted a passionate appeal not to give up the idea of integration. He defended his "Initiative on Race" programme which was attacked a year after its launch for not producing any new ideas [TM 9 July 98]. Three decades after the civil rights movement and more than a decade of affirmative action, racial divisions are still visible. Glazer may be right about American civic loyalty, but until that has been demonstrated, and recognising that indigenous blacks are a special feature of the United States, multiculturalism should be approached with caution by those societies that are still able to avoid it. Having reviewed the multicultural and multiethnic problems of the United States and their relevance to Western Europe, Glazer observes [1981:15] "Perhaps Europe can learn from the United States what we have not yet learned from our own experience and our own efforts . . . Alas, [13] while the United States offers a terrible example, it has almost nothing to suggest as to means to avoid it." John O'Sullivan [1996:18–19] observes that the American black-white divide may eventually be resolved (that is, diluted) by the continuing influx of other races and ethnicities, so that the United States will no longer be a black/white divided society, but more multicultural and maybe even more divided. Nonetheless, under what "might best be called 'cultural conservatism' [which includes seriously enforcing laws against illegal immigration but also reducing legal immigration; supporting English as the official language and, more generally, opposing multiculturalism; and defending the concept of an inclusive 'American' identity against the second coming of hyphenation] . . . gets support varying from sixty-five to eighty percent in opinion polls . . . [and includes] black Americans who face competition in the labour market from low-paid immigrants."

Stanley Fish [1994] attacks anti-multiculturalists and Arthur Schlesinger's book *The Disuniting of America* [1992]. He says [81–83] correctly that the threat of multiculturalism has been echoed in a series of essays and books written between 1870 and 1925 which were anti-immigration, anti-excess, anti-Catholic, and out-and-out racist, to which the solution was seen as assimilation and the Anglo-Saxon triumph of language. He says [87–88] that "their appeal is not to prejudice but to national unity in the face of the danger posed by ethnic balkanisation" and adds that "it is not yet certain that he [Schlesinger] will be able to complete the passage from the heritage of his Jewish grandfather to total assimilation." The fact that the multicultural threat has not materialised, although some would say that the evidence in some cities of the United States is already there, does not negate the contention that it will not.

It may be that with time, and provided that multiculturalism is successfully managed by gradualism during a period of transition, that voluntary assimilation will take place as future generations of migrants affiliate into the economic and social structure and institutions of the mainstream society. Nevertheless, this discussion contends that a "doomsday scenario" for multiculturalism should not be summarily dismissed. In the absence of assimilation, the potential, or maybe the probable, consequence of unrestrained separatism is that it could lead to a destabilisation of society and latent internal ethno-national conflict, with claims for self-determination, or even territorial claims by external states to protect their kith and kin. Alexis Heraclides [1991: xv and 11] studied self-determination movements post-WW2. He concluded that "not a day passes without some report of action by secessionists, be they Sikhs, Basques, Tamils, the Baltic peoples—or any host of others . . . the whole process towards separatism can thus be seen as a path from a quest for meaning and group identity through disadvantage or inequality to a group demand for respect as a group and ultimately political effectiveness and control."

In times of internal or external threat to the stability or security of the nation-state, the primary loyalty of migrant Others to the values and interests of their "adopted" country may become suspected of being neutral or even disloyal, particularly if there is also a strong messianic religious affiliation, as has been shown by British Muslims. Will migrants conditioned by cultures that differ radically from the democratic individual liberalism of the West believe in, or in any event, support, the host culture? What is questioned here is unconditional loyalty in a national crisis, and not the superficial test of support for their national sports teams playing away from home. In the national emergency after Dunkirk, up to about 70,000 German, Austrian, and Czech refugees, including Jews, living in Britain were interned, most temporarily [Lynn 1989:165], as were 110,000 American-Japanese after Pearl Harbour. This was done en masse, because clearly the time and the resources were not available to establish their individual allegiance. The more numerous American-Italians and American-Germans during WW2 were also evacuated from military areas, put under curfew and had their homes searched, but were not interned. Escapees from the Channel Islands were interrogated under armed guard. Kuwait expelled its foreign nationals during the Gulf war. A similar concern occurred in peacetime in the McCarthy era during the Communist threat that at the time seemed real enough to many Americans. Israel has drawn up plans to expel its foreign workers who they fear might demand to establish non-Jewish communities. A militant minority may seek to take advantage of the liberal individual traditions of the West, whilst within their own communities continue to practice a tradition of illiberal values. A fundamentalist religious ethnic group may promote a hidden political agenda, whilst the mainstream society continues with a tolerant political complacency. This may be overlaid by a "wait and see" approach, in the belief that minorities will eventually fragment and defeat themselves and no longer have a common "enemy," namely the passive and tolerant majority. Or that the threat of multiculturalism is unreal or unproven, because there have always been subcultures, meaning political, class or status divisions in the country which have been tolerated without harm. A response to this is that what is new is the potential scale of multiculturalism together with its militant politicisation, supported by appeals to the relatively recent concept of universal claim rights. The cultural divide may remain quiescent and unresolved until it erupts into a conflict. Paradoxically, if the world consisted entirely of multicultural states having the same ethnic makeup, there might be no future wars, because there would no longer exist a national will to defend it or to wage war. Larry Siedentop [TM 30 May 00] believes that the influence of the inherited political culture of a minority cannot be dismissed. For sixty years some 17 million people in East Germany had been subject to despotic government, first of the Right and then of the Left. "Can anyone doubt that the habits and attitudes formed under such regimes survive or that a prolonged education in representative government and constitutionalism may be needed to root out authoritarian attitudes? . . . The attraction of the extreme Right to younger people in eastern Germany amounts to an inversion of the previous communist order. It is the liberal Centre which may not hold."

Since the end of the super-power era the world has become more unstable. Nation-states continue to be prepared for threats to their independence and sovereignty. Should such a threat arise, the presence of a significant proportion of a separatist ethnic minority owing a latent or covert allegiance elsewhere could be seen as undermining or at least being indifferent to the security of the nation-state—a "fifth column" or a "threat from within." A Ukrainian, Tatyana Koshechkina [1992:137], observed that "national culture is often bound with war and international relations as well as with international sport. It is supposed to be a focus of loyalty and patriotism. Those who feel this loyalty most strongly regard immigrant and ethnic minority culture as a threat." Nazi Germany created the conspiracy threat of a worldwide Jewish diaspora—supposedly supported by assimilated German Jews, who considered themselves to be "Germans by birth but of the Jewish faith."

Optimists might say that major wars between nation-states are in the past, but the future is unpredictable and wars could arise from embargoes on vital natural resources, as between the United States and Japan in 1941, and between the Arabs and the West in 1973—the effects of which would be serious. The current known world reserves to production ratio for oil and gas at present price levels is about fifty years. The successful independence movement in East Timor was mirrored in the strongly Islamic province of Aceh at the northern tip of Sumatra. The West feared that the whole of the Indonesian archipelago, centrally controlled by Jakarta, might face national disintegration with dire economic consequences to oil supplies, and trade with Japan and the Far East. A fragile situation continues to exist in East Timor, which shares a common border with West Timor and is sovereign Indonesian territory. The UN has the difficult task of rebuilding a shattered local economy in a political and institutional vacuum.

Military intervention in a long-standing ethno-national conflict is unlikely to resolve the divisions. The minutes of a secret British Cabinet discussion in 1969 said "the Irish problem after fifty years of relative stagnation was on the move again [TM 1 Jan. 00]." As in Bosnia/Herzogovina and Kosovo, international peace-keepers, be they under a UN or NATO (North Atlantic Treaty Organisation) flag, or both, may become in the foreseeable future a quasi-colonial, occupying, administrative and policing power, with support by the "European Community" waning. The Kosovo conflict ended with a deal brokered by Russia that preserved the fiction of Serbian sovereignty over multicultural Kosovo. The NATO Secretary-General has warned the foreign ministers of forty-five nations that if they do not start giving the UN the money to "get the administration going, then we'll lose the peace." The cost to Britain is estimated to be £866 million by 2003. The U.S House of Representatives passed a resolution which required the president, by April 2001, to withdraw its troops if the European nations have not paid their dues; the Senate is considering an even stronger measure. Reportedly [STM 30 Dec.00], the new administration of President Bush is planning to withdraw all U.S. ground troops from Bosnia/Herzogovina (Sfor-Stabilisation Force—4,400), and Kosovo (Kfor-Kosovo Force—5,600) within the next four years. Like Clinton, Bush has become concerned about America's "imperial overstretch" and more sceptical about humanitarian missions that were not in the American national interest, or seen as being secondary to its military priorities.

It is being conceded that the future of Kosovo will not be a multiethnic state, but the establishment by the UN of Serbian cantons in an Albanian state. Of the nineteen NATO members, only three, Britain, France and Italy have not imposed limits on where their troops can be sent and the responsibilities they should be given. The United States, no doubt mindful of the effect of body bags on the 2000 presidential election, said that they did not want their troops operating out of their sector of Eastern Kosovo.

In the United States it would seem that the objective of some activists has been to erase the European WASP (White Anglo-Saxon Protestant) inheritance and to replace it with an infusion of other cultures. Tocqueville observed in 1835 that "a democracy can obtain truth only as a result of experience; and many nations may perish while they are awaiting the consequences of their errors"—this observation could also be applied to escalating multiculturalism.

The divisive effect of separatism in the United States was recognised by Professor Robert Nisbet [1976:9–10] twenty-five years ago: "there is the upthrust of ethnicity . . . the 'unmeltable ethnics' . . . with its only too clear implications for the American myth of the melting pot, yes, but also for the political bond itself which, after all, has justified itself during the past century or more largely on its capacity to divert tribal loyalties from ancient tribalistic unities and to reunify these loyalties in the political community. We might have learned a general lesson from the profound change of black militants and intellectuals shortly after the civil rights revolution commenced in the late 1950s: a change of orientation or mission from the once hallowed 'integration' to something far more nationalistic, so far as blacks were concerned, and more pluralistic in thrust for the America. Conceivably we could have sensed something coming even earlier from the renascence of the Jewish community . . . Ethnicity is, along with the family, locality, and religion, among the most ancient and powerful of bonds for mankind. Only the political illusion could have caused us to forget this fact. We are relearning it today."

Fukuyama [1996:318–9] observes that "immigrants have been extremely important to the United States, but they have been valuable because the diversity has been harnessed to central American institutions . . . the more one is familiar with different cultures, the more one understands that they are not all created equal. An honest multiculturalist would recognise that some cultural traits are not helpful in the sustenance of a healthy democratic political system and capitalist economy. This should not be the grounds for barring certain peoples with cultures deemed unacceptable but, rather, grounds for the assertion of the positive aspects of American culture like the work ethic, sociability, and citizenship as immigrants move through the educational system."

A supposed multicultural threat, to some, is alarmist, inasmuch that multiculturalism might claim to "work" in the New World societies of the United States and Canada, but there is evidence to question this. Nor should the claim that the new multicultural societies of Australia and post-apartheid South Africa are existing harmoniously be taken as a guarantee of their future stability. It is too early to judge Mandela's inherited multicultural "Rainbow Republic" which is now a racially polarised, ghettoised, and criminalised state, having a murder rate about ten times that of the United States. The Australian James Jupp [1998: vi] notes that "in 1991 it was widely agreed that Australia was a multicultural society, that immigration was beneficial, and that a planned increase in population was a necessary feature of economic growth. By 1997 some of these propositions were under serious challenge . . . The government elected in March 1996 was much more hesitant than its predecessor about even using the word 'multicultural.'" The anti-immigration One Nation party, formed in 1997, which reflected the cultural and linguistic concern, had some success in the elections after which two major multicultural agencies were abolished. Since then [TM 12 Feb.01] it has gained two or three seats in the Western Australian parliament and has unseated its coalition. In 2001, Australia refused to accept any more illegal migrants. Jupp [146 –7] says that "throughout the 1990s there was a growing scepticism about multiculturalism. This scepticism was most strongly expressed in the United States. Even in Canada, where the concept was first developed, a major political party, Reform, was highly critical of what many had come to think of as a Canadian 'core value.'" Concern about the Australian identity was also expressed in the book *The Australians—In Search of an Identity* [Terrill:1987]. Similar concerns about national identity and social cohesion have been voiced by some of Australia's and Canada's foremost politicians and prominent others in radio discussions [BBC Radio 4. 22 May/ 5 June 1996].

In Canada, the high turnover of its population, mainly to the United States and the low level of national identification, has rarely in recent years been recognised by the Canadian state as a serious problem. The official policy of multiculturalism acquiesced to by the two original and major indigenous groups was destined to last only as long as it did not rebound on their particular aspirations. At the last general election, the new Reform Party, which opposes multiculturalism and non-selective immigration, obtained eighteen percent of the votes, and is now the third largest party. In Canada there are two volatile ethno-national issues: Quebec and Native-Indian rights. There is a recurring Francophone movement in the province of Quebec in which two thirds of its six million population are of French origin, with its last separatist referendum in 1995 narrowly defeated. The Francophones who seek "true affirmation of their separate (French) identity" demanded fifty/ fifty equality with the whole of the rest of Canada, and all Quebec residents would have lost their Canadian citizenship. The Quebec immigration law of 1985 favoured French speaking Francophones. The alienated Anglo-Quebecers are officially discriminated against linguistically, and have a partitionist movement to stay within the rest of Canada—as do the Native-Indians. Over the last twenty years, large numbers of Anglo-Quebecers have left Montreal. The Canadian government has granted to a Native American tribe a greater degree of autonomy and self-government than Quebec—there are fifty other tribes in British Columbia with potentially similar claims (TM 6 Aug. 98]. By 1991, Canada had admitted 586,000 migrants from Hong Kong/China to its West coast, and Chinese is now the third largest language in Canada. Vancouver now has about 250,000 Chinese, about one third of its population [BBC 2 31May 97]. Reactions to this plurality and lack of identity is to ask "what is a Canadian?" and "we can have no Canadian nation when we have no Canadian patriotism," and "so long as the majority of Canadians have two countries, one here and one in Europe, national unity will remain a myth and a constant source of internecine quarrels" [BBC Radio 4. 5 June 1996].

No one multicultural society has the same origins and characteristics. They differ widely, and need to be carefully examined before any universally applicable judgement, if any, or if ever, can be made. Jupp [187] supports this view but concludes that "none of the disasters predicted by opponents of immigration in the past have materialised. Nor are they likely to do so in the future. The world will become more crowded, and parts of it will become so overpopulated as to threaten the political stability and economic viability of some nations. The most rational Australian response would be to continue a planned and controlled intake rather than to try to shut the world out altogether." His conclusion that there will be no "disasters" is historicist, and unlike Australia, the relatively small island of Britain could become overpopulated. Jupp proposes [186] "a planned and controlled immigration programme with an annual intake just below 100,000. Something like 30,000 are likely to leave permanently each year, many returning to their original homelands, especially to New Zealand." A net intake of about 70,000 a year would be unlikely to have a significant impact on the world's population growth, but would this intake continue indefinitely? Australia's "overseas non-white born" population in 1996, that is, excluding Europeans, North Americans and New Zealanders, was about 6.9 percent, out of a total of 17.9 million. After New Zealand, Britain is still the largest source of Australian immigrants.

Israel is a unique multiethnic secular/religious state with a population of about 5.9 million, of whom about one million are Arab (mainly Muslim) citizens with whom they are engaged in low-intensity war. The United States has a higher Jewish population than Israel. Israeli Jews come from seventy different countries with ninety different languages from a worldwide Jewish diaspora of about twelve million. It was created at the end of the British mandate in 1948 at the insistence of President Truman, after nationalist violence and massive "illegal" immigration. It comprises Western secularised and Ashkenazic and Sephardic Orthodox Jews from the diaspora, and ultra-theocratic sects whose minority political wings have at times held the balance of power and key Cabinet posts in the Knesset. Israel is inventing and defining a national identity—it is an American surrogate supported by American financial aid ($3 billion annually) and military support, and threatened by three million Palestinians.

Belgium is bi-cultural and has a population of 10.1 million with 2.8 million Moslems. It has no national culture—being half Flemish and half French. It became federalised in 1993 into the semi-autonomous regions of Flanders, Wallonia, and Brussels, with three official languages. The main racial/ethnic groups have compromised with bi-partisan control of the national government and the public institutions, but each group periodically agitates for a dominant or completely separatist hegemony over their ethno-national region. There is continuing ethnic rhetoric—the Flemings talk about confederation, whilst the Francophiles say that this would lead to a schism like that between Slovakia and the Czech Republic, with Wallonia becoming part of France. Belgium's enthusiasm for a European political federation, and the Schengen agreement which scrapped passport controls in 1995 between eight other EU countries (France, Germany, Austria, Spain, Italy, Portugal, Luxembourg and the Netherlands), may be because it has no discernible national culture or identity to lose. Additionally its national government has devolved largely to its regions. This may explain why ninety percent of Belgians voted in the EU elections compared with twenty-four percent British. The Flemish Party, which opposes non-European immigration, seeks independence for Flanders and its MP obtained nearly thirty percent of the vote in Antwerp, which has an immigrant population of about fourteen percent [BBC2 14 May/TM 13 Sept.00]. Other prominent anti-immigrant parties exist elsewhere in Western Europe, and attract between thirteen and twenty-seven percent of the vote, in Denmark, Switzerland, Norway, Germany, and notably in France (Le Pen). In Austria (Haider), the anti-immigrant party is in its coalition government.

Switzerland should not be seen as a multicultural success. It is a loose federation of twenty-six cantons of three different national/cultural groups (sixty-four percent German, nineteen percent French and eight percent Italian) with a small and prosperous population (7.3 million). It fulfils a unique international role, is isolationist, neutral, not a member of the UN, and has recently voted against joining the EU [TM 5 March 01]. It has never been under a direct threat from its neighbouring states and its nationhood has not been put to the test. Switzerland is a signatory to the 1951 UN Convention on Refugees. A referendum was recently held on whether to limit immigration of non-Swiss foreigners (including asylum seekers) to eighteen percent, and to make greater efforts to expel illegal immigrants [TM 15 Sept.00]. This was supported by thirty-six percent of the electorate [TN 25 Sept.00].

There are about two million Muslims in Britain, although Muslim was not an official category in the 1991 census, together with twenty million in the West and 1.3 billion worldwide—Islam being the fastest growing faith in the world. Contrary to claims of its apologists, the compelling religious loyalty of Muslims could conceivably result in a rejuvenated British Muslim Parliament, or the British Islamic Action Movement, or even the American/British separatist, anti-white, anti-semitic Nation of Islam, becoming influential in British politics. There are reports [STM 17 Jan. 99/TM14 April 00] that there are training camps in Britain funded by terrorists from overseas preparing young Muslims to fight in conflicts in Kashmir, Chechnya and Afghanistan, or for a holy war: "it is an obligation upon all Muslims to train and prepare to protect themselves for the inevitable conflict." Five young Muslim Britons were given long jail sentences by the Yemeni authorities for an alleged plot to bomb British targets in Aden during Christmas 1998, which it is alleged was masterminded by a fundamentalist cleric in London [TM 9 Aug. 99]. Islamic law, in those states where they can be strictly applied (such as in Afghanistan) by the fundamentalists, are grossly intolerant according to Western standards. A major threat to the West would arise if the diverse and divided Muslim world united. It comprises Arab and non-Arab, pro-Western and anti-Western, secular and non-secular Muslim communities. Although there is no evidence of it at present, a pan-Muslim movement of the fifty-four Muslim states could be initiated by healing the divisions between the majority Sunnis who predominate in Saudi and the minority Shi'ites who predominate in Iran and are about one sixth of the global Muslim population. Turkey is at the frontier of the East/West cultural divide and presents a political/ cultural problem for the EU and in particular for Greece, which was a very reluctant NATO ally during the Kosovo (Albanian) campaign. This was because Greece does not want to be encircled by Muslim states and because of Turkey's formal candidature for membership of the EU [TM 9 Dec. 99]. Although Turkey is an important member of NATO, it has had an Islamic fundamentalist government in recent years; its human rights record is not good; it has a long-term sovereignty dispute with Greece over Cyprus and the Aegean islands and is a gateway for drugs and illegal immigrants. Germany in particular is concerned about the immigration implications if Turkey is admitted to membership of the EU.

Albert Weale [1985:26] erroneously argued that "there are obvious practical objections to the state pursuing a policy of [tolerant] neutrality. For example, any society would appear to need for its survival a set of common cultural standards. Although this objection to the principle of neutrality has some force, it typically underestimates the ingenuity that societies can show in coping with cultural diversity. A multilingual and multiethnic society like Yugoslavia may exhibit considerable frictions between its constituent units, but those frictions will not necessarily threaten the existence of the society itself." Minority groups are not always powerless as is sometimes supposed. It is not necessary to be numerically significant to have a disproportionate influence in a legislative assembly or other institution if there is a loss of self-confidence or a contented apathy by the majority in its determination to retain power. In the lead up to a general election, politicians can have an opportunist incentive both nationally and locally to gather marginal votes from either right or left, or from gays, greens, or ethnic groups, although once in power and in the absence of proportional representation, the main political parties tend to absorb any radicalism. If there is a "hung" parliament, made more likely wherever there is proportional representation, then deals or coalition bargains may be made by the majority party on issues of particular importance to a minority, who achieve a disproportionate influence. Minority parties have had a significant influence on marginal constituencies and the government in power. This is not simply a question of the overall proportions nationally, which may be modest. The 1991 census in Britain classed about 5.5 percent of the population as ethnic, although today's figure, due to later migration and illegal immigration is higher, and increases disproportionately due to higher birth rates. With ghettoisation, the ratio in some inner-city London districts and constituencies was up to about forty-five percent. Some academics estimate that the 2001 census will show two inner London boroughs as having a non-white majority. Bradford City Council estimate that twenty-one percent of its population is ethnic compared with 15.6 percent a decade ago, its Asian population nineteen percent compared with fourteen percent, and its whites seventy-eight percent compared with eighty-four percent [TM 8 Dec. 01]. By 1999/2000 an official estimate [Regional Trends 2000:54] of the ethnic population of Great Britain showed overall seven percent, with eight percent in England (including twenty-five percent in London), with two percent both in Scotland and in Wales.

An example of the influence of a politically powerful religious minority on United States policy is the American-Jewish vote. The president has to balance the small but influential Jewish minority vote (about 2.5 percent of the population) with the United States national interest in maintaining stability in the Middle East with its oil supplies. Zionism and Israel are said to be central to the life of many Jewish Americans, even if they have not been born there and do not live there—it is often said that "without America there would be no Israel" and it is "a place to go in time of need." This may reveal a complex dual identity which is characteristic of partial "two-domain" multiculturalism. But will the United States future global military power and political will be able or wish to continue to guarantee the security of Israel, which has become the American Ulster—with the United States becoming less ethnically Jewish and more multicultural? How long will the United States be able to do this if Iran, Iraq, or Syria are able to match Israel's nuclear capacity?

Another example is the approximately forty million Americans who claim Irish descent, and have an influential nationalist Irish-American vote. The U.S. president was, with Senator Mitchell, the third party in the Ulster peace talks. In Ulster (population 1.69 million, about the same as the county of Hampshire), the political ambitions of the numerically near equal "minority" for integration with the Irish republic, is responsible for an ethno-national bicultural conflict going back over 100 years. The body count of around 3,500 over the last thirty years has been higher than the lowest estimate (2,500) of the Albanians killed in Kosovo. Some years after its peak, there are still

13,500 troops in Ulster—about one soldier to every one hundred inhabitants—approximately double the number in the late 1960s. This situation of numerically evenly balanced people of different religions, cultures and national loyalties, but racially indistinguishable, financially supported from outside (Britain), and occupying the same disputed territory is potentially the most explosive.

Whenever an indigenous society has displayed generous toleration towards a minority, it cannot be assumed that this will necessarily be recognised or reciprocated, if and when the dominance is equalised or reversed. Separatism can be reinforced by politically motivated and determined terrorism, sometimes self-justified by a perverted utilitarian or theocratic rationalisation. Until the moderates of an ethno-national conflict effectively deal with their own extremists, no amount of negotiation by a peacemaker is likely to lead to a permanent resolution of the conflict. If disparate groups do not share a love of the same nation, it is not enough to simply inhabit the same territory, even given mutual trust and toleration. Such conflicts have to be resolved from within and external intervention is largely ineffective. In Yugoslavia, by rejecting the original Carrington/European Commission peace plan, the president of Serbia prolonged the Bosnia/Herzegovinan conflict. All the other former Yugoslav provinces agreed to independence, with Germany recognising Croatian independence prematurely in 1991. Serbia refused on the real, or more probably, the tactical grounds that the Serbian minorities in provinces like Kosovo could not be properly protected, other than by direct Serbian intervention. This imitated the Nazis in 1938, with the 3.25 million Germans in the Sudetenland; or the takeover in 1998 of Kosovo by the Serbian (ten percent) minority; or with the territorial claim over Ulster by the Irish republic, written into Articles 2 and 3 of its constitution from 1937 to 1999, which have not being completely abolished but reformulated [DT 8 May 00]; or de Gaulle's exhortation to the separatist French-Canadians "Vive le Quebec libre."

The Swann report [1985:19–20] makes the contentious comment that "those immigrants who came here for economic betterment and to enhance the prospects for their children, came on the understanding that they had every right to come to this country and, once they and their families were established here, they would not only be entitled to full equality of opportunity in terms of housing, jobs and education, but would also be in a position to seek changes in existing systems and procedures where these took no account of their presence here." "No account" and "changes in existing systems and procedures" could be euphemisms for what in their view is an insufficient account in seeking to relativise the mainstream culture and its values. Swann also suggested that "refugees may simply accept this (racism) as the price to be paid for being allowed to remain in this country." This is likely to be more true of illegal immigrants and economic refugees claiming asylum, who for the time being at least, would be unlikely to make demands. Equality of opportunity is a necessary, but not always seen as a sufficient condition for political and social harmony. The 1976 Race Relations Act did not extend to Ulster. Nevertheless, equal opportunity essentially existed in Ulster during the years 1972–1999 of direct rule from the central government in London, but a climate of mutual toleration and trust did not follow from this. This has been exemplified by the makeup of the former RUC (Royal Ulster Constabulary): eighty-eight percent Protestant and eight percent Catholic, in a population that is forty percent Catholic. In its seventy-seven year old history, the RUC has never had more than twenty-one percent Catholic officers, although originally one third of places were reserved for them [TM 6 Sept. 99].

NOTES

Banton, M. "Modelling Ethnic and National Relations." In *Ethnic and Racial Studies*. vol. 17. no.1, January 1994. 9.

Bernstein, R. *Dictatorship of Virtue—Multiculturalism and the Battle for America's Future*. New York: Alfred A. Knopf, 1994. 4–9.

Connor, W. "Beyond Reason—The Nature of The Ethno-National Bond." In *Ethnic and Racial Studies*. vol.16. no.3, July 1993. 373.

Fish, S. *There's No Such Thing As Free Speech*. Oxford: Oxford University Press. 1994. 81–3/87–8.

Fukuyama, F. *Trust—The Social Virtues and the Creation Of Prosperity*. London: Penguin Books, 1996. 318–9.

Mauk, J and Oakland, J. *American Civilization*. London: Routledge, 1997. 77.

Glazer, N. "The Universalisation of Ethnicity." In *Encounter*. vol. 44. February, 1975. 17.

_____ "The Ethnic Factor." In *Encounter*. July 1981. 13 and 15.

_____ *We Are All Multiculturalists Now* Cambridge, Mass: Harvard University Press, 1997. 4.

Ibid. 6.

Ibid. 7.

Ibid. 21.

Ibid. 47.

Ibid. 91.

Ibid. 120.

Ibid. 123.

Ibid. 136.

Ibid. 145–6.

Gray, J. "Toleration and The Currently Offensive Implication of the Loss of Judgement." In *The Loss of Virtue*. London: Social Affairs Unit, 1992. 40.

Jupp, J. *Immigration*. Oxford: Oxford University Press, 1998. vi.

Ibid. 146–7.

Ibid. 186–7.

Koshechkina, T. *Political Tolerance—From General Principles to Concrete Application*. M.A. Dissertation. Canterbury: University of Kent, 1992. 137.

Lynn, V. *We'll Meet Again*. London: Sidgwick and Jackson, 1989. 165.

Nisbet, R. *Twilight of Authority*. London: Heinemann, 1976. 9–10.

O'Sullivan, J. "Reaching the Right that Bill Can't." In *New Statesman*. 9 August 1996. 18–9.

Schlesinger, A.M. *The Disuniting of America—Reflections On a Multicultural Society*. New York and London: W.W. Norton, 1992.

Siedentop. L. *Democracy in Europe*. (Book Review). London: Penguin, 2000.

Stationery Office. *Regional Trends*. NO. 35. 2000. 54.

Swann, Lord. *Education for All—The Report of the Committee of Inquiry Into the Education of Children from Ethnic Minority Groups*. London: Stationery Office, 1985. 19–20.

Ibid. 36.

Terrill, R. *The Australians—In Search of an Identity*. London: Bantam Press, 1987.

Weale, A. "Toleration, Individual Differences and Respect for Persons." In *Aspects of Toleration*. Horton, J. and Mendus, S. (Eds). London: Methuen, 1985. 26.

Wieseltier, L. *The Trouble with Multiculturalism*. (Book Review) In *The New York Times Book Review*. 1994.

BBC Radio 4. *Diverging Dominions—Australia*. No. 1. 22 May 1996.

BBC Radio 4. *Diverging Dominions—Canada*. No. 3. 5 June 1996.

BBC 2. *Under Fire (Correspondent)*. December 1999.

BBC 2. *Out of the Melting Pot*. 18 February/30 September 1995/6.

BBC 2. *Correspondent Europe*. 14 May 2000.

7

Cultural Imperialism and
Cultural Nationalism

The cultural hegemony of a nation-state can be self-contained without aspiring to actively export its culture. Hegemonists are not cultural imperialists; they seek to preserve and to protect a culture within their society. They need have no missionary, interventionist, or evangelical ambitions, but rather an attitude of "live and let live" based perhaps on indifference. It is a case of not wishing to be judgmental or exclusive, or not wishing to invite the accusation of imperialism, or simply, "minding their own business." This is comparable with the value pluralism of the philosopher Isaiah Berlin [1995:29] which rejects the liberal dream of a universal civilization of like-minded, high-minded men and women with a single version of what constitutes a good society—if not nationally, then globally—and is, at least sometimes, incommensurable and incompatible. Berlin was said to be sympathetic to some nationalist hopes for cultural independence and political sovereignty.

Post-imperial Britain was for years seduced by the aspirational and culturally imperialist myth of its fifty-four member multiracial Commonwealth of 1.6 billion people. It has no formal constitution and includes a fictitious and amorphous concept of citizenship—"subjects of the Crown." It was not originally intended or envisaged as promoting migration and a legal right of entry into Britain, with a subsequently politically embarrassing liberal agenda. A legacy of this remains in the fact that citizens of the Commonwealth (and the Irish Republic) residing in Britain, but not citizens of EU member states, have voting rights in British general elections. Unlike the United States, which recognises it only in individual cases, Britain has no restrictions on dual nationality. Reverse racists associate imperialism with victimhood, and requires Britain to apologise for its history and to compensate for its alleged past sins—often after fifty years of self-inflicted political and economic blunders. The Commonwealth ethos assumed that the British tradition of parlia-

85

mentary democracy, incorruptible institutions, and basic human rights would rub off on to the "New" Commonwealth states as they reached political maturity, and would overcome the culture gap. The reality is that some of them have become among the world's cruellest and oppressive regimes, prone to corruption, bankruptcy and military dictatorship. Max Beloff [1992: 121] observes that "Once the way was open for countries with no nominal allegiance to the Crown and with independent and sometimes antagonistic cultures to become full members of the Commonwealth, the difficulties inevitably multiplied. From being an organ at least of inter-governmental cooperation on major issues of world economics and politics, the Commonwealth rapidly became no more than an umbrella for covering a limited number of technical, educational and aid projects which could probably have come into being or have subsisted without it."

Walzer observes [1992:169] that "it often seems as if the chief motive for national liberation is not to free oneself from minority status in someone else's country, but to acquire (and then mistreat) minorities of one's own." When the internal affairs of these countries do not conform to the ethos of the West, any reaction by Britain can be labelled colonialism and used by the local despots to reinforce their regime. The perception of Britain as having a divided loyalty to its Commonwealth and a special relationship with the United States, influenced de Gaulle's vetoing of the British applications to join the European Common Market (later the EU) in 1961 and 1967, although it has recently been disclosed that the Dutch government was the most forceful in objecting to Britain's entry, fearing that immigration from the Commonwealth would flood the Netherlands [TM 8 Sept.00]. This delayed entry until 1973, a decision confirmed by a national referendum in 1975 with sixty-seven percent in favour. On a more modest scale, Scottish, Welsh and Irish nationalists have made accusations of cultural imperialism or even "white on white racism" on English holiday home-owners or retired incomers/settlers who are perceived as being "foreigners" [BBC 2 July 94].

Another global organisation is the 135 nation WTO (World Trade Organisation), formed in 1995, to liberalise trade and whose meeting in Seattle in 1999 ended up in chaos and without agreement. Amongst the disparate problems was the move supported out of self-interest by the AFL-CIO (American Federation of Labor-Congress of Industrial Organizations)—the United States' largest trade union—to introduce U.S. labour and environmental standards into the talks on free trade, although if this were done it would deprive many of the developing countries of their competitive economic advantage. Self-interest took precedence over the moral imperative of universal equality. Others saw economic globalism as Western protectionism and a neo-colonialism infringing upon the sovereignty and culture of developing countries. It could be argued equally that the developing countries are infringing the sovereign rights and culture of Western nation states as economic and illegal refugees by taking advantage of the loosely worded and liberal 1951 UN Convention.

Before WW2, cultural imperialism went hand in hand with evangelising missionaries, but since then it has been largely seen as "Americanisation." Some regard some aspects of the Western consumerist culture—Coca Cola; junk food; Hollywood; Rambo; the Ricki Lake and Jerry Springer shows; television soaps—as being decidedly bland, lightweight, decadent, or even nihilistic, with which they have no wish to assimilate. This became evident in post-Communist Russia and some other emerging nation-states, who, although they were ready to adopt capitalism and consumerism, resisted the erosion of their traditional cultures, as in the 1960s, when de Gaulle tried to counter the "Americanisation" of France. The American Culture Centre in Paris, which intended to disseminate American culture, closed some years ago with huge debts [TM 14 Dec. 96]. The French are now more concerned about the Islamisation of France. There is today less overt cultural imperialism, other than crusades for human rights. When there are gross abuses, although the West does not remain passive, it is regionally selective and distinctly non-universal, as with the NATO armed humanitarian intervention in Kosovo, but not in Chechnya or Tibet. Humanitarian aid in the man-made disasters of civil wars can be abused by one faction using it as a weapon of war, with aid workers seen as political agents. There are limits to the toleration of internal "culture wars," but the autonomy of sovereign states has to be respected, and there are physical, political and financial limits of the West on its global obligations and influence. Sceptics might say that moral imperialism has little effect other than to satisfy the domestic audiences of politicians, and can be labelled by its recipients as interference, arrogance or imperialism. Trade sanctions can be counter-productive and can range from being incomplete to ineffective and can create a national victimhood. Sanctions and diplomatic rhetoric are often the limit of the West's global influence. Nevertheless, whereas the West preaches globalisation and human rights, much of the world sees itself being increasingly run by, and for, the benefit of the West. The 1993 Bangkok Declaration [Michael Davis 1995:206] of the Asian states declared that it "discourage(d) any attempt to use human rights as a conditionality for extending development assistance," and it "emphasize(d) the principles of national sovereignty and territorial integrity as well as non-interference in the internal affairs of states, and the non-use of human rights as an instrument of political pressure." China's description [175] of its rights tradition "emphasized economic developmental concerns, sovereignty, and the pre-eminence of collective over individual interest as a basis of rights." The Chinese probably recall that Western religion in the form of Christian missionaries acted as a spearhead for foreign colonisation around the 1900s.

The former Cabinet Minister Healey [1989:219] observed the different approaches in their African colonies between the British policy of cultural dualism and the French policy of cultural assimilation. After the tragedies in Ghana, Nigeria, and later Uganda, Zimbabwe, and Sierra Leone, he was less sure about the British model. Although a different culture may be temporarily or partially assimilated by Others, it is unlikely to remain so after independence. He noted [223] that "most of the military coups which have proliferated in British Africa since independence were led by men trained in British military schools [Sandhurst] and staff colleges [and at the English Bar]; but their regimes have not necessarily accepted British influence." Nonetheless, Nelson Mandela said [DM 5 Nov. 94] that "I was brought up in a British school, and at the time Britain was the home of everything that was best in the world. I have not discarded the influence which Britain and British history and culture exercised on us."

In Zimbabwe, President Mugabe's land grab threats started about four years ago, and there followed the murder of five farmers in a total of at least thirty-seven killings. The British High Commission dealt with a flood of passport applications, and the Foreign Office updated contingency plans to evacuate British nationals [TM 25 March 00]. In a population of more than 12.5 million, there is less than one percent of whites who own about seventy percent of the prime agricultural land [TM 8 April 00]. Mugabe also threatened to deprive about 86,000 Zimbabweans of their citizenship, who had held dual nationality before this was abolished in 1985—ethnic cleansing by another means. An edict legalised the seizure of 841 white owned farms and left compensation, other than for "improvements" to the British government as the former colonial power [TM 25 May 00]. Britain had previously provided £40 million for compensation [TM 27 April 00]. Nonetheless, on Zimbabwe's twentieth anniversary of independence, the Queen, as head of the Commonwealth, sent a message of congratulation to President Mugabe [TM 25 May 00]. The Secretary General of the Commonwealth exhibited similar duality in saying that no action should be taken against Zimbabwe because "this is African politics. This is not unusual. African politics is volatile at the best of times" [TM 28 April 00]. This echoed the remarks of the last British governor about the validity of its first general election after independence in 1980: "this is Africa . . . they behave differently." After the 2000 parliamentary election, the predictable disagreement took place as to whether the election had been free and fair. The UN withdrew its team sent to coordinate the international observer missions [DT 10 June 00]. After ten months of violent anarchy and after international aid had been almost entirely cut off, the land grab was temporarily ended in December 2000, having urged his supporters to "strike fear into the heart of the white man," because Mugabe said that "we have reached our target." More probably it was to rescue his shattered economy.

Zimbabwe's five remaining white supreme court judges have been threatened with violence unless they surrender their posts immediately [TM 5 March 01], and 26,000 Britons are to have their dual nationality revoked [TM 27 March 01]. The trust of the Zimbabwean whites in the multiracial ethos underlying the Commonwealth has been destroyed. Nevertheless, a British army team continues to train Zimbabwean troops as Mugabe increasingly uses his security forces to keep his regime in power. This was set up to turn his guerrilla army into a professional force even though one third of this army is now fighting in the civil war in the neighbouring Democratic Republic of Congo [TM 4 March 00]. The West has poured billions of dollars of aid into Africa with little apparent benefit both politically and economically. Twenty countries in Africa are at war with one another or suffering internal civil conflicts, and the combined debt of African countries rose from $122 billion in 1983 to $350 billion in 1999. Under the current debt relief initiative, Uganda was the first country to receive from the IMF's (The International Monetary Fund) debt relief initiative, the first $31 million package of aid in 1999. Its parliament promptly approved the purchase of a $35 million jet aircraft for the President's use [DT 8 May 00]. It seems that the political leaders of these countries have not absorbed much of the Western ethos.

The world has changed in radical and largely unforeseeable respects in the last fifty years. The UN Charter reflected the then world order still largely colonised by the West, and idealised American political and cultural imperialism set the moral standards for the rest of the "old" and unawakened world. Repeating the failed messianism of President Wilson, it constructed a system of universal rights based on a cosmopolitan liberalism. Today some UN member states still lack mature democratic governance and political structures. Capitalism without the tradition of democracy and its institutions can lead to crime and corruption as has became evident in the new Russian Federation.

Professor Edward Said [1993:407–8] claims that "No-one today is purely one thing . . . Imperialism consolidated the mixture of cultures and identities on a global scale. But its worst and most paradoxical gift was to allow people to believe that they were only, mainly, exclusively, white or black, or Western, or Oriental . . . It is more rewarding—and more difficult—to think concretely and sympathetically, contrapuntally, about others than only about 'us.' But this also means not trying to rule others, not trying to classify them or put them in hierarchies, above all, not constantly reiterating how 'our' culture or country is number one (or not number one, for that matter)." If this "gift" was true in the past, it reflected and accepted the then status quo, and most people would not recognise the validity of this accusation today. Nevertheless, whenever the United States has been called upon by the UN under its "authority" to act against third world states, it has been accused of imperialism.

Like the historian Max Beloff, Arthur Schlesinger [1987:156–7] is an American who defends Western imperialism: "it was only when the under-developed world bestirred itself after the Second World War that the subject peoples began to edge into the analytical picture. The conviction of their impotence survived, however, from the Euro-centric phase of imperialism theory . . . the idea of 'cultural imperialism' arose to explain how Western culture doomed them to permanent spiritual emasculation . . . cultural aggression had not always accompanied political and economic aggression. Colonial administrators and imperial apologists often sought to protect the native culture, including even the traditional religion, against westernization . . . the most benign and selfless of the Western intruders—missionaries, doctors, educators, social reformers—sometimes roused the most resentment . . . ironically, it was the missionaries who, in order to prove the native's spiritual equality, were most prepared to destroy his cultural identity . . . the French determination to free Algerian women from the veil appeared an attempt to make them an 'ally in the work of cultural destruction' . . . as nationalism began to awaken the non-Western world, the rising bitterness came in the end more from cultural than from political or economic wounds. The most humiliating kind of defeat is a cultural defeat." The British colonial policy was one of cultural dualism—not cultural extinction. Moreover, the supposed unilateral economic benefits of imperialism to the imperialists should be set against the diversion of their talented manpower and resources. In the years 1951–1973, when decolonization was at its height, the real GDP of the UK was increasing. The annual average growth rate of three percent outstripped that of any period since early Victorian times. The only possible conclusion is the economically "the Empire was more burden than benefit" [Davies 1999:950].

Multinational corporations now have an influence second only to governments except in the global financial markets, but their objectives differ. Some Japanese companies [STM 13 Aug. 00] are trying to put pressure on the British government to join the Euro currency which has major political, as well as economic, implications for Britain. Some of the press is labelling this "blackmail" and noting that Japan only accounts for about four percent of British inward investment. Noam Chomsky [1966:6] attacks as "hypocritical moralism" American economic and cultural imperialism, principally through the use of rights diplomacy—"recent history shows that it makes little difference to us what form of government a country has as long as it remains an 'open society,' in our peculiar sense of this term—a society, that is, which remains open to American economic penetration or political control. If it is necessary to approach genocide in Vietnam to achieve this objective, then this is the price we must pay in defence of freedom and the rights of man." But developing countries can sometimes adopt the alternative of jointly owned capital ventures. There has been a sizeable inward investment and export of employment to Western Europe by Pacific Asian countries, which is not seen as "reverse imperialism" nor "exporting" their cultures. In 1997, of the total inward investment into Britain, this was about ten percent [STM 9 Aug. 98]. Britain is seen as being politically and socially stable, incorruptible, and a low wage economy. Given the absence of latent ethno-national conflicts, if these same conditions were met in developing countries, the incentive for economic migration from them to the West would be reduced by foreign investment, overseas aid, liberal trade policies, and the acceptance of birth control.

The philosophical basis of cultural nationalism was developed by the German Enlightenment philosopher Herder, who assumed the God-ordained uniqueness of nations, and that a nation must have a state of its own. Cultural nationalism is a feature of the politics of identity recognition, and is the integration of an indigenous culture into a territorially defined nation-state that maintains a cultural hegemony within its social, moral, and political life. It seeks to preserve and to strengthen its cultural identity and will defend it, if it is felt to be threatened. The essence of the nation is regarded as being the product of its unique history and culture, and is manifest by a collective solidarity endowed with unique attributes. It can originate in movements led by historians, philosophers, intellectuals and artists who formulate its ideology. Cultural nationalism, however, may be perceived by separatist Others as racist.

This discussion argues that without the bond of a national identity, an undivided loyalty to the nation-state cannot be assumed to exist. It makes the case for the maintenance and protection of a British traditional cultural hegemony, faced as it is with the present-day threats of mass migration and politicised separatist multiculturalism. A shared culture is inclusive of a common history, language, legal system, traditions, customs, and political and moral institutions which applies to people born and nurtured within the same racial/ethnic group, together with those Others who have assimilated its culture. The background of a nation, be it historic, cultural, physical, symbolic or emotional, provides a link with the past and a sense of continuity and belonging. A shared culture and history, together with its heroes and achievers, provide its people with a sense of national identity. It may be minimised as a representational construct of a stereotype, but for many people it is a psychological reality. Kosaku Yoshino, in his enquiry into cultural nationalism in contemporary Japan and the means by which its national identity has been reinvented, highlights a particular feature that also applies to cultural nationalism in other island states, including Britain. He notes [1992: 68] that "The Japanese archipelago has been almost entirely immune from territorial wars. In other words, the territorial question is not an issue of which the majority of Japanese are actively conscious. The issues of Japan's [cultural] nationalism have centred around the notion of the uniqueness of Japanese ethnicity shared by its members, a uniqueness which is a function of culture, religion and race."

A sense of national identity, tradition, heritage and pride does not imply arrogance, superiority, or a contempt for Others. It is not attempting to set a pattern for others, although others may choose to imitate or to adopt it—but to preserve and to protect its cultural preference. Raz [1994:75] defends this preference: "one's devotion to and love of one's culture in no way depends on believing it to be better than others. It is rational and valid whether or not it is better than others, so long as one loves one's own culture for what is truly good in it . . . one should certainly be acquainted with the cultures that inhabit one's country—this is so whether or not they are the equal of one's own—that is one of the duties of citizenship . . . compare one's attitude to one's culture with one's love of one's children . . . one loves one's children because they are one's children." In a democracy, national pride does not mean putting some extremist theology or perverted "interest" of the state, above concern for human life, as in August 2000 with the doomed submarine Kursk in the authoritarian Russian regime.

A cultural hegemony values the importance and the benefits that it perceives in the traditional order, conformity, and coherence of a national society. It is "felt" that in order to constitute a stable society, its members must have common laws, customs, standards, values and a culture that includes basic moral beliefs. John Dewey [1963:12] says that "to form anything that can be called a community in its pregnant sense there must be values prized in common. Without them, any so-called social group, class, people, nation, tends to fall apart into molecules having but mechanically [politically?] enforced connections with one another." The predominantly visceral response of a cultural hegemony to multiculturalism with its different lifestyles is to perceive it as presaging undesirable and unnecessary tensions, giving rise to feelings ranging from being "uncomfortable," to seeing it as a positive threat. These responses can remain relatively unaffected by the arguments rational or otherwise as to its supposed benefits, economic or otherwise, or whether they are characterised as being objective or subjective. The American philosopher Thomas Nagel [1979:196] observes that "there is a tendency to seek an objective account of everything before admitting its reality. But often what appears to be a more subjective point of view cannot be accounted for in this way. So either the objective conception of the world is incomplete, or the subjective involves illusions which should be rejected."

A cultural hegemony is not based on the belief that other cultures do not merit respect, and it is not inconsistent with the acceptance of cultural relativism provided that it is on a global dimension. It is the argument, belief or feeling, that within the confines of the nation-state, the culture of some Others can be contrary to, and may be destabilising and minatory to, the identity which the majority have inherited, are accustomed to, and do not wish to have eroded. Breaking away from a culture, a tradition, or a morality is often anathema particularly to the older generation, and rejecting the status quo can be unpredictable and disturbing, but may be more attractive to the young, at least in the short term. Dewey [1963:36] discusses how human nature relates to (idealistic) ideologies: "among the youth in particular . . . of being engaged in creating a pattern for new institutions which the whole world will in time adopt . . . satisfaction [is] derived from a sense of sharing in creative activities . . . there is the satisfaction that comes from a sense of union with others . . . The satisfaction obtained by the sentiment of communion with others, of the breaking down of barriers."

Societies that espouse a cultural hegemony believe that maintaining a definitive national/ethnic culture is a natural right. The make-up and reinforcement of this culture, which may in part be of their own creation, is not seen as immutable but will change and develop with time in an evolutionary and not a revolutionary way. This gradualism will be in its own direction and at its own pace. Nevertheless a cultural hegemony has to address the issue "should people of other cultures who make the choice of living, or seeking to live here, be expected to assimilate into our 'way of life?' If not, what limits including those of toleration should we extend to them?"

The integrative role of cultural nationalism with political nationalism, is particularly apparent in self-determination movements. John Hutchinson (1994:41–2) distinguishes between "two distinctive and sometimes competing types of nationalism: a political nationalism that has as its aim autonomous state institutions; and a cultural nationalism that seeks a moral regeneration of the community . . . by comparison with political nationalist movements, those of the cultural nationalist variety are relatively small in numbers and must give way to state-orientated movements since their models can only be implemented through the state . . . in practice, of course, it is often difficult to distinguish between cultural and political nationalists, for both put forward what, since the eighteenth century, has been in many contexts a revolutionary doctrine; that sovereignty is located ultimately in the people, and that the world is divided into distinctive peoples, each with unique homelands. Cultural interests have often provided a useful cloak for the political struggles of rising social groups hostile to the established polity."

Political nationalism is led by elite politicians and opinion formers who transform a philosophical ideology into positive political, economic, and social programmes, which generate grievances among different, even competing groups, against the existing polity. Their objective is to create a recognised and centralised nation-state based on common citizenship, which participates as an equal in the world. Political nationalism founded on cultural nationalism took place early in the twentieth century first in the Habsburg Empire with the Czechs, Slovaks, and Slovenes, and later in the Ukraine/Belarus/ Baltic/Caucusus, and in the former Yugoslavia with Serbia, Slovenia, Croatia, Bosnia, Herzogovina, Kosovo, Montenegro, and Macedonia. Nationalism is always latent where there is a colonial or occupying power. It was directed against the British in Ireland in the nineteenth century Gaelic revival, and in Irish political nationalism from the mid–1860s to the Anglo/Irish Treaty of 1922 leading to the creation of the Irish Free State [O'Day:1987]. Plaid Cymru, the Welsh nationalist party set up as a cultural organisation in 1925, became a serious political force during the 1960s. The British, French, Dutch, Belgian and Portuguese empires yielded to nationalism in the second half of the twentieth century. In India nationalism was a by-product of the Hindu and Muslim intellectual revivals of the nineteenth century and the founding of the Indian National Congress in 1885. It was inevitably anti-British, and like other nationalistic movements, had its militant factions, and later a Hindu/ Muslim religious split resulting in ethnic cleansing. Accounts of nationalism may be relevant to ex-imperial and colonial states, but they are not applicable to Britain, which has been a territorially defined and independent political nation-state for centuries.

Cultural nationalism can be promoted by the film industry, particularly if it is state subsidised. Those of Hollywood and Britain have a largely commercial ethos, though the latter is now subsidised by the National Lottery, and neither is beyond occasional myth making. Some Australian revisionist films have disparaged Catholicism and British colonisation, but paradoxically do not reflect the present-day Asianisation of Australia. In Britain over the last two or three decades, national heroes have tended to be removed from school history books and debunked by anti-racist education progressives and political correctness. This is aimed at destroying the reputations of prominent figures of the last century—who cannot respond. The former Chief Executive of the Schools Curriculum and Assessment Authority called for children to be taught to believe what it means to be British, whatever their cultural or ethnic background. He said [DM 18/19 July 95] that there is an "embarrassed silence, ill-focused hostility, or a kind of cosmopolitan disdain" when it is suggested that a sense of national identity should be taught in schools.

Creeping multiculturalism and cultural relativism are self-fulfilling prophesies, which lend support to the claim that there is no such thing as a British culture and national identity. It also leads to the integrationist proposition that a novel but ill-defined national identity should be sought, which does not involve the annulment of other loyalties, whilst sharing some common, but unspecified, ethical and civic values. There are indeed aspects of the liberal individualistic culture of the West, such as overt self-interest and loss of shame, which some other cultures regard as socially lacking. On the other hand, there are features of other cultures such as family values, respect for elders, rejection of gambling, drug addiction, materialism and consumerism, which many Britons find commendable. Desirable features, though, cannot be selected and adopted piecemeal, because cultures have to be lived in their totality. Nevertheless, it could be said that the Western democratic individualistic way of life is achieving something of a cosmopolitan hegemony, inasmuch that other societies throughout the world are emulating it, or parts of it, with the exception of those dominated by fundamentalist religions.

NOTES

Beloff, M. *An Historian in the Twentieth Century.* New Haven: Yale University Press. 1992. 121.

Berlin, I. *Are There Limits to Liberalism?* (Book Review). In *The New York Review.* 19 October 1995. 29.

Chomsky, N. "The Responsibility of Intellectuals." In *American Power and the New Mandarins.* London: Pelican Books, 1969. 256–7.

Davies, N. *The Isles.* London: Macmillan, 1999. 950.

Davis, M.C. (Ed.)—*Human Rights and Chinese Values—Legal, Philosophical and Political Perspectives.* Oxford: Oxford University Press, 1995. 175.

Ibid. 206.

Dewey, J. *Freedom and Culture.* New York: Capricorn Books, 1963. 36.

Healey, D. *The Time of My Life.* London: Michael Joseph, 1989. 219 and 23.

Hutchinson, J. *Modern Nationalism.* London: Fontana Press, 1994. 41–2.

Nagel, T. *Mortal Questions.* Cambridge: Cambridge University Press, 1979. 196.

O'Day, A. (Ed.) *Reactions to Irish Nationalism.* London: Hambledon Press, 1987.

Raz, J. "Multiculturalism—A Liberal Perspective." In *Dissent.* Winter, 1994. 75.

Said, E.W. *Culture and Imperialism.* London: Chatto and Windus, 1993. 407–8.

Schlesinger, A.M. *The Cycles of American History.* London: Andre Deutsch, 1987. 156–7.

Walzer, M. "The New Tribalism." In *Dissent.* Spring. vol. 39. 1992. 169.

Yoshino, K. *Cultural Nationalism in Contemporary Japan.* Routledge: London. 1992. 68.

BBC 2. *Scottish Nationalism.* July 1994.

8

The Appeal of Nationhood and Kinship

Nationhood is a sentiment that moulds together the public and private lives of a society into a national identity. Kinship is the feeling of belonging to, and sharing a communal and exclusive identity, which human beings consciously and explicitly use to define their social relationships. A national identity satisfies a desire to conform to the common characteristics of a collective—the opposite of diversity, which implies complexity and multiple identities. As Liah Greenfeld [1992:489] observes, "Nationality elevated every member of the community which it made sovereign. It guaranteed status. National identity is, fundamentally, a matter of dignity. It gives people reasons to be proud." Jonathan Glover [1988:196–9] says that "the nation-state is one of the clearest expressions of group identity . . . perhaps a national or group identity is defended so strongly because of the part it plays in the sense people have of their individual identity." Hutchinson [1994:22] says that "nationalism arises not just as a means to achieve [industrialisation] modernity, but rather to (re)create a sense of distinctive identity and autonomy that will enable populations to survive in a modern world in which unpredictable change is the norm . . . It is this enhancement of threat produced by modernization that helps explain the spread and deepening of ethnic politics, manifested in modern nationalism." The expectations of some economists that nation-states would be eroded and would suffer a leakage of political authority due to the multinational corporations and globalisation is beginning to look less credible and inevitable (apart from financial independence), as does the belief that a cultural cosmopolitanism would evolve. Given a global free market, capitalism will take advantage of the economic differentiation between states—which cannot be avoided—but cultural diversity within a nation-state is another matter.

Human associations require qualifications to join a group or institution and continue to belong—there are rules, responsibilities, and a culture which its members must accept in return for certain privileges, and to be accepted by its other members One of the most important of these is to be supportive and loyal to the aims and objectives of the organisation (extremists demand absolute obedience), and to the character (culture) of the kinship network. This does not imply that there is no scope for individuality or eccentricity, but that the diversity has to be kept within tolerable limits, otherwise the offender is not trusted, and as a result, excluded. Experience suggests that whenever excessive individualism lacks a binding structure such as an accepted culture or discipline, the viability of a group erodes. Citizenship, with its implied social contract of loyalty, are aspects of the kinship of nationhood.

Thomas Hobbes, the seventeenth-century English philosopher, believed that self-preservation was central to human nature, which led the individual to implicitly transfer authority to the state in exchange for its guarantee of personal safety. This social contract was based on the collective will of all individual members of the state, and applied not only to external, but also to internal threats which might disrupt its social cohesion. There is no more potent stimulus to the bond of kinship than when the group or nation is threatened and is in need of protection. A lack of national coherence and resolve on the victim's part to defend its people and its territory can be perceived as weakness, and can attract an aggressive war. However, William Pfaff [1993:238] recognises a society's own potential for aggression in that the "affirmation of the nation is an international disturbance to the extent that a nation [may] conceive itself licensed to validate itself by the victimization of another society. But the geographical sweep of this is usually limited." Neil Maccormick [1979:100–2] says that "States are legalistic impersonal entities, nations are communities with culture and personality . . . a positive elucidation of nationhood is that nations are constituted by a form of popular consciousness, not by a mode of legal organization . . . Consciousness of belonging to a nation is one of the things which enables us as individuals in some way even in our earthly existence to transcend the limitations of space, time and mortality, and to participate in that which had meaning before us and will continue to have meanings beyond us . . . Families and a 'sense of family' can have similar significance." National identity, like racism, is to some extent belief validated, but this does not make it a less real and potent psychological force. It cannot be satisfactorily defined other than to generalise its association with a shared history, together with components of race, aesthetic culture, language, religion, beliefs, traditions, taboos, dress, appearance, customs, rituals, symbols and practices, which may in part be "invented" by over-laying an objective structure on to a subjective experience. People will give differing interpretations and selective examples of what it means to them, but this imprecision should not be used to deny its existence and compelling influence. It is not only what people are: it is what they feel themselves to be.

The notion of nationhhood can be dismissed as a "common misconception" or "a community of people who think that they are a nation." Benedict Anderson [1991:6–7] proposed as a definition of a nation: "it is an imagined political community—and imagined as both inherently limited and sovereign. It is imagined because the members of even the smallest nation will never know most of their fellow-members, meet them, or even hear them, yet in the mind of each lives the image of their communion . . . no nation imagines itself as coterminous with mankind." Connor [1993:373] calls nationhood *ethnopsychology* and says that "both statesmen and scholars have failed to comprehend the non-rational, emotional well-springs of ethno-nationalism and, consequently, have tended to under-estimate its capacity for influencing group behaviour." Communism suppressed nationhood in the former USSR, and after the Berlin Wall came down in 1989, these nations led by the Baltic states reasserted their independence. Latvia, for example, which until 1991 was colonised by the USSR and is twenty-six percent ethnic Russian, is determined to reassert its Latvian nationhood. To achieve homogeneity, the dominant ethnic group may "cleanse" its territory of Others by massacre, forcible expulsion, apartheid, or more gradually by a selective policy of land purchase and/or housing, or by disparate procreation. A separatist minority in a multicultural society will not readily find this status as being a satisfying, or permanent, expression of its nationhood. Lloyd George correctly foresaw at the 1919 Peace Conference that Germany's frustrated nationhood could give rise to an aggressive nation-state, reclaiming from their neighbours their "oppressed" minority and their "lost territory and lost people"—being repeated today with Kosovo, Macedonia, Montenegro and Albania calling for a "Greater Albania."

Lord Devlin (1965), a High Court judge some thirty years ago, argued that a shared morality is essential to the existence of a society—the infringement of which was analogous to treason, and if allowed, would destroy that society. Although the law accommodates changes in morality, it codifies society's moral expectations, and the containment of immorality (however that is defined) is arguably as much the law's business as the suppression of the more obvious criminal activities. How the law could reflect the moral diversity of a separatist multicultural society with no coherent culture and arbitrate between disputes is problematic. An appeal to the traditional moral (cultural) values of British nationhood was made by the Archbishop of Canterbury [DM 16 March 96]: "honesty, truth, justice—all these have made our country great in the past and will continue to do so if we return to them."

Social anthropologists believe that kinship (sometimes pejoratively labelled "tribalism") and the formation of closed and selective societies is a part of a predictable and permanent human need for an identity. Others view nationhood as an irrational atavism, reverting to an earlier type. Kinship involves establishing a connection between individuals or groups of individuals by finding other members common to that individual or group. The natural accompaniment of loyalty to all in-groups is the exclusion of out groups, and self-regulation, including expulsion, which may relate to their race/ethnicity/class/status. The scope and intensity of kinship may range from the street gang, the old school, to the club, to the religious cult/sect, to the old boy/old girl network, to fellow expatriates, to the regiment, to any elitist group to the nation. Kinship and camaraderie are strongest wherever the physical and emotional relationships and dependence such as shared risks are closest. Citizen armies are no longer ready to die for "King and Country." Nevertheless, no matter how irrational it may seem, loyalty and tradition remain important enough for professional soldiers to be prepared to risk their lives within the supportive kinship/comradeship of their regiment, as were their predecessors.

Fukuyama [1996:314–5] observes that "rights based individualism is deeply embedded in American political philosophy and constitutional law . . . communities tend to be intolerant of outsiders in proportion to their internal cohesiveness, because the very strength of the principles that bind members together exclude those who do not share them. Although each of the individual steps taken (by the courts against discrimination against minority groups) could be justified in terms of the country's basic egalitarian principles, the cumulative and unintended effect was for the state to become an enemy of communal institutions—virtually all communities saw their authority weakened."

The most direct bonding (kith and kinship) is between parents, siblings and blood relatives—namely, a relationship that includes a reproductive genetic characteristic. Friendship is a non-genetic bonding that extends into other social domains. Steven Grosby [1994:164–7] contends that "from everything we know historically and anthropologically about the human species, the infant has never merely belonged to its immediate family; the child has also belonged *from birth* to the larger cultural collectivity, whether a lineage, a clan, a tribe; a city-state, a nation, or a national-state . . . the infant develops into a person through its participation in the objectified, both past and current, achievements of the lives of the many individuals of the larger cultural collectivity; it does this by participation in, for example, the language of the larger cultural collectivity; in learning the language of its society. The infant participates in the culture of the larger society; it becomes a member of that society; it shares in its collective consciousness through the assimilation and use of the language. The life and the development of the life of the infant have always been dependent upon both of the immediate family and the larger collectivity." A nation may well be an "imagined or a presumed community," or an "idealised abstraction," in the sense that its members never know the other members, but it has a collective identity brought about by language, history, education and the media. People need a recognisable framework of similarity and difference from others, to reinforce the identity of their collective and individual selves, and will seek approval from their "significant others."

Evidence today in Eastern Europe and elsewhere, supports the hypothesis that mankind is likely to continue to live in social and territorial communities, be they nations or peoples. Their identity is largely determined by the community and the territory in which they live, bestowing upon them a kinship for the common good which manifests itself as loyalty and patriotism, which they are prepared to defend. National or regional groups vary in the way in which they cohere, but tend to be racially, culturally and religiously homogeneous, and the territory they occupy conditions them to what they are. Without a national identity there can be no nationhood. If nations lose their sense of identity, they lose their self-confidence, their self-esteem, pride in their culture—and become destabilised. National unity and love of country are emotive themes which politicians repeatedly employ to mobilise electoral support. The first appeal for "One Nation" was 150 years ago by Disraeli, in response to the social divisions of the time. The rhetoric of a unified society has been repeated by incoming Prime Ministers at least from 1979 until today. Blair, at the 1995 Labour Party Conference [IMD. 4 Oct. 95], portrayed Labour as the 'patriotic party' and called for national unity and love of country. In 1998 he called for a "patriotic alliance" between political parties to promote Britain's interests in Europe. In the lead up to the 2001 general election, Blair made the bizarre assertion that to be an Eurosceptic was to be "unpatriotic"[DM 26 May 01]. After devolution, Britain is no longer "One Nation" politically. President Clinton, in his 1997 inaugural address, appealed for national unity: "Our greatest responsibility is to embrace a new spirit of community for a new century." Separatist multiculturalism raises the issue of whether a disparate society can develop a genuine sense of nationhood and kinship. It is axiomatic that a nation-state based on a cultural hegemony, even with its class divisions, cannot be compatible with a separatist multiracial, multicultural, divisively religious society.

Associated with the term *nation* are the nation-state, nation building and national self-determination. Political and diplomatic rhetoric will use "nation" or the more populist "people." To most Europeans, a "nation" refers to a territorial group sharing a common culture, and a "state" is a political organisation that grants citizenship. The "American people," which means the state, is used more frequently than "American nation"—maybe reflecting the United States' disparate make-up. Strictly speaking, a "country" refers to a geographical area and "nation" refers to its political and social features.

Yael Tamir [1993:65–6], who discusses the concept of nation building, argues that "it is important to distinguish between the two closely related terms: a nation and a people. Although in the literature they often appear interchangeably, a nation is a community conscious of its particularistic existence, whereas the concept of 'people' belongs to the same social category as 'family' or 'tribe,' that is, a people is one of those social units whose existence is independent of their members' consciousness. It follows then that there must be some objective fact, such as relations of blood, race, a defined territory, or the like, which will allow an outsider to define a people without reference to the awareness of its members. The endurance of peoples, unlike that of nations, does not depend on the presence of a national consciousness or on the will of individuals to determine themselves as members . . . a group is defined as a nation if it exhibits both a sufficient number of shared, objective characteristics—such as language, history, or territory—and self-awareness of its distinctiveness . . . Drawing the boundaries of a nation involves a conscious and deliberate effort to lessen the importance of objective differences within the group while reinforcing the group's uniqueness vis a vis outsiders." On this analysis, owing to their complex diversity, Israeli Jews, from their diaspora having few objective features, may feel themselves to be less of a distinct nation than the Palestinians. Cosmopolitan, citizens of the world, could be regarded as rootless citizens of nowhere, and give rise to the question: who would they turn to for protection or would they support in a crisis? have they no imagery of "going back home," no haven of the familial and safe? The feelings of kinship in a small and close national community must be stronger than a tenuous connection with an imaginary globalised community. Does a totally committed cosmopolitan feel isolated and insecure if the comfortable values of his inherited culture have been discarded and he is left with nothing?

Nationhood is facilitated if the state can readily define its territory. Such is the case with Britain (and Japan), which are not landlocked and have no artificially created or redefined borders (other than Ulster) that are difficult to define and police, and that may be occupied by an ethnic minority. A territorial "place" is essential for the sentiment of nationhood, the significance of which is often maintained and magnified at a distance by expatriates. Some strongly bonded migrant ethnic or religious groups such as Irish-Americans, Jewish-Americans, and British Muslims who, although they have sacred sites or homelands, do not feel these places are an integral part of their local group identity. They do not feel that they need to permanently occupy their "homelands"—their co-ethnics provide the insurance of doing this. The possession of outlying island territory, some with independence movements, can be a continuing source of conflict between states. Such are the disputes between Russia and Japan over the Kurile Islands; between Turkey and Greece over Cyprus and some tiny Aegean islands; between France and Corsica; between Britain and Argentina over the Falklands and South Georgia; and more ominously between China and Taiwan. For Argentina, the Falklands are a focus of national identity; for China it is Taiwan; for Spain it is Gibraltar; for Ireland it is Ulster, even though the majority of its inhabitants have no such affiliation.

A feature of federalised states, particularly if multiracial/ethnic, is that their inhabitants feel there has been an erosion and subsuming of their national identity and culture. They also feel they have lost much of their influence on decisions that materially affect them to a remote and much less directly politically and fiscally accountable and centralised institution. This can result in disenchantment with the democratic process itself, as has been experienced in the federalised United States, Canada, and the EU. France, which is an important EU member state, has a highly centralised government remote from the electorate. French people, if they deem it necessary, take "direct action" on the streets and usually get what they want, as did the French farmers when protesting against the tax on fuel—a move that was subsequently imitated by British farmers and hauliers. With a politically federalised Europe, if the limits of tolerance are breached, then direct action is likely to become more frequent. The regional Celtic devolution of Scotland and Wales may be a response to a Freudian narcissism of localised and by no means universal ethnic differences. This narcissism may eventually emphasise differences between these in-groups themselves, i.e. between the Scottish and Welsh inhabitants of their industrialised and rural regions. Devolution may be a step towards a gradual or a rapid fundamentalist secession towards complete regional independence and British quasi-federalism. This, together with increasing Europeanisation, may lead to the effective dissolution of the unitary British sovereign state. The likelihood is that more independence will be demanded both if devolution works and if it does not. If so, it may give rise to a positive resurgence of English separatism as opposed to British nationalism—as evidenced by the re-emergence of the flag of St George, calls for an English national anthem, and the "detartanisation" of parliament. If so, English devolution could become a serious concern for the Scottish and Welsh. In the House of Commons there are 529 English seats out of 659. The Conservative Party has called for removing the right of Scottish and Welsh MPs to vote on English laws. There have been demands for an English parliament, and for English regional EU and central government subsidies, which can be up to twenty-five percent lower per head, to be similar to those for Scotland and Wales [DM 28 April 01]. London has also become effectively devolved since May 2000 with the Greater London Assembly—it now being twenty-five percent ethnic [2000:54]. It is unlikely that a debate on the constitutional future of England can be avoided indefinitely.

In an attempt to sideline Scottish and Welsh nationalism after devolution, Treasury Minister Gordon Brown (who is a Scot) said that "Britain now had the potential to become the first successful multicultural, multiethnic and multinational country" [TM.2 Dec. 99]. Arguably few people in Britain would consider that the inhabitants of Scotland and Wales merit this separatist label, and immigrants might feel uncomfortable with this resurgence of separate regional identities in Britain. Neither the Scottish parliament nor the Welsh Assembly includes a black or Asian member. Prime Minister Blair, the architect of devolution, appears to be following the law of unintended consequences, namely, the break-up of Britain. He declared [TM 12 Feb. 00] that he is "proud of our [Labour Party] commitment to decentralisation. Devolution does not create new identities within Britain. It simply gives expression to existing ones." And then, inconsistently, "it is just not possible to construct any practical and meaningful national basis of ethnicity, as some of those arguing for the separation of the nations of the United Kingdom would wish to see." This might seem credible insofar as the indigenous population of Britain is concerned, but is less convincing if applied to multicultural ethnic separatism. The official forum in Britain that adjudicates racial discrimination claims is the Employment Tribunals. Two of these have made conflicting rulings [TM 15 Feb/28 Mar. 97] on whether employment discrimination cases could proceed under race relations laws, either because Scots are deemed to have, or not to have, a different ethnicity to the English. It is difficult to accept that being born in England or Scotland results in a racial difference. If anything, there may be minor cultural differences. With devolution, language can become a discriminatory racial weapon. Over a six month period of the jobs advertised in a Welsh daily newspaper, seventy-nine percent required a knowledge of the Welsh language, which only twenty percent of the population speak [MoS 16 April 00].

At the 1997 Labour Party Conference, Blair used the words "Britain" or "British" forty-five times, and in a later speech nineteen times. William Hague, the Conservative leader at its 1998 Conference, used them seventy-four times. It is therefore ironic that with the devolution of Scotland, Wales, Ulster and London, Blair has done more to undermine the sense of identification with Britain and Britishness than any other Prime Minister. Max Beloff states [TM 3 May 99] that "When Blair argues that sovereignty pooled can be sovereignty enhanced—or at least power and influence renewed—he reveals a total misunderstanding of sovereignty. It is not the same thing as 'power and influence,' not least in economic affairs. His attitude defies both logic and history." There was strong opposition and apathy in Britain at the June 1999 European Parliament election to further Europeanisation—after seventy days of a "European" (Kosovo) war, only about twenty-four percent of the British electorate found Europeanisation relevant compared with ninety percent in Belgium, and with the EU average of forty-nine percent [Social Trends 2000: 220]. In 1999 the EU election was for the first time on a proportional representation basis, with Britain divided into twelve regions electing almost fourteen percent of the EU parliament—no doubt a first move towards European regionalisation. If this voting apathy and cynicism fuelled by disillusionment and resignation continues, and a political vacuum ensues, then the apathy could be filled by political extremists. It is a bizarre fact that those Europhiles who complain about the loss of authority by the Westminster parliament nevertheless promote the sharing of Britain's sovereignty with the EU.

Symbolism is an important component of national identity. Ideological manipulation based on representations was effectively used by the Nazis by using evocative titles, uniforms and insignia such as those of the S.S. (Shutzstaffel). Symbolism persists in Ulster with the ritual marches and uniforms of the Orangemen to recall and to reassert their dominance of the past, and the controversy surrounding the retention of the badge and title of the RUC, and flying the Union flag in Ulster. Symbolism may be inherent in an act—for the IRA (The Irish Republican Army) the complete decommissioning of arms would be a symbolic defeat for the republican movement. When British Airways decided in 1997 to replace its Union Jack tail fin with "world images" at a cost of £60 million, it was accused of "dropping the Britishness." It has since abandoned the scheme, but not before the Union Jack symbol was adopted by the Virgin Atlantic fleet [TM 1 Mar. 99]. The British car manufacturer MG Rover, which almost closed down two years ago, is to have a Union Jack emblem on all its new cars. Its chief executive said [TM 28 Feb. 01] that it is "symbolic of the renaissance of our company, of the triumph of British spirit and courage to overcome the most difficult of situations." Nationhood can be fostered by emotive epithets for a prosaic "sense of belonging." These include the Mother Country; Mother Russia; the Welsh Hiraeth; the German Heimat; the pre-WW1 (World War One 1914–18) German Fatherland; and the pre-WW2 (World War Two 1939–45) Das Reich. The Japanese government has passed laws that for the first time give legal status to Japan's national flag and anthem. National dress, dances, insignia, flags and anthems are not always chauvinistic—the shamrock of Ireland, the daffodil of Wales, and the thistle of Scotland, are bland symbolism. The emotive memories of "ghosts of the past" can be aroused, years afterwards, by visiting familiar physical surroundings.

A benign sense of nationhood and national pride is in evidence at international sports events such as the Olympic games, football matches, or in prestige construction projects such as the Crystal Palace of the 1851 Great Exhibition, the pre-war German autobahns, the 1951 Festival of Britain, Concorde, the 1969 American "man on the moon," the two Riyahd super-skyscrapers, or the national stadium built for the 1998 Commonwealth Games in Malaysia (which was said to be about "building a sense of national pride and self-confidence"). Support for a national athlete or team in an international sporting event provides an opportunity to lose, albeit temporarily, a sense of individuality, and to identify with a national group. Conversely, a major sporting failure can be seen as an indication of national decadence. Arguably, the violence of some football supporters at international matches may offer one of the rare occasions when a suppressed but perverted sense of national pride can find a shared outlet. The 2000 Millennium Dome in London has been judged a failure. In contrast to the 1951 Festival of Britain, it paid little attention to British history and cultural achievements, and in striving to represent diversity in Britain, tried to be all things to all people, and meant nothing to everyone.

NOTES

Anderson, B. *Imagined Communities—Reflections on the Origin and Spread of Communities.* London: Verso. 1991. 6–7.

Anon. *Social Trends 2000.* London: Stationery Office.

Connor, W. "Beyond Reason: The Nature of the Ethno-National Bond." In *Ethnic and Racial Studies.* vol. 16. no.3. 1993. 373.

Devlin, P. *The Enforcement of Morals.* Oxford: Oxford University Press, 1965.

Eller, J.D. and Coughlan, R.M. "The Poverty of Primordialism: The Demystification of Ethnic Attachments." In *Ethnic and Racial Studies.* Vol. 16. no. 2, April 1993. 183.

Glazer, N. "The Universalisation of Ethnicity." In *Encounter.* vol. 44. February 1975. 10.

Glover, J. *The Philosophy and Psychology of Personal Identity.* London: Penguin Books, 1988. 196–199.

Greenfeld, L. *Nationalism—Five Roads to Modernity.* Cambridge, Mass: Harvard University Press. 1992. 489.

Grosby, S. "The Verdict of History: The Inexpungeable Tie of Primordiality." In *Ethnic and Racial Studies.* vol.17. no1. January 1994. 164 –7.

Hutchinson, J. *Modern Nationalism.* London: Fontana Press, 1994. 22.

Maccormick, N. "Nations and Nationalism." In *The Crown and the Thistle—The Nature of Nationhood.* Maclean, C. (Ed.), Edinburgh: Scottish Academic Press, 1979. 100–2.

Pfaff, W. *The Wrath of Nations—Civilization and the Furies of Nationalism.* New York: Simon and Schuster, 1993. 238.

Stationery Office *Regional Trends 2000.* London. 2000. 54.

Tamir, Y. *Liberal Nationalism.* Princeton: Princeton University Press, 1993. 65–6.

9

The Nation-State, Sovereignty, and the European Union

The formation and re-emergence of nation-states and the appeal of nationalism, sometimes subsuming a religion, is likely to continue in the foreseeable future, and the hypothesis that these have peaked and will decline is improbable. The more uncertain and unstable geopolitics become, the greater the importance of the nation-state, there being about 190 autonomous polities worldwide. Nationalism is the emotional attachment to one's own ethnonational group, and according to Peter Alter [1985:2 and 9], "To conceive of nationalism as a political aberration, or as an inevitable but ultimately transitory historical phenomenon is to disregard its unabated impact upon politics. Though we might justifiably abhor its extreme forms, which were especially rampant in the years directly before and after the First World War, we cannot conveniently forget it as a pathological manifestation in the history of modern societies, nor dismiss treatment of its historical impact as irrelevant . . . the tenet of Enlightenment philosophy—that the individual is principally a member of the human race and thus a citizen of the world—no longer holds: individuals perceive themselves, rather, as members of a particular nation. They identify with its historical and cultural heritage and with the form of its political life."

Ernest Gellner [1964:147–8] observes that "Marxism contained the anticipation of the decline of nationalism. So did nineteenth-century liberalism . . . those who had heralded the decline of nationalism, had under-estimated the power and hold of the dark atavistic forces in human nature. They over-estimated the power of reason. They operated with a shallow psychology . . . The theoretical problem is to separate the quite spurious 'national' and 'natural' justifications and explanations of nationalism, from the genuine, time-and-context-bound roots of it." Gellner, writing in 1964, claimed [152] that

"There are various ways of bringing home to oneself that, contrary to the current preconception, nationalism is not something obvious, natural, manifest." The experience of the 1990s demonstrates that these "preconceptions" are more than ever valid.

Professor Elie Kedourie [1966: 9 and 90–1] notes that "Briefly, the doctrine (of nationalism) holds that humanity is naturally divided into nations, that nations are known by certain characteristics which can be ascertained, and that the only legitimate type of government is national self-government . . . [90–91] [the] confusion, whether nationalism is a right wing or a left wing movement, has become greatly prevalent owing to the triumph of Bolshevism in Russia, and the wide popularity and respect which the writings of its leaders, Lenin and Stalin, have attained . . . Such a line of reasoning (the socialist class struggle) makes it easy to understand why to Bolshevists nationalism is a right wing movement in contemporary Europe, and a left wing movement in Asia and Africa. But it also ought to become clear that the wide acceptance of such classifications depends on a tacit, uncritical acquiescence in the Marxist interpretation of history." Kedourie's remarks about the popularity of the writings of Lenin and Stalin, brings home the fact that political philosophy, in particular, can provide the intellectual rationale to initiate or to subsequently support an ideology which has an emotive and intellectual appeal, but can be misused to provide the justification for amoral extremism. As late as in the era of Nazism and fascism, the Volkish and Roman ideologies, with their mythology and legends, were intellectually underwritten and given a dubious legitimacy by some German and Italian archaeologists and anthropologists.

The beginnings of English cultural nationalism found expression in Locke's political philosophy, but the Romantic movement heightened the sense of national identity in Europe. This followed the French revolution and the writings of Rousseau, Edmund Burke and the German Enlightenment philosophers. Herder first used the term *nationalism* in 1774, and his version of a Romantic cultural patriotism evolved into the political nationalism of Fichte and Hegel. Before then, *nation* referred to the ruling political class. Subsequently, *nation* came to mean a wider territorial community sharing civic rights. A people did not have to comprise a political entity for their nationhood to be recognised. The state was no longer conceived as an accident of territory, but as an expression of a popular will for self-determination with the nation seen in monocultural terms.

From the early nineteenth century, the principle began to be accepted that national self-determination was to be the basis for the new political order in Europe. A person could be educated in his mother tongue, instead of in the classical languages, or by means of the literary creations of other peoples, who supposedly had reached a higher degree of civilisation. As education and travel became more widespread and local speech and local loyalties became weaker, poets and scholars began to emphasise their culturalism. Under the influence of the new theories of sovereignty of the people and the rights of man, the "people" replaced the monarch as the centre of the nation. The state became the people's state, and as it became identified with its national culture, the nation-state. Professional armies replaced the untrained citizen or mercenary armies which had fought without the motivation of nationhood. American nationalism found its expression through Jefferson and Paine in the Declaration of Independence which emphasised liberty, equality and happiness, and which subsequently influenced the French revolution.

Before the French Revolution, Germany imitated the French in language and culture. Napoleon's conquests spread the spirit of nationalism throughout Europe and into the Near East, but turned the latent nationalism of other Europeans against France. In Germany the movement was initiated by Enlightenment philosophers and writers, who provided the conceptual philosophical underpinning for German nationalism, and who rejected the liberal and humanitarian principles upon which the American and French revolutions had been based. Herder linked nationalism with human nature through its embodiment in its culture, and which can only be understood in terms of that culture, with every society growing and developing in a distinctive manner. Language was the most important attribute, or expression of, a different culture, and gave people their identity. Since there is no universal norm of human nature or universal recipe for "happiness," each culture has its own merits, and any universalised judgmental comparison between them of ranking is meaningless. Herder believed each society should respect the culture of other societies, whilst remaining true to its own culture. Hegel also had an important influence on nationalist movements in Europe outside of Germany. Since the French Revolution up until the present day, new nation-states have emerged in Europe and elsewhere. Between 1830 and 1922, eighteen new European states were founded.

The philosophical rationale of nationalism initiated by Herder, Fichte and Hegel was that the sovereignty of the nation-state and its sense of national identity and community are essentially based on a cultural hegemony. They considered nationalism the highest goal to which all Germans should aspire. Probably most Germans were influenced by the romantic nationalism of the patriotic poet and pamphleteer Arndt and Jahn, a Prussian, who urged the creation of a German Fatherland and the maintenance of racial purity. Nevertheless, the German nation-state was eventually formed not by ideology, but by wars, annexations, alliances, and a customs union, and was based on the military-authoritarian tradition of Prussia. After the defeat of France and Austria in 1871, Bismarck's Germany was founded not on the principles of political philosophy, as was the American Union, but on radical pragmatism.

Two distinct types of nationalism have emerged. The benign civic version typified by the American revolution or Britain's SNP and Plaid Cymru (the Scottish and Welsh National parties), and the territorially aggressive and autocratic version typified by the Nazi and fascist regimes in Germany and Italy. Although nationalism can be used in a hostile sense, it is a political movement to secure or maintain national independence. It is a potent and complex force in the world today with varying degrees of generality and specificity. It requires a self-identity attained through differentiation and separatism from Others through a continuity of time. Its features are: (a) loyalty (patriotism) to the nation; (b) priority given to the interests of the nation, especially if competing with other nations; (c) an attitude of attaching high importance to the distinctive characteristics of the nation; (d) a doctrine of preserving the national culture; and (e) a political/anthropological theory that mankind is naturally divided into nations and that each nation is entitled to a government of its own. Nationalism might be considered to be irrational because it delights in the symbolic rhetoric of "blood and soil," and that, enormously important as it is for the historian and sociologist, [and it has been argued that] it would be mistaken to treat it as if it invited serious rational criticism. [S. I. Benn 1967:442–5].

Will Kymlicka [1995:130–7] wants to distinguish between indigenous national minorities and immigrants. He says [130] that "There are few examples in this century of national minorities—that is, national groups who share a state with larger national groups—voluntarily assimilating into the larger society . . . [whereas] (immigrant groups) do not think of themselves as separate nations alongside the mainstream society and do not seek to establish their own autonomous homelands and self-governing political institutions . . . An immigrant group will adopt a nationalist agenda only if it prevented from integrating into the mainstream society, through mandatory segregation and legal discrimination." In some cases, however, voluntary separatist ghettoes are in fact national mini-homelands for minorities, who were originally immigrants. Kymlicka [131–3] also wants to distinguish between civic, ethnic and cultural nationalism. In practice, all three of these can imbricate and have differing priorities. Even though civic nationalism describes an allegiance to a political system, and although its citizenship is inclusive, it can also have both ethnic and cultural loyalties that can resist assimilation.

Historicism suggests that things today are what they are because of their historical development over the last two hundred or so years, and that this is likely to continue. This hypothesis could be likened to the relationship between history and science, namely "the philosophy of science without history of science is empty; history of science without philosophy of science is blind" [Imre Lakatos 1994:244]. Nevertheless, the nation-state has been the predominant societal organisation in Europe (apart from the Austro-Hungarian empire and Yugoslavia), and the resurgence of ethno-nationalism supports historicism in this respect, not as a given pre-determinant, but as a probability. The government of the nation-state is the legal entity invested with power, and is the political expression of its nationhood. The ultimate responsibility of the nation-state is to defend its security and independence, both from external and internal threats, and to maintain its social coherence. The defining characteristics of the nation-state are its territory and its qualifications for citizenship, both of which are its sovereign domain. A prospective citizen or a visitor requires the consent, and accepts the conditions laid down by that nation-state, and which are not determined by any external/international institution.

The commonly accepted criteria among jurists for a state are a national territory, a people coming together as a nation, and a sovereign state authority. The nation-state is defined in this discussion as a territorial and political nation, whose citizenship reflects an essentially monocultural nationhood, and that is dedicated to preserving its sovereignty. Few authors, other than Jules Coleman and Sarah Harding [1995:19–23] and Jean Hampton [67–8], include in their discussion on multiculturalism the influence of the requirements for granting citizenship to immigrants and their families which gives multiculturalism its permanence. Hannah Arendt [1963:279] recognised that a nation-state has natural boundaries, inasmuch that "Freedom, wherever it existed as a tangible reality, has always been spatially limited. This is especially clear for the greatest and most elementary of all negative liberties, the freedom of movement; the borders of national territory or the walls of the city-state comprehended and protected a space in which men could move freely. Treaties and international guarantees provide an extension of this territorially bound freedom for citizens outside their own country, but even under these modern conditions, the elementary coincidence of freedom and a limited space remains manifest."

Rainer Baubock is an Austrian, who sets out to challenge [1992:1] Arendt's view, that freedom of movement (migration), should be restricted to citizens within their own territory. He looks at [115–6] "societies tied together by continuous flows of migration, as if forming a single community of citizenship with different statuses for internal and external citizens, for aliens and long-term resident immigrants. The egalitarian and universalistic thrust of citizen rights provides us with a guideline for policies of equalizing unjustifiable differences. Establishing rights of transition between unequal statuses can itself be an important contribution to such equalisation. Resistance to denizenship [foreigners given certain rights in their adopted country], naturalisation rights and dual citizenship finds its legitimation in nationalist, rather than democratic, principles . . . I [Baubock have] pleaded for rights of transition between the statuses of illegal immigrants, legal aliens, denizens and internal citizens within the society of residence. Could this argument not be extended to transitions between societies as well, in other words support a general right of immigration? . . . He concludes [123] "Only within the ideologies of nationalism can present societies still imagine themselves as islands of free citizens, whose freedom depends on their sovereign right to exclude outsiders . . . there is yet little sign that historical evolution in going this way." There is an implication that nationalism cannot be democratic, and the unlikely proposal that sovereign states will grant citizenship rights to migrants who breach their immigration legislation. There is no acceptance as yet of universal immigrant citizenship rights, or that immigration should be uncontrolled or is uncontrollable.

Pluralism was inherent in the large artificially created multiethnic states of Yugoslavia, Czechoslovakia, the USSR and some of the Western colonies. This was contrary to their need to maintain a unifying national identity, and, at least, posed a potential threat to their political and social cohesion, stability and security. Recent years have seen the emergence of smaller, predominantly monoethnic, monocultural, monoreligious nation-states, sometimes created at the cost of an economic penalty. Social cohesion and stability are also seen as the characteristics of an established democracy, which would otherwise have to be authoritarian and impose a coercive stability. The emergence of nationalism often reflects the latent fracture lines in societies when under strain. Although it is never entirely independent of the class and status structure of its particular society, national self-determination has a special and resilient appeal as a mobilising ideology. It will be stimulated whenever there is a sense of repression imposed by an oppressor, ranging from cultural deracination and colonization, to economic domination.

It appears that the appeal of the nation will persist, even though it may be temporarily suppressed or overlaid by a political dogma, or by the imposition of artificial territorial boundaries. Before the collapse of Communism, Marxist ideology saw nationalism as an exploitative, socio-psychological instrument of the ruling classes that obtained its principal support and expression in an organised capitalist state. It believed that the nation-state would disappear under a Marxist regime. Nonetheless, that which a society enjoys in common and wishes to preserve is more important than its class stratification. Communication makes political frontiers more transparent, but racial and cultural barriers remain. Healey [1989:98–9] observed as early as 1945 that "whether I [Healey] liked it or not, the basic unit in world affairs was the nation-state. Attempts to base (Marxist) policy on the international solidarity of social classes had broken down in two world wars. A common ideology was no more likely than class solidarity to override the realities of national feeling." Malcolm Rifkind a former Foreign Secretary also emphasised [TM 24 Jan. 97] the affinity to the nation-state: "it is not a hangover from a more nationalist era, but a tradition rooted in the experience and culture of the British people. It will not go away."

Every citizen of a nation-state owes it an implied allegiance which in a national crisis should take precedence over individual or sectarian interests. A democracy also depends on the support of its citizens for the polity on which its government is based and which it can change. Charles Taylor [1996:120] sees democracies as common enterprises in self-rule which need patriotism: "They require a great deal of their members, demanding much greater solidarity toward compatriots than towards humanity in general. We cannot make a success of these enterprises without strong common identification. And considering the alternatives to democracy in our world, it is not in the interests of humanity that we fail in these enterprises." The usual objection or fear of nationalism is that it turns into a nationalistic egoism and territorial aggression. Although it is true that in most international conflicts this century, nationalism has been a factor in its causation, these conflicts have often been those of self-determination rather than outright territorial aggression of one state on another—except for Germany, Italy and Japan during WW2. Since records began, 1997 was expected to be the second year in which there would be no "hot war" between states. However, the last report of the Stockholm Institute for Peace Research [TM 1 Jan. 97] listed twenty-four internal conflicts. According to the London Institute for Strategic Studies [TM 15 Oct. 97], nearly 18 million people were killed in wars and armed conflicts between 1945 and 1994. Arguably, the current trend towards national self-determination has not led so far to overt extra-territorial aggression. The experience of German National Socialism during 1933–1945 could be used as a powerful criticism against cultural nationalism. However, after WW1 there existed special and well recognised political, economic, and social factors which brought the Nazis into power, and the hegemony of Nazi Germany was not founded on an established tradition of a liberal democracy. The safeguard against aggressive nationalism resides in democratic traditions and institutions—founded on history, heritage, and the values incorporated into a political constitution. It is when democracy does not exist, or if it fails to deliver, that dictatorships ensue. There can be no guarantee of this, but it would also require the take-over of an extremist ideology arising from an unusual combination of circumstances, such as occurred in Germany, Italy, Spain, and the USSR prior to WW2. It also requires a charismatic and sometimes psychopathic leader, supported by the secret police and the military, who offers an ideology and an ultimate goal that satisfies a political void to a disenchanted nation which has become destabilised and dissatisfied with severe and adverse economic and/or cultural change, and is facing a threat from another ideology. In Germany and Spain's case, this threat was communism. Almost any ideology, whether political, religious or sociological, if it is unrestrained and becomes absolutist, can become repressive.

Nationalism, when associated with an absolutist religion, as in Islamic Iran, Afghanistan, and Chechnya, or a political ideology, as in Communist North Korea and Vietnam, is a powerful combination. The United States did not justify its containment policy in the civil war in Vietnam by appeals to American nationalism but to "democracy"—saving Vietnam from Communism [Putnam 1996:147]. In spite of the supposed and nebulous "international community," it would be naive to assume, because history teaches otherwise, that sooner or later territorially or ideologically aggressive or natural resource hungry states, such as Japan during 1941–45, will not use force. Ironically, the West still bolsters its intervention with the rhetoric of "democracy." It is unlikely that the American public would today tolerate casualties to save say Taiwan from communism as it did in Vietnam, or in Somalia, where the U.S. Army had fourteen peace-keepers killed. Edward Luttwak [1995:9] observes "society's tolerance for war casualties tends towards zero in the absence of obviously compelling reasons to fight," because (Western) families now "invest their entire emotional capital in 2.2 children," and cannot afford to lose them. Moreover, the debilitating psychological effect on the ability of Western armies to fight a future conventional war after acting as passive peace-keepers and aid-workers in ethno-national conflicts has yet to be tested.

Tamir [1993:4–5] takes a more benign view of nationalism: "even when viewed from a liberal perspective, nationalism advances an important claim, which can hardly be dismissed as manifestly and utterly irrelevant, false or morally reprehensible. This is not to say that certain types of nationalism are not morally repugnant, but the same could be said about almost any other political theory . . . liberals are challenged to accommodate (its) worthy elements, and lend substance to national values within the boundaries of liberalism." Professor Tudur Jones [1974: Preface and 2] provides an example of benign nationalism, or more realistically, Welsh regionalism. He says "This [book] is not meant to be a dispassionate of neutral study. It is written by one who is committed to the national struggle in his own country and who views nationalism with sympathy, even if on some specific points there is room for disagreement with what nationalists do or say . . . To achieve full maturity as a nation and to receive international recognition as such, Wales must be constituted into a nation-state. Not to possess one is not to exist in the modern world."

Nation-states have in the past co-existed peacefully and continue to do so, and aggressive wars have been the exception. This supports a basic contention of this discussion—that a benign nationalism, albeit assertive and protectionist, founded in a democracy is unlikely to be territorially aggressive. It will be proud of its history, heritage, culture, customs, traditions, and nationhood, and its military security limited to that which it deems necessary to protect its way of life. It will aim to be economically strong but will pose no threat to other states, peoples or cultures. This contention does no more than reflect toleration of the diversity and difference which exists globally between the peoples and states of the world. A territorially majority racial/ethnic group has an a priori claim to self-determination wherever it has a genuinely distinctive language, social practices, and history. It may interpret this claim as giving it a right to self-determination, complete political independence, and the use of force to achieve this. However, it has to be pragmatically accepted that self-determination movements (such as Greater Albania and Kurdistan) for the creation or re-emergence of nation-states which disturb the existence of a geopolitical/regional stability, cannot be supported by international coercive diplomacy. The best they can hope for is a separatist multicultural modus vivendi. Most attempts in the recent past to impose multinational, multiethnic, and multireligious super-states or federations have eventually failed, or are at risk of breaking up, including the former USSR, Yugoslavia, the Central African Federation, Canada, Ulster, Czechoslovakia, Kashmir, Nigeria, Indonesia, Fiji and Sri Lanka, and maybe Afghanistan.

Malcolm Shaw [1997:876] observes that "developments that have been seen in recent years have demonstrated an acceptance of a far broader conception of what constitutes a threat to international peace and security, so that not only external aggression but certain internal convulsions may qualify, thus constraining further . . . the exclusive jurisdiction of states." This reflects the fact that the principal member states use the UN to provide a pseudo-legitimacy for some of their interventions, and provides the UN itself with a pseudo-legitimacy for some of its resolutions. The UN has difficulty in reconciling its principles of sovereignty with those of national identity and self determination, particularly if the territory in question is non-contiguous with that of either party. In 1965 the General Assembly approved Resolution 2065, which called upon Britain and Argentina to resolve their dispute over the Falklands without delay. This made reference to ending colonialism but ignored the islanders right to self-determination. This conflicts with Article 73 of the UN Charter which enjoins member states to develop self-government of non-self-governing territories taking into account "the political aspirations of the peoples." UN Resolution 502 in 1982 was based on Article 2 of the Charter which enjoins members from "the threat or use of force against the territorial integrity etc." Britain had occupied the Falklands in 1833; its population was entirely British and was opposed to Argentinian rule, influenced by the fact that Argentina had a military junta in 1976 during which 10,000 to 20,000 had "disappeared" [Blakeway 1992:15]. This "conventional" war contrasts with the internal war in Chechnya against the Muslim separatists. This conflict is said to be supported by most Russians, and was characterised by the President Vladimir Putin, when he visited troops near Grozny in Chechnya on New Year's day 2000, with the statement "This is about how to bring an end of the break up of Russia—that is your fundamental goal" [TXT 1 Jan. 00]. He implied that the West ought to be grateful to Russia for combating an international terrorist movement of Islamic fundamentalists. The Russians realise that there is little future in negotiating with separatists insisting on independence, which they believe would have a domino effect throughout the Russian Caucasus. There is also Russia's strategic and economic incentive of access to the vast oil and gas reserves in Chechnya and the Caspian basin.

Although there are today globally about 190 states, it is sometimes said that the nation-state is no more than an imagined or invented community, which derives its appeal from historical and sentimental myths. The national independence movements in Europe of Slovenia, Croatia, Bosnia/Herzogovina, Montenegro, Macedonia, Kosovo, the Baltic states, the Ukraine, Belarus, and Chechnya, let alone those elsewhere in the world, show the strength of these "sentimental myths" that some nations have been "imagining" for the last 200 years or more. Although they can be factually flawed, myths can be just as powerful as the truth (assuming that a single truth can be unquestionably established), and can be created or destroyed by historiography. What cannot be denied is the psychological appeal of nationalism. There is also the criticism that the appeal of the nationalism rests on some widely held fallacies. These fallacies include a state being only able to mobilise its citizens in its defence by invoking an appeal to nationhood, and that homogeneity is essential to its social and political stability. If these are fallacies, then it poses the counter-question: "if it is not nationhood based on a cultural hegemony that is conducive to the promotion of these desirable ends, then what does?"

Winston Churchill forecast [1929:203–4] that "the almost complete exclusion of religion in all its forms from the political sphere has left nationalism the most powerful moulding instrument of mankind in temporal affairs." Harold Macmillan, the then-current PM (Prime Minister), said [Cohen 1980: 218] in Cape Town in 1960: "The wind of change is blowing through this continent, and whether we like it or not, this growth of national consciousness is a political fact." France's national pride recovered from the humiliation of WW2 because of Gaullist nationalism, the myth of the Resistance, and the support of Churchill. President Kennedy [Schlesinger 1987: 414] also "saw nationalism as the most powerful political emotion of (his) time. His abiding purpose was to adjust American policy to what he called the 'revolution of national independence' he saw going on around the world. His vision was of a 'world of diversity'—a world of nations varied in institutions and ideologies 'where, within a framework of international cooperation, every country can solve its own problems according to its own traditions and ideals . . . If we cannot now end our differences, at least we can help make the world safe for diversity." This is precisely the international scenario for which this discussion argues.

Nationalism has had a bad press and arouses powerful prejudices, some of which reflect a fixation with the past. It is blamed for promoting aggressive wars, racism and genocide. It allegedly gives rise to the verbal violence and accusations of extremism, bigotry, fascism, Mosleyism, xenophobia, paranoia, parochialism, tribalism, racism, jingoism, chauvinism, sovereignty neurosis, and bunker mentality, and to the existence of "little Englanders." Paradoxically, it is acceptable to have an ex-Communist past, but not an ex-fascist past. Ironically, and in contrast to its pejorative use today, "little Englanders" were the Liberal politicians in Victorian times who opposed the Crimean and Boer wars. Jingoism is a music-hall term coined in the hysteria of 1876, when Britain and Russia nearly went to war over Turkey. Since WW2 these demonising and obfuscating epithets have inhibited political discourse on nationalism except at an academic level. Geoffrey Parkins [1984:31] notes that some of these epithets suggest that anyone with such views is either racist, or unaware that his thinking is based on racist tendencies. This "language labelling," together with memories of the territorially aggressive regimes which led to WW2, and the frequent and well-publicised reminders of its associated Holocaust, can give rise to an intellectual polarisation. Not surprisingly, nationalism has tended to be closely identified with Nazism, fascism, racism and territorial aggression. After WW2, the victorious allies avoided blaming the whole German nation by employing the device of demonising the Nazis, namely, the followers of a political ideology. Political regimes such as that of Milosevic in Serbia can be readily labelled as "Nazi" without too much attention being paid to detail or to history with the result that the Serbs as a nation became demonised internationally. The pejorative connotation of Nazism inhibited rational dialogue about nationalism, until the collapse of the Communist empire presented a respectable opportunity to support the rise of latent nationalism in Eastern Europe, Central Asia and Yugoslavia. In contrast to nationalism, and as Peter Caws observes [1994:381], "'multicultural' is a good adjective; it has a generous feel to it; it is welcoming, inclusive, embracing; like 'international,' or 'pluralist' or 'ecumenical,' it suggests a largeness of conception, a transcendence of sectional interest, an openness to the variety of human pursuits and achievements."

A characteristic of a nation-state is its sovereignty and independence from any external authority, ruled by its co-nationals, making its own laws, controlling its own borders, and determining its own foreign policy, economy and defence. The erosion or denial of sovereignty is a feeder for nationalism. Economic nationalism can give rise to a sense of satisfaction, in the ownership and control by co-nationals, and in the case of socialism, ownership by the state itself, of the basic national industries and services—although in the era of economic globalization this is less likely. The apparent inability of the British government and other EU states to control asylum seekers and economic refugees, and the creeping influence of EU legislation, gives the impression that Britain no longer has control of its own borders and is surrendering its sovereignty. In addition to the Hague's UN International Court of Justice, set up in 1946, which adjudicates on civil disputes between states, Britain, unlike the United States, is also subject to the judgements of two other Courts whose decisions take precedence over its Parliament and the judicial Committee of the House of Lords (the highest level of Britain's Supreme Court): the European Court of Justice and the European Court of Human Rights, although the last mentioned is now less likely since Britain enacted its own Human Rights Act. Nigel Nicholson [1997:151–2], a one time MP, publisher, and a member of the British delegation to the Consultative Assembly of the Council of Europe, makes a revealing comment: "it was regarded by (his constituents) as a distraction from our proper role, which was to defend our constituency's interests . . . once at a sub-committere meeting in Paris, we spent a whole morning discussing the first line of the first clause of a European Charter of Human Rights—'Every man has the right to work'—each word of this doctrine was challenged: 'every,' 'man,' 'right,' 'work.' National philosophies were paraded at considerable length. The British were pragmatic, the French cynical, while Greeks and Icelanders committed their governments to social reforms which they had neither the will nor the cash to implement."

Forfeiture of sovereignty is why some strongly oppose moves towards a European Franco-German-dominated political federal state, run on the French bureaucratic model and lacking a culture of public consent, including a diminution of immigration control typified by the Maastricht Treaty and the Schengen/Dublin/Amsterdam Conventions. The opposition in Britain to federalisation by stealth, and support for the complete independence from Europe, is represented politically by the UK Independence Party. When Britain joined the then-EEC in 1973, it was the European Economic Union, a free trade area, and was not, as some Europhiles now claim, with the recognised intention of ultimately entering into a political federation with diminishing national sovereignty (known as the "process of integration"). Cabinet papers recently released [TM 01 Jan. 01] under the thirty-year secrecy rule show that the government in 1970 suppressed evidence that taking Britain into the European Common Market in 1973 could lead to political and monetary union. The British public believed that in the 1975 referendum they were signing up to a trading bloc and not to a political entity. Owen [1991:176 –7] observes that "By exposing that a unified monetary policy meant a big step towards a United States of Europe, Jim (Callaghan, PM 1976–79) also drew attention to the way Heath (PM 1970–74), throughout this period, sold entry to the British public as joining a Community of nation states. I never realized that Edward Heath was hiding his own federalist opinions at every stage of the negotiations as well as during the passage of the legislation."

The European Union currently has fifteen member states speaking eleven languages, with a bureaucracy in Brussels of about 17,000 people. After enlargement to twenty-seven member states, it would have twenty-two official languages. It has a total electorate of 372 million and an annual budget of £55 billion, of which Britain's net contribution is £4 billion. In 1999, its then-commissioners were allegedly found guilty of malpractice, disorganisation and fraud, and had to resign. Year after year, including 2000, its Court of Auditors, which oversees EU expenditure, reports that the commission's accounts are so imprecise that they cannot account for billions [BBC 2 10 Dec. 00/STM 21 Jan. 01). The Court rejected the EU's accounts as "incorrect or incomplete" and declined to give them a "positive statement of legality and regularity" for the fourth year running" [DT 17 Jan. 99]. Recently, at least twenty incidents of waste, mismanagement and subsidy frauds were disclosed amounting to millions of pounds [STM 8 April 01]. The EU could be enlarged in the millennium to up to twenty-seven/twenty-eight member states of diverging interests—a substantial increase from, and seemingly even more remote than, the present relatively homogenous fifteen. The EU Parliament meets in Brussels, and also four days a month in Strasbourg (at the insistence of the French). It has at present 626 MEPs, of which Britain has almost fourteen percent of the members. After the next twelve member states join there will be 738 MEPs, of which Britain will have ten percent. The first six states—Poland, Hungary, Czech Republic, Slovenia, Estonia and Cyprus—hope to join by June 2004, followed by another six states—Bulgaria, Latvia, Lithuania, Malta, Romania and Slovakia, and possibly later by Turkey. This expansion of the EU might appeal to those member states who would like to dilute the French German influence. At the December 2000 Nice EU summit meeting, Britain abandoned more of its right of veto, but retained some of these as opt-outs. Unanimous voting is still required on matters relating to taxation, social security and most immigration policies. Qualified majority voting applies to all other EU decisions [STM 11 Dec. 00]. After the full twelve member EU enlargement, a passing majority would be achieved with at least 255 votes (seventy-five percent) in favour out of a total of 342, when those countries have sixty-two percent of the EU population, with Britain, France, Germany and Italy each then having twenty-nine votes [TM 12 Dec. 00].

Compliance by the states varies, with France heading the list of those who have allegedly breached EU laws and treaties. Of the 1,459 directives issued by the EU Commission, France has not implemented 4.5 percent of them;

Italy 3.2 percent; Germany 3.1 percent; and Britain 2.7 percent. Formal notices of recorded breaches of EU rules during 1998–99 show France receiving
eighty-nine, Italy seventy-two; Germany sixty-six, and Britain thirty-four.
These warnings are the first move in a three-step legal process which can end
up in the European Court [DM 25 Nov. 00]. Proposals for EU tax regulation
and harmonisation would be difficult in Italy where tax avoidance is part of
the national culture. Furthermore, the illegal avoidance in the national interest
of EU competition laws on state handouts to beleaguered industries is not
unknown. The EU's latest proposal is to form an EU army—the European
Rapid Reaction Force—amidst an ongoing debate as to its effectiveness and
its relationship to American led NATO. Max Beloff [1992:106–7] feels that
"the example of the United States as a working federal system is wholly
inapplicable to the European scene . . . in particular the word 'federalism'
which had a precise meaning in an Anglo-Saxon context, meant something
quite different to continental Europeans. It is not a difference that has gone
away . . . no doubt racial and colour prejudice play a part, since these are
human failings all over the world. But it is rather that the doctrine of assimilation which has been the key to dealing with past migrations (into Europe)
cannot be easily applied to self-conscious adherents of other cultures than the
European, cultures in some cases with a long pedigree."

Tony Judt, a Professor of European Studies, [1996:9] observes "There is
very little tradition in Europe of effective assimilation . . . or, alternatively,
'multiculturalism' . . . when it come to truly foreign communities . . . there is
a certain self-fulfilling advantage in speaking of Europe as though it already
existed in some stronger, collective sense. But there are some things it cannot
do, some problems it does not address. 'Europe' is more than a geographical
notion but less than an answer." The psycho-political objections, namely the
emotive and intuitive desire to close ranks and to have control over "our own
affairs" will compete with the supposedly objective arguments against them
together with the diminishing proposition that an EU would prevent future
European wars. Monetary union, the "Euro," about which very few people in
Britain have any informed opinion, is seen as another step towards creeping
Europeanisation, eroding its democracy and independence and contributing
towards the twilight of Britain.

Euro-sceptics argue that a European political federal state or confederation, which is commonly but incorrectly labelled a "super-state," could result
in an irrevocable loss of political sovereignty, a loss of national identity, and
democratic accountability by its member states. This view has been reinforced by comments such as that made by the German Chancellor [Jan. 99]:
"the time for individual nations (in Europe) having their own tax, employment and social policies is definitely over. We must finally bury the errone-
ous ideas of nations having sovereignty over foreign and defence policies.

National sovereignty will soon prove itself to be a product of the imagination." Unlike other European states, Britain is, physically, territorially separate, and has been undefeated and unoccupied. It also has a language affinity and an Atlanticist "special relationship" with the USA (The United States of America). These must influence its semi-detached relationship with continental Europe.

The evidence is that when an important self-interest or traditional loyalty of a member nation-state of a "reluctant coalition" is involved, such as with the "European community," there will be no success in overcoming its partisanship or opting out of UN or other international initiatives. This was demonstrated by the failure and impotence of the European diplomatic "initiatives" on the Yugoslav and Kosovo civil wars. EU collective action sometimes follows national self-interest, or attempts to interfere in the domestic politics of an EU or UN member state. This occurred when Austria formed a right wing coalition government early in 2000, largely resulting from Austria's reaction to its major refugee problem. The EU imposed sanctions which have since been withdrawn [TM 13 Sept. 00], but it implied that a country is not free to choose its own government. Austria accepted more than one million refugees between 1989 and 1998 in a total population of just under eight million, and took 120,000 refugees from the Balkans and Kosovo [TM 15 May 00]—in 1999, 43,000 immigrants were arrested, double the figure for 1998 [TM 17 May 00].

Denmark has rejected joining the Euro currency, voting 53.1 percent against and 46.9 percent in favour, with an eighty-eight percent turnout of its 5.2 million population [29 Sept. 00]. This happened in spite of the support for the Euro given by all the Danish mainstream political parties, business interests, trade unions and opinion formers. The Danes, and later, the Irish Republic, were unimpressed by the economic arguments for joining and refused to sign up for a political union in which their sovereignty and democractic tradition would have been lost to a federal European government. This is counter to the claim of the historian Professor Davies [1999:1054]: "Perhaps the main source of optimism lies in the existence of an European Union. Unfortunately, the most positive aspect of the EU is rarely noticed . . . But it is this: it gives a place in the sun to Europe's smaller and middle-sized nations. Economics were never at the top of the agenda of the fathers of the European movement, It was always a means to a higher end . . . The European ideal is despised by those who wish to hang on to vestiges of superior status and of national domination." Reportedly the most notable experience among others which influenced the "No" vote was the imposition of sanctions on Austria by the other EU members. The Danes have no particular affection for Austria's right wing party, but they objected to the outside interference in the domestic affairs and sovereignty of a small member state.

Critics of nationalism label it as Right wing or maybe fascist. The fascist labelling does not recognise the differences between the populist and popular regimes in Italy, and that in Nazi (National Socialist) Germany. Although they were both totalitarian and authoritarian, Italian fascism originally had no racial fanaticism—in 1933 the Chief Rabbi of Italy was a member of the fascist party. Italy embarked half-heartedly on anti-semitic legislation in 1938, some five years after Germany. Because they embrace certain aspects of fascism, as in fact do both left and right wing political parties, it can be convenient to label some countries and organisations as being fascist. Nevertheless, the ideology of fascism is difficult to readily define and can be misapplied. Fascism can be seen as being less politically and morally acceptable than communism, although both employed evil methods, possibly because communism supposedly contained no racial ideology. At least in the West, fear of the far right is now more potent than fear of the far left. Hugh Purcell [1977:18–9] observes that "Fascism provides a fusion of right-wing and left-wing policies . . . fascism and communism converge at many points and are in some ways hard to distinguish." The so-called "third way" pragmatic policies of the present New Labour government defy categorisation. It "spins" Old Labour (left wing socialism), but increasingly practices conservative (right wing) ideology. No single model can be applied to both the Nazi and Italian fascist regimes because there were significant differences, but they could be said to have included to a greater or lesser degree, the following: they were politically totalitarian and autocratic, and led by a demagogue having a mass appeal; nationalistic in respect of their own nation; they both had extra-territorial ambitions; they strove to be economically self-sufficient; they were socialist to the extent that national resources were mobilised for the benefit of the state and distributed for the common good; they controlled the mass media; and they were anti-Communist because they were nationalistic and not international, and did not promote the ideology of the nation nor a revolutionary class struggle.

According to Oswald Mosley [1968:341], he was not anti-semitic because of race or religion, but because of dual loyalties, which was a similar argument to that used by Hitler: "Our quarrel with the Jewish interests is that they have set the interests of their co-racialists at home and abroad above the interests of the British state. An outstanding example of this conduct is the persistent attempt of many Jewish interests to provoke the world disaster of another war (WW2) between Britain and Germany, not this time in any British quarrel, but purely in a Jewish quarrel." As with all political parties be they major or fringe, the British fascist movement, the BUF (British Union of Fascists) contained radical dissidents who did not conform to the official party line, and it more closely resembled the Italian model. James Gregor [1969:265] concludes that "Perhaps the most striking feature of the Fascist

Manifesto was the rejection, in principle, of any a priori ascription of superiority or inferiority to any given race." The Italian fascists forged national unity on the basis of an integrated nation, and worked within the established social, aesthetic culture and religious structure of the state, whereas the Nazis were less tied to these institutional constraints. Throughout the 1930s other European countries had fascist movements, and most of Europe, including the Vatican and Britain, (and later the United States during the early 1950s), reacted strongly against the threat of the "godless and Jewish" ideology of Communism. Many Germans hated the "Bolshevists" as much as they did the Jews. The pre-WW2 British Union of Fascists led by Mosley, formed in 1932, never had more than 40,000 members, nor became an electable party. It owed its demise to its perceived violence, its crude anti-semitism, and from 1936, its alliance with Hitler's Nazi Germany. It was renamed in 1936 the British Union of Fascists and National Socialists, and the term fascism was replaced by *national socialism*, which had both right and left wing connotations. In the inter-war years, several sincere and prominent people in Britain joined the fascist and communist parties—the then Prince of Wales was allegedly a supporter of Mosley. If it were not for its pre-war association with German and Italian territorial aggression, its anti-semitism, its cult of the leader, and the street violence (most of it between the police and the communists rather than the fascists), arguably a more benign form of fascistic movement might well have had a similar electoral success as Communism did in post-WW2 Europe.

NOTES

Alter, P. *Nationalism*. London: Edward Arnold, 1989. 2 and 9.
Arendt, H. *On Revolution*. Faber and Faber: London, 1963. 279.
Baubock, R. *Immigration and the Boundaries of Citizenship*. Coventry: University of Warwick, Centre for Research in Ethnic Relations, 1992. 115–6.
Ibid. 123.
Beloff, M. *An Historian in the Twentieth Century*. New Haven: Yale University Press. 1992. 107–8.
Benn, S.I. "Nationalism." In *Encyclopedia of Philosophy*. (Ed.) Edwards, P. London: Macmillan, 1967. 442.
Ibid. 445.
Blakeway, D. *The Falklands War*. London: Sidgwick and Jackson. 1992. 15.
Caws, P. "Identity: Cultural, Transcultural, and Multicultural." In *Multiculturalism*. (Ed.) Goldberg, D.TM. Oxford: Blackwell Publishers, 1994. 381.
Churchill, W.S. *The World Crisis—The Aftermath*. vol.5. London: Thornton Butterworth, 1929. 203–4.
Cohen, J.M. and M.J. *Dictionary of Modern Quotations*. London: Penguin Books. 1980. 218.
Coleman. J.L. and Harding, S.K. "Citizenship, The Demands of Justice, and the Moral

Relevance of Political Borders." In *Justice in Immigration*. Schwartz, W.F. (Ed.) Cambridge: Cambridge University Press, 1995. 19–23.

Davies, N. *The Isles—A History*. London: Macmillan. 1999, 1054.

Gellner, E. *Thought and Change* . London: Weidenfeld and Nicolson, 1964. 147–8. Ibid. 152.

Gregor, A.J. *The Ideology of Facism—The Rationale of Totalitarianism*. New York: The Free Press, 1969. 265.

Hampton, J. "Immigration, Identity, and Justice." In *Justice in Immigration*. Schwartz, W.F. (Ed.) Cambridge: Cambridge University Press, 1995. 67–7.

Healey, D. *The Time of My Life*. London: Michael Joseph, 1989. 98–9.

Jones, T. *The Desire of Nations*. Llandybie: Dyfed. 1974. Preface and 2.

Judt, T. "Europe the Grand Illusion." In *The New York Review*. 13 June 1996. 9.

Kedourie, E. *Nationalism* . London, Hutchinson. 1966. 9 and 90–1.

Kymlicka, W. "Misunderstanding Nationalism." (Book Review) In *Dissent*. Winter. 1995. 130–7.

Lakatos, I "Boston Studies in The Philosophy of Science." In *A Dictionary of Philosophical Quotations*. Ayer, A.J. and O'Grady, J. (Eds.) Oxford: Blackwell Publishers. 1994. 244.

Luttwak, E.N. "Great Powerless Days." (Book Review) In *Times Literary Supplement*. 16 June 1995. 9.

Mosley, O. *My Life—Sir Oswald Mosley*. London: Thomas Nelson, 1968. 341.

Nicholson, N. *Long Life—Memoirs*. London: Weidenfeld and Nicolson. 1997. 151–2.

Owen, D. *Time to Declare*. London: Michael Joseph. 1991. 176–7.

Parkins, G. "Positive Racism in Britain." In *Reversing Racism—Lessons from America*. Holland, K.M. and Parkins, G. London: Social Affairs Unit, 1984. 31.

Putnam, H. "Must We Choose Between Patriotism and Universal Reason." In *For Love of Country*. Nussbaum, M.C. Boston: Beacon Press. 1996. 147.

Purcell, H. *Fascism*. London: Hamish Hamilton, 1977. 18–9.

Shaw, M.N. *International Law*. Cambridge: Cambridge University Press, 1997. 876.

Schlesinger, A.M. *Cycles of American History*. London: Andre Deutsch, 1987. 414.

Tamir, Y. *Liberal Nationalism*. Princeton: Princeton University Press, 1993. 4–5.

Taylor, C. "Why Democracy Needs Patriotism." In *For Love of Country – Debating the Limits of Patriotism*. Nussbaum, M.C. Boston: Beacon Press, 1996. 120.

10

The Obligation of Loyalty
and Patriotism

A nation-state is shaped by the social coherence of its people, manifested in its national pride and by its patriotism—the loyalty to one's country is the ultimate social loyalty, and nostalgia is the mother of loyalty. This, together with a respect for one's national history, heroes, and artefacts, are deeply felt instincts, and are important components of the human psyche and motivators of patriotism. Loyalty and patriotism arise from a pride in the inherited tradition and history of a culture. Sceptics claim that these merely objectivise an emotional nostalgic belief, and historical revisionism will attempt to diminish its objective rationale. Without this foundation it is doubtful whether any culture would survive, even in a multicultural society. Hilary Putnam [1996:97] believes that "Because reason calls for such endless renegotiation, it cannot function as a neutral source of values for 'world citizens' to live by . . . And that is why the best kind of patriotism—loyalty to what is best in the traditions which one has inherited—is indispensable." Patriotism in a democracy should be seen as a civic responsibility, and not an unintelligent, uncritical emotion, typified by "my country right or wrong," or in a blind kamikase obedience to a godlike leader. Loyalty and subjection to sovereignty is a mode of Hobbsean response, which protects the individual's self-interest against the threat of others. A patronising view is that it is only in backward societies that individuals exhibit an uncritical loyalty towards their unchosen identity: the group into which they are born, and which takes precedence over their individual self-interest. This is evidentially not the case in Ulster, Quebec, Basques, Corsica, Chechnya and Yugoslavia—all "imagined communities" engaged in "mindless" conflicts. Bosnia/Herzogovina and Kosovo exemplify how what is perceived as being disloyal, in this case by Muslims, can create long-standing divisions and conflict. Tudiman, the president of Croatia, said that "The Muslims are only Serbs and Croats who were too weak to stand up to the Turks" [TM 26 Oct. 00].

Patriotism is a positive emotion of pride in the nation without which its people are unlikely to harmonise and cohere. When the homeland is under threat, a patriotic appeal can have a powerful influence, albeit with the better-informed society of today, this has to have a firm foundation. It is no longer enough, as it was in WW1, to wave a Union Jack or the Stars and Stripes at soldiers going off to be killed, or to wave the Confederate flag, as during the American Civil War (which had the highest death toll in American history). Vietnam finally ended all that. Nationalism, the emotional attachment to a nation or ethno-national group, and patriotism, tend to merge. Patriotism can be undermined if there exists a loyalty to another race, ethnicity, religion and/or political ideology.

Patriotic rhetoric became tainted by Nazism, and for years became intellectually down market largely for those "intellectuals" whose disloyalty George Orwell [1995:11–15] attacked. Archbishop Carey said [TM 12 March 97] "I realise how much I take for granted the sense of belonging and identification in being British and being part of a proud and confident nation." It is unfortunate that he does not see a discontinuity between this sentiment and unrestrained multiculturalism. Pride can be aroused and focussed on successes, ranging from winning a war to winning an Olympic gold medal. Populist patriotism is in evidence if, like the United States, the country is perceived as being a world super-power, a perception the Russian Federation is also trying to restore. The sentiment of patriotism and allegiance are not as is sometimes supposed—the exclusive concern of the political right—nor, as might have been so until WW1, is it confined to the uninformed and unintelligent.

We live in an era of anti-heroism. Professor Anthony O'Hear [DM 25 Jan. 1995] comments that "today many . . . seem to prefer national humiliation to national self-respect, and out of national humiliation, still expect a sense of community to mysteriously arise . . . a country whose subjects do not have a sense of pride in their nation is unlikely to inspire feelings of co-operation and harmony among its peoples. Ultimately, the very existence of a community depends on the willingness of its members to sacrifice their own interests in defence of others, even if that means making the supreme sacrifice of life itself." And the modern historian Anthony Sampson [1982:434] observed that "the nation is still the chief focus for people's identity, the source of much of their security and confidence: the more uncertain the world climate, the more important the nation will seem. The Falklands crisis was a reminder of how rapidly patriotic emotions can be re-awakened . . . was the national consciousness, like the human brain, divided between the fore-brain which can calculate and reason, and the primitive hind-brain which reacts only to simple stimuli and dangers? If so, the Falklands brought the old brain back to the forefront [431]." Although WW1, WW2, the Falklands, and the Gulf conflicts remain alive in the memories of the British public, arguably because they were perceived as having a positive national interest, the UN-inspired Korean War, in which 80,000 British troops served, is (like Vietnam) a "forgotten war," and those that served see themselves as "forgotten heroes."

Alasdair MacIntyre [1993:180] defends patriotism. "[It is] a moral virtue, against what he took to be the critique of liberal philosophy, that patriotism engenders an unhealthy indifference to the requirements of international justice, a chauvinistic repudiation of the international norms of morality, and a dangerous blindness to the faults of one's own nation . . . the true patriot does not bear allegiance to his country because of something independently attractive about the norms and ideals that it stands for: the American patriot does not stand by the United States just because of its commitment to constitutional democracy . . . Instead, the true patriot stands by his country first and foremost because it is his country, and it is only in the light of this prior and particular allegiance that he sees any virtues (or for that matter any vices) that it has. The virtues of his fatherland are for him matters of particular pride, and its vices—if they can be recognised as such—are a matter for guilt and shame rather than an occasion for exercising the easy mobility of the liberal conscience."

Even in peacetime politicians make rhetorical appeals to patriotism and call for strong leadership, social solidarity, and seek to identify their party with a supposedly classless "one nation." At their 1996 conference, the then-leader of the Liberal Democrat party portrayed himself as the strongest leader in Britain, and that the country had not had a tough leader since the war-time Churchill. The conservative government, he said, had been racked with division and indecision. He described his party as the home of "true patriotism," and he attacked the "false patriotism" of the Tories, who had abused its "real meaning" [TM 25 Sept. 96]. In the 1997 general election campaign, he accused both the Tories and Labour of "phoney" and "designer" patriotism. Blair, in his speech to the 1997 Labour Party Conference, claimed that his government would be one of "enlightened patriotism." Established patriotism and traditions can, however, be an embarrassment if the political ideology of a state changes, and may have to be re-invented. In the USSR, the post-revolution Communist government tried to make the traditions and patriotism of Tsarist Russia unfashionable. However, during WW2, in order to resist the German invasion, they found it expedient to allow the Russian church and religion to re-emerge, the Red army to restore its traditions, and encouraged the glorification of national heroes. Appeals to loyalty such as "Buy British" have been used in psychological marketing campaigns, and disloyalty stigmatised.

Martha Nussbaum [1996:4] wants loyalty to be to global cosmopolitanism.

She says that "this emphasis on patriotic pride is both morally dangerous and, ultimately, subversive of some of the worthy goals patriotism sets out to serve . . . These goals, I [Nussbaum] shall argue, would be better served by an ideal that is in any case more adequate to our situation in the contemporary world, namely the very old ideal of the cosmopolitan, the person whose allegiance is to the worldwide community of human beings." Gertrude Himmelfarb [1996:77] counters this with "Identity is neither an accident nor a matter of choice. It is given, not willed. We may, in the course of our lives, reject or alter one or another of these givens, perhaps for good reason. But we do so at some cost to the self . . . To pledge one's 'fundamental allegiance' to cosmopolitanism is to try to transcend not only nationality but all the actualities, particularities, and realities of life that constitute one's natural identity. Cosmopolitanism has a nice, high-minded ring to it, but it is an illusion, and, like all illusions, perilous." Individuals have a plurality of loyalties, with ever widening and over-lapping, but diminishing, circles—from family to friends, school, political party, and so on up to the nation-state—but it does not often extend to a multi-national region, let alone to the world at large. It condenses into a single loyalty when the nation-state itself is threatened. The supposed loyalty inherent in global cosmopolitanism is weak to non-existent even if it sounds good, makes no real demands, and remains untested.

To some there is little merit in patriotism, seeing it as xenophobia or a willingness to kill and be killed for trivial reasons, presumably because of its emotional component. The outward display of national pride can be judged by some as being nostalgic or even racist. This might be explicable by applying one of Betrand Russell's [1990:99] observations, namely "Cynicism such as one finds very frequently among the most highly educated young men and women of the West, results from the combination of comfort and powerlessness." Loyalty to the nation-state, with its political and associative obligations, can give rise to a conflict with personal morality, notably conscientious objection. Helmut Schmidt [1991:13–5], the ex-German Chancellor, admitted that he was in the Wehrmacht not because he was patriotic, but because fear (of punishment) was more potent than moral principles.

Lord Tebbitt gave as his criterion for immigrant loyalty: "See which way the chap cheers at the cricket match. They should uphold their allegiance to that new country completely and absolutely, with no looking back." The Pakistani captain of the English cricket team has called upon young Asians who support India and Pakistan at Test matches to support England instead [STM 27 May 01]. The black broadcaster Darcus Howe [Channel 4 July 1/4 Aug. 00] talked to British Caribbeans, Indians, and mixed race supporters about their national identity and loyalty at cricket matches with England. He found that, with few exceptions, their loyalty lay with their ethnic origins and not with the English team, because of their different culture and colour:

"English means whiteness." He concluded that this evidence of "unshakeable roots will take a considerable period of time to disappear . . . black Caribbeans cannot hold on to their roots for ever, something has got to give, and it's soon." Of mixed race supporters he concluded that "Race comes before nation. Those of mixed race parentage will follow the lead of their black or Asian bloodline." This anecdotal but limited evidence indicates that race, culture, and colour can be perceived as barriers to national loyalty and assimilation.

Some believe that the only patriotism possible and acceptable in multicultural societies is patriotism based on the values of the polity. Maurizio Viroli [1995:179 and 181] describes civic patriotism: "American patriotism is not based on blood or religion, on tradition or territory . . . It is a 'political idea' that was better articulated by Lincoln . . . In this tradition, patriotism means democratic citizenship. It describes a love for a republic that the citizens feel as their own business and as their own creation; a love coupled with self-interest and pride, but still an essentially political love which translates not into desires for purification, but into the practices of participatory democracy." Adlai Stevenson [1990:268] also believed that "[American] patriotism is not short, frenzied outbursts of emotion, but the tranquil and steady dedication of a lifetime." Accordingly, [American] patriotism might be said to be less ardent than the patriotism that springs from the attachment to the place where one was born, but is more creative and lasting. Walzer [1995:178] also contends that "the concept of 'patria' has never captured the American imagination, probably because so many of us were fathered in other lands. Nor is the [American] nation a source of commitment and loyalty; American society lacks the cultural, ethnic, and religious unity that nationalist allegiance requires. The only kind of commitment that is compatible with the pluralism of American society is a commitment to the republic; it is a political allegiance." Walzer [1994:185] notes that in relatively homogeneous countries like France, Germany and Japan, "whatever regional differences exist, the great majority of the citizens share a single ethnic identity and celebrate a common history." And in the territorially based heterogeneity of the old multinational empires like the former Soviet Union and Yugoslavia, "a number of ethnic and religious minorities claim ancient homelands . . . The United States differs from both these sets of countries: it isn't homogeneous nationally or locally: it's heterogeneous everywhere—a land of dispersed diversity, which is (except for the remaining Native Americans) no-one's homeland." This gives rise to the questions: do hyphenated Americans and Britons with multiple identities have both a cultural allegiance to the left of the hyphen and a political allegiance to the right? And in the event of a war, who would they support? Although the Stars and Stripes flag remains a powerful symbol, does the WASP look-a-like "Uncle Sam" icon officially adopted by Congress in 1961 as the national symbol now represent the United States?

It would seem to be a delusion that loyalty can accrue to a multicultural state founded on the political concept of its being a democracy, otherwise its minorities would not seek separatism and/or self-determination. The theory of American civic patriotism as opposed to ethno-national patriotism/nationalism is suspect inasmuch that less than half of all Americans vote in Presidential elections. The theory of civic patriotism may be a search for an integrating and inclusive patriotism in a multicultural society—no other concept of national allegiance is available. Nevertheless, the United States, unlike Britain and Canada, does not generally allow its citizens to hold dual nationality, maybe because multiple loyalties are not credible, and because U.S. immigrants could readily opt out of the ultimate loyalty of their oath of allegiance.

Predictably there is a heightened concern about the loyalty of aliens in a national crisis, which can result in some human rights legislation being derogated. This led to the internment in WW2 of the Japanese-Americans and most of the German and Austrian Jews in Britain. Between WW1 and WW2 some European countries passed "denaturalisation" legislation to deprive suspects of their citizenship. At the outbreak of WW1, Germany and the Austro-Hungarian empire expected their Jewish citizens, many of whom were descended from mid-to-late nineteenth-century Polish, Russian, and Ukranian refugees, to loyally support them in winning the war. A Jewish Legion was recruited to fight the Turks, and Jews had been active in organising a strike of German munitions workers in January 1918. Hitler did not forget that the head of the short-lived (March-May 1919) Bavarian breakaway Soviet style republic was a Jew, as was most of its ruling council. This again became emphasised after Germany attacked "Jewish" Communist Bolshevist Russia. Hitler was convinced that world Jewry had acted in unison, and for its own benefit, to destroy Austria and Germany, and should not be trusted again. After WW1, the Jews in Germany and Austria attracted the envy and dislike that almost always attaches to the materially successful alien. Even though many Jews were fully assimilated Germans and Austrians, the separatist and "high visibility" Orthodox Jews provided a stereotype for hatred and were seen as a "nation within a nation." The toleration or indifference, at least at the official level, changed to ethnic cleansing because of the perceived disloyalty that the Jewish minority, through their influential diaspora, presented to the German nation-state. Nevertheless, Nazi Germany had to "tolerate" only one indigenous ethnic/religious cultural minority (the Jews). The relative proportion of these increased enormously from 275,000 as Germany expanded into Poland (with its three million Jews) and Eastern Europe, and which led to ethnic cleansing.

Galbraith [1992:129] notes that when the United States suspended military conscription after Vietnam in 1973 (although students could get temporary exemption), "It was accepted that the contented (majority) should not be forced into military service . . . [advertising] abandoned patriotism as a plea and promised instead immediate economic advantage and subsequent advance." Minorities outside of the contented majority are now "over-represented" in the armed forces, particularly in the American army, where the dangers of battle are the greatest, in 1989 they were more than twenty-five percent of the total [131]. Galbraith [173] believes that "A deep recession could cause stronger discontent in the areas of urban disaster in the aftermath of some military misadventure in which, in the nature of the modern armed forces, the unfortunate were disproportionately engaged." The unspoken implication is that the patriotism and loyalty of the "grunts" of the U.S. army borders on the mercenary, and could not be relied upon.

The United States has never been under a direct military threat since Pearl Harbour, which arguably was the last time that the United States with a nonprofessional army, was motivated by patriotism. Since then, American society has become more pluralistic and the effect of this, and the erosion of Eurocentrism as a focus for loyalty, remains to be seen. In Vietnam, the reasons why the United States suffered an ignominious defeat were because it was not under direct attack; the domino threat was too remote; the containment strategy questionable; and conscripted and disproportionately black Americans, were not ready to die to "save Vietnam from Communism," which eschewed Western style democracy. McNamara, then Secretary of Defence, said that the mistake made in Vietnam after the experience of Cuba was to interpret a patriotic nationalist movement as being Sino/Soviet Communist imperialism. Since Vietnam, which the United States could not win with its part-conscript army, it has, like Britain, used only professionals—but has been seen by some as imperialist mercenaries and liable to be accused of war crimes. It has been provided with overwhelmingly technically superior and remotely operated weaponry, requiring the minimum personal commitment and risk. The West has become insulated against the effects of real warfare by casualty-free and bloodless films and computer games. The UN has tried to prevent at arm's length the ethnic cleansing of Kurds in North Iraq and the Shias in the South by "no fly" zones, and of the Albanians in Kosovo by air and missile bombardment. The test for a nation-state arises when the threat is such that it has to rely on its citizen conscript army as ground troops committed to battle. The duality and extent of loyalty inherent in a multicultural society would then be put to the test.

Recruitment by the British army is now around 8,000 short of its target of 108,000—predominantly in the "teeth arms" such as the infantry—and at the current rate of recruitment it would take at least until 2005, and possibly until 2008, before the army was fully manned [TM 30 April 01]. Consideration has been given to recruitment from young offenders institutions, the Commonwealth [TM 8 Nov. 99], and Gurkha mercenaries [STM 11 June 00]. The rate of desertion and absence without leave in the British army in 1999 was 2,000, equivalent to one in every forty-eight soldiers [TM 5 June 00]. The principal problem is one of retention, particularly of commissioned ranks, and in 1999 the army recruited only seventy-nine percent of its needs [STM 5 Sept. 99]. Official reasons do not include that of job satisfaction, and there are multiple reasons for this, including the low level of unemployment, but the Shadow Defence Secretary suggested that these include the increasing level of commitment in peace-keeping regions such as in Ulster, Bosnia/Herzogovina and Kosovo. Arguably risking one's life, and the problem of family separation as global peace-keepers or involuntary aid workers, is not seen as a patriotic role. The Chief of the Defence Staff, no doubt concerned that the ethos which has heretofore sustained the army is being undermined, has warned that involvement in humanitarian operations must not be allowed to mar the combat efficiency of the British army [TM 11 Aug. 00]. It would also be ingenuous to believe that future draftees, although brought up with the Hollywood myth of "bloodless wars," would be as the WW1/WW2 propaganda suggested: ready to die for "the war to end all wars" or "to make the world safe for democracy," which the G.Is in Vietnam were not.

The British army has recognised that a rapidly changing society requires a moral and ethical basis, which is shared and understood by all and has published its first moral "covenant" [3 April 00]. This makes clear that "soldiers will be called upon to make personal sacrifices—including the ultimate sacrifice—in the service of the nation," but that they must have reassurance that in this event "the nation will look after them and their families," which begs the question as to what the nation will in fact be after another generation gap. As Ignatieff [BBC 2 25 Mar/1 April 00] has opined, there is no convincing evidence that with increasingly diversified nations, ex-servicemen would, in such an event, be "looked after," nor is it clear who will defend the defenders.

Although the 1907 Hague Convention would probably not have been applicable in such an event, the British "nation" was sued through the ECHR by relatives of the 323 sailors who died when the Argentinian cruiser General Belgrano was sunk during the Falklands conflict [TM 30 June 00]. Conveniently, the claim was rejected as time expired [20 July 00]. It is conceivable that the next step would have been to accuse the captain and crew of the submarine responsible as being war criminals. In 1992, as a result of a book published by a Falklands war veteran, the then-Secretary of State for Defence initiated an investigation by civilian police into an allegation that Argentinian prisoners of war had been massacred. This accusation had already been dismissed by the army. It did, however, set a precedent against the unwritten principle that a soldier who risks his life for his country on the battlefield is answerable to the military authorities alone and would have involved the army in being answerable to a civilian court. The charges were wisely subsequently dropped [Brazier 1998: 70–1]. The government is also being sued and accused of participating in war crimes by families of victims of a NATO bombing raid on Belgrade. This action is under Article 2 (1) of the European Convention that states "everyone's right to life will be protected by law" [STM 16 July 00]. The army, in recent years, has been principally engaged as agents for the British government's foreign policy, sometimes in a "foreign" cultural environment, in conflicts in which their "peace keeping" presence is not welcome. In Ulster they were welcomed for less than two years 1969–71. As Schlesinger observed [1987:73–4], "The problem is not only that simplistic moral principles are of limited use in the making of foreign policy decisions. It is that a moralistic foreign policy may well add troubles of its own creation . . . And moralization often ends by combining the most lofty intentions with the most ghastly consequences."

NOTES

Arendt, H. *The Origins of Totalitarianism*. London: George Allen and Unwin, 1958. 278–9.

Brazier, J. "Who Will Defend the Defenders?" In *Not Fit to Fight*. (Ed.) Frost, G. London: The Social Affairs Unit. 71.

Galbraith, J. K. *The Culture of Contentment*. London: Sinclair Stevenson, 1992. 129.

Ibid. 173.

Himmelfarb, G. "The Illusions of Cosmopolitanism." In *For Love of Country—Debating the Limits of Patriotism* . In Nussbaum, M.C. Boston: Beacon Press, 1996. 77.

Ignatieff, M. *Future War*. BBC 2. 25 March /1 April 2000.

Lynn, V. *We'll Meet Again*. London: Sidgwick and Jackson, 1989. 166–8.

Macintyre, A In *Liberal Rights*. Waldron, J. Cambridge: Cambridge University Press, 1993. 180–1.

Nussbaum, M.C. "Patriotism and Cosmopolitanism." In *For Love of Country—Debating the Limits of Patriotism*. Boston: Beacon Press, 1996. 4.

Orwell, G. "The Freedom of the Press." In *New Statesman and Society*. London, 1995 Aug. 18. 11–15.

Putnam, H. "Must We Choose Between Patriotism and Universal Reason?" In *For Love of Country—Debating the Limits of Patriotism*. Nussbaum, M.C. Boston: Beacon Press, 1996. 97.

Russell, B In *Book of Quotations*. (Ed.) Fitzhenry, R.I. London: Chambers, 1990. 99.

Sampson, A. *The Changing Anatomy of Britain*. London: Hodder and Stoughton. 1982. 431 and 434.

Schlesinger, A.M. *The Cycles of American History*. London: Andre Deutsch, 1987. 73–4.

Schmidt, H. In *Voices of the Third Reich*. Steinhoff, J. Pechel, P and Showalter, D. London: Grafton Books, 1991. 13–5.

Stevenson, A. In *Book of Quotations*. (Ed.) Fitzhenry, R.I. Edinburgh: Chambers, 1990. 268.

Viroli, M. FOR *Love of Country—An Essay on Patriotism and Nationalism*. Oxford: Oxford University Press. 179 and 181.

Walzer, M. Ibid. 178.
Walzer, M. "Multiculturalism and Individualism." In *Dissent*. Spring, 1994. 185.
CHANNEL 4. *The Cricket Test*. 31 July/ 1/4 August 2000.

11

The Re-Emergence of
Ethno-National Conflicts

A separatist multicultural/racial society is susceptible to dormant ethno-national, cultural, or religious conflict that may become politicised. O'Leary [BBC Radio 4: 5 May 94] observed about self-determination that "the world's political order dictates [that] the difference between a nation and a national minority [is that] . . . the latter is told to accommodate to the powers that be. If national minorities do not accept that fate, their plight or their fight is theirs and theirs alone." Ethno-national disputes may initially be presented to the mainstream society, or interpreted internationally, as issues of human or civic rights like oppression or injustice. In Ulster, an ethno-national movement developed from a civil rights campaign, reinforced by religious sectarianism. This is a basis for the contention that wherever it is still possible, a nation-state should neither acquire nor promote multiculturalism, which could lead to separatism, or ultimately, demands for self-determination. The demands on the still essentially homogenous nation-states of the West to acquire, or to accept, increasing multiculturalism, and the future likelihood of ethno-national conflicts, arise from:

1. The pace of change in the world's economy, and particularly the need to generate employment, both nationally and internationally. Although the West is relatively prosperous, it has had, and is likely to continue to have, periods of long-term unemployment and a permanent underclass, which can be as much as about twenty percent of the working population. These high levels of unemployment could be due to the increasing world population, a decline in unskilled/low skilled employment, the ease of transfer of technological manufacturing know-how from the West, the global mobility of investment, and the longer-

term rise of China and India as major trading competitors, with world demand remaining static.

2. A heightened awareness of human rights that promote enhanced claims for political, socioeconomic, and other rights in multicultural societies by immigrants and minority groups, and the self-determination aspirations of stateless national groups.

3. The growing tide of people on the move—from agricultural regions to cities, and across national borders and continents. This has given rise to substantial economic migration and increasing numbers of economic refugees. Inward migration can be eased by the export of manufacturing investment to developing countries, but at the cost of domestic employment and social welfare in the developed countries, with their longer-term political and social repercussions.

4. The collapse of Communism and the break-up of the former USSR and its satellites, which has resulted in the re-emergence of independent nation-states in the Baltic/Belarus/Ukraine/Caucasus and of the Islamic states of its former Central Asian republics.

5. The probable longer-term geopolitical incentive to secure supplies of non-renewable, and as yet undeveloped, natural resources needed by the industrialised West, notably energy.

During its fifty-year imperial retreat from India to Hong Kong, Britain policed and paid a body count for the internal conflicts in Malaya, Borneo, and Kenya; against the Haganah, Lehi, Irgun and Stern Gang in what was then called Palestine; Flosy in Aden; Eoka in Cyprus; and the IRA and its splinter groups in Ulster. The United States, like the rest of the West, learned from its experiences in the Lebanon and the Sudan, no doubt influenced also by the emotional exhaustion from a succession of ethno-national conflicts. If Britain had agreed in 1948 to Truman's request to prolong its thirty-one year mandate, and to prepare a "composite state," or to police the UN partition of Palestine, British troops might have been there until today. This involvement continues with Israel reportedly asking the U.S. to enter into a treaty to upgrade its relationship to that of a "strategic ally" [TM 13 Nov. 00]. Britain currently has about 2,700 peace-kepers in Bosnia/Herzogovina (down from 13,000), 3,900 in Kosovo, 3,200 in Cyprus, 900 in Sierra Leone and 1,650 in the Falklands [TM 21 Nov. 00].

Franjo Tudjman [1981:245] reviewed the ethno-national "questions" in Europe in 1981, some of which have since erupted. He recognised that "The fact that a nation does not accept the dissection of its national being, even if it is small and even if its division has lasted for centuries, is seen in the example of the Basques, while the full range of disastrous effects that can be caused by a foreign rule and territorial and religious division is seen in the nightmare events in Northern Ireland . . . In the group of multi-national state communities in which the national question has been solved through the legal and political recognition of national individuality and through a certain degree of self-government and national sovereignty—Switzerland, the USSR, Yugoslavia, and Czechoslovakia—we also find a specific and very different situation in each of them" [248]. Apart from Switzerland, federation and limited self-government did not solve their national question. In sensitive regions such as in Yugoslavia and Kurdistan, the causes of some of these have remained latent for decades, or erupted when a former "imperialist" power tried to reassert its hegemony, as Russia did in Chechnya, where separatists want to set up an independent Muslim state. Russia has made it clear that it would accept no criticism from "outsiders," let alone intervention [TM 19 Nov. 99]. If some of these conflicts had occurred during the Cold War, they might have escalated into confrontations between the super-powers. The radical "solution" to some of these conflicts has been ethnic cleansing up to and including genocide—originating as an inter-ethnic threat, heightened by the breakdown of trust. Although arms embargoes and the deployment of a peacekeeping force can temporarily stabilise the situation, it does little to resolve it, and experience has shown that humanitarian aid can be hijacked by the combatants.

Paul Hockenos [1993:314], who favours intervention, and writing in 1993 before the experience in Kosovo, asserts that "the West's failure to respond constructively to the new realities in Eastern Europe has nowhere been more blatant than in former Yugoslavia . . . As early as 1991, during the war against Croatia, the West could have intervened and stopped the fighting and shown the Serbs that it was serious about enforcing democratic standards in post-Communist Europe . . . Rather than insist upon a multiethnic solution to the crisis in Bosnia/Herzogovina, Western policy makers endorsed the logic of nationalists by proposing to divide Bosnia/Herzogovina into ethnically based provinces. The Vance-Owen plan and its successors represented clear capitulations to Serbian and Croatian nationalists and to the rationale of ethnic nationalism in general. The plans for partitioning the state admit that peoples of different ethnic and national backgrounds cannot live together in multinational states." If Hockenos means that, in the unlikely event the disparate group of nation-states, loosely termed the "West," would have had the political and military will to occupy and administer the former multiethnic Yugoslavia and convert it to multiculturalism, particularly in the face of the opposition by Russia—then the subsequent experience and addition of Kosovo, Macedonia, and Montenegro would have shown how mistaken this intervention would have been.

NATO's "coercive diplomacy" in Kosovo, which was followed by illegal but moral military intervention, was ostensibly undertaken to prevent ethnic cleansing and to promote Serbian/Albanian multiculturalism. The original estimate of 100,000 dead was subsequently reduced to 10,000 and may end up as 2,500 [STM 31 Oct. 99]. It ended as a hollow moral victory, first with the temporary ethnic cleansing of the Albanians, and was followed by the virtually complete ethnic cleansing of the Serbs, who are unlikely to return. This was in addition to the 300,000 Serbs who were ethnically cleansed from Croatia [STM 10 Oct. 99]. The humanitarian intervention became inextricably involved in supporting the Albanian secessionist political movement. At the Rambouillet conference, the KLA (Kosovo Liberation Army), which became a NATO ally, demanded independence and not autonomy. It is alleged [TM 29 Dec. 00] by the Albanian Foreign Minister that the U.S. Secretary of State made informal commitments about eventual Kosovan independence and the KLA, of which the other Rambouillet participants were apparently unaware. The final, and clearly unacceptable, ultimatum made to the Serbs by NATO at Rambouillet demanded immediate autonomy for Kosovo, with an independence referendum three years later (the outcome of which was self-evident), and the "unrestricted and unimpeded" freedom of movement and immunity from Serbian law for NATO troops both in Kosovo and Serbia itself. These were clear infringements of Serbian sovereignty. There followed seventy-eight days of bombing that killed 1,500 civilians and ended with a peace deal actually brokered by Russia. At the height of the conflict forty-seven percent of all British forces were engaged [TM 12 Feb. 01], and NATO were within twenty-four hours of invading. The demands for an independence referendum and free movement of NATO troops in Serbia were withdrawn. The Serbian leader Milosevic was subsequently toppled not by NATO, but by the Serbian electorate, and the threat of the withholding of $50 million in aid and threats of trade sanctions [STM 1 April 01]. After extraditing Milosevic to the Hague (allegedly in violation of the Yugoslav constitution), a total of $1.28 billion of international aid was pledged [TM 30 June 01].

The Serb population of the capital Pristina, being protected by the NATO Kosovan force (Kfor) from 400,000 Kosovans, has fallen, according to a UN report, from about 40,000 to less than 2,000 [TM 12 Aug. 99]. The Serbian victims of Albanian intimidation are estimated to be 130,000—about seventy-two percent of the original Serbian population [STM 8 Aug. 99]. There are reports that Catholics are being persecuted, and that Orthodox Serbian churches and monasteries have been damaged or destroyed [18 Jan. 00]. Drug dealing, prostitution and smuggling are rampant with an all-Albanian judiciary of dubious impartiality. The British troops who were sent into Kosovo to prevent the Serbs persecuting the Albanians are now attempting, but often failing, to prevent the Albanians persecuting the Serbs, some of who are now claiming asylum in Britain. In 1998/99 most asylum seekers in Britain were from the former Yugoslavia. The "domino effect" in this region may reinforce Albanian demands for national independence from Serbia, civil war in Montenegro, and possibly also in Vojvodina. Macedonia, with its thirty percent Albanian population, has been hovering on the brink of civil war [TM 30 May 01]. The Macedonian prime minister called for the declaration of a state of war, saying that "everyone must understand that we are at war and that strong military action is the only solution for reaching peace" [TM 7 June 01]. Although genocidal ethnic cleansing has been highlighted by the Balkans, this has taken place on a massive scale on other occasions in Europe and elsewhere during the twentieth century. Predictably, the Serbs accuse the Americans of ethnically cleansing the Native-Americans from the West.

Disparate procreation can be another long-term threat to the indigenous majority in multiethnic/racial societies. In Serbian/Muslim Bosnia/Herzogovina a demographic ethnic inversion took place between 1961 and 1991, and this is expected to occur in Ulster. Territorial partition and a siege mentality can be only a partial and temporary remedy, because it leaves behind a vulnerable minority. This was recognised in the 1993 Israeli/Oslo "land for peace" Accords when up to 100,000 Jewish settlers were to be moved out of the Gaza Strip and the partially Israeli-occupied West Bank by May 1999. This has been only been partially implemented, and in spite of strenuous efforts and failed "peace initiatives" sponsored by the United States, has deteriorated into a mini-war with the PLO threatening to unilaterally set up a Palestinian state. This ethno-national conflict could escalate and draw in the Middle Eastern Arab states. As long as the U.S. is perceived as being the patron of Israel, the end game of this ethno-national conflict could deteriorate into a scenario foreseen in Samuel Huntington's book *The Clash of Civilizations*.

An optimism at variance with reality is that negotiation will peacefully resolve ethno-national disputes, often articulated by diplomats as "ultimately the conflict will have to be resolved by negotiation or a political settlement." This is true, but what does "ultimately" entail? If the resolution of a long-standing and polarised ethno-national conflict is to be by negotiation, sponsored by the mediation of an "honest broker," it is only likely to succeed given certain conditions. These include prolonged and widespread experience by the combatants of human misery, terrorism, and war weariness; or the temporary exhaustion of the resources needed for the continuation of the conflict; or the declining expectation of military success; or "peace" being enforced/policed militarily by a powerful third party, such as NATO, and usually financial aid. A genuine and lasting negotiated settlement also requires the absence of political dogmatism and threats, mutual trust, reciprocal toleration, and shared basic values on both sides.

A review of a book on Ulster [Ruane and Todd:1997] dismissed "the widely held view among academics that understanding, if pursued with sufficient vigour, is bound to produce workable solutions to the problems that beset humanity. In fact, this is rarely true. Money and power speak louder than understanding" [STM 2 Mar. 97]. The thirty-year civil war in Ulster, let alone its earlier history of 100 years or more, provides one example among many that this is so. The partial ethnic cleansing of Ireland by partition in 1922 did not resolve this intractable conflict, which has since cost Britain billions of pounds. From 1969, it has taken more than 3,600 lives and 40/50,000 injured—58.8 percent were killed by republicans, 28.9 percent by loyalists, 6.6 percent by the army and 1.4 percent by the RUC [TM 4 Aug. 00], who had an overwhelming superiority in both manpower and weapons. The implementation of the 1998 Good Friday power sharing agreement, which included the decommissioning of weapons, was in a state of paralysis for three and a half years. The impasse arose because the Irish/Catholic nationalists have no real allegiance to the Protestant/British nation-state—a situation reminiscent of both Henry VIII and John Locke who both were aware of this feature of Catholicism. Independence is their ultimate aim—not power sharing nor a climate of mutual trust. Open civil war had been prevented by the unwelcome presence of the British army. Like most military interventions in civil wars, the army was initially perceived as an ally and then as the enemy. The British troops, called in to quell the riots in which ten people were killed and 100 wounded, were initially welcomed by the nationalists, and were told by their commanding officer that it was a "temporary operation" [TM 01 Jan. 00]—they are still there after thirty years. A sceptic might think that a solution to this long-standing conflict would have occurred earlier, if it had been allowed to escalate into a full civil war, or at least, a voluntary and financially-assisted ethnic cleansing in 1922 by two-way migration between Ulster and the Irish republic.

It is a mistake to assume that more or less numerically evenly balanced ethnic groups, with no dominant majority, particularly having outside support, will necessarily seek negotiated compromises. Experience shows that some issues cannot or will not be compromised. If this were so, there would be no wars and diplomacy and rational objectivity would succeed. Michael Ignatieff, [1993] in his book *Blood and Belonging*, studied six such territories ridden with ethno-national disputes: Croatia/Serbia; Germany; Ukraine; Quebec; Kurdistan and Ulster. The extremist elements of a separatist group may resort to terrorism, which victimises the innocent and/or any peace-keeping third party, but this violence usually pays a negotiating dividend. Extremists sometimes have the covert support, or at least the tacit connivance, of otherwise peaceful communities, including donations from expatriates who are possibly guilt-ridden, and who at a safe distance see it as an effective way of loyally publicising and advancing their ethno-national cause, i.e. the end justifying the means. Ignatieff [STM 22 Feb. 98], in his book *The Warrior's Honour: Ethnic War and the Modern Conscience*, observes that "liberal internationalists have had to learn that force is the only language which authoritarian populism actually understands . . . Never has the instinct—"something must be done"—stood in greater need of precision [namely an exit strategy]."

The setting up of national boundaries by the early Western imperialists, encompassing differing but sizeable cultural groups, has often postponed the eventual ethno-national confict—hence the post-colonial civil wars in Africa. Nigeria gained its independence in 1960. Its population in a 1993 census was 92.6 million, consisting of over 250 distinct ethnic groups, including three dominant Muslim and Christian groups. The Christian Ibo tribe declared Biafra independent in 1967 and there followed a thirty-month civil war, in which estimates vary from 100,000 to two million being killed. The resolution of an ethno-national conflict in mature liberal democracies such as Ireland, Canada, and Spain is particularly difficult, because the culture of the West does not permit the exhaustion of large-scale and prolonged violence to produce the climate for a solution.

If the prerequisite of mutual trust has been lost over time, and both parties are intransigent, the division becomes irreconcilable, and neither toleration nor negotiation on their own are likely to resolve the conflict. Croatia, whose independence was insisted on and recognised by Germany as early as December 1991, continued to ethnically cleanse the Serbs from its Krajina territory, and this influenced the Serbs to take over most of Bosnia. The boundaries drawn up by the American-brokered, NATO-enforced 1995 Dayton Accord recognised that the future of this region is one of smaller hegemonic nation-states, and not a multiracial federation. The Dayton Accord retained the external borders of Bosnia/Herzegovina, but with a multiethnic "national" government: Slav Muslims 44%, Serbs 31% and Croats 17%, population 4.6 million. This was partitioned into two administrative entities each presiding over half the country—a joint Slav Muslim/Croat federation and a Serb statelet of Republika Srpska. The Dayton Accord seems to have become a quiescent truce under a NATO "stabilisation force" (Sfor) in this effectively NATO protectorate. Nevertheless, the bitter conflict showed what the alternative might once again be. After Dayton, Kosovo erupted. It has a population of 1.96 million and is about the size of the county of Devon.

The Federation of Malaysia, founded in 1963, is an ex-colonial Asian nation-state that inherited a multicultural/racial society. It was formed from the Malayan peninsula, North Borneo and Sarawak. Singapore left the federation in 1965 because of the imbalance of its seventy-seven percent Chinese, fifteen percent Malay population. North Borneo and Sarawak have a predominantly Malay population, and the present ethnic mix of Malaysia is sixty percent Malay who are Muslim, thirty-one percent Chinese and eight percent Indian. Serious rioting took place in 1969 with hundreds being killed, and again in 1998. The target was the Chinese who control business and much of the economy. Before 1969, the Malay majority was an under-privileged and largely rural community. State-imposed social engineering was used to avoid future conflict between its multiethnic groups—reverse discrimination—but in favour of the indigenous Malay majority. The Chinese were also targeted by the Muslim majority in the 1998 uprising in Indonesia—they are only about three percent of the 200 million population (which has 600 ethnic groups) but own seventy percent of the country's wealth [STM 1 Feb. 98].

If the above and similar experiences have a general validity, it suggests that latent ethno-national conflicts will continue to erupt and the UN will be powerless to prevent or to effectively resolve them. Mestrovic [1994:176] has challenged "The smug but probably false, optimistic faith that the Enlightenment narratives of the so-called West will help to achieve the utopian goals which were promised by Marxists and communists. These modernist, utopian goals include, but are not limited to, the victory of tolerance over racism and sexism, globalization, and the triumph of rationality over culture . . . the existing divisions within both Islamic and Christian nations and the civil religions derived from these faiths will probably worsen." He warns [192] that "The [then] current crisis in former Yugoslavia is a microcosm not only of the fate of much of the post-communist world, but of Europe and the rest of the world as well. Everywhere, it seems, including recently Afghanistan, postmodern forces in the sense of post-Enlightenment narratives are clashing with genuinely post-modern or anti-modern forces such as tradition, nationalism, fundamentalism, racism, and what the West calls human rights abuses."

The former multiracial/ethnic USSR had a population of around 240 million, of which about fifty-four percent were ethnic Russians, seventeen percent ethnic Ukrainians, with the balance made up of thirteen or more sizeable ethnic groups, not counting those groups without a distinct ethnic region. Under the Soviet constitution, all nationalities were supposed to have equal rights in the participation in the country's economic, cultural, and political life. The break-up of the Soviet Union dramatically changed its concept of the national identity of its peoples. With the demise of its Communist centralist government, eleven states of the former USSR declared their national independence. One of the main sources of the present instability of the rump of the Russian federation, most of whose landmass is not in Europe, is its ethno-national diversity, as in the multiethnic Muslim republics, which include Chechnya. *Ukraine* means frontier, borderland, the edge, and is a divided and cleavaged multiethnic country. It has a population of fifty two million which is seventy-three percent Ukrainian, with a ten million, twenty-two percent Russian minority in the east, Poles in the west and Muslim Tartars in the Crimea. Its western city of Lvov is the centre of Polish nationalism, being at one time in a Habsburg and then a Polish province, before becoming part of the Soviet empire in 1945. Poland itself looks to the West, to EU membership, and the Catholic Church and the authority of Rome are at the centre of its identity.

Koshechkina [1992:150] investigated the prospects for promoting political toleration in the post-Soviet republics after Ukrainian independence in 1991, where the Soviet colonial ethos of universalism and assimilation had supposedly given way to a post-colonial multiparty pluralism. She concluded that "there is no doubt now that the USSR was an empire in which diverse ethnic and social groups were held together with the help of total control and engineered (economic) disasters . . . one of the main sources of instability are inter-ethnic conflicts [155]. The split of the Soviet Union dramatically changed the national identity of people . . . the reconstruction of national identity which was suppressed not only during the seventy years of Soviet power, but for a long time before in the Russian (Czarist) empire as well." She posed the question [158]: "can one exclude the possibility that being promoted and used as a means of power redistribution, as a weapon in a fight for power, tolerance in ex-Soviet societies will mean (anything) more than yesterday's political fashion?"

This analysis may be relevant to the durability of the toleration that has been displayed towards multiculturalism in the West. In France, which has more than three million third world immigrants [TM 10 May 97], the extremist neo-Nazi National Front took control of four large towns, and its share of the vote in the presidential elections increased from 0.74 percent in 1974 to more than fifteen percent [TM 11 Feb. 97]. It is said to be attracting sophisticated voters who, although they deny being racist, are opposed to multiculturalism, immigration, mass unemployment, corruption, Europeanisation and significantly, the loss of traditional French rights and beliefs.

NOTES

Hockenos, P. *Free to Hate.* London: Routledge.1993. 314.
Ignatieff, M. *Blood and Belonging.* London: BBC Books and Chatto and Windus. 1993.
Koshechkina, TM. *Political Tolerance—From General Principles to Concrete Application.* M.A. Dissertation. Canterbury: University of Kent, 1992. 150.
Ibid. 155.
Ibid. 158.
Mestrovic, S.G. *The Balkanisation of the West—The Confluence of Post-Modernism and Post Communism.* London: Routledge, 1994. 176.
Ibid. 192 .
O'Leary *The Fate of Nations.* (Analysis). BBC Radio 4. 5 May 1994..
Ruane, J. and Todd, J. *The Dynamics of Conflict in Northen Ireland.* Cambridge: Cambridge University Press. 1997.
Tudjman, F. *Nationalism in Contemporary Europe.* New York: Columbia University Press. 1981. 245 and 248.

12

The Education and
Understanding Fallacy

Education, together with family, role models, and peer pressure, are the principal influences by which a sociocultural system can be impressed upon receptive youth before their critical faculties and experience have fully developed. This process of socialisation makes a social being out of human beings born cultureless. Those wishing to promote an ideology will seek to do this through "education led" social engineering, through schools and universities. As with the Jesuits, it was recognised that if one can seduce and convert the young, one can be sure of the adult. Ideologues recognised that this would control the future—hence the Hitler Youth, the Italian fascist Nazionale Belilla Youth, and the Russian Communist Young Pioneers. In Britain prior to WW1, the schools of the established Church reinforced the social order, and imparted religious and moral values. Today, state-financed education is an effective tool of governments. Those opposing the "battle for hearts and minds" will call it propaganda, indoctrination, "spinning," information management, or brainwashing.

Knowledge has two interactive components. One is cognitive and passive, which can be improved by better understanding, the other is reactive and affective/emotional, which can remain relatively unaffected by better knowledge. It can assume that an opinion is due to ignorance, and if so, education will change it. Education and understanding is cognitive inasmuch that it recognises that there can be a discontinuity between simply knowing and understanding a difference, and accepting it. Whilst understanding requires knowledge, knowledge in and of itself does not necessarily result in understanding. In any case, education cannot be complete without experience. In the same way that familiarity does not necessarily breed affection, and although having an interest is a necessary condition, it is not sufficient if it does not also satisfy a genuine need. A fine line also exists between neutral educa-

145

tion and positive promotion, as evidenced by the political controversy over the repeal of Section 28 in Britain, banning the teaching of homosexuality in schools. Cosmopolitans believe that benefits follow from an improved knowledge and understanding of other cultures. They claim that if the extremes of uncoordinated chaos or imposed uniformity and conformity are to be averted, cultures will have to evolve a new level of understanding of themselves, and toleration of others. This may be so with global culturalism, but it is not the answer to cultural separatism, within the confines of a national society.

The unquestioning acceptance of the supposed benefits arising from better understanding takes an unrealistic view of human nature, and it raises the issue as to whether toleration can be taught and learnt. Although understanding another culture may remove misconceptions, provide explanations and insights, and facilitate negotiation by empathising with a belief, custom, or practice, it does not necessarily lead to their uncritical acceptance or toleration. There is evidence [Koshechkina 1992: Preface] that although education "still remains significant for general [political] tolerance, but has no significance for applied tolerance," meaning that although it will be supported generally, this is not necessarily the case when it is applied to a specific or personal situation. Arguably, this conclusion also applies to other fields of tolerance. For example, moral philosophers have a good knowledge and understanding of the abortion issue, but either oppose it for theocratic beliefs, or support it for pro-choice reasons. It also raises the question as to whether Western values of democracy, toleration, and individualism are culture bound. A homophobic heterosexual could be educated in homosexual practices, but it does not necessarily follow that he will become homophilic or more tolerant, he may still feel revulsion, namely, an absolute interdiction.

Flew [1995:3] proposes that "if the urgently needed critique of the documents and doctrines of Islam is to be produced and published, then the work will have at least to be begun by rationalists and humanists in the countries where the same job was done for Christianity. Once it is well and truly begun we may hope that the influences of Muslim immigrations into these countries will not be felt exclusively by the host countries but will be felt also in the countries from which they came." The former Archbishop of York [TM 18 June 00] has accused the Islamic faith of refusing to allow internal criticism of itself, or the Koran, and being unable to deal with social and political systems not under its control. An objective of this study should be to disentangle what it is claimed by Muslim apologists and fundamentalists as to what the Koran says, with the way in which the religion is seen to be practised. Flew's proposal might help to avoid unjustifiably demonising an entire faith followed by up to about one billion Muslims worldwide. A provocative culture block which education and understanding will do nothing to reconcile was expressed by Jehangir Mohammed, the deputy leader of the radical Muslim parliament in Britain, as reported by Gareth Smyth [1996:31]: "We [Muslims] must establish our own political base outside the political system . . . Islam is a very modern political system. Democracy is the Western style of representation—which we don't accept. In Islam we represent the will of God." The Muslim parliament bans members of British political parties from joining its ranks and rejects all "establishment" attempts at dialogue. A prominent Pakistani mufti, or scholar, allegedly decreed [TXT 21 Aug. 99] that all Muslims should boycott the U.S. and its Western allies, and that "the shedding of American blood is permissible."

The 1948 UN Universal Declaration enjoins its signatories to "promote understanding, tolerance, and friendship among all nations, racial and religious groups." Ervin Laszlo [1993: ix and 185] sees UNESCO's role not as diluting individual cultures, but blending regional and national cultures, saying, "We are one species; one family. We are many societies; many cultures. Can we live as one (society) even while we are many? The answer to this question is central to human survival at the dawn of the twenty first century . . . in viable systems, differentiation is always balanced by integration . . . we have much 'world diversity' but little world order. How can the chaos that is always attendant on unordered diversity be averted or overcome? How can diversity become integrated without becoming flattened? How can we find the oneness in multiplicity that humanity needs to discover if it is to survive? . . . it is ultimately culture that decides the order or disorder of this world. If we are to evolve into a global species, we must evolve a global culture—a culture that is not globally uniform but globally rich, and globally united in its tolerance, co-operation and common purpose." Some would think that this is a tall order.

Laszlo [203] wants UNESCO to become "the crucial and as yet still undeveloped information link between the world's cultures—a link capable of ensuring an unbiased flow of information, able to promote dialogue without fear and to convey the understanding that is the pre-condition of unity within the world's diversity . . . [201–2] a [global] cultural message can create understanding and solidarity; it can enhance diversity with new found unity. Unity is very different from uniformity; it is not based on the eradication of differences, but on their integration within a harmonious whole . . . As uncoordinated diversity spells chaos, so undifferentiated uniformity spells not merely stultifying boredom but also critical instability: monoculture in society . . . may seem efficient in the short term but it is unsustainable. Humanity needs diversity and it needs unity. Presently the great cultures are a source of diversity, but they are not—not yet—an inspiration for unity."

Laszlo's analysis of culturalism is valid, but not its solution. There is little evidence to support the assertion that cultural diversity, at least globally, has at least to date, been uniquely responsible for chaos. Nor is the suggestion that a monocultural hegemonic society is unsustainable—in fact particularly since the 1990s, the reverse appears to be the trend. What first needs to be demonstrated is that the conflicts in existing multicultural/ethnic states are capable of resolution. It is not obvious that diversity needs to be, should be, or indeed can be, co-ordinated, and whether any organisation is capable of doing this. The dissemination of unbiased information on differing cultures is unrealistic, because aspects of some cultures are repugnant to other cultures, and provocative information would have to be sanitised or censored. There could also be doubts about UNESCO's objectivity and impartiality—because of its anti-Western bias, the United States left UNESCO in 1984 as did Britain in 1985, but rejoined in 1997. Moreover, the UN does not improve its credibility in the field of education, by employing a circus of pop/film star and other celebrities as "goodwill ambassadors" for issues ranging from safe sex to nuclear disarmament.

In discussing ethnic revival, Anthony Smith [1981:3–4] argues that "Communications, too, have only accentuated ethnic antagonisms and heightened the visibility of national differences. Far from creating a single world culture, the mass media have been ready instruments of state authorities, who have used them to mould or instil a national culture in every citizen and every household . . . Travel and education can just as easily bring home to men and women their cultural differences and reinforce their national loyalties as erase them; and all too often, this is what has happened So that, far from being merely transitional phenomena, the nation-state and nationalism have become more firmly entrenched within the world order, even in the most advanced industrial societies. Indeed, within Europe itself, in the industrial heartlands of the West, we are witnessing a resurgence of ethnic nationalism in the wake of an era of massive economic growth." Contrary to the cosmopolitan claims made for modern information technology, satellite television and the unregulated Internet may well strengthen, rather than weaken, ethnic and cultural affinities globally between expatriates, clinging nostalgically to a culture which they left behind. If so, it will weaken the likelihood of assimilation, and promote rather than eliminate separatism.

It may be that the solipsism brought about by television and computers means that people no longer need to or want to communicate with their immediate and different "neighbours" and prefer arms length cultural contacts. It seems that whenever globalisation might eradicate national identities, there follows an ever-increasing yearning, at least for the cultural past. Sean Connery, the Scottish film actor, after forty-five years of self-imposed tax exile, and not registered as a British resident since 1973, gives about £50,000 each year to the SNP and has appeared in their political broadcasts [STM 4 July 99]. Ireland is a country that has in the last few decades forged a new identity as a modern, industrial, and increasing secular European state. Nevertheless the myth of a Gaelic country of idealised bucolic, almost backward insularity, finds a ready audience in the Irish diaspora [STM 12 Nov. 96], and is being enhanced by the Irish Internet [BBC 2 10 July 95].

An international organisation that believes improved knowledge and understanding will create an integrated global community is the British Commonwealth. It has fifty-four member states, representing about one third of the world's population, of different races, cultures and populations, ranging from a few thousand to several hundred millions. Its members have a spectrum of political systems from Western style industrialised democracies to de facto one party states and near-dictatorships with basic economies. It meets biennially with the British monarch as its titular Head—who vacuously has "no strict constitutional significance . . . [but] remains crucial as the symbolic link uniting all member states." This allows the monarch to continue posturing as the head of a sort of multiracial neo-Empire of highly differentiated members, reinforced every Christmas with a "message to the Commonwealth." The banal principles enshrined in its 1991 Harare [Zimbabwe] Declaration [Commonwealth Secretariat 1995:47–52] pledge its members to pursue Western principles including "the protection and promotion of democracy and the equality of women." Paradoxically, sixteen years on, nowhere were these principles being violated more than in Zimbabwe itself. Some of its member states, such Nigeria, Sierra Leone, Zambia, Zimbabwe and now Fiji, and before that Uganda and Kenya, could not behave more differently. Blair is said to believe that the Commonwealth uses time and money on business over which it can have little influence [TM 15 Nov. 99], but at best this international "talking shop" serves to dilute divisions.

Other cultures can only be understood through values and concepts that are derived from one's own culture. This is not intended to justify ethnocentrism based on Western values, which it is assumed ought to be universal, but that one's own culture is preference based. It is this compelling preference which makes it difficult for a society to tolerate some aspects of other cultures, and is a cogent reason why multiculturalism can be divisive and lead to conflict. The most worthwhile outcome of better knowledge, might be a wider recognition of the differences between global cultures and their different value systems. Although some aspects of other cultures might be judged to be better or worse relative to indigenous values, they should be seen as being intrinsic features and specific to that particular region and/or ethnicity. Value should not lie principally in its moral relativity as judged by Western standards, but in relation to its origins and relevance to the political, religious, and socioeconomic life of that particular society. It should be recognised that each society has its own culture, practised within its own cultural/national boundaries. Moreover, taking the moral high ground on global issues can be provocative and culturally imperialist, and no messianic attempt should be made to export (or to import) a culture.

Wittgenstein observed that one can only genuinely understand and value a culture if one grows up and lives within it—locked into a given consensus of morality and values. Bassnett [1997: xviii] also notes that "someone who is born into a culture and grows up in it will necessarily have a different perspective from someone who learns about that culture in their adult life . . . although anyone can study a culture there are fundamental differences between those who see themselves as 'native' and those ('outsiders') who are encountering the culture though another language." It is also true that if an individual has a connection with the history of his past, it will at the very least influence his view of the future.

Professor Edward Said (1995) argues that the West understands Oriental cultures and history only in Western political and not pure terms, and distinguishes between politicised and pure knowledge: "[11] For if it is true that no production of knowledge in the human sciences can ever ignore or disclaim its author's involvement as a human subject in his own circumstances, then it must also be true that for a European or American studying the Orient there can be no disclaiming the main circumstances of his actuality; that he comes up against the Orient as a European or American first, as an individual second. And to be a European or an American in such a situation is by no means an inert fact . . . [26–7] Three things have contributed to making even the simplest perception of the Arabs and Islam into a highly politicized, almost raucous matter: one, the history of popular and anti-Arab and anti-Islamic prejudice in the West, which is immediately reflected in the history of Orientalism; two, the struggle between the Arabs and Israeli Zionism; and its effects upon American Jews as well as upon both the liberal culture and the population at large; three, the almost total absence of any cultural position making it possible either to identify with or dispassionately discuss the Arabs or Islam." Said is highlighting the perceived support and lack of sympathy by the West of Palestinian self-determination, no doubt conditioned by the fact that he is an American Palestinian Christian Protestant Arab. More generally, Said's argument is a criticism of the value of arms length cultural education.

Universities have traditionally been seen as institutions principally devoted to the transmission of their national culture. Cultural studies in academia are worthwhile for specialists, but not by non-specialists. There is much to be learnt and enjoyed from the study of the aesthetics of other cultures—their art, music, and literature. These appeal to the sentient side of human nature and do not conflict with the student's indigenous culture and values. This is not to argue that an improved knowledge of other cultures is valueless as most knowledge is worthwhile, but practical limits are imposed by time and resources, namely the difference between "what should be" and "what can be."

There is however, a positive commercial incentive to understand other cultures as a pre-requisite to international trade. Nevertheless, there can be a dichotomy between the acceptance of whatever leads to economic prosperity, versus an enhanced tenacity in retaining the non-commercial aspects of an indigenous culture. Asian and Arab elites are knowledgeable about the West—where many have been educated. Although they belong to a global professional and commercial elite, they remain firmly rooted in the preservation of their own political and social cultures, and are not divorced from the bulk of their non-elite society. Samuel Huntington [1996:76] recognises that "In the early phases of change, Westernization promotes modernisation. In the later phases, modernization promotes de-Westernization and the resurgence of indigenous culture in two ways. At the societal level, modernization enhances the economic, military, and political power of the society as a whole, and encourages the people of that society to have confidence in their culture and to become culturally assertive. At the individual level, modernization generates feelings of alienation and anomie as traditional bonds and social relations are broken and leads to crises of identity to which religion provides an answer."

The Swann report [1985:36–7], being a multicultural integrationist study, saw education as a means to counter racism, and to promote multiculturalism-"[the schools] should be capable of leading to change by creating an overall unity of purpose which will encompass the concept that to be British you do not have to have a white skin nor to have family origins only in this country . . . Much of what we recommend will require a fundamental shift in attitude [of teachers] . . . this will involve expenditure in 'psychological' terms over and above the direct financial outlay needed." This obligatory shift in attitudes might be perceived by some teachers as patronising, brainwashing, and/or an infringement of their autonomy.

In an earlier report, Lord Scarman [1981:104] recorded that criticisms "chiefly voiced by West Indian parents were . . . [the] lack of understanding by teachers of the cultural background of black pupils; and failure of the [school] curriculum sufficiently to recognise the value of the distinctive cultural traditions of the various ethnic communities." No explanation was offered as to the supposed benefits of this trans-culturalization or to whom it is valuable. Scarman also said [105] that "teachers must, however, be warned against a danger of a 'reverse racialism' in attributing all the ills of black people to exploitation by white people. A balanced approach, in this, as in much else, is needed."

The Swann report [772–3] on education recommended that "we are in favour of a non denominational and undogmatic approach to religious education . . . [and concluded that] there should be no conflict between the role of the schools in providing religious education and the role of the community institutions in providing religious instruction." This would appear to

152   **The Twilight of Britain**

have been a neat way of dealing with multicultural diversity. In any event, the Muslim community rejected multi-faith education in state schools [DM 5 Feb. 96], with the Head of the Birmingham Moslem Welfare Adssociation and a parent-governor describing it as a "confusing mish-mash . . . It ends up as a dilution of their faith, they end up with no faith at all." The outcome of multi-faith education can be religious relativism, and as with cultural relativism, all beliefs and values would be deemed to be equal, with confused young people rejecting them all, and becoming indifferent or amoral. On the other hand, religious denominational schools lend themselves to ethnic separatism.

NOTES

Bassnett, S. (Ed.) *Studying British Cultures.* London: Routledge, 1997. xviii.
Commonwealth Secretariat. *The Commonwealth Yearbook 1993–1994.* London: Stationery Office, 1995. 47–52.
Flew, A. "The Menace of Islam." In *The New Humanist.* vol. 11, no. 3. August 1995. 3.
Koshechkina, T. *Political Tolerance—From General Principle to Concrete Application.* M.A. Dissertation. Canterbury: University of Kent, 1992 Preface.
Laszlo, E. (Ed.) *The Multicultural Planet.* Oxford: One World Publications, 1993. ix–185.
Ibid. 201–3.
Huntington, S.P. *The Clash of Civilisations and the Remaking of World Order.* New York, Simon and Shuster, 1996. In *Decline of The West* Book Review. McNeill, W.H.
New York Review. 9 January 1997. 19.
Said, E.W. *Orientalism.* London: Penguin Books, 1995. 11 and 26–7.
Scarman, Lord. *The Brixton Disorders 10–12 April 1981.* London: Stationery Ofice, 1981. 104.
Scruton, R. "Homosexuality and the Liberal Consesus." In *Morality and Religion in Liberal Democratic Societies.* Anderson and Kaplan. (Eds.) London: Paragon House, 1991.
Smith, A.D. *The Ethnic Revival.* Cambridge: Cambridge University Press, 1981. 3–4, 36–7.
Ibid. 772–3.
Smyth, G. *On Mohammed's Side.* London: New Statesman. 1996. 31.

13

The Fiction of Global Idealism, Cosmopolitanism, and the United Nations

Both the UN and the failed League of Nations set up after WW2 and WW1 embodied the ideal of global cosmopolitanism, mankind, and an "international community." The credibility of the UN is relevant to multiculturalism to the extent of its ability to prevent or resolve ethno-national conflicts; the effectiveness or otherwise of its international agreements and its military intervention; its universal human rights and refugee conventions; and whether it can be an effective promoter of global cultural cosmopolitanism. Given that it has no powers of enforcement and in spite of its resolutions which can sometimes be little more than an expression of disapproval, the UN is virtually impotent without the support of the U.S. and NATO. Its fifteen-member Security Council, whose permanent members are the USA, Britain, Russia, China, and France have a veto and act largely in their own self-interest. A particular issue at present, debated by David Luban [1985:238], is the situation of humanitarian intervention or liberal imperialism, including the waging of war on other nation-states and breaching their sovereignty to enforce universal basic human rights. A justification claimed for this is that it is permitted under international law to restore democracy, and was used by the United States for its intervention in Panama in 1989. Shaw [1997:803] says that "apart from the problem of defining a democracy, such a proposition is not acceptable in international law today in view of the clear provisions of the UN Charter." Sometimes a "democratically" elected government can subsequently behave undemocratically, as in Nazi Germany and some member states of the British Commonwealth. What is suspect is that intervention will be influenced by the geo-political interest of the enforcer.

This scepticism is regrettable, but its validity should be recognised not only in respect of the internal security and sovereignty of nation-states, but with regard to the UN's idealised and far from universally enforced "standard setting" Charter and Human Rights and Refugee Conventions. The UN monitors these obligations in a two-tier manner, sometimes to the detriment of the sovereignty and cultural hegemony of its conforming member states. The UN Committee on the Elimination of Racial Discrimination recently [TM 23 Aug. 00] criticised Britain's record on racial attacks and asylum seekers, demanding that "more should be done." It published its report before sending a copy to the government. A UN Committee on Children's Rights issued a report accusing Britain of seriously breaching the 1991 Convention, ratified by 171 countries [DM 28 Jan. 95]. It included members from Burkina Faso, Zimbabwe, the Philippines and Brazil. In Western societies, this causes an increasing tension between the self-evident claims of their own nationals, and its obligations to illegal migrants and bogus refugees claiming their universal rights.

The 1945 UN Charter established a guideline standard-setting for a stable international order and justice, and a foundation for human rights. The idealism of the immediate post-WW2 era was that the UN would resolve conflicts, but this soon faded with the Cold War and adverse experience. As with the League of Nations, which failed to deter Japan, Italy, Germany and the USSR, the UN cannot be a guarantor of the sovereignty of a state, and its moral influence counts for little with those countries whose culture and priorities differ. Nevertheless, it provides a convenient forum to make judgements and to imply legitimacy on those international conflicts on which it formulates resolutions. Its specialised agencies have been effective in global environmental and health matters, and in a humanitarian role, albeit sometimes abused by its recipients because of its perceived politicised dimension. However, it lacks the unequivocal political support and the resources to resolve conflicts, to impose its resolutions, and to compel compliance, and its peacekeepers risk being taken as hostages, as occurred with 500 British peacekeepers in Sierra Leone [STM 4 June 00].

The General Assembly that makes resolutions had, at the last count, in excess of 210 member states, each having a vote—which means that the United States has the same voting power as say tiny Monaco, which joined in 1993, and Antigua, which has a population of 70,000 and is effectively owned by a Texas billionaire [TM 31 July 00]. Decisions sometimes require a simple majority, although on important issues a two-thirds majority is needed, so the Afro-Asian-Arab voting bloc can marginalise the West. The UN borders on bankruptcy and is under intense pressure to reinvent itself. By 1997 [TM 17 Nov. 97] the U.S. owed $1.3 billion, or sixty percent of its dues, to the UN. It also required [TM 12 June 97] the UN to reduce the U.S. contribution from twenty-five percent to twenty percent of the UN budget, reflecting the U.S. share of world GDP (Gross Domestic Product). In 1999 [TM 16 Nov. 99] Clinton signed legislation authorising the payment of $926 million (£570 million), Because Congress said that the UN bureaucracy is riddled with waste and corruption, it finally agreed to this compromise and demanded in return that the UN accept this as full payment of American dues, provided that $385 million of foreign family planning aid is not used to promote abortion. Senator Jesse Helms warned the Security Council against trespassing on American sovereignty and that the UN must accept U.S. proposals for reform or risk extinction, and listed UN failures in Bosnia, Kosovo and Iraq [TM 21 Jan. 00]. The irony is that the UN has been seen by much of the non-Western world and by Soviet Russia and China as existing primarily to give legitimacy and respectability to Western geo-politics, and a fashioning of the world in the Western image.

Healey [1989:99] concluded long before the demise of the Communist bloc that a nation-state cannot rely on world order to guarantee its sovereignty and security: "In a world of nation-states, order could not be maintained by (international) law alone; nor could treaty obligations by themselves guarantee how governments would behave in a crisis. The League of Nations had failed to prevent nations from breaking its Charter by resorting to war; and the alliances which followed its failure, had been ignored by their members when their obligations fell due." Interestingly, the covenant of the League of Nations contained guarantees for minority rights, which were used by Germany to justify its eastward expansion. Healey [115] had no more faith in federalism: "Europe's history of separate national existence has produced clearly defined interest groups. When such groups do exist, no written [federal] constitution can by itself compel them to act against their perceived interests." This was demonstrated by the failure of the first (Carrington) "peace plan" in Yugoslavia, which the European Commission rejected in 1992. Laura Silber and Allan Little [1995:222] observed "Thus the EC's (European Commission) first confident experiment in common foreign policy-making ended in a shambles, the Community's own carefully formulated legal and diplomatic mechanisms shot down by old-fashioned political expediency." Since the end of WW2 the evidence is that federal or composite states are less stable. Although communication technology may provide better knowledge, the political, social, racial, and cultural barriers remain intact.

The United States was a principal promoter of the UN at its inception, and during the Cold War used it to good effect. Ethical foreign policies can be seen as being geo-politically and economically selective with self-serving double standards, and having an instrumental purpose in undermining authoritarian regimes. Civil rights movements can become subsumed into terrorism. Ulster indicated that without outright war, a terrorist organisation, even if it amounts to only a few hundreds, namely the "army" of a minority of a minority, can only be contained, and cannot be defeated. The one-time adverse perception of terrorism has been undermined, because recent world events have shown that erstwhile terrorists who are indistinguishable from civilians become "freedom fighters," who then become "representatives" demanding independence—one man's patriot is another man's terrorist. Some terrorist groups finance their operations with the proceeds of crime. Terrorism cannot be morally right, but the political reality is that violence or the threat of it works. It "gets one noticed," and criminality is often rewarded. To "solve" the ethno-national conflict in Ulster, violence was effectively legitimised, and the serial concessions made for three years to the paramilitaries after the 1998 Good Friday Agreement obtained nothing in return, with IRA arms said to be that of two army battalions and nearly three tons of explosives [TM 7 Aug. 01]. After renewed and strenuous efforts in July 2001 by the British and Irish prime ministers, Sinn Fein could not fulfil their equivocal obligation under the 1998 Good Friday Agreement. This was "to use any influence they may have to achieve decommissioning of all paramilitary arms within two years." Ulster could, for the foreseeable future, become as dangerous and unstable as Israel and Palestine. Hard line terrorists may feel no obligation to conform to the terms negotiated by their diplomatic representatives or a mediator, let alone an arbitrator, and are the "empty chair" at negotiations. In Ulster, the "armed struggle" by the Official IRA, was continued by the Provisional IRA and the INLA (Irish National Liberation Army), which was taken over by the Real IRA and the Continuity IRA. Without violence and the resulting media interest, Ulster would never have become an "issue" with the British public. Terrorism condoned by morally ambivalent sympathisers can neuter the resources of international diplomacy and domestic democracy. Ex-patriates in the West can fund civil wars in their country of origin. For example, there are said to be more than 450,000 Sri Lankan Tamils living abroad, contributing £1.25 million per month worldwide, including 50,000 in Britain contributing what is believed to be £0.25 million a month, most of which funds the conflict. The Home Secretary, using his powers under the new Terrorism Act 2000 [DT 01 March 01] has published a list of twenty-one militant groups from around the world which he proposes to ban from Britain. Their activities include maintaining offices, fundraising, recruiting people to travel abroad to be active in terrorism, and many members use London for transferring money for terrorist actions. Sixteen of these are Islamic groups from the Middle East, Turkey and Kashmir. They include the al-Qaeda group led by Osama bin Laden, which attacked New York and US embassies in Nairobi and Dar es Salaam in 1998, the Islamic army of Aden, the Basque separatist group ETA, and the separatist Tamil Tiger group.

Arguably the dubious legality of NATO's humanitarian intervention or moral war in Kosovo could be seen as modern day neo-imperialism. Military intervention has so far seemingly been restricted to smaller nation-states, such as Kosovo, in which the West has a regional, but not a global interest.

Nevertheless this risked the resumption of the Cold War with Russia, and was not necessarily and unequivocally in the national interest either of the U.S. or Britain. Reportedly [TM. 26 Nov.99] intervention in Yugoslavia had, up until that time, cost $11 billion in warfare alone, with maybe another $60 billion in damage. In Kosovo about eighty percent of the war effort was American and about ten percent British, even though there are nineteen NATO member states. During its later stages, it remained unlikely that most of these other member states would allow their ground troops to be used.

The United States is the member state which the UN sub-contracts to implement its resolutions, and has the capability of quickly putting large numbers of peacekeepers on the ground in distant places. It is not surprising that with the number of intractable ethno-national conflicts in the world and the accusation of cultural imperialism (and now war crimes), that the United States is rethinking its post-Cold War role as the international peace keeper, the crusader for democracy, and the guardian of human rights. Extremist militia groups in the United States believe that the UN poses the greatest take-over threat to its sovereignty. After the 1993 debacle in Somalia, the U.S. became disillusioned and has not continued as the UN global military enforcer of mission-creeping UN resolutions outside of NATO and Western Europe. Subsequently, and in 1994, President Clinton issued a directive for a new U.S. peacekeeping policy, and did not commit U.S. ground troops in Rwanda. Moreover, it is alleged that in the first three years of the Balkans civil war that the U.S. engaged only rhetorically, and not diplomatically or militarily, in the UN peacekeeping operation [BBC 2 24 June 01]. Although Europe had learnt that there is no future in fighting someone else's civil war, this policy was not applied to the Balkans. This was deemed to be part of Europe under NATO, but it did apply to Chechnya, Sierra Leone, and East Timor, to which the U.S and Britain provided only token support—in Britain's case, Gurkha mercenaries, or to other independence movements such as the Kurds, and the eighteen year civil war in Sri Lanka in which 64,000 have died [TM 25 July 10].

There is an accusation of colonialism, inasmuch that Britain declined a UN request to send combat troops to Sierra Leone. Troops were sent to help evacuate British, Commonwealth, and EU citizens with the Foreign Secretary, saying that they were not joining the failed non-Western UN peacekeeping force in a combat role—because he believes that the African states should send more peacekeepers. The Security Council proposed to increase the peacekeeping force from 13,000 to 20,000 to "decisively counter" the rebels [TM 24 Aug. 00]. The Conservative party see Sierra Leone as yet another potential UN mission creep into a civil war, as had occurred in Bosnia and Kosovo. The United States became involved in Vietnam with an initial policy of detached support by logistic assistance, weapons supply and military advisers. However, British military "trainers" have been provided and there are increasing numbers of British service personnel in and around Sierra Leone after the proposed withdrawal of 3,000 Indian and 1,800 Jordanian troops from the UN force. The number of UN peacekeepers around the world now totals more than 37,350 [TM 24 Aug. 00]. Britain now has about 8,300 peacekeepers in Bosnia/Kosovo [TM 9 Nov. 99]. The United States could be moving away from globalism towards disengagement, or at least to short-term or regional responses. This demise of the Pax Americana towards an ungrateful world parallels the demise of the Pax Britannica after Suez. After the debacle of its global political idealism in Vietnam, probably the only reason why the United States (or the West) would commit its ground troops to a war other than to defend its own territory would be if other vital interests were at stake—such as during the 1992 Desert Storm campaign. The 1995 Dayton Peace Accord, which ended the forty-four-month conflict in Yugoslavia after the failure of the UN had to be enforced by NATO.

The International (UN) War Crimes Tribunal for the former Yugoslavia, set up in 1993 by the Security Council in the Hague under Articles 2 to 5 of the 1949 Geneva Convention, is an ad hoc court. It has criminal jurisdiction only over individuals, and has a number of legal anomalies [TM. 17 June 99]. It has twelve judges from as many nations who make the rules, hear appeals, and decide the verdict, and like the UN has no powers of enforcement and its processes are prolonged. It is a compromise between *realpolitik* and justice by virtue of its mix of legal and political objectives, but many of the principal perpetrators still remain free. It is conceivable that if the Allies had lost WW2, Western political and military leaders could have been tried for committing war crimes. The ad hoc Tribunal set up in Rwanda was described by the UN watchdog as a management "shambles" [TM 13 Feb. 97]. It took four years to secure its first conviction (a guilty plea), and since then has concluded only seven trials in two years [TM 26 Sept. 00]. There are still thirty-five defendants awaiting trials, which at the present rate of progress will take years to complete [TM 22 Aug. 00]. A U.S. Supreme Court Justice highlighted the realpolitik dilemma saying [TM 13 Sept. 00] that "The need to stabilise a new democratic regime in the short run may counsel against aggressive efforts to prosecute the perpetrators"—this can be by ignoring the issue, blanket amnesties, truth and reconciliation committees, or prosecuting minor offenders. To maintain order a new regime may have to make "deals' with the army and police of the previous regime to not arrest their war criminals. In Britain, out of the 380 investigations into Nazi war criminals in the 1990s, two were prosecuted and one convicted. [TM 6 Jan. 00]. Moreover, professional soldiers acting as UN peacekeepers do not like being seen as international mercenaries or facing the threat of prosecution as war criminals [TM 20 July 98]. The Rome 1998 Treaty [TM 10 April 01] required 120 countries to sign up by the end of 2000, and 137 had done so, including Britain and the United States. The proposed International Criminal Court will open in the Hague when sixty countries have ratified the statute. So far twenty-nine have done so, including international lightweights such as Mali, San Marino and the Marshall Islands, but China, Japan, India and Pakistan have not, and it is doubtful whether the U.S. Senate will ratify the agreement. The court would be empowered to prosecute those states that have accepted its jurisdiction in respect of three classes of crime: genocide, war crimes and crimes against humanity—this last category being capable of a wide interpretation.

Idealistic globalism is unlikely to be a powerful influence on the foreign policies of governments, but rather self-interest and particularisms, which are subject to the vagaries and incompatibilities of their domestic electorates. States have differing attitudes towards their ability and obligations to comply with international agreements when their national sovereignty and domestic interests are affected. When the UN identified a gross violation of human rights by the abduction of children from the black African tribes in the Sudan by the ruling Islamic fundamentalists in the North, the claim was flatly rejected by the Sudanese government. Schlesinger [1987:72] recognises that "Until nations come to such a common morality, there can be no world law to regulate the behaviour of states as there is law within nations to regulate the behaviour of individuals. Nor can international institutions—the League of Nations or the United Nations—produce by sleight of hand a moral consensus where none exists. World law must express world community; it cannot create it . . . [86] moral values do have a fundamental role in the conduct of foreign affairs. But, save in extreme cases, that role is surely not to provide abstract and universal principles for foreign policy decisions. It is rather to illuminate and control conceptions of national interest."

Those who advocate cosmopolitanism and universalism see themselves primarily as "citizens of the world" and wish to see the abandonment of particularity for universality. Nevertheless, Nussbaum says [1996:135] that "cosmopolitanism does not require, in any case, that we should give equal attention to all parts of the world. None of the major thinkers in the cosmopolitan tradition denied that we can and should give special attention to our own families and to our own ties of religious and national belonging. Cosmopolitans hold, moreover, that it is right to give the local an additional measure of concern." This begs the question as to the magnitude of the "additional measure." She uses a personal example [136–7]: "may I give my daughter an expensive college education, while children all over the world are starving and effective relief agencies exist?" and responds: "these are hard questions, and there will and should be much debate about the proper answers." She remains silent as to what is the "proper" answer. This illustrates the reductio ad absurdum of cosmopolitanism. Common sense and human nature dictate that responsibilities to family and friends come first, and global humanity comes last—as it always has been, cosmopolitanism notwithstanding. It might be remembered that just prior to WW1, a best selling book, *The Great Illusion*, was published, which argued that a major war was impossible because of global integration. Malcolm Waters [1995:126 and 136] says that a "globalized culture [would be] chaotic rather than orderly—it is integrated and connected so that the meaning of its components are 'relativised' to one another but it would not be unified or centralized . . . globalization does not necessarily imply homogenization or integration. Globalization merely implies greater connectedness and de-territorialization. The possibility arises therefore of an increased measure of ethnic pluralism but in which ethnicities are not tied to any specific territory or polity . . . it weakens the putative nexus between nation and state releasing absorbed ethnic minorities and allowing reconstitutions of nations across former state boundaries. This is especially important in the context of states that are confederations of minorities." An example might be an ethnic coalition between the blacks of the United States, the Caribbean, and Africa. Samuel Scheffler [1996:8] criticises the cosmopolitan "discrepancy between the humane values they largely share and the cold realities of current political life . . . [and] warns against a moralistic cosmopolitanism, which everywhere feels superior."

Intellectual migrants to the West may find that cosmopolitanism provides an answer to the identity question *who am I?* Once devoid of a national identity, a person becomes a "citizen of the world." Cosmopolitans will typically have been employed by a non-commercial and/or international organisation; their ancestry will be diverse by intermarriage; and they may have peripatetically migrated to different regions of the world, before retiring to their homeland. As Ignatieff [1994] comments, a cosmopolitan is "someone who's got a passport in his pocket," or preferably, dual nationality. Kymlicka [1995:133] has another view of citizens of the world (which also applies to some migrants): "Confronted by nationalists who care deeply about borders, and indeed who often wish to redraw them so as to create smaller units, many cosmopolitan liberals feel threatened and confused." For the nativist citizen, dual nationality implies a lack of commitment, and sees the cosmopolitan as someone who has been uprooted and seeks to mentally uproot others. Moreover, the wealthy cosmopolitan can avoid the tax regimes of his country of origin whenever convenient, and can always afford to return to his country of origin if need be.

McConnell [1996:79–80] warns that "cosmopolitanism may turn out to be more destructive than constructive. It is more likely to undermine coherent moral education, which in the real world is rooted in particular moral communities with distinctive identities, by substituting a form of moral education that is too bloodless to capture the moral imagination . . . A student who cares not a whit for his own culture's accomplishments is unlikely to find much value in the accomplishments of others. A student who has no religion is unlikely to respect the religious commitments of others. One who knows no heroes in his own land will feel nothing but contempt for the naivete of those who honour heroes elsewhere. Before a child can learn to value others he needs to learn to value." These remarks are also a criticism of any global eclectic culture.

"One World" cosmopolitans assert that human rights should not be contingent upon culture, tradition, place or time in history, which is valid, insofar that these relate only to basic rights. Nevertheless, the UN, the amorphous concepts of the "international community," and "world opinion" cannot enforce even basic human rights. Non-Western states criticise human rights campaigns as being an imperialist imposition of Western cultural values and priorities, notably those of liberal individualism. The global cultural relativist would argue that rights can only be understood and evaluated by reference to the rules and norms which make up that particular culture. Smith [1991:175] puts a case for "tiered" nationalism/cosmopolitanism: "It must be apparent by now that the chances of transcending the nation and superseding nationalism are at present slim. It simply is not enough to point to the powerfully transnational impact of the new economic, political and cultural forces at work today, nor to the various global inter-dependencies that they undoubtedly create. A growing cosmopolitanism does not in itself entail the decline of nationalism; the rise of regional culture areas does not diminish the hold of national identities. There is nothing to prevent individuals from identifying with Flanders, Belgium and Europe simultaneously, and displaying allegiance in the appropriate context; or from feeling [that] they are Yoruba, Nigerian and African, in concentric circles of [diminishing] loyalty and belonging. It is, in fact, quite common, and very much what one would expect in a world of multiple ties and identities." This observation is equally true of regions of Britain, who can identify themselves in the appropriate circumstances as Scottish, Welsh, Irish, or English, or British.

Since the threat of communism has receded, the West has moved away from a political stance of global idealism to realpolitik. Diplomatic concessions which began in the geopolitics of the Reagan era can be seen in the pragmatism towards authoritarian as distinct from totalitarian regimes. The authoritarian regime in China is tolerated, or rather has to be tolerated, because of the fear that its precipitation into democracy of which it has no tradition could result in instability, as occurred in the USSR. In the Middle East and in developing countries such as Singapore, Malaysia, and Indonesia, the authoritarian and nominally democratic regimes have been accepted because they provide political stability. The much-vaunted promise of the New Labour Party's "ethical" foreign policy did not lead to the revoking, which was said to be on legal grounds, of British arms export licences inherited from the previous administration for exporting to countries guilty of human rights abuses. Hong Kong, given the stability of 155 years of authoritarian but paternalistic British rule, became the world's eighth largest trading economy. The question may then be posed: "Which is the highest Benthamite 'good:' instant democracy or stability with economic prosperity?"

Global cosmopolitanism without a super-power enforcer cannot resolve or significantly influence a protracted, intense, or latent ethno-racial conflict. UN peacekeepers have become involved in ethno-national conflicts and civil wars where no peace exists, or is likely to exist, unless they enforce it and then maintain it. The UN was unable to prevent genocide in Yugoslavia, Rwanda, and elsewhere in the world, and accepted blame for the massacre in 1995 of 7,300 Muslims in the UN safe haven of Srebrenica in Bosnia [TM. 17 Nov. 99]. It then made the revealing comment that "We tried to keep the peace and apply the rules of peacekeeping when there was no peace to keep." In other words, the peacekeepers were not mandated to be peace enforcers. The UN has also accepted the blame for its failure in Rwanda in 1994 which cost 800,000 lives [TM 17 Dec. 99]. Rwanda symbolises for some the argument for leaving (Africa's) periodic tribal civil wars to resolve themselves. International intervention can be seen as a partisan political act which only serves to stabilise the endemically unstable and influences the balance of power. UN intervention sometimes does no more than stabilise a civil war, or limit external involvement, such as in Cyprus, without removing the underlying cause of the conflict. Some strategists believe that at times war should be given a chance, because it alone can resolve the problem. Otherwise, until one side is defeated, no lasting peace will be attained, if for no other reason than the combatants will conceal their military hardware until the peacekeepers have left. Conor Cruise O'Brien, the historian and politician, saw Zaire as semi-anarchic for many years and now completely so. He said [TM 19 Nov. 96] that "it should be allowed to assume such shapes as the energies and aspirations of its various peoples may eventually assign to it. The energies of international diplomacy should be confined to holding the ring and discouraging the internationalisation of the conflict."

NOTES

Healey, D. *The Time of My Life*. London: Michael Joseph, 1989. 99.
Ibid. 115 .
Ignatieff, M. *The Fate of Nations*. (Analysis) In O'Leary, BBC Radio 4. 5 May 1994.
Kymlicka, W. *Misunderstanding Nationalism*. (Book Review) *Dissent*. Winter 1995. 133.
Luban. D. "The Romance of the Nation-State." In *International Ethics* . Beitz, C.R., Cohen, M et al. (Ed.) Princeton: Princeton University Press. 238.

McConnell, M.W. "Don't Neglect the Little Platoons." In *For Love of Country—Debating the Limits of Patriotism*. Nussbaum, M.C. Cohen, J. Boston, Mass: Beacon Press, 1996. 79–80.

Nussbaum, M.C. "Reply." In *For Love of Country—Debating the Limits of Patriotism*. Boston: Beacon Press, 1996. 135.

Scheffler, S. "Family and Friends First." (Book Review) *For Love of Country—Debating the Limits of Patriotism*. Nussbaum, M. In *Times Literary Supplement*. 27 December 1996. 8.

Schlesinger, A.M. *The Cycles of American History*. London: Andre Deutsch, 1987. 72.

Ibid. 86.

Shaw, M.N. *International Law*. Cambridge: Cambridge Universitry Press. 1997. 803.

Silber, L and Little, A. *The Death of Yugoslavia*. London: Penguin and BBC Books, 1995. 222.

Smith, A.D. *National Identity*. London: Penguin Books, 1991. 175.

Waters, M. *Globalization*. 1995. 126 and 136.`

BBC2. *Correspondent—Allies or Lies?* 24 June 2001.

14

The Misappropriation of
Universal Human Rights

Human rights are normally understood to reflect a universal global morality requiring obligations to all humanity—the natural rights of all people, in all situations, and not to be withheld. In practice, this principle is not universally recognised throughout the non-ideal world, and never has been. Its abuse and partiality can undermine the sovereignty and cultural hegemony of the nation-states of the West, because multiculturalism can be acquired by strictly conforming to the "oughts" required by unqualified universal claim rights. It may, though, be argued that a nation-state, whilst rigorously maintaining the human rights of its own citizens, should not be duty or morally obligated, let alone capable of, attempting to enforce these rights outside of its own territory. Nor, in having regard to its own national interest, should it be obligated to harbour illegitimate asylum seekers claiming rights violation in their country of origin. A further contention is that some of the universal claim rights seemingly acceptable fifty or so years ago at the time of the UN Conventions are now outmoded, and should no longer be regarded as absolute and unchangeable—at least insofar as they give support to the unqualified and effectively unverifiable claims of migrants. These Conventions need to be revised to update their relevance and legitimacy in the changed circumstances of the millennium. Arendt [1958:279] observed that "no paradox of contemporary politics is filled with a more poignant irony than the discrepancy between the efforts of well-meaning idealists, who stubbornly insist on regarding as 'inalienable' those human rights, which are enjoyed only by citizens of the most prosperous and civilised countries, and the situation of the rightless themselves."

The principal feeder of multiculturalism are economic migrants and sham asylum seekers who are able to claim the same rights and benefits as citizen residents of the Western nation-states. Economic migrants on entry to the West allegedly having a "well-founded fear of being persecuted" simply claim asylum. The Balkans experience shows that the migration of refugees will continue after the situation in their home country has been normalised, or perhaps even after the threat has been removed or reversed. The culture of rights and the social benefits in their country of origin are often not remotely comparable or reciprocal. This occurs in reverse when Britons abroad find themselves in difficult situations. They often expect their own domestic standards of legal, social and moral treatment to apply in other cultures that do not recognise them. This has been the case with capital punishment for drug smuggling in Malaysia, or in Singapore with the prohibition on public speaking by foreigners or the dropping litter. Rights are globally diverse because the nations, races, and cultures of the world differ in their value systems, though regionally, some basic rights, obligations, and duties do have a degree of commonality. But the moral principles of the West are not absolute and fixed for all time. This is exemplified by the way in which the morality of issues concerning life and death are being up-dated and modified, taking account of discoveries in medical science and genetics and, to an increasing extent in Britain, on the prioritisation of health care resources.

It is contended that parts of the UN Conventions are outmoded, inasmuch that nation-states should only undertake to have a direct and recognised absolute responsibility for the basic natural rights of their own citizens, or at least to those of fully reciprocating member states. Given the diverse systems of cultural values across the world, can all mankind expect to adopt, and if need be, lay claim to, the Western culture of rights? And is the ethos of rights simply a particular facet of Western cultural imperialism? An ever-widening interpretation and extension of claim rights, which threaten the sovereignty of the nation-state, underlies much of the present concern and opposition in Britain to the political federalisation of Europe: "wants" can become "needs," and "needs" can become "rights." Britain is opposing making the EU's contentious Charter of Fundamental Rights legally binding. Human rights, at least in their idealised and universalised form, have been made increasingly untenable by rights-based, single-issue pressure groups. Like the British social security system devised in 1948, most Western governments have accepted that since then the world has radically changed, and have imposed limits on the welfare rights of their own citizens, let alone to the world at large—the age of unlimited resources is over.

The universalisation of rights gives rise to anomalies:

1. Declarations or Covenants of Human Rights have by definition to be formulated by an international body as standard setting principles. In order to have the necessary authority, these principles have to be

translated into systems of jurisprudence that may differ from nation to nation, otherwise they cannot be implemented. In practice therefore, these may or may not be subsequently recognised—in their entirety, incompletely, or not at all—in the diverse national domestic systems of jurisprudence. In the absence of this recognition, they become in effect, unenforceable and not universal.

2. Even within a given state and culture, the application of differing human rights may conflict with one another, or may even be mutually exclusive, and in practice their relative priority will have to be decided. The exercise of one right by some may result in harm being done to the rights of others. Human rights tend to be seen as being individualistic and dutiless, whereas a utilitarian account may not always perceive this outcome as being to the communal good of the majority.

3. Human rights are stated as general principles and may well be interpreted in an open-ended manner. In practice, wide-ranging interpretations are counter productive and a limit should be imposed on their application.

4. There is an implicit assumption that what is essentially the Western concept of human rights is universally the correct one. Other cultures may believe that these are really no more than the conventional beliefs of Western society, and are not applicable to their own particular values.

5. There is a tendency to extend the scope of human rights into the area of socioeconomics, which in some non-Western countries is clearly impractical, although migrants to the West will claim them.

Human rights are founded in Western culture, originating in: the Magna Carta 1215; Habeas Corpus 1679; Thomas Paine and John Locke; the English Bill of Rights of 1689; and the French Declaration of the Rights of Man and Citizens of 1789. Rights were originally intended to protect the autonomy of the individual against an autocratic state. In the Hobbsean tradition, natural rights did not impose duties on others, but in return for transferring an individual's authority to the state, provided a right to act in one's self-interest, even if this conflicted with the liberty rights of others. The later Lockean tradition of natural rights presumes that the individual has a basic right to life, liberty and property, and who has a reciprocal duty not to harm the life, liberty, and property of others. Further, it is the primary function of government to uphold these natural rights for all of its citizens. Locke recognised that some aspects of the liberty rights of individuals have to be surrendered to the state in return for its protection.

Flew [1988:4] suggests that "Like other currencies, the currency of rights has in recent years been subject to inflation . . . so the more that is said to be a matter of natural or universal human right, the less force any such particular claim will have . . . But since WW2 such Declarations . . . on the part of so many of the new signers totally insincere, have embraced ever-lengthening lists." He argues that it has been forgotten that rights are really about protecting the autonomy of the individual and that claims to rights have become vacuous and counter-productive and are subverting cultures. And there has been a subtle shift from protecting the autonomy of the individual to forcing equality on people.

Flew distinguishes between positive rights, which are essentially the right to be left alone and unharmed, and are equally valid at all times and in all places, and socioeconomic rights which are claims to be provided with various services and goods. He argues that claims to welfare rights should be challenged by questioning "At whose expense?" and "What is the basis of the obligation supposedly falling upon the unspecified providers of all these desired and desirable benefactions?. . . [and that] the total available resources could not satisfy even half of these fashionably proliferating welfare claims." Positive rights have correspondingly reciprocal and equal obligations, whereas welfare rights do not. If there are insufficient resources to provide welfare rights, then they must remain aspirational, the alternative being to compel the claimant to contribute—so diminishing his autonomy. A natural/basic right exists in the nature of things because it is deemed to be God-given, or because tradition has made it so. This is something that all individuals possess, irrespective of their nationality, race, religion, and culture, and whether or not it is recognised in their own society or in that of others. These positive or "first generation" rights are associated with life, liberty, and property. Socioeconomic rights, sometimes termed "second or third generation" rights, attach to whole groups or classes of people. Clearly there can be a conflict between a claim right made by an individual that is rejected because it is not in the best interests of the community, and the claimant who argues that it is his positive or basic right which must be universally acknowledged. The strict application of the European Convention for the benefit of alleged "victims" who were themselves gross victimisers can seem to be perverse and contrary to natural justice [DM 5 May/TM 5/18 May 01]. The families of IRA terrorists killed by security forces whilst blowing up a police station were awarded compensation by the ECHR. This was because of shortcomings in the proper procedures for ensuring accountability of agents of the state in terms of its transparency and effectiveness. In what was essentially a civil war, this meant having to disclose highly confidential intelligence information.

Basic human rights are inherited as positive rights by the citizens of many, but not all, nation-states, because they are recognised and enforced by the law of the land. Once a right has been sanctified by legislation, the state has a legal as well as a moral obligation to grant it without question. A feature of a legal right for the benefit of a minority is that the interests of the majority cannot be protected by a maximising utility evaluation, as might be the case if the right was only prima facie. Government institutions and NGOs (non-government organisations) are the targets for pressure groups who have, or claim that they have, a grievance because for them, the best outcome is for the state to abandon its neutrality and to intervene. It is a tactic of these special interest groups that as more legal rights are obtained, further rights are demanded, often on the grounds of precedent either at home or elsewhere. Lobbying groups with special pleadings tend to dilute a direct relationship between the electorate and their elected representatives, who otherwise become the agents of sectional interests.

The propagation of an ethos of universal human rights by the United States and the West during the Cold War, and the demise of colonialism, was not entirely altruistic or moralistic. It had, in part, a geopolitical motive in emphasising the authoritarianism and economic privations of the communist regimes, but with little risk then of extensive migration to the West. Some claims should not qualify as rights because they can be essentially aspirational. They assume that *ought* implies "can" and "will." These are claims people would like to have, or they perceive as being "needs." This weakens the notion that rights are absolute, and tends to debase their validity. Human rights campaigns do not have a universally accepted moral foundation and derive from a plurality of reasons, including geopolitical. The validity of univeralised claim rights is central to the issue of multiculturalism. Are universal "rightists" trying to engender a sense of self-flagellating guilt, or accepting the accusation of intolerance, discrimination, or racism on those nation-states who prioritise rights obligations of their own citizens? They may do this in order to preserve their own cultural hegemony or to prioritise their resources, but do not accept that these rights can be automatically claimed by other peoples. Well-meaning attempts to universalise the Western tradition of liberal individualist rights and values can be rejected by other societies as insidious cultural imperialism, meddling, interventionism, or intolerant conformity. Or they may suggest double standards or outright hypocrisy. Did it border on moralistic hypocrisy to impose a trade embargo in 1985 on the South African regime, when apartheid had also been practised in some parts of the United States before 1965? And because the West's commercial interests were now at stake, not to impose trade restrictions on China, which has a non-Western culture and is a gross abuser of human rights? The issue of animal rights typifies a political and cultural dilemma even within Western Europe. British culture is perceived as being kind to animals, and if the animals are cruelly treated, it can excite a reaction that belies the reserved British character. Some other cultures perceive such sensitivity as a luxury, and see the animal kingdom as a natural resource to be exploited. Nevertheless, even if the British electorate so expressly wished, its government would not be able to ban the cruelty in exporting live animals, because this would be contrary to overriding European law.

Conflicts between the prioritisation or hierarchy of rights can occur within the same state. In the United States, where basic rights are guaranteed by the Constitution, and also in Britain now that the 1998 Human Rights Act is in force, this is resolved by litigation or creative interpretation by the supreme judiciary. In the United States this sometimes involves extrapolation of the Constitution and can change with time. Nadine Strossen [1995:14], a one time president of the American Civil Liberties Union, opposes pro-censorship feminists in banning pornography, because "Women's rights (such as eliminating violence and discrimination) are far more endangered by censoring sexual images than they are by the sexual images themselves." Mestrovic [1994:10] argues that "The post-modern programme promoting organized tolerance is fundamentally flawed, and doomed to failure. This is because any and all organized systems of tolerance will automatically be intolerant of some groups and of all traditional cultures." This paradox occurs with discrimination claims, such as a white lesbian employer being accused of unfairly or racially discriminating against a black male employee. Single-issue groups will sometimes temporarily join forces to reinforce their claim to a common right. A well-intentioned government policy of discriminating in favour of minorities, and favours one racial/ethnic group, will not always satisfy the claims of another group. If the common "enemy" of the (white) mainstream group is losing its dominance, minorities can be equally prejudiced and intolerant of one another, as the violence between African-Americans and Latin-Americans, or between Sikhs and Muslims and Hindus, or between (African-Caribbean) blacks and (Nigerian) blacks has shown. In the 1992 Los Angeles riots, Arthur Hu [1992:13–4] found that Asians were "often a strategic target (of black violence) . . . [and that] "Korean entrepreneurs ran a 1 in 250 chance of being killed . . . about the same odds as a tour of duty in Vietnam." A Nigerian social worker, who was a former mayor of the London Borough of Wandsworth, said [DM 2 Dec. 00] "The sad reality is that there is no single black community. There are a number of communities of black people which are all too often violently prejudiced against each other, against ambitious Asians and against the host community." The Swann report [1985:27–8] also noted "instances of racist attitudes between ethnic minority groups . . . (and) actual racial attacks."

Peter Jones [1994: 223] observes that "If we shift our focus from a single society to the whole of humanity, [the] practical problem is magnified. If human rights are to be recognised and implemented across the entire globe, they have to secure a consensus amongst a much larger and much more diverse population and also across nation-states each of which is jealous of its sovereignty and independence. If the content of human rights is radically disputed, the attempt to impose any particular version of human rights upon all societies will seem little more than an exercise of power by some over others—an exercise of power that will be all the more resented because it will be conceived as violating the autonomy of societies and the sovereignty of political systems . . . [Although] there may not be a full worldwide agreement about any aspect of human rights, but there is at least very widespread acceptance of the idea of human rights and also a measure of agreement about their content . . . [Although] the lip-service that people pay to human rights is not always reproduced in their conduct."

This is true, but it leaves unresolved another important practical issue. Although a government clearly has a duty to uphold socio-economic claim rights for its own "local" citizens within its particular nation-state, to what extent if any, does it also have a duty to afford those same socio-economic rights to its non-citizen immigrants, originating from literally anywhere in the world? Thus, should the term "universal" apply only "locally," or should it also apply, or is it indeed practical for it to apply, to all people, wherever they originate from, and to wherever they choose to migrate to. The UN Convention on Refugees, at least as it is interpreted and applied by the British judiciary, clearly adopts the latter view.

Rights raise the dilemma both for the national and international polity of distinguishing between those issues which are the legitimate, rational, and practical concern of the governance of international or national society, and those which are the principally the concern of individuals and not of governments. Knee jerk claims to rights made under the abstract principles of equality, fairness, liberty, or justice have become as much a matter of sentiment as objectivity. These can allege discrimination and are often made litigiously to promote the objectives of minority social, political, ethnic, or religious groups, to replace toleration or to formalise consent. Rights phrased in abstract principles or guidelines may conflict, and in the EU may require legal interpretation by the majority opinion of a third party judiciary, namely, by the ECHR—although this is less likely now that Britain's Human Rights Act is now in force, which still has to take the ECHR's intepretation of human rights "into account" [TM 29 June 00]. The latest move is the European Charter of Fundamental Rights, which would commit the EU to its endorsement and its institutions to a binding commitment to the European Convention on Human Rights through the ECJ (European Court of Justice). Although a third party judiciary may claim to be neutral and objective, its interpretation of the law and the "spirit in which it was made" may be culture-bound, or reflect their domestic political tradition, and can lead to interpretative differences between domestic judges and those of international courts. Human rights have gone beyond the right of individuals to equality before the law, colour blind justice, and qualification by merit, into the sociopolitical arena of claim rights by any group or class, both national and international.

The rights ethic of the West is likely to continue to be misappropriated by migrants, unless the validity of the doctrine of "unqualified and universal claim rights" is rethought. Who would be entitled to claim which rights, what limits and entitlements should apply, and who (and under what circumstances), is obliged to honour them? Namely, those that apply to all human beings irrespective of their origin and identity, and those a society recognises only for its own citizens, and are inherent in their implied social citizenship contract. The French Declaration of 1789 for example, distinguished between the rights of man and the rights of citizens. The Home Secretary has argued [TM 2 March 00/DM 17 June 00], as does this discussion, that the 1951 UN Convention on the Status of Refugees should no longer apply without qualification, because it reflects the outmoded historical circumstances and the geopolitics post-WW2 and the Cold War.

Experience has shown that the acceptance of the rhetoric of rights by delegates at international forums, even if they are subsequently ratified, has not reflected the depth of political consensus or commitment by their present or future governments. Oppressive regimes pay lip service in international forums to declarations and conventions, but continue to detain, cleanse, torture, execute and "disappear" their dissidents. Mestrovic [1994:79–80] noted that in 1993 Vienna "In an atmosphere strangely removed from reality, the first World Conference on Human Rights in twenty five years opens here [Vienna] with a broad mandate to discuss human rights in the world—as long as it avoids naming any government known for abuses . . . Nor is any discussion expected of political prisoners in say, China or Cuba. Instead, 5,000 delegates from 111 countries will debate human rights in the abstract." It is ironic that most of the member states of the former Communist bloc (including Yugoslavia) took a pride in formally granting in their constitutions, but not in practice, explicit rights to their minorities. Saudi Arabia, although recently acceding to the 1984 UN Convention Against Torture and Other Cruel, Inhuman, and Degrading Treatment or Punishment, usually enters a reservation that no UN Treaty provision contravenes Islamic law. Japan has never signed this Convention. Israel has reportedly [TM 7 Aug. 99] used torture under its emergency powers. India has been accused of discrimination by human rights organisations who want the issue of caste put on the agenda of an international conference on racism in South Africa (TM 14 Feb. 01). The response of India's External Affairs Minister was "We must ensure that the conference does not lose sight of its focus on racism—racism should not be confused with discrimination in general."

The 1948 UN Declaration of Human Rights, devised in 1942, did not receive unanimous support from those of the then thirty-six member states who were outside of the American sphere of influence. For the second time this century, the influence of the United States was at its strongest and Europe at its weakest. A liberal, Eleanor Roosevelt, presided over the drafting of the Charter, which was aimed at preventing abuse by future dictatorships and was modelled on individual liberalism, and was to be the antithesis of the 'Old' World. William McNeill [1997:18–22] observes that "Ever since [the Declaration of Independence] Americans have liked to think of themselves as showing other peoples how to bring public affairs into harmony with eighteenth century Enlightenment conceptions of universal human rights." And Fukuyama observes [1996:316] "For Americans, rights have an absolute character that is not balanced or moderated by constitutional language outlining duties to the community or responsibilities to other people . . . what is particularly insidious about the American culture of rights is that it dignifies with high moral purpose what often amounts to low private interests or desires." Articles 1 to 30 of the UN Declaration were a statement of general and idealised principles, of which Articles 1 to 20 were first generation rights, including some derivative rights. Some are "rights to claim" as distinct from "rights to be given." The standard setting Declaration was followed in 1966 by two UN International Covenants, which promoted civil and political rights (eighty-eight signatories), and the economic, social and cultural rights (ninety-two signatories) included in the 1948 Declaration. Whereas the 1948 Declaration was not binding, these Covenants have the legal force of treaties for the signatories to them. Since then the Declaration has been given "prominence" in the Proclamations of Tehran (1968) and Helsinki (1975). Human Rights Conventions in Latin America and Africa came into force in 1978 and in 1986 respectively—but with little effect.

Schlesinger [1987:95] notes the inconsistency of Western geo-politics following WW2: "The idea of human rights like nearly everything else, was soon caught up in the Cold War. The democratic states assailed the communist world for its abuse of civil and political rights; the communist world assailed the democratic states for their neglect of social and economic rights. Human rights began to emerge as a theme in American foreign policy in this context." This was a clash in political cultures to which neither side fully subscribed, even though the UN Declaration was supposedly universal. He also notes [80] that "A democracy is in bad trouble when it keeps two sets of books—when it uses one scale of values for its internal polity and uses another in foreign affairs . . . it happened to the United States during the Vietnam War." He asks [100] "was not the whole concept of political and civil rights ethnocentric and culture-bound and therefore the American determination to cram it down the throats of the world an adventure in cultural imperialism? A nation's supreme interest is in self—preservation. When national security and the promotion of human rights come into genuine conflict, national security must prevail" [102]. Thus Schlesinger is adopting the same principle as did John Locke. Nevertheless, globalisation has resulted in a "missionary diplomacy" of human rights, by which the West has attempted to export a Kantian form of moral imperatives. Although the United States is a signatory of the Vienna Convention on human rights, in one case the Supreme Court decided not to intervene. This was in spite of appeals from the Secretary of State and a unanimous decision of the International Court of Justice, because of the Tenth Amendment gives independence to the states from the federal courts [TM 17 April 98].

The European Convention of Human Rights came into force in 1953 and its judiciary (the ECHR) was set up in 1959. It is the only effective supranational institution that can uphold human rights, but with its fifteen EU member states its jurisdiction is limited to a region having compatible cultures. It was intended that the role of the ECHR should be that of a review body, for many years was of little practical consequence, and it generally left matters of human rights violations to national courts. However, it progressively became another level of appeal from the decisions of national courts. Since 1966 British citizens could take individual cases to the ECHR and by the end of 1998, fifty-two out of a total of ninety-nine had been allowed and prompted changes in British law [TM 3 Nov. 98]. Because of its 12,635 backlog of applications, with possibly another 15,000 pending [TM 15 Feb. 00], it could take an average of five years and cost some £30,000 to take an appeal to the Strasbourg Court. Britain has been unhappy with the ECHR in respect of the selection criteria and experience of its seventeen judges, and the extent of their allowable national discretion: the "margin of appreciation" [TM 25 Nov. 96]. This was intended to allow national courts flexibility as long as they did not breach fundamental principles. Its judges' tenure of office is perpetual and their decisions can be on a majority basis. One judge is from tiny Andorra, another from Luxembourg, and one from Turkey which has a questionable human rights record [TM 17 Dec. 99]. Like the UN, the enforcement of its decisions requires the co-operation of the member state concerned.

As a result of its dissatisfaction, and the anomaly apparent in the increasing number of appeals to the ECHR, Britain enacted its own law. This was the 1998 Human Rights Act, which came into force in October 2000 in England and Wales, with which its legislation and common law will have to conform. British courts will now be obliged to interpret domestic legislation consistently with the European Convention. Where this is not possible, the judiciary must still apply the existing law, but can make a "declaration of incompatibility," which will serve to advise/assist parliament to decide whether to change the law accordingly. British courts will, however, be able to make their own interpretation and application of the British tradition in judging appeals on human rights and their sometimes conflicting principles, which will be less likely to go to the ECHR. This is in effect resistance to the growth of European jurisprudence. Scottish law had incorporated the European Convention earlier, and although over 600 cases had been brought since it came into effect in July 1999, less than three percent had been successful [TM 23 June 00].

A number of problems are apparent, such as the balance between the conflicting rights of the individual versus the rights of society, and the unintended consequences of particular decisions. There is a potential conflict between the freedom of expression including that of the press, and the right to respect for private and family life. The dichotomy between individual rights and social responsibilities has allowed the supporters of known terrorists to claim .from the nation-state, through the ECHR, the right to life of those that did not allow this reciprocal right to their victims. A European anti-discrimination directive backed by the government, which is potentially alarming for a multi-religious society, will force all religious schools and charities—Christian, Jewish or Muslim—to employ atheists and practising homosexuals and face legal action if they do not [TM 30 June 00]. Another issue is whether Muslims as a religious group should have a right of protection under proposed new legislation against inciting religious hatred, which they do not have at present. This is in contrast to the Christian, Jewish, and Sikh religions, which are recognised as ethnic groups. The ECHR had also ruled by a majority decision, that a domestic judge must conduct detailed enquiries into what went on in a jury room, if any allegation of racial bias among jurors is brought to his attention, and if so, order a retrial [TM 10 May 00].

It is regrettable that the post-war international organisation discussed by Roosevelt, Stalin, and Churchill followed Roosevelt's idealism. Originally they proposed, instead of a League of Nations global replicate like the UN, that power should be concentrated into three regions—European, American and Pacific—under a supreme global council, and that power should not reside above or below. The UN placed an emphasis on state's rights and individual rights, and the right of all "peoples" to self-determination [BBC 5 May 94]. In so doing, it created a tension between these rights. With the NATO intervention in Bosnia and Kosovo, Western governments took a selective view of their international obligations to legitimise their actions, which was to prevent a humanitarian disaster. This was justified under international law rather than the UN Charter, and obtained twelve out of fifteen votes of the Security Council with Russia, China, and Namibia opposed. Expert legal opinion holds that the Kosovo intervention was illegal under treaty law both under the 1942 UN Charter Articles 2 (3) (4) and (7) and Article 53, and the corpus of modern international law. The founding charter resolves that force should not be used to resolve international disputes and that the basis of international order must be the sovereignty of UN member states. For example, Article 2 (4) states "All members shall refrain in their international relations from the threat or use of force against the territorial integrity or political independence of any state etc." Article 2 (7) prohibits the UN from intervening "in matters which are essentially within the domestic jurisdiction of any state or shall require the members to submit such matters to settlement under the present Charter etc" [Brownlie 1994:4].

Since the Bosnia/Kosovo internal human rights abuses, intervention is clearly no longer deemed to be prohibited or excluded. Britain was a signatory to the 1965 UN Declaration on the Inadmissibility of Intervention in the Internal Affairs of States and the Protection of their Sovereignty. Moreover, Britain and Yugoslavia were signatories to Articles ii and vi of the OSCE (Organisation for Security and Cooperation in Europe) 1975 Final Act of the Helsinki Conference of European States. This agreement was clearly conditioned by the Cold War and requires signatories to "refrain . . . from the threat or use of force against the territorial integrity or political independence of any state . . . No consideration may be invoked to serve to warrant resort to the threat or use of force in contravention of this principle" [391–5]. Shaw [1997:902] notes that "The Helsinki Final Act laid down a series of basic principles of behaviour among the participating states, including sovereign equality; inviolability of frontiers; prohibition of the threat or use of force or violence; territorial integrity of states; non-intervention in internal affairs etc . . . (however) the Helsinki Act was not a binding treaty but a political document." The non-negotiable Rambouillet Accord presented to the Serbs/Albanians before the NATO intervention contained clauses which infringed the sovereignty of the whole of the Federal Republic of Yugoslavia, and not just Kosovo [TM 29 Nov. 99]. For post-Kosovo, which is still part of the Yugoslav state, the UN has affirmed its right to intervene in the internal affairs of its member states "if they threaten regional security," which includes humanitarian grounds.

After the Russian sponsored peace deal, the UN restored the principle of the sovereignty of Serbia over its former multiethnic Kosovan province by UN Resolution 1244—thus the fiction of the UN not being seen to be supporting secessionist movements was maintained. Most conflicts today are ethno-national civil wars that limit the UN's direct intervention to third world states unable to resist. Otherwise it is confined to diplomatic rhetoric and largely ineffective sanctions. It is unsurprising that no powerful member state of the UN is likely to allow any external authority to infringe its sovereignty—it can only be done if the offending state is virtually powerless to resist, as in the Balkans, Africa and Afghanistan, and is also deemed to be of sufficient strategic importance—as with the U.S. invasion of Grenada in 1983. The present trend is to by-pass the UN, and to otherwise attempt to legitimise the armed intervention in the ethnic conflicts of small and relatively power-less nation-states. Intervention did not take place in Chechnya, Russia, and China after their recent strategic alliance had warned against foreign intervention in what they regard as their "domestic terrorism" [11 Dec. 99] Their powerful military and nuclear potential result only in UN resolutions. Kosovo should not be taken as a guide to future interventionism because of its unique casualty-free nature, although more than 54,000 British ground troops were due to be committed less than twenty-four hours before Milosevic surrendered [STM. 29 Oct. 00]. Nor did it achieve its objective of averting a humanitarian disaster, and it did not directly force out Milosevic.

The downside of the intervention in Kosovo was the temporary ethnic cleansing of almost one and a half million Kosovan Albanians, followed by the cleansing of the Serbian minority, together with massive destruction in both Kosovo and Serbia, and the setting up of another long term NATO military and economic protectorate. According to a U.S. State department estimate [TM 11 Nov. 99], 10,000 Serbs were killed between March and June 1999. If and when NATO withdraws, the Kosovans will no doubt demand independence, even though this was specifically rejected by UN Resolution 1244 and the new Yugoslav president. The British general who led the 50,000 peacekeeping force in Kosovo has come to this view [TM. 24 Nov. 99]. About half the NATO effort is spent in protecting the imprisoned Serbian minority with eight Americans killed to date, and amounts too little more than a enforced Albanian/Serbian co-existence with the Serbs living in NATO protected ghettoes. Although officially disbanded, the 20,000 strong KLA independence movement is still in being, some with the Macedonian NLA (National Liberation Army), and its authority conflicts with that of NATO and the UN police force. It has ambitions to become the Kosovan national army—an option specifically ruled out by the UN Security Council. Without independence, elements of the KLA could become the Kosovan IRA.

NOTES

Arendt, H. *The Origins of Totalitarianism.* London: George Allen and Unwin, 1958. 279.

Brownlie, I. (Ed.) *Basic Documents on Human Rights.* 3rd edn. Oxford: Clarendon Press, 1994. 4 and 391–5.

Cranston, M. *What Are Human Rights?* London: The Bodley Head, 1973. 21.

Flew, A. "The Artificial Inflation of Natural Rights." In *Vera Lex.* vol. 2, 1988. 4.

Fukuyama, F. *Trust—The Social Virtues and the Creation of Prosperity.* London: Penguin Books, 1996. 316.

Hu, A. "Us and Them." In *The New Republic.* 1 June 1992. 13–4.

Jones, P. *Rights.* Basingstoke: Macmillan Press. 1994.

Mayall, J. *The Fate of Nations* (Analysis). BBC Radio 4. 5 May 1994. 7.

Mestrovic, S.G. *The Balkanisation of the West—The Confluence of Post-Modernism and Post Communism*. London: Routledge, 1994. 10.

Ibid. 79–80.

Mc Neill,W.H. "Decline of the West." (Book Review) In *New York Review*. 9 January 1997. 18–22.

Schlesinger, A.M. *The Cycles of American History*. London: Andre Deutsch. 1987. 95.

Ibid. 80.

Ibid. 100.

Ibid. 102.

Shaw, M.N. *International Law* . Cambridge: Cambridge Universitry Press. 1997. 902.

Strossen. N. *Defending Pornography*. New York, Scribner: 1995. 14.

Swann, Lord. *Education for All—The Report of the Committee of Inquiry Into the Education of Children from Ethnic Minority Groups*. London: Stationery Office, 1985. 27–8.

15

Global Migration and Refugees

This book argues that the principal threat to the preservation by the European nation-states of their national coherence and their cultural hegemonies is multiculturalism, which is being reinforced by global migration. Migration arises from escape from ethno-national conflicts, the gross disparity between the living standards of the "first" and the "third" worlds, and the world's population growth. According to the UN [TM 3 Sept. 98], this is growing at a rate of eighty million a year with Europe alone running counter to the trend with a declining population that by 2050 is set to return to the same figure of 600 million as twenty years ago. In the year 2000 in England and Wales, the birthrate was 1.66 children per woman, the lowest level (with 1977) since records began in 1924 [TM 11 May 01]. This reflects a similar trend throughout much of Western Europe. By 2000 the world population had reached 6.055 billion compared with 2.524 billion in 1950 [Social Trends 2001: 38]. The population of Nigeria in 2050 is forecast to be larger than that of all the present EU countries—in 1997 it was less than one third [TM 2 March 98]. According to the UN, the population of India has reached 1 billion and China has reached 1.248 billion [TM 13 Aug. 99]. Dr. Coleman, Reader in Demography at Oxford University, casts doubt on recent official population projections for the U.K. [TM 23 Nov. 01]. These tell us that net immigration into the U.K. will increase the population by 135,000 every year, which is equivalent to a new London borough every two or three years. Even this figure understates the most recent immigration figures (a net addition of 180,000 in 1998 and 1999). We are not told why such a sharp reversal of recent upward trends should be expected . . . Inflows on the current scale threaten housing provision, countryside protection, and any prospect of a cohesive society. Does the government have any policy at all on these matters, or is it hoping that no one will notice? To this list might be added the additional strain on other social resources, particularly those of education, health, and the police.

179

The official figure [Social Trends 2001:37] for 1994–1998, excluding asylum seekers, averaged 73,000 per year. However, the majority of migrants particularly since 1997, have been asylum seekers, visa over-stayers, marriage migrants, and dependants, who also have a higher rate of fertility. If migrants add predominantly to the welfare underclass, they will eventually adversely affect the already disturbing dependency ratio, namely the ratio of old people to those in work.

Population pressures and ethno-national conflicts lead to instability and poverty and to environmental degradation. Most migrants to the West are economic migrants in search of better living standards, welfare benefits and political security, absence of institutional corruption and organised crime, an ethos of human rights, and a tolerant culture. Migration has grown to alarming proportions since colonial independence and the breakdown of the Russian hegemony over Eastern Europe and Central Asia. The number of immigrants into the U.K. is growing, encouraged by cheap travel and facilitated by the criminalisation of migration, awareness of universal human claim rights, particularly asylum rights, and the global dissemination of Western life styles by television. Economic migration could be eased if the standard of living in these regions was improved, and by their trained elite not emigrating and depriving their homelands of their skills. Migration will have a major influence on what sort of society and what sort of culture or cultures, the Western nation states will have in the new millennium.

A doomsday scenario for Britain, given the continuance of the 1951 UN Refugee Convention, would be one in which mass migration would destroy all that is currently understood by its way of life. The probability of this will be increased if a country cannot control its borders, and if it grants amnesties to illegal immigrants. A letter writer to the Times [12 Feb. 00] whose parents were Jewish refugees from Nazi Germany in 1934 noted that that under the UN Convention "perhaps half a million Kosovans would be eligible; well over a million Kurds; and perhaps 100,000 Roma. In Africa, virtually the entire populations of Rwanda, Congo and Angola would appear to have equally valid claims, as also the inhabitants of Somalia, Tutsi and Hutu in other African states could also be added to the list. Every unmarried woman [and homosexual] from the fundamentalist Islamic states could legitimately claim to be oppressed and deprived of her rights. Nor is this list anything like exhaustive . . . We have bound ourselves by an undertaking which we simply cannot honour. It could break us."

Migrants usually know and care little about the culture into which they enter, and into which they may or may not subsequently assimilate to an indeterminate degree. Controlled selective immigration coupled with gradual assimilation is one thing—an unchallenged ideology of multiculturalism, coupled with the ethos of universal claim rights is another. The principal considerations that should influence immigration policies are their effect on the national identity and culture; their macroeconomic gain or penalty; and the impact of asylum seekers. Under the 1951 UN Convention, refugees, together with economic migrants and illegal immigrants posing as refugees, essentially bypass the normal immigration controls. A Czech visitor noted [TM.16 Aug. 99] that on entry to Britain, he has to satisfy immigration officials as to the purpose of his visit, the address at which he would be staying, and his cash resources. If he failed this interview, for example, if he was intending to work illegally, he would be returned to the Czech republic within days with no appeal. On the other hand if he claimed asylum he would be given permission to stay with accommodation and benefits. This highlights the impracticality of the political rhetoric that Britain will always accept "genuine asylum seekers" and the relative ineffectiveness of the rhetoric of "tightening immigration controls" when the basic principle remains flawed, let alone the practical problem of verifying the credibility of asylum claims. Britain enacted five immigration-related acts in the last twelve years with little effect on the control of immigration, with many of the Home Office Minister's immigration decisions being ruled invalid on appeal to the courts on judicial review. The Head of the UN Mission in Bosnia/Herzogovina estimates that there are 42,000 Chinese in Serbia waiting to cross the virtually unpoliced border, and these, together with Iranians, Turks, Kurds, and so on, are entering this open backdoor to Fortress Europe at a rate of up to 10,000 a month [TM 31 Aug. 00]. Salins [1997:211] points out that "If the right to immigrate to the United States is a kind of 'property right,' illegal immigration represents a form of theft . . . First, it is being taken from the native Americans who have the power to grant it, but ultimately—and perhaps more significantly—it is being seized from those who are waiting to enter the United States lawfully."

Refugee lobbies call on the West to solve the refugee problem, often in terms of the language of "something must be done," as members of the "international community." This could mean effectively acquiescing to an open door, or "no borders" policy, and providing limited resources in response to an unlimited demand. Solving the refugee problem could also mean that the West should become more involved in resolving ethno-national conflicts, in spite of the experience of accusations of imperialism and colonialism. The questions which the nation-states of the West will have to address, if they wish to preserve their cultural hegemony in the millenium are: what are the principles which underwrite their immigration policies (or lack of them), and what should be its numerical scale and basis for its selectivity? This involves issues of practicality as well as philosophical principles. The attitude of British governments towards immigration this century, particularly since the 1950s, has been characterised [Garrard 1971:7] as "There is an underlying ambiguity in British attitudes towards immigrants, extending even to the juxta-position of sentiments of tolerance and intolerance in the same statements. Thus, in a situation where we are all a little scared of being thought to be illiberal, and where none want to appear prejudiced, the accusation of racial prejudice becomes as potentially powerful a weapon as the exploitation of prejudice itself."

The 1951 UN (Geneva) Convention on Refugees reflected the post-war global political stability, albeit sometimes under totalitarian or colonial rule, and the pre-Cold war idealism of the American and British founders of the UN. Article 1 A (2) of the original 1951 Convention, applied to those who became refugees "as a result of events occurring before 1 January 1951, but this limitation was removed by the (New York) Protocol that came into force in 1967. Daniel Steinbock [1999:13] says that "[It is] adhered to—at least formally—by 133 nations [now 137]—Though the [1951] Convention and its 1967 Protocol do not so require, it has inspired many states to employ the definition in their domestic asylum systems . . . [17] the text of the refugee definition constitutes what might be described as the boundary of its applications. Within those limits textual analysis can only take us so far towards a workable interpretation of the refugee definition . . . [14] As a result of its great practical impact, virtually every word of the core phrase of the refugee definition has been subject to interpretative dispute." This has certainly been the case in Britain, where no doubt encouraged by free legal aid, almost every aspect of this Convention has ended up in the Court of Appeal and been interpreted by the judiciary, sometimes over-turning asylum decisions by the Home Secretary. It is a bizarre fact that when the 1951 UN Convention was coming into force, the McCarthy Committee was at the same time politically "persecuting" American communists. Until at least its failure in Vietnam, and the collapse of the USSR, American foreign policy reflected the belief that it had an altruistic duty together with a self-interest, to combat Communism, and to promote its version of democracy and human rights, wherever it could project its power and influence. It also reflected the essentially problem free earlier assimilated migrations from Europe including the 1930s Jewish migration from Germany—the number of these refugees had been relatively small, Britain taking 52,000 from a total of 250,000. These were not economic migrants, but were genuinely apolitical, involuntary and persecuted people, who sometimes brought with them exceptional talent. For many years the words *refugee* or *exile* created a sympathetic response, especially after the experience of the German Jews and the displaced Europeans immediately after the war. Nevertheless, the stereotyping of migrants as a group as being either talented or otherwise is specious, inasmuch that examples can be readily found to the contrary.

Since the 1990s most refugees are economic migrants who are using the outdated UN Convention. The standard setting 1948 UN Declaration of Human Rights included the obligation under Article 14 –1, which gave "everyone the right to seek and enjoy in other countries asylum from persecution"— a right to "seek" but not a right to "obtain or be given" asylum. This was followed by the 1951 UN (Geneva) Convention Relating to the Status of Refugees, which came into force in 1954, before which economic migration into Britain was relatively rare, amended by a Protocol coming into force in 1967 and accepted by 137 states, although the problem which they face, their interpretation of it, and their compliance with it, varies. Article 1. A.(2) obliges signatories to offer asylum to refugees, who are defined as any person who "owing to well-founded fear of being persecuted for reasons of race, religion, nationality, membership of a particular social group or political opinion, is outside the country of his nationality and is unable or, owing to such fear, is unwilling to avail himself of the protection of that country; or who, not having a nationality and being outside the country of his former habitual residence (as a result of such events), is unable or, owing to such fear, is unwilling to return to it." This definition is vague and all embracing. For example, the Convention contains no explicit restriction on a refugee's right to choose their country of asylum, and on the other hand, of the right of a sovereign state to refuse asylum on the grounds of their coming from a "safe third country." Members of "persecuted" political groups suspected of terrorism have obtained asylum in Britian. A refugee can claim to be a member of a group rather than simply an individual, and the persecution/discrimination can be social, as well as political or religious. Persecution based on gender and sexuality is also grounds for asylum according to the UNHCR, even though they are not mentioned in the Convention. Nevertheless, the House of Lords ruled that it can apply to any social group, as in the case with two abused Pakistani women [TM 26 March 99], and may also apply to homosexuals. The phrase "well founded fear of persecution" is open to a variety of interpretations. Refugees are also entitled under the UN Convention Articles 16 and 21 to 23 to legal aid, housing, education, and social welfare benefits including health service treatment, no less favourable than accorded to nationals. Some EU states do not recognise non-state persecution, and recently [TM. 7 July 00] the House of Lords also ruled that migrants were not eligible for asylum on the grounds of persecution if the state offered protection through the rule of law, but only if the state was unwilling or unable to do so. Perversely, the law lords have overruled the Home Secretary's decision that Germany and France are safe countries and refugees can be returned there, because both countries recognise as refugees only those who face persecution in their own country [TM 20 Dec. 00]. The Home Secretary (an ex-barrister) also lost on appeal [TM 13 Mar. 01] his decision to return hundreds of Kosovan Albanians to Germany, because it "frustrated their legitimate expectations," and would cause them "significant hardship." In 1998, Germany granted only three percent Albanians refugee status. In Britain sixty percent were granted refugee status or given leave to remain.

The 1990 Dublin Convention Determining the State Responsible for Examining Applications for Asylum Lodged in One of the Member States of the European Community came into force in 1997. The Dublin Convention replaced the Schengen Agreement (to which Britain had opted out), as the governing European law, and was another attempt to coordinate EU control of refugees. This Convention supposedly determines which EU member state decides an asylum application, but its compliance and some aspects of its interpretation by member states remain to be established. The Amsterdam Treaty (of the EU), on the harmonisation or the so-called "communitarianisation" of asylum determination and procedural remedy policies, was agreed to by twelve out of the fifteen member states, and is due to come into force in 2002. The U.K., Ireland, and Denmark have negotiated "opt in" protocols. The aim, as in the earlier Schenger agreement, was to have a common EU frontier which would replace the internal frontiers of member states. This partial EU harmonisation is likely in practice to remain selective, or reach a consensus at the level of the lowest commonly acceptable denominator. If EU immigration laws are federalised, Britain would have to insist on uniform regulations and strict enforcement becoming a "must" for all EU members—Britain being an island relies on border controls, whereas some other EU countries rely with more difficulty on internal controls.

Even freedom of movement for its citizens within a large geographical region is not enough for some. Kum-Kum Bhavnani [No. 45 Autumn 93:35] saw a racialised threat in the formation in 1993 of the EU from EEC nation-states: "It is this European internationalism which is a racialized internationalism, in the sense that 'black/Third World' people are always defined as immigrants, and therefore not citizens, and therefore not Europeans, and therefore not desirable . . . [33] this very 'European identity' strengthens the distinction between European and non-European." One might ask where else in the world is such an extensive free movement of people within a group of nation-states possible? Daniele Joly [1999: 353–4] recognises that "Individual [Western European] governments have more discretion on decisions determining [refugee] status, and are breaking away from the influence and control of international instruments. However these bodies do not enjoy a completely free reign in their decisions . . . It is possible to find differing views and interpretations according to the institutional and social actors involved. Fundamentally, there is a tension between, on the one hand, those who have a more liberal interpretation of the institution of asylum coupled with a greater concern for human rights in countries of origin, while promoting the integration of refugees into the host community and, on the other hand, those who want to restrict asylum and integration." This discussion argues the case for selectively restricting immigration, and at the same time promoting assimilation.

The first immigration legislation in Britain was the Aliens Bill of 1905. Since 1987, there have been six items of legislation relating to immigration and its control. In the United States, serious political concern about immigration goes back until at least the 1850s. Economic migration into Britain was not on a significant scale until post-WW2, although substantial cheap labour Irish migration took place during the first half of the nineteenth century, which was largely free of racial overtones, as well as the Jewish pogrom migration (1890–1905). The post-WW2 African-Caribbean influx was in part due to the unemployment arising from Britain buying sugar from Cuba, and the virtual banning of West Indian immigration to the United States after 1952. Prior to this nine out of ten West Indian migrants embarked for America [Humphries and Taylor 1986:117]. In the mid to late 1950s when economic migration into Britain was high, unemployment was only about a quarter of a million, but by the 1970s the situation was changing. The expectation of the 1950s and early 1960s was that New Commonwealth immigrants would be temporary "sojourners" or would be assimilated into the white urban class—by the mid–1960s this was clearly not the case. Rex [1991:8] recalls that "The first official British response . . . was simply to declare that they [immigrants] must be assimilated to a unitary British culture . . . This policy was very quickly abandoned, however, and in 1968 the [liberal] Home Secretary [Roy Jenkins] said that what he envisaged was 'not a flattening process of uniformity, but cultural diversity, coupled with equal opportunity, in an atmosphere of mutual tolerance.' Since these policy aims have never been formally abandoned, it may be assumed that, in some degree at least, they still influence government policy." It was unlikely that the Jenkins policy would be "formally abandoned" by any government since 1968. Government policies have been those of imposing increasing restrictions and controls on non-visa immigration, backed up by equal opportunities and race relations legislation, but subject always to the loophole of the UN Refugee and Human Rights Conventions.

Immigration reappeared as a publicised, albeit local political issue in Birmingham, during the 1964 general election. That year the Home Secretary had reported to a government committee that there was widespread evasion of immigration controls. The then Labour government planned to curb the "flood" of immigrants [TM 25 May 98] which was greater than the rate at which they were being assimilated, and in 1968 enacted the second Commonwealth Immigrants Bill. But it was not until April 1968 that the first senior politician (Enoch Powell) publicly expressed serious concern about immigration, supported by five Privy Councillors, and called for immediate legislation to curtail the influx. His "rivers of blood" speech resulted in his being sacked from the Shadow Cabinet and politically ostracised. He was credited by some for breaking the government's "conspiracy of silence" and performing his duty as a politician, but criticised by others for "making racial intolerance respectable." He proposed that firstly, illegal immigrants should be deported; secondly, there should be control over the immigration of dependants; and thirdly, there should be generous financial assistance for voluntary repatriation. The disaster scenario that Powell forecast did not come about, namely "civil strife of appalling dimensions, and that institutions and laws, let alone exhortations, will be powerless to prevent." Both Conservative and Labour politicians distanced themselves from Powell's inflammatory rhetoric, but subsequently expressed it in acceptable political terms, realising that the public had to have confidence that the government had immigration under control. The 1971 Immigration Act followed, and governments have since legislated firmer controls, including some of those proposed by Powell, in an attempt to pragmatically relate immigration to societal toleration and the avoidance of abuse. Miles [1989:120] believes that although Powell's speeches in the 1960s expressed racism, "their ideological content was as much, if not more, nationalist than racist. Powell was seeking to reconstruct a sense of Englishness in the context of economic decline and the failures of Labourism as a political alternative to Conservatism." Nevertheless it is still true that without confidence in a government to control all immigration both legal and illegal, including asylum seekers who have a prima facie right of entry, societal toleration is threatened.

MORI interviewed 2,118 British adults face-to-face aged fifteen plus [MORI July 00]. This found that sixty-three percent of people agreed with the statement that "too much is done to help immigrants at present," compared with twenty-two percent who disagreed. Sixty-six percent believed that "there are too many immigrants in Britain," compared with seventeen percent who thought not. Eighty percent thought that "refugees come to Britain because it is a soft touch," compared with twelve percent who thought not. And thirty-eight percent thought that "those settling in this country should not maintain the culture and lifestyle which they had at home," whilst forty-four percent thought that they should. The adverse reactions to immigrants in these polls were weighted towards the older (aged sixty-five plus) generation, compared with the younger (fifteen to twenty-four) generation; those living in the North East of England compared with London; and supporters of the Conservative party, compared with Liberal Democrat and Labour party supporters. MORI also found that thirty-seven percent felt that there was generally more racial prejudice in Britain now compared with five years ago, compared with twenty-one percent who thought that there was less. In five years time, thirty-eight percent thought that there would be more racial prejudice than now, compared with twenty-three percent who thought that there would be less.

In another poll, MORI interviewed 1,005 British adults by telephone aged fifteen plus [MORI Jan. 01]. This indicated that sixty percent thought that asylum seekers should be detained in reception centres until their cases had been settled, whilst thirty-three percent thought not. Eighty-four percent thought that the existing system for processing applications should be speeded up so refusals could be expelled more quickly, compared with nine percent who thought otherwise. Both forty-four percent of people thought that Britain should take, or should not take, any more asylum seekers. In both polls data were weighted to the population profile.

The multiracial Commonwealth, with its myth of common citizenship, had a considerable influence on immigration legislation in Britain. Although the issue had been first brought to Cabinet attention in 1954, there was vacillation, ambivalence, and concealment of the issue from the public by the government prior to the 1962 Act. This has, to some degree, continued ever since. The Conservative government admitted [TM 3 Feb. 00] to this continuing conspiracy of silence in granting amnesty in 1992–93 to 26,000 asylum applicants without advising parliament. This was then followed by what is effectively an amnesty by the present Labour government for another 10,000, with exceptional leave to stay for up to four years for another 20,000 [TM 28 July 98]. The granting of amnesties is in effect an acceptance of the failure of immigration control. Prior to 1962, and also, to some extent, until very recently, and for reasons which are not made public, successive British governments have been reluctant and too late in imposing effective immigration controls. From 1984–88 the annual rate of immigration did not exceed about 4,000 per year, but by 1989 it had risen to a rate of about 45,000 per year and has been rising steadily ever since [Social Trends 1992:35]. In 1999 it had reached 71,200 excluding dependants and South East Asian refugees [Social Trends 2001:38]. Possibly this governmental reticence has been due to: the predictable fear of being labelled racist; concern about offending the ethnic vote; reluctance to abandon the myth of the multiracial Commonwealth; and the continuing strict adherence and judiciary interpretation of the UN Conventions. An exception was when the government resisted the proposal by its last governor (Patten) to grant British citizenship to the 5.75 million (or ten percent of the UK) population of its former colony Hong Kong prior to its independence. Politicians of all the major parties have for over the last forty years remained essentially impotent over this sensitive issue, or have tried to stifle debate ("involuntary toleration"?). When in opposition, they have opposed proposals for immigration legislation, which they then implemented when in power. It was not until April 2000, when Britain was again being "flooded" with illegitimate asylum seekers, and the lack of public confidence in the control of asylum seekers became a matter of serious concern, that calls were being made to have a more open debate on immigration. Michael Heseltine, a former Deputy Prime Minister [TM 01 Jan. 01], drew attention to the fact that bogus asylum seekers are depriving British citizens of housing and health care: "Let's not mince our language here. Why on earth should British citizens go without the houses they want, or take longer to get treatment they need, in order to make way for people who have cheated on the immigration rules." Until recently such a comment by a prominent politician, normally constrained by the rhetoric of "playing the race card," would have been unthinkable and such concerns would have been confined to the middle pages of the tabloid press. Nevertheless, a former Chairman of the CRE (Commission for Racial Equality) [STM 3 Jan. 99] believes that Britain is a "fair and tolerant place, in many ways more so than most others." This is unprovable, as is the hypothesis that if this is so, then it is the outcome of progressively modest restrictions on immigration imposed by British governments, and equal opportunity and anti-race legislation since the early 1960s.

Open door immigration and unrestricted multiculturalism is incompatible with national self-determination. The self-understanding and self-regard of a nation is potentially undermined by an uncontrolled and unselective influx of migrants, because it alters its cultural composition. This may become apparent only when the pressure for continuing liberal immigration meets the subconscious limits determined by the indigenous society in asserting its natural right to maintain its political-cultural lifestyle. Given that the ordering of a nation-state is shaped by its culture, its autonomy should include the right to affirm its identity vis-a-vis those Others who could give an unwelcome cast to its traditional culture. In addition to its political, social, economic, and environmental aspects, uncontrolled and unselective immigration has a psychological influence. Native citizens can resent their cities changing into "occupied territories" and looking like the Punjab, Jamaica, Hong Kong or Nigeria, and becoming exiles in their own land. Although this might be a visceral reaction, supposedly objective counter-arguments are counter-intuitive. The electorate has never been asked whether it wanted to become a multiracial/cultural society, which arguably has been its most significant change since WW2. The multicultural lobby that routinely criticises immigration restrictions as being those of "middle England and racist" never indicates what restrictions, if any at all, they would impose. Some nation-states have immigration policies which are designed to preserve their characteristics: the United States had this until the 1965 Act, which thereafter favoured non-European immigrants; Israel regards every Jew as a potential citizen; and Germany grants automatic patrial citizenship to anyone deemed as being of German blood.

Glazer [1996:62–3] discusses the limits of obligations of "host" countries to migrants/refugees: "Any immigrant or refugee policy presupposes a state, with rules that differentiate among those who are allowed entry, in what status and with what rights. This presupposition does not mean that those outside the boundaries of the state are without human claims, indeed rights—rights that have been in large measure specified and defined by international protocols. So we [the United States] will join in feeding Rwandan refugees, perhaps join in protecting them, but we will not, for example, give them rights to enter the United States. All these commitments to others' claims and rights involve costs, in money and lives, and these costs are not assessed against the world, but against the citizens and soldiers of a specific country, the only entity that can lay taxes and require soldiers to obey orders. It is perhaps this reality that also gives the citizens of a state the ethical right to make distinctions. It is hard to see, practically, how to move beyond a situation in which the primary power to grant and sustain rights rests with constituted sovereign states."

Nevertheless, some philosophers debate immigration in terms of the morality of justice, equality, fairness, and rights from a universalist viewpoint in contrast to those of a particular society. They seemingly ignore the capability and resources of a host country, and that this altruistic proposition would be unlikely in practice to find the requisite domestic political support. Some philosophers argue that Rawls idealised "distributive justice" approach should be adopted. A selection process would be constructed behind a veil of ignorance unaware of migrants race, class, religion, culture, so as to be all of the same moral worth, which raises the question "who's moral worth?" When the veil is removed, people would be unreservedly accepted free of any preferences and other characteristics. Rawls has been defended [1995 Perry:106–8] on the grounds that what he intended was a "social contract" within a society, and not between globalized societies, and "it is for this reason that the scope of the original position is limited to persons within a single society."

Another argument is that the liberal norms of justice and democracy require that there should be a time threshold after which illegal immigrants should either be granted the full rights of citizenship, or should be awarded nationality automatically, without any conditions or tests. "Distributive justice" would also require "social goods" to be distributed preferentially to reduce inequalities below the median level. It would be difficult to imagine better incentives to promote illegal immigration. This illustrates the irrelevancy of attempting to apply an idealistic philosophical theory into a real situation, employing ideal Rawlsian persons, who are apparently devoid of human nature. Gray observes [1995:4] that "[the category of the Rawlsian 'person'] is a cipher, without history or ethnicity, denuded of special attachments that in the real human world give us the particular identities we have. Emptied of the contingencies that in truth are essential to our identities, this cipher has in the Rawlsian schema only one concern—a concern for its own good, which is not the good of any actual human being, but the good we are all supposed to have in common, which it pursues subject to constraints of justice that are conceived to be those of impartiality."

It would not be possible for some states such as Norway, Denmark, or Ireland, which have a small population but a high standard of living, to accept as many refugees as might claim that they had a right to settle there. This absence of selectivity neglects the economic value, the language and culture, the propensity for separatism, the political assertiveness, and the ability of the host country to accept certain categories of refugees. Arendt [1994:169] recognised that the effect of a critical mass may be felt, albeit subconsciously, even by the established pre-WW2 Jewish immigrant minority in Holland, towards new immigrants/refugees, as well as by the indigenous majority. This sensitivity about the effect of numbers was shown by the restrictions imposed in 1939 by the British government on Jewish immigration into Palestine. Britain itself, admitted 50,000 Jewish refugees from Germany prior to WW2, of whom 10,000 were unaccompanied children [IND 8 April 00].

Pressure for liberal immigration is mainly from refugee, civil liberties, and humanitarian organisations and charities, who allege breaches of international standards on immigration/refugee rights, or because they are discriminatory, or stigmatise. Some employers also benefit indirectly from a supply of cheap manpower. In Britain, some pressure groups have long experience of exploiting the complex legal machinery of human rights, coupled with an opportunist textual analysis of the legislation. This has resulted in the judiciary allowing under the UN Convention, some non-political social group categories of migrants to qualify for asylum. The refugee voucher scheme which was introduced in April 2000, and is similar to that used elsewhere in Europe, is to be reviewed because of accusations of racism and stigmatisation [TM 30 Oct. 01]. This criticism could equally be said to apply to the indigenous underclass children, who are given vouchers or tokens for free school meals. Restrictions on immigration are predictably labelled racist, prejudiced, or discriminatory by anti-racists. The indigenous majority can become progressively intimidated into a state of impotence by historical revisionism or obfuscation, inherited guilt, self-flagellation, shame, and accusations of racism and injustice. This induces the political correctness of silence, acquiescence, and pressure to be even more permissive. In contrast, this was not said about the restrictions on threatened influx of hundreds of thousands of economic migrants from mainland China, whom the over-populated Hong Kong sought to impose after its reversion to China in 1997 [TM 20 May 99].

An immigration policy based on "liberal nationalism" has been proposed by Tamir [1993:159–160], no doubt with the moral dilemma of Zionism in mind. She says that "Although they [Tamir's guidelines] cannot bridge the gap between the ideal of free immigration and the ideal of national self-determination, together they may lead to a reasonable balance between them. First, a clear distinction should be drawn between the rights of refugees and the rights of immigrants. Although certain restrictions on immigration could be justified, they could never rescind the absolute obligation to grant refuge to individuals for as long as their lives are at risk. Second, after individuals have entered a certain territory under the justified impression that they will qualify for citizenship, it is unjustified to change these terms retroactively . . . third, liberal democratic principles dictate that, if a majority of its citizens so wishes, a national entity is justified in retaining its national character. On these grounds, a national entity might be seen as entitled to restrict immigration in order to preserve the existence of a viable majority . . . restrictions on immigration constitute a violation of the right of national minorities to equal treatment, as they only serve the needs of the majority. Therefore, they can only be justified if members of the minority have materialised their right to a national entity of their own, to which they could immigrate if they desired to live as members of a majority, and as long as family reunions are allowed. Hence, the Israeli 'Law of Return,' which actively encourages immigration of Jews and grants them automatic citizenship and financial assistance on their arrival in the country, would only be justified if the largest minority in the state, namely, the Palestinians, would also have a national entity in which they could enact a similar law . . . wealthy nations [162], concerned with avoiding pressure to open their gates to immigrants who are apt to change the national and cultural status quo, should, therefore, embark on efforts to improve standards of living in poorer countries, on both moral and prudential grounds."

This idealised argument accepts that a nation is justified in restricting immigration to achieve/preserve its homogeneity, but only if other nations have established their own nation-state—a "state to each nation." In practice, restrictions would have to be applied selectively to non-conforming nations and not to others. Moreover one has to translate into political/legal terms a "reasonable balance," a "justified impression," and the practical distinction between a refugee and an economic immigrant. This exhortation may be a plea for a Palestinian state and influenced by the plight of the Palestinians in Israel, compared with Israel's incentives to returning Jews. The 1950 Law of Return contrasts with the escape/emigration of the one third Palestinian population of Jerusalem which the Israelis unified in 1967 despite a UN resolution to withdraw, and made their capital city. When land is bought from Palestinians in the Old City, the unequal application of planning laws prevents Palestinians from buying back or leasing land. Since the creation of Israel in 1948, its population has grown from about 0.8m to 5.9 m, with about forty-three percent of this increase being due to immigration [TM 29 April 98].

This discussion argues that the gradual evaporation of prejudice and discrimination is dependent on tight and selective immigration controls, together with public confidence that immigration, in all its forms, is under control. This, it is argued, is more likely to ensure increasing toleration, which itself depends primarily upon the West maintaining its traditional liberal culture, in which loose controls, or the absence of any definitive immigration policy, whether by intent or by default, would put at risk. Inevitably, selective, quota, and visa-based controls on immigration would predictably be labelled racist by anti-racists and some ethnic pressure groups—which in a sense they would be. Otherwise this would require the indigenous society to continue to support, or to passively tolerate, a government condoning effectively an open door policy—no government in the world does this. It is unrealistic: neither the numerical intake of migrants nor its composition can be separated from one another, and it would eventually give separatist ethnic minorities an effective control over political power, with unforeseeable consequences.

Chain migration, ethnic pride, racism, and discrimination promote the formation of urban ghettoes. In the American ghettoes, the poor white, black, Hispanic, or illegal migrant underclass is largely multiracial/ethnic and accentuate violence, crime, alcohol and drug abuse, and social disorder. High crime rates may, though, be a feature of any underclass irrespective of race/ethnicity, and has become a semi-permanent rather than a generational phenomenon. These migrants provide the largely non-voting and non-participating labour that is required by modern capitalism for its less-agreeable, unskilled urban, agricultural, seasonal, and service occupations. A static economy, and the movement of industry and work to economically more favourable global locations, could deny to the underclass the secure employment once available in large cities. More importantly, in the past, several generations escaped to a more rewarding life, and this upward movement arrested discontent. If the process of generational escape comes to an end, greater resentment and social unrest are to be expected. Charles Murray, of the American Enterprise Institute, sees Britain as being blind to the problems of the underclass, which he says points to the growth of a class of "violent, unsocialised people who, if they become sufficiently numerous, will fundamentally degrade the life of society" [TM 23 April 00]. According to Linda Chavez [1993:18–9], the American Latino National Political Survey, possibly the most comprehensive opinion study of its kind ever done, concluded that "U.S. citizens of Hispanic origin (who will shortly outnumber blacks)—like most other Americans—think there are already too many immigrants in the United States. It found that seventy five percent of Mexican-Americans share that view, as do seventy nine percent of Puerto Ricans and sixty five percent of Cuban-Americans, compared to about seventy four percent of non-Hispanic whites."

Nevertheless, an economic argument advanced in favour of liberal immigration is that the low wage rates paid to unskilled immigrant labour is a way of keeping inflation under control—it is a short-term alternative to fiscal methods and which some would regard as immoral. In Britain, this is less likely to increase the labour market and restrain wage increases, because the welfare benefits both direct and indirect are relatively generous. Although the expectations of economic immigrants may initially be satisfied and be better than those they left behind, if their lack of education and skills persists, they become unemployable and add to the underclass, claiming discrimination. Selective economic immigration can be justified where there is an urgent need for a highly specialised skill, and this cannot be met in time by training the domestic workforce. Belatedly the British government has recognised a downside of unselective immigration, at least on the economy. For three decades, legal immigration with British residency has only been on familial grounds, or to bring in investment [TM 12 June 01]. Since 1994 this amount has been at least £1 million, of which at least £750,000 has to be invested in a UK trading company or in government bonds and maintained for at least four years. If after four years applicants continue to live in Britain they can, with some exceptions, obtain permanent residency [STM 3 June 01]. The work permit system has been eased to facilitate the entry of migrants from outside the EU classed as Shortage Skills, Key Workers [DM 12/30 Sept. 00] and entrepreneurs [STM 30 July 00]. Overseas workers permits are to be increased from 90,000 in 2000 to 120,000 in 2001 [TM 17 Oct. 00]. This could be extended to a scheme similar to the U.S. "green card" system which gives a limited number of workers the right of entry and permanent residence [TM 12 June 01]. This has caused concern about the "brain drain" from developing countries. Currently, out of just over 110,000 doctors working in the national health service, about 25,000 are from outside of Britain, and by 2019 this proportion is expected to rise to about one third [TM 8 Nov. 99]. Britain has about 630,000 registered nurses and about 22,000 vacancies, which are being filled with foreign nurses, particularly Filipinos. About 30,000 foreign nurses work in the NHS (National Health Service), with thousands more in the private sector, and make up about one quarter of the London population of nurses [TM 12 March 01]. It could be a reflection on the government's preoccupation with Ulster, Europeanisation, and immigration that it has failed to address the problems of the National Health Service—in particular the low pay, conditions, and status of nurses. It is expected that the NHS will receive over 30,000 applications from foreign nurses in the year 2001. This will exceed, for the first time, the 15,400 British nurses who qualify this year [DM 21 July 01].

Most, if not all, polities place a high priority on the economic prosperity of the society they represent, and consequently the economic benefit argument about immigration is important. However, instead of basing the evidence on non-specific generalities and/or individual high profile cases, the statistical research should attempt to differentiate between the country of origin of immigrants, their employment and language skills, and their age, health and dependants. Also taken into account should be the overall cost to the host country of the welfare benefits to the immigrant and family, together with all other less direct costs and expenditure. Galbraith [1992:37] is an exponent of the economic benefit of a cheap labour immigration policy. He says that "In the [U.S.] immigration legislation of 1990, there was at last some official recognition of the more general and continuing need for immigrant labour . . . It is not thought appropriate to say that the modern economy—the market system—requires such an underclass, and certainly not that it must reach out to other countries to sustain and refresh it." He argues [1996:91] that immigration is necessary "for upward economic and social movement . . . to refresh the labour force in the area of monotonous, non-prestigious toil," and claims [89] that "without this [immigrant] labour supply, there would be grave economic disorientation, even disaster." He says [90] that "Britain has replenished its industrial workforce and staffed its service industries, including numerous small retail establishments, with former residents of its erstwhile empire." Galbraith's analysis is open to accusations of "reverse/internal colonialism" and "exploitation," and reads like twenty-first century mercantilism—that a growing population and low wages are necessary to maintain national prosperity. This is questionable inasmuch that economies may not necessarily continue both to expand and require more unskilled labour, and governments can provide fiscal and other incentives to offset a low birth rate. The small retail establishments in Britain once largely owned by Asians, are rapidly going out of business because of supermarket competition and their adoption of longer opening hours. The African-Caribbeans who were recruited by London Transport during the 1950/60s have now largely been replaced by one-man buses and a largely automated Underground system. Indians and Pakistanis were recruited in the 1960s to man the textile industry, which has now disappeared, and the same is now happening to the automotive industry. Unskilled immigrants can result in an economy becoming technically obsolescent, with social cohesion being maintained in the meantime by generous welfare grants. Failing industries would call for protection and would seek dramatic remedies.

If the economy does not expand, then the underclass will not indefinitely tolerate the immigration of illegal immigrants/asylum seekers who will work for less. Yet flawed arguments persist. An editorial [TM. 17 July 00] argued for the relaxation of restrictions on migrants to relieve the shortage of seasonal strawberry pickers and to reduce the price of imports. This season lasts for about three weeks in the year and rural communities are already strongly resisting the accommodation of dispersed asylum seekers. Lessons seem not to have been learned from the Californian experience, and about forty years ago, seasonal hop pickers were completely displaced by machinery.

Galbraith [89] accepts that "There is a strong current of thought . . . that deeply deplores immigration, is deeply resentful of the migrants and campaigns ardently against their entry and continuing presence." Nevertheless, he advocates more of the same, but warns [1992:180] of its long-term social implications: "The present and devastated position of the socially assisted underclass has been identified as the most serious social problem of the time, as it is also the greatest threat to long-run peace and civility." He proposes a higher progressive taxation, lower defence expenditure and more welfare, social, and educational services and benefits for the underclass. He recognises that [12] "It is the nature of [the culture of] contentment that it resists that which invades it with vigour and often, as in very recent times, with strongly voiced indignation."

Rex [1986:132] supports Galbraith's economic analysis in that "The whole primary community of the ethnic minority, including its associations, has a function in relation to the larger society . . . this is why the idea of a multicultural society is supported to the extent that it is. In crude Marxist terminology it may be said to provide the essential social machinery for the reproduction of the labour force." Such was 1993 "Nannygate" affair, when a nominee for U.S. Attorney General withdrew because of her employment of two illegal immigrants as nannies, and did not pay their social security. The United States has created a federal task force to combat the modern day slavery of exploiting illegal immigrants [TM 25 April 98].

Galbraith [1996:95] recognises that the nation-state has a responsibility to control migration in favour of its own workforce, provided that "there is no discrimination, actual or implicit, as to ethnic identity or race," and appears to recognise that increasing multiculturalism is not without a social penalty. He accepts selective immigration controls in favour of the professional/artistic classes, because [96] "No country can be burdened with a large surplus of workers beyond the demands of the lower levels of employment." He accepts [93] that the melting pot theory applies only to earlier migrants, and "toward current arrivals there is a strongly negative attitude that is manifested in political oratory, discriminatory legislation and occasional outbursts of community hostility." He also accepts [92] that "the newly arrived are thought to bring a different and presumptively defective racial, religious, familial, hygienic or civic culture to the established community." Nevertheless he [95] believes that "life in the advanced countries would be difficult without a steady foreign contribution . . . to the lower, more arduous levels of labour force . . . who should be both welcomed and encouraged and should encounter no discrimination or hostility based on race, colour, language of cultural difference."

These views, including the economic arguments, are problematic. Firstly, any form of selective immigration control, which Galbraith now accepts, is unlikely to meet non-discriminatory criteria. Secondly, over the last twenty years and with the demise of industrial nationalisation, there have at times been levels of high unemployment and constant "downsizing" throughout the industrial West. Thirdly, there has been a clear economic incentive since the 1960s to replace unskilled and semi-skilled manpower with technology and investment. Fourthly, public reaction and legislation in the West to migration is hardening. Prior to its reversal in 1989, and it has continued to deteriorate ever since, Japan's post-war economic success was often attributed to its uniquely homogeneous and harmonious social culture, largely maintained and reinforced by its illiberal immigration policy which avoided its dilution. Clearly, this hypothesis of attributing either enhanced or poor economic performance to the level of unselective immigration is no longer tenable.

The Immigration Act 1971 Section 29(1) (2) attempted to reduce migrant numbers by voluntary assisted non-patrial repatriation. Prior to that, in 1968, the Labour government Home Secretary had announced that it was willing to repatriate any immigrant family that was unable to pay for itself and wanted to return home. Between 1965 and 1967, 243 heads of families had done so [TM 30 April 01]. The black MP Bernie Grant also proposed to the Home Secretary in 1995, that each black Briton should be allotted £100,000 [TM 10 April 00] to return to Africa or the Caribbean. A similar scheme for Jamaicans was financially supported by the EU [DM 29 Aug. 95]. During the 1980s, unemployment in Britain had been up to three million, with factors of about five to ten times the 1950s level, but during the current boom it is just under one million [Office for National Statistics July 2001], which is about 3.2 percent of the labour force—its lowest level for twenty-five years, given that the statistical bases are directly comparable. Claimant unemployment in Britain was about four percent in 1980; eleven percent in 1987; 5.5 percent in 1990; 10.5 percent in 1993 and four percent in 2000 [TM 20 May 00]. In Britain and elsewhere the economy has been cyclical, and unless a permanent answer to the problem can be found, it could be repeated. Some economists believe that high levels of unemployment and/or low wage levels for the underclass, are an endemic and permanent feature of capitalist economies, and the demand for unskilled labour will not arise again. Advanced manufacturing technologies and capital intensive industries in the developed world have reduced the demand for both unskilled and semi-skilled manpower, the only demand for which is low grade service employment.

A Harvard Business School study reported by Paul Kennedy [May 96:28], estimated that there were then 250 million workers in the United States and EU earning about eighty five dollars per day (roughly £15,000 per year). Over the last few decades, these workers, who in France and Germany also have a high social wage, have already faced competition from about ninety million workers in the Asian "tiger" economies. The challenge now emerging is the shift in manufacturing to the 1.2 billion Third World workers in South America, Indonesia, India, and China earning less than three dollars per day. This export of jobs will no longer be confined to "blue collar" manufacturing workers, because of the levelling of education and skills and modern information technology, with call centres leading the way. This will exert a depressive effect upon real wages in the richer countries with possibly, even probably, strong nationalist or protectionist policies and/or unionised labour unrest against globalization. Business interests have in the past when unemployment is low, justified economic immigration by "what is good (cheaper) for business is good for the country." There is an incentive to source the marginal labour market from immigrants, including illegal ones, the unskilled, and the disabled, in an expanding economy—but only while it lasts. This also applies for seasonal work such as picking crops, but subsequently the problem will remain. Business will distance itself from the national cost and political/social effect, by saying that these matters are for the government. Experience over the last forty years or so indicates that migrant manpower is not in fact cheap when the indirect and long-term social costs, such unemployment and welfare benefits are taken into account, along with the disproportionate demands on education, health care, and other resources, such as housing. Such resources are spent on remedying facilities in deprived areas to avoid social disturbances. Since the 1980s Britain has been a high-skill, high-investment, and low-taxation economy, because no other alternative is globally viable, and is now the world's fourth largest economy. The response should be to stop unnecessarily adding to the underclass, maybe at a temporary economic penalty, and accept that any quota based selective policy of immigration will be labelled racist.

In Britain, the United States, and Europe there has been a right-wing backlash against immigration. Typical rhetoric is "we are a haven, not a honey-pot," and "we provide a safety net, not a hammock." The state legislature of multicultural California passed legislation—Proposition 187—denying illegal immigrants all public services and non-emergency medical care, and bars their children from schools [DT 10 Nov. 94]. The now defunct Republican "Contract with America" would have gone further and denied welfare to legal immigrants as well, cutting off taxpayers money for medical care, school education, and social security from the growing number of illegal immigrants. Heightened concern has led to the enforced repatriation of Cuban and Haitian refugees, and probably the American financial aid to Honduras. It took five years for American troops to leave Haiti. Immigrants seem to favor the Democratic Party, which is more likely to accommodate their concerns; thus it has been predicted by two political analysts that if the current level of Third World migration continues, it will be virtually impossible for a Republican president to be elected after 2008—"a matter of simple political survival" [TM 7 June 97]. According to another forecast by Zillah Eisenstein [1996:67–8], "By 2005 the United States will probably be 15.8 percent black, 10.1 percent Asian, 27.8 percent Latino, and 46.3 percent white ... these demographic shifts have little to do with who votes. In the 1992 presidential election, eighty two percent of voters were white." The U.S. Census Bureau has recently announced that in California, the most populous U.S. state, Anglo-Saxons now account for only 49.8 percent of the population [TM 4 Sept. 00]. The number of Hispanics has increased by sixty percent in the last decade largely due to immigration, much of it uncontrolled from Mexico., and now accounts for about twelve percent of the U.S. population, about the same as African-Americans [TM 8 March 01]. Much of this arises from President Johnson's 1965 Immigration Act, which abolished quotas by national/racial origin, enacted in 1924 with the National Origins Quota System, thereby effectively destroying the Eurocentric hegemony. The loss by Californian whites of their majority status can be expected to be repeated within the next few years in Texas, Arizona, New Mexico, and Florida [STM. 9 July 00].

The reservoir of economic migrants quickly take advantage of new migration opportunities. After Canada had imposed visa restrictions on Czech/ Slovak Gypsies posing as "tourists," they turned their attention to Europe and the well-publicised welfare benefits of Britain, which received a sudden influx of Eastern European Gypsies. As with the long delay in implementing the new restrictions in the 1962 Commonwealth Immigration Act, this influx of Czech/Slovak Gypsies was probably intended to "beat the ban" following the initial publication of the Asylum and Immigration Act which introduced tougher asylum regulations, but which was not due to come into effect until April 2000.

When the EU Dublin Convention came into force in 1997, asylum seekers traveling without a visa became the responsibility of the first EU state where they elected to claim asylum, and not of the first EU country which they entered. Before then, an asylum seeker who passed through the first "safe" EU country could be sent back, because his application for refuge should have been lodged with that country. This Convention was intended to prevent asylum seekers from applying for asylum in more than one EU state, either simultaneously or consecutively, by taking advantage of unrestricted access between the internal borders of many of the EU states. Prior to 1997, member states with extensive land borders with refugee countries were likely to receive the most asylum seekers. However, asylum seekers now seek refuge in the EU state with the most favourable immigration controls and benefits, usually Britian, and travel across Europe unhindered until they reach the

Channel port of Calais. Another self-inflicted problem was when the Asylum and Immigration Appeals Act of 1993 conferred the right of "in-country" appeals, prior to which an appeal against refusal of entry could not be made before removal.

NOTES

Arendt, H. *Eichmann in Jerusalem*. London: Penguin Books, 1994. 169.
Bhavnani, K.K. "Towards a Multicultural Europe?" In *Feminist Review*. no. 45. Autum 1993. 33, 35.
Brand, H. "Inequality and Immigration." In *Dissent*. Summer 1994. 405.
Chavez, L. "Just Say Latino." In *The New Republic*. 22 March 1993. 18–9.
Eisenstein, Z. *Hatreds—Racialized and Sexualiized Conflicts in the 21st Century*. London: Routledge. 1996. 67–8.
Galbraith, J. K. *The Culture of Contentment*. London: Sinclair Stevenson. 1992. 12.
Ibid. 37.
Ibid. 180.
Galbraith, J.K. *The Good Society*. London: Sinclair Stevenson. 1996. 89.
Ibid. 89.
Ibid. 90.
Ibid. 91.
Ibid. 92.
Ibid. 93.
Ibid. 95.
Ibid. 95.
Ibid. 96.
Garrard, J.A. *The English and Immigration 1880–1910*. Oxford: Oxford University Press. 1971. 7.
Glazer, N. "Limits of Loyalty." In *For Love of Country—Debating the Limits of Patriotism* Nussbaum, M.C. Boston: Beacon Press, 1996. 62–3.
Gray, J. *Enlightenment's Wake*. London: Routledge, 1995. 4.
Horne, A. *Macmillan 1957–1986*. London: Macmillan, 1989. 421–3.
Joly, D. "A New Asylum Regime in Europe" In *Refugee Rights and Realities*. Nicholson, F and Twomey, P. (Eds.) Cambridge: Cambridge University Press, 1999. 353–4.
Kennedy, P. "Forecast: Global Gales Ahead" In *New Statesman and Society* May 31 1996. 28.
Miles, R. *Racism*. Routlege: London. 1989. 120.
MORI/Readers Digest. *Britain Today—Are We an Intolerant Nation?* London. 2000. July 20–24.
MORI/Mail on Sunday. *Asylum Poll*. London. 2001. January 4–5.
Steinbock, D. J. "The Refugee Definition as a Law: Issues of Interpretation." In *Refugee Rights and Realities*. Nicholson, F and Twomey, P. (Eds.) Cambridge: Cambridge University Press, 1999. 13.
Ibid. 14.
Ibid. 17.
Rex, J. 'The Political Sociology of a Multi Cultural Society." In *European Journal of Inter-Cultural Studies*. vol. 2. no. 1, 1991. 8.
Rex, J. *Race and Ethnicity*. Buckingham: Open University Press, 1986. 132.

Salins, P.D. *Assimilation, American Style*. New York: Basic Books. 1997. 211.
Perry, S.R. "Immigration, Justice and Culture." In *Justice in Immigration*. Schwartz,
　　W.F. (Ed.) Cambridge: Cambridge University Press, 1995. 106–8.
Stationery Office. *Social Trends 1992*. London. 35.
Ibid. 2001. 38.
Stationery Office. *British Nationality Act*. London. 1948.
_____ *Commonwealth Immigrants Act*. London. 1962.
_____ *Commonwealth Immigrants Act*. London. 1968.
_____ *Immigration Appeals Act*. London. 1969.
_____ *The Immigration Act*. London. 1971.
_____ *Race Relations Act*. London. 1976.
_____ *Supreme Court Act*. London. 1981.
_____ *British Nationality Act*. London. 1981.
_____ *British Nationality (Hong Kong) Act*. London. 1985.
_____ *The Immigration (Carriers Liabilty) Act*. London. 1987.
_____ *The Immigration Act*. London. 1988.
_____ *Education Reform Act*. London. 1988.
_____ *The Asylum And Immigration Appeals Act*. London. 1993.
_____ *The Asylum And Immigration Act*. London. 1996.
_____ *The Special Immigration Appeals Commission Act*. London. 1997.
_____ *Criminal Justice (Terrorism And Conspiracy) Act*. London. 1998.
_____ *Immigration And Asylum Act*. London. 1999.
_____ *The Race Relations (Amendment) Act* . London. 2000.
_____ *Terrorism Act*. London. 2000.
Tamir, Y. *Liberal Nationalism*. Princeton: Princeton University Press, 1993. 159–162.
Channel 4. *Gypsies, Tramps and Thieves?* 30 January 2000.
Channel 4. *Girl Friends from Pristina*. 6 February 2000.

16

The Failure of Immigration Control

Since the migration surges of the post-colonial 1960s and the post-Communist 1990s transitional eras, the UN (Geneva) Refugee Convention has been exploited, and Western Europe has become a "fortress." Immigration has an important influence on the toleration of multiculturalism because of the effect of the numbers and the origin of migrants. Paradoxically, it is not normally easy to enter Britain. Visas are intended to control overseas visitors, students, au pairs, and those seeking work permits. Refugees bypass all of these controls. Economic migrants may enter the country on a student or visitor visa, or be "over-stayers," or be illegals, and then claim asylum, as "in-country applicants." In February 2000, these made up almost sixty percent of the total claiming asylum [TM 25 March 00]. Refugees and economic migrants are not selected, difficult to administer, add predominantly. to the underclass, and claims for asylum are difficult both to refuse on entry and to subsequently validate. The seemingly uncontrollable flood of refugees which has increased over the past ten years or so make nonsense of any otherwise restrictive or selective immigration regulations. The financial returns for smuggling asylum seekers are high, and the risks acceptable. In Britain, until recently, any discussion of immigration (often labelled playing the "race card") had become negatively loaded, almost a taboo—usually said to be a "matter of principle." If a matter of principle is accepted as a reason for not doing something, then the implication is that only an unprincipled person would do so. In the run-up to the 1997 general election, the then-PM, when invited to comment on "strict control of immigration was the key to good race relations" [TM 5 Mar. 97], gave the response that "he was not going to lend his voice to anything that imperilled improving race relations." By the next general election (2001), the issue of immigration could no longer be swept under the carpet. Asylum applications remained relatively modest until

1991, when applications rose from 4,300 in 1986 to about 45,000. They then declined to 22,000 in 1993, reached the 45,000 level again in 1995, declined to 30,000 in 1996 and in 1999 sharply increased to about 72,000 and are still rising. What are major causes for concern are the widening gap between the applications and the number of grants of asylum, exceptional leave to remain, and refusals. The scale and cost of immigration into Britain is belatedly giving the government cause for serious concern [TM 15 Mar. 00]. In the lead up to the 2001 general election, the Labour party was proposing a place a "cap" on the number of asylum seekers allowed to remain each year, but subject to EU approval. The Conservative party was proposing that all asylum seekers would be detained in "secure reception centres" while their applications were processed, and that immigration officers would inspect documentation immediately on arrival so as to prevent asylum seekers from dumping their paper work before passing through immigration control, and then lie about their identity, nationality and airport of origin [TM 7 May/STM 20 May/DM 19 May 01].

Immigration administration in Britain, after years of neglect, political indecision, and the lack of a clear policy, has been variously described as being a shambles, collapsed, or in a state of meltdown. The director-general of Immigration and Nationality recently said [TM 8 Nov. 00] that the number of asylum seekers secretly living and working in Britain could not be calculated "and were very substantial," and could run into hundreds of thousands. The Home Secretary has admitted [TM 22 Nov. 00] that the whereabouts of more than 72,000 asylum seekers is unknown—they only give their address at the time they lodge their application. Because of the incompleteness of official statistics on immigration, unofficial estimates reported in the press vary from about 120,000 to up to twice that figure. This hidden pool of illegal immigrants is a major and uncontrolled feeder of multiculturalism. The official statistics on refugees are confused, confusing, and also suspect, because the information is often not complete and the figures do not usually include dependants. In many cases they should be multiplied by a factor of three or four, because migrants will bring in their families or future partners by later chain migration. Some ethnic groups have more children than other groups. The Asylum Aid Organisation [TM 22 May 00], says that "Home Office figures greatly underestimate the numbers who actually secure refuge in the U.K. The statistics issued by the Home Office refer only to initial decisions, and omit the many people who are allowed to stay following an successful appeal against refusal of asylum, or successfully petition the Home Office to re-examine their claims . . . the Home Office does not know how many people it grants asylum to each year, because it simply excludes large numbers of them from its calculations . . . a fairly conservative estimate for the proportion who are allowed to stay after initially being refused would be 20 to 30 percent." The most recent figures have been released by the Immigration Service Union [TM 17 June 01]. Since 1989, 484,525 asylum applications have been made not including dependants. Fewer than ten percent have been granted asylum, while removals and voluntary departures account for a further ten percent. Almost 175,000 are either awaiting appeals or have been granted temporary leave to remain in Britain. The rest are missing. More than half had travelled through other "safe" EU countries, including Greece, Italy and France. More than 130,000 have vanished without trace and this number, which has doubled since 1998, is equal to the population of the Isle of Wight.

The Home Secretary has acknowledged that there is a huge problem with deportation. Many illegal immigrants will have married over the years and had children, and it would not be politically acceptable to return them to their country of origin. In the period 1989 to 1997, 268,595 people applied for asylum of whom 14,685 were given refugee status, 51,140 were given exceptional leave to remain, 19,782 left the country, with a 91,870 backlog of appeals or applications or withdrawn applications. This left 91,118 who failed to make contact or unaccounted for [TM 6 Mar. 00]. These figures do not reflect the immigrant surge since 1997. The number of illegal immigrants rose nearly five fold in the first seven months of 1998 to 1,484 from 317 the previous year. Perhaps twenty percent of all applicants will be granted either refugee status or will not be accepted as refugees, but granted exceptional (temporary) leave to remain. This allows residence for four years with the possibility of an indefinite extension of leave to remain. In 1999 almost 100,000 people were accepted to live in the UK, the highest figure for twenty years, this being mainly due to refugees and those given exceptional leave to remain [TM. 13 Oct. 00]. The remainder have no right to stay, but more than half will do so. Most of the rejected applicants cannot be deported, because they "disappear," confident that they will never be found. According to the Immigration Services Union (TM 14 Feb. 01), since the new Human Rights Act came into force in October 2000, asylum seekers are using it to delay their deportation from Britain, claiming that that their right to life would be breached if they returned to their country of origin. Every month about thirty are escorted back to their country of origin and a further 620 are escorted on to planes at British airports. A further 100 a month leave under a voluntary repatriation scheme. If so, this equates to about only 9,000 per year. The latest government scheme is to offer illegal immigrants a £400 "settlement payment" and free flights to persuade them to go home [DM 24 March 01].

In 1999 there were 102,870 asylum seekers awaiting an initial decision on their application, with new applications in that year at a record 71,160—over fifty percent up from 1998 [TM 15 Mar. 00]—which excludes their dependants. To relieve this backlog, nearly 10,000 asylum seekers who have been waiting since before 1996 to have their case decided were made eligible for exceptional leave to remain, even if their claim proved to be unfounded, or they are coming from a state that is in turmoil or civil war. It is estimated that it would take the Immigration and Nationality Department almost four years to clear the backlog if no more refugees arrived. After the initial asylum application has been refused, the applicant has the right to lodge an appeal within seven days to a Special Adjudicator. If this fails and another appeal is lodged within five days, the application can go to an Immigration Appeals Tribunal. By February 2000 there were 3,339 applications waiting for an appeal before special adjudicators, and 2,258 contesting a point of law [TM 11 Feb. 00]. In 1996 more than 1,748 applications were made for judicial review of the appeal ruling of which 301 were allowed. As an emergency measure, the government is belatedly taking steps to reduce this backlog [TM 11 April 00]. The number of Immigration Tribunal adjudicators and Immigration Appeal Court judges have been substantially increased, a new national administrative centre was due to open in July 2000, and extra government funding provided for immigration lawyers. The government is to give £600 million emergency cash and 900 extra staff to the Immigration Service to a total of almost £1.2 billion, to clear the backlog of 89,000 applications. These extra resources had succeeded in reducing the backlog of applications, which had reached a record of 101,000 last year, to 24,315 by June 2001, following initial decisions having been processed at a rate of up to 10,000 a month. Predictably, there were, though, a record number of nearly 47,000 applications waiting for an appeal hearing [TM 26 July 01]. The government had previously announced a target of 12,000 deportations in 2000 and 57,000 by 2003, which seemed unlikely inasmuch that only 5,000 were deported during 1999. It also announced the intention to increase the number of detention centres for those considered likely to abscond [DM 8 June 00]. With deportations last year at only 8,900, the government failed to meet its target, but has set a new target for the year ending March 2002 of 24,000 "overstayers" plus 6,000 dependants. Three 500 member teams have been formed to arrest "overstayers" [TM 26 April 01]. The cost to the taxpayer of supporting asylum seekers in 1999 was £590 million and is expected to be £604 million in 2000 [DM 25 Nov. 00], and presumably excludes the £600 million emergency cash promised earlier [TM 24 July 00]. This expenditure contrasts with the government's reluctance to replace clinically sub-standard Victorian hospitals, a deteriorating national health service with long waiting lists, ageism discrimination against old people in hospitals and care homes because of lack of resources, and homeless couples refused Council housing.

Economic migrants and refugees are unlikely to return voluntarily—history in the twentieth century teaches otherwise [TM 6 April 99]. In addition to those who had arrived independently, during the Kosovo conflict, an official quota of 10,000 was authorised, of whom 4,346, mainly Kosovan Albanian refugees, were temporarily evacuated to Britain. Of these, only 1,527 accepted the offer of free flights back to Kosovo plus £250 resettlement allowance a year after the conflict ended [TM 12 June 00]. More than 1,900 are seeking permission to extend their twelve-month permission to stay, and if refused, face deportation [TM 20 June 00]. It is noteworthy that when the dependants of the 410 individuals who had applied for extensions to their twelve-month permits is taken into account, the total number becomes 2,050 [TM 12 June 00].

The number of asylum seekers in April 1999 during the Kosovan conflict was 4,905, which in October had increased to 6,295—the largest single group of 1,220 being from Yugoslavia [TM 26 Nov. 99]. In the whole of 1999, there were 11,535 such applications [TM 26 Feb. 00]. The flow of refugees had not diminished several months after hostilities and persecution had ceased. Germany took in some 350,000 refugees during the Bosnia war, around half of whom have returned. Tens of thousands more arrived during the Kosovan conflict. Germany is reported to be ready to deport tens of thousands of these 160,000 Kosovan refugees who have not returned [TM 21 April 00]. Britain is faced with the grotesque situation of accommodating Albanian refugees coming from Kosovo, some of whom came from Albania itself, now policed in part with British troops sent to protect them. One of the arguments for intervening in the Balkans was to prevent a mass influx of refugees who could disturb the social and political stability of Western Europe.

In the London Register Offices, illegal immigrants are marrying strangers within hours of arriving to obtain a UK passport. It is estimated that there are between 7,000 and 10,000 of these marriages a year. This was made easier by the scrapping in 1997 of the "primary purpose" rule, whereby an immigration officer could refuse entry if he thought that the reason for entry was not marriage, but to settle. From April 2001, a new law will require registrars to call an immigration officer if they suspect the wedding to be a sham [TM 25 Jan. 00/DM 12 Feb. 00]. The Foreign Office is also considering changes to immigration procedures, which would require a British woman believed to have been forcibly married overseas to attend an interview in person with her husband before he is granted admission to the UK.

Well-organised criminal gangs operate an illegal immigration racket. The latest Home Office estimate [TM 31 Oct. 00] suggests that the profits from smuggling total between £8 billion and £13 billion a year. The prices range up to £16,000 from China, and between £6,000 and £9,000 from India, to be paid out of future earnings, which, together with the exorbitant interest, means that they arrive in deep debt to the smugglers. If unpaid, the Chinese Triad gangs can arrange for a beating for their families in Britain, or in the country of origin. From March 2001, Hong Kong residents can stay in the EU for up to three months without visas. The price of fake passports has risen because criminal gangs tell mainland Chinese that this entitles them to apply for permanent resident status in Europe [TM 27 March 01].

The police have noticed that illegal immigrants have been less likely to surrender of late and claim asylum because criminal gangs can provide them with a clandestine life independent on any grant of asylum. In 1991 sixty-one people were found trying to enter Britain clandestinely, but in 1999 16,000 were apprehended. The Head of the Immigration Service said "the gangs have infrastructures, communications, and surveillance capabilities, far in excess of anything that the law enforcement agencies in transit and source countries can muster. The ease with which they operate across international boundaries means that the chances of their activities diminishing are negligible." The government called an unprecedented summit of its three intelligence agencies to counter international organised crime, including illegal immigration, which may now be the biggest threat to national security [STM 5 Dec. 99]. A failed attempt by the government to prevent the abuse of the immigration regulations was the proposal to ask visitors to Britain from India, Pakistan and Bangladesh to lodge a £10,000 bond if officials suspected that a visitor intended to settle illegally, and which would be forfeited if they failed to leave on time. These visitor visa applications slumped after the announcement from a record 255,000 in 1999 [MoS 16 April 00]. This proposal was dropped after protests of racism from immigrant communities.

It is bizarre that Britain is having to underwrite some Western European signatories of the 1951 Refugee Convention. They have at various times not been considered to be safe countries, because the British judiciary, on appeal from the Home Secretary's deportation decision, do not see them as fulfilling their obligations under this Convention. There were about 175 asylum seekers every month from the Czech Republic and Poland claiming persecution [TM 19 April 00]. It was agreed [DM 31 March 01] that British immigration officers could interview suspected asylum seekers in Prague, but this was abandoned after only three weeks [TM 8 Aug. 01]. At the same time, some of these countries supposedly having the rule of law and good government are seeking to join the EU. The situation is not made easier by some decisions by the British Courts, whereby the judiciary seems intent on overturning asylum decisions made by the Home Secretary. The High Court quashed the Home Secretary's refusal to grant asylum to five applicants who had entered Britain via Belgium, a refusal which had been upheld by the Appeal Adjudicators on the grounds that Belgium was no longer a safe country [DM 20 April 96]. In some cases, the Courts have ruled unlawful the Home Secretary's decision to return asylum seekers to France and Germany as safe countries [18 May 01]. But in another case, the Court decided that a Kurdish refugee could be returned to France as a safe third country [TM 24 Feb. 97]. It has also been ruled that Pakistan (now a suspended member of the Commonwealth) cannot be included on the Home Secretary's list of approved safe countries, although ratified by Parliament, because his decision was irrational [TM 18 May 01]. The Courts have also ruled that asylum must be given to those escaping "non-state persecution" [TM 2 March 00]. Two abused Pakistani women were allowed by the House of Lords, on appeal, to claim asylum because they formed a particular social group unprotected by the Pakistani state [TM 26 March 99]. This means that other social groups, including homosexuals, could be entitled to claim asylum. There are practical difficulties in verifying the claims made for asylum. A Turkish visa "overstayer" claimed asylum on the grounds of political persecution and abuse of human rights, but an independent and unofficial (BBC) investigation in Turkey found that these claims were false [BBC 2 22 April 01]. The Turkish police had issued a warrant for his arrest for questioning about the death of an English girl [DM 28 April 01]. Article 1 F (b) of the UN Convention makes such an immigrant ineligible for refugee status if he has committed a serious non-political crime.

Lawyers, on appeal, exploit loopholes in the Convention, and judges make creative interpretations, which can vary from one appeal to another, of the imprecise language of the UN Convention, and can dismantle the Home Secretary's intentions. A recent Court of Appeal decision related the significance of a semicolon before the word "or" in the 1951 Convention [TM 8 Sept. 00]. It is no exaggeration to say that virtually every word and conceivable nuance of the definition of a refugee has been contested in the High Court. The UN Convention on illegal immigrants, i.e. covert migrants or undeclared asylum seekers, is unclear [DT 2 March 00]. It allows illegal immigrants to apply for asylum, but only if they have come directly from a country where they are in danger. Some EU members will return these people only back to a "third" safe country, whilst others will send them back to their country of origin. Many of these immigrants cross Western Europe, having passed through other safe countries, and claim asylum only when they reach Britain.

Migrant opportunism in not confined to Britain. The Irish Republic, which for 150 years was a major exporter of its people and until recently one of Europe's poorer and most homogeneous countries, has also experienced an influx of migrants from Eastern Europe and Africa. There were thirty-nine applications for asylum in 1992, compared with 4,000 in 1996, and 6,000 predicted in 1997 [STM 15 June 97/TM 14 Jan. 98]. Ireland has a population of 3.5 million, and has generous welfare benefits and liberal immigration laws. An anti-immigration group has been formed [TM 14 Jan. 98], and tougher penalties have been introduced against illegal immigrants, who made up ninety percent of the entries [TM 15 June 97]. Immigration officials have found that hundreds of claimants are crossing between Britain and Ireland, which have no border checks, and are receiving welfare payments in both countries [TM 19 March 00].

In spite of the problem of the "disappeared" refugee, civil liberty pressure groups campaign against the detention of a relatively small proportion of immigrants whose claims are deemed to be "manifestly unfounded." In February 1998, 427 detainees were held in prison custody, which represents about half of those then in detention [Ellis.1998: 4]. Detention takes place while claims for asylum are being verified, or because of claims that human rights and/or the Immigration Acts have been contravened, and/or are seeking appeals and judicial reviews of Ministerial decisions. In response to the refugee surge, two new detention centres are to be opened to increase the capacity from 1,000 to 3,000 asylum seekers, but the problem is to find suitable sites free of local opposition [TM 27 Nov. 00]. The U.S. solution was to plan to confine its 20,000 Kosovan refugees in its Guantanamo Bay naval Base in Cuba [TM 7 April 99].

Economic migrants and their advisers can be well-versed in Western "rights talk." If their applications for entry are refused, they can apply for temporary residence on the grounds of education, family separation, and other humanitarian claims, with appeals that can take four years or more. This gives time to bring in dependants who then commence their own appeals. The Home Office [TM 23 Jan. 98] identified about 250 individuals or companies banned from legal aid work, and more than 100 solicitors [18 May/1Sept. 99] who exploit asylum seekers by advertising expensive and unnecessary assistance for unfounded and abusive claims, including legal aid, welfare benefits, fraud, falsifying documents, and the evasion of immigration laws. Dishonest immigration advisers provide forged travel documents and sham marriages. Many asylum seekers still choose to remain in London and the South East. This is reflected by the fact that of the 423 immigration law firms in Britain, more than half are in the London area. More than 100 of these firms were to be banned from legal aid work as incompetent or giving bogus advice [TM 1 Sept. 99]. The Home Secretary has said that "Many [asylum] claims are just a tissue of lies," and that some solicitors and "bent immigration advisers . . . are wholly abusive and say 'just put in another appeal, the longer you are here the more difficult it will be to remove you.'" Serial automatic legal appeals undermine the credibility of immigration control. It takes at least three months, and usually years, to carry out a verification, and if exceptional temporary leave to remain is granted on humanitarian grounds, or as a result of coming from an unsafe state that is in turmoil or civil war, some asylum seekers fail to attend for interview and cannot be traced. Some destroy their passports, knowing that it is time consuming and sometimes futile to try to return them to their country of origin without identity papers, or to countries such as China, which may refuse to accept them. At least 60,000 "overstayer" asylum seekers "disappeared" between 1989 and 1997, probably living clandestinely and working in the black economy, although some may be awaiting the outcome of judicial reviews. They are sometimes exploited as "slaves" by dishonest employers, both white and non-white [STM 26 April 98]. Although it has been given consideration, to date no sanctions have been imposed on employers employing illegal immigrants. The motivation of the Immigration Service and the police to carry out forcible deportation orders had no doubt been undermined [Ind. 9 May 99] by the barrage of racist accusations that they faced over the high profile enforced deportation fatality in 1993—the illegal Jamaican immigrant Joy Gardner, who was canonised as a black victim. Three police officers were acquitted of her manslaughter [DM 15 June 95].

The 1999 Asylum and Immigration Act was the most comprehensive reform of the legislation for many years, contained more restrictive regulations, and closed some loopholes. A national, in the place of the existing local authority system of maintenance and support (The National Asylum Support Service), was set up, together with a compulsory dispersal scheme for refugees. Appeal procedures were also streamlined using a 'two tier" process, through a Special Adjudicator, then an Immigration Appeals Tribunal, and then possibly a judicial review. Under the new regulations, which came into effect in April 2000, to dissuade economic refugees, national social security cash benefits were replaced by a voucher system—which was labelled racist by anti-racists and is to be abandoned. Existing refugees can continue to claim income support and housing benefits until a decision is made on their asylum claim. New asylum seekers are entitled to voucher support, equal to 100 percent and seventy percent of national income support levels for children and adults respectively, of which £10 per week per person is received as cash.

This lower adult rate reflects the fact that utilities, furniture, furnishings, and other living essentials are provided with the offer of accommodation if needed [IND 8 April 00]. Asylum seekers are banned from working during the first six months of their stay; after that they can apply for work, and are supposedly taxed in the normal way. These benefits, although not generous, compare favourably with the national benefit entitlements, such as the basic state retirement pension, and the statutory minimum wage, let alone the poverty and misery suffered by some elderly people and the homeless. Having paid national insurance premiums throughout the whole of their working lives, the state benefit for half of Britain's pensioners constitutes seventy-five percent or more of their total income, and twenty-two percent are living below the "poverty level" in households with incomes below half of the national average before housing costs [TM 20 Aug. 00]. An apologist wrote to the press [TM 5 April 01] claiming that in the 1999–2000 financial year, the cost of all asylum seekers to the British taxpayer was less than fifty pence a week, although the basis of this calculation was not given. This compares with the increase in the payment to millions of state pensioners from April 2000, which was seventy-five pence per week.

In the year 2000, the government supposedly planned to disperse new refugees. To do this, it needed to provide 4,200 new homes every month, at a cost of £300 million. Nine regions of the country were supposed to take 300 refugees each month. This scheme had to be scaled down from the original estimate of 65,000 to 38,000 after only 5,000 refugees volunteered for it after the first five months. It is estimated that at least eighty-five percent of all asylum seekers and refugees live in London [TM 1 June 00]. According to the Home Office [TM 23 May 99], nearly 10,000 Kosovan refugees have settled in London in the last two years, and leave reception centres elsewhere in the country for London. Kent County Council, which includes the channel port of Dover, will be spending £52 million on asylum seekers this year [TM 21 Sept. 00]. These 1999 Asylum Act proposals were first published in July 1998, twenty-one months before they came into force in April 2000, which no doubt contributed to the subsequent "beat the ban" surge of refugees. This new Act so far appears to have had a modest effect on the number of economic migrants, asylum seekers, illegal immigrants, and the number of "disappeared." In October 2000 there were almost 7,000 asylum applications, which was the highest total for the year [DM 25 Nov. 00]. In March 2001 there were 5,815 new applications, with a total of 88,510 asylum seekers, with their dependants arriving in the ten months to February 2001 (equivalent to an annual rate of 106,000) [TM 26 April 2001]. In spite of the reduced level of benefits introduced the previous April, this suggests that many work illegally [DM 21 Sept. 00].

The Refugee Council objected to the dispersal scheme because it is a "massive piece of social engineering"—as if uncontrolled immigration, and its acquired multiculturalism, were not. It wants refugees to be located in "an area that has an existing multi-ethnic population"—which means increasing ghettoisation. This relocation is sometimes being done without consulting local residents, who complain that the housing and facilities provided are sometimes better than their own. A remote village in Somerset of 300 residents vigorously protested with NIMBYism when it was required to accommodate seventy-four asylum seekers, plus a staff of fifteen [TM 14 June 00]. There was a similar reaction in a village of 4,000 residents in South Yorkshire, when Rotherham Borough Council proposed to build an extendible hostel to house 180 asylum seekers [TM 15 March 00]. The plan was dropped in the face of these local protests because of "changed circumstances" [TM 28 March 00]. Glasgow City Council refused to accept busloads of about seventy refugees sent by the London Borough of Wandsworth. A disused holiday motel in an Essex village of 850 residents was required to house 120 asylum seekers [TM 17 June 00]. The government planned to compulsorily disperse 65,000 people across Britain in so called "cluster areas" in its first year of operation. In fact only 21,072 were successfully relocated, with about

14,000 "gone missing"—no doubt living with relatives or friends [TM 25 April 01]. It was found that tension resulted when 1000 asylum seekers were dispersed in the city of Hull. A report concluded that they should have instead been sent to cities with a high minority population, i.e. with ghettoes [TM 4 July 01]. The lessons from this are obvious.

Hijacking aircraft is a premeditated act of international terrorism, punishable under the 1982 Aviation Security Act with up to life imprisonment [TM 10 Feb. 00]. However, under the 1951 UN Convention, a criminal conviction, even for hijacking, is no bar to a subsequent asylum application—the only exclusion is for crimes against humanity or international peace. In 1996, six Iraqi hijackers held 197 people hostage in a Sudanese Airbus that landed at Stansted airport. After a successful legal appeal against prison sentences, they are living in Britain as asylum seekers, receiving legal aid, and five are receiving welfare benefits [TM 9 Feb. 00]. The impotence of the British authorities towards hijackers may have led to the latest hijacking incident in February 2000, also at Stansted. The latest hijack of 173 passengers and crew cost Britain more than £4 million [STM 30 Dec. 00], and is believed to have been expertly planned: more than forty of the passengers brought mountains of luggage with them. The hijackers demanded asylum, immunity from prosecution, and the right to set up an Afghan political opposition base in London [TM 10 Feb. 00]. At the time, the Home Secretary said [TM 30 Dec. 00] "I am utterly determined that nobody should consider that there can be any benefit to be obtained from hijacking." Fifteen months later, eighty-one passengers and crew had left voluntarily; four people and thirteen dependants were granted asylum; another thirty-five and their five dependants were refused asylum, but have appealed; and eleven have been on trial defended by twenty-four barristers with estimated legal costs to date of £12 million at the taxpayers expense [TM 19 April 01]. This incident is indicative of the impotence of the current system of immigration control and legislation. All Afghans in recent years have been granted "exceptional leave to remain" even if their asylum claims are rejected [DM 25 Nov. 00]. The exclusion of hijackers is a clear example of a necessary amendment to the 1951 Convention.

Official figures for the year 2000 [DT 26 Jan. 01] show that Britain has now become by far the most attractive destination in Europe for asylum seekers. Principal applications numbered the highest ever at 76,000, an increase of seven percent on 1999, which, including dependants, gave a total of 97,000. This is in spite of the more restrictive regulations imposed in April 2000, although there are signs that the rate of increase is slowing when compared with the rise of fifty-five and forty-five percent in 1999 and 1998 respectively. The figure for Germany was 78,564—a fall of seventeen percent. Britain now accounts for around twenty percent of the EU total of asylum seekers, and now takes in more than the United States, illegal immigrants apart. In Britain last year two thirds of the applications for asylum were from people already in the country [DT 26 Jan. 01]. A total of 110,000 initial decisions were taken, but only 10,185 were recognised as refugees and a further 11,365 were given exceptional leave to remain, plus a further 3,300 were given asylum on appeal. Nevertheless, the crucial fact is that between March and September 2000, only 4,870 asylum seekers were removed [TM 26 Jan. 01], adding to the growing year-on-year total. Insofar as the Government's refugee dispersal scheme is concerned, of the 65,000 dispersals planned during its first twelve months, only 13,500 were successfully dispersed over the first nine months [DM 26 Jan. 01]. The Immigration Minister had to admit that "What we are seeing in the EU is unfortunately the concept of asylum being undermined by these people using it as a backdoor route to migration" [TM 26 Jan. 01] and has now called for a "sensible debate" about immigration [TM 23 Jan. 01]

Dover in Kent is the principal cross-Channel port of entry and has become Britain's new "land border". On a normal day it has about thirty illegal immigrants [TM 20 June 00]. Immigration by cross-Channel ferries, trains, lorries, and cars is more difficult to control than by airlines. The French officials make only token efforts to curb asylum seekers [TM 1 April 00]. Over the last three years Dover has had Slovak Gypsy asylum seekers, then Kosovans, then Albanians, Chinese, and now Somalis, Iraqis and Afghans [TM 27 June 00]. Dover has 33,000 residents who remain almost universally hostile to refugees, which peaked at 1,200 in 1999 [TM 24 June 00], and resulted in local disturbances [TM 5/DM 16 Aug. 99]. Local residents see legitimate causes for concern inasmuch as economic refugees divert scarce resources and put pressure on local schools and health services [TM 9 Aug. 99]. Dover may represent a microcosm of the outcome of exceeding a critical mass in sensitive areas. The government belatedly decided to spread ethnic clusters of asylum seekers from Kent and London around the country, ostensibly because of a shortage of housing. The Chief Constable of Kent [TM 23 Jan. 01] has warned that Britain faces significant public disorder unless police quell tension and violence between asylum seekers and local communities and within refugee communities, because of their mix of nationalities that are in conflict in their own countries. The Shadow Home Secretary has also warned [TM 28 Jan. 01] that the number of asylum seekers entering Britain has become "unsustainable," and a senior immigration official revealed that some countries, such as Iraq and Serbia, are encouraging the outflow of refugees to Britain in retaliation. Blair has cautioned that the Balkans had "become Europe's capital for the illegal traffic of human beings" [DM 20 Jan. 01].

There is also exploitation of children sent to Britain who have been coached in how to claim protection on their arrival. Six thousand unaccompanied children are now being looked after in England and Wales compared with

2,500 in 1999 [TM 8 Aug. 01]. In 1996 477 children aged seventeen and under, who were unaccompanied, and not known to be joining a close relative, applied for asylum at the ports of entry [Ellis 1998: 8]. In the county of Kent, the number of unaccompanied minors aged up to seventeen increased from 115 in April 1999 to 850 in February 2000, and the annual cost of social and educational services to help them is estimated to be £8.1 million. In Britain in 1999, the total number was 3,349, mainly from Yugoslavia [TM 17 March 00]. The cost in the neighbouring county of Surrey of educating asylum seekers is said to be 2.5 times higher than the average pupil [TM 19 April 00]. Anecdotal evidence suggests that some local schools were resisting accepting refugee children because of the adverse effect on their position in the government education league tables. Permission has since been given to exclude pupils from these tables whose first language is not English [TM. 21 July 00], but this does not altogether remove the problem. The government estimates that it will cost £4,416 per year in education and health costs for each asylum seeker family per year, and some doctors report that their consultations are taking an average of three to four times longer than other patients [TM 1 June 00]. A study for the British Thoracic Society showed that tuberculosis infection rates among asylum seekers coming through Heathrow are twenty-two times higher than the rest of the country [DM 15 Dec. 00]

Lorry drivers, both British and non-British, are offered up to £1,000 for each illegal immigrant brought in. One driver denied all knowledge when 101 such immigrants were found on his lorry [TM 1 April 00]. Britain's largest ferry firm is now employing forty security guards to check every lorry coming into Dover. Ferry companies and lorry drivers face a fine of £2,000 for each clandestine illegal brought in at any British port, and their vehicles impounded. This has since been declared on appeal to be illegal and disproportionate. These penalties did however have the desired effect [TM 5 April 01]. In the three-month period of January to March 2000, before the penalties were introduced, the number of illegal immigrants caught at Dover was 3,908. In the first three months of 2001, the number fell to 2,271. Up to the end of March 2001, 837 penalty notices had been imposed on hauliers, in respect of 4,666 people found in vehicles. The penalties amount to £9.3 million, although only £1 million has been paid. These regulations were extended to the Channel Tunnel rail freight trains from March 2001. A freight train operator has said that with the current rate of these immigrants, it could be facing a fine of £5 million a year and may go out of business. The French will not allow them to inspect the trains in France, and French and Belgian operators are not subject to the fines [STM 25 March 01]. Another entry route which has been used to evade immigration controls is via the Eurostar passenger train. Until recently, immigration officials could only begin checking passenger documents when the train had entered British territory. In the first three months of year 2000, 825 asylum seekers used this route. Governments have now agreed to post their immigration officials to check documents at French, Belgium, and British Eurostar stations [TM 30 May 00/TXT 31 March 01]. A concern of those who opposed the Channel Tunnel when it was agreed to by the British and French governments in 1986 and then opened in 1994 was that it would endanger the military security of the British Isles. It is ironic that what was not then envisaged was that approximately 1,000 immigrants per month would use the Eurostar freight and shuttle services from Calais to enter Britain illegally. Eurotunnel is now facing fines of £2 million a month for its failure to properly secure its rail terminal at Calais [STM 23 July 01].

It is not unknown for a political refugee, instead of having being the oppressed, has in fact been the oppressor. A refugee living on four categories of benefit in London since 1998 was arrested on behalf of the UN International Criminal Tribunal of Rwanda. He was facing charges of genocide and crimes against humanity, being allegedly responsible for the slaughter of more than 100,000 Rwandans in 1994 [TM 16 Nov. 99]. His presence had been reported in the national press four months beforehand. He was due to be deported. Or a former leader of the rebel government in Sierra Leone, whose tactics allegedly included hacking off the arms of his opponents, was granted temporary leave to stay in Britain as an asylum seeker. Activist, anti-British, anti-American and sometimes racist political and/or terrorist "sleeper" refugees have continued their domestic power "struggle" within the tolerant haven of London, and publicly demonstrate for support. Today's political asylum seeker can be tomorrow's Downing Street/Whitehall protester. The Independent Television Commission revoked the licence of the Kurdish Met television satellite channel because it was using Britain as a platform for inciting violence [TM 24 April 99]. Russia has accused Britain of being a "hotbed of Chechen sympathisers," who issued a death threat fatwa on the Russian President. It took until 1998 for the government to enact legislation to punish terrorist conspiracy in Britain, or to incite people overseas to commit a terrorist act. This has been reinforced by the Terrorism Act 2000 with another Act pending. In 1999 eighty-three people were charged in connection with international terrorism under 1998 Act. This illustrates the lack of reciprocity between the claiming and the respecting of rights, and how politically motivated migrants can appeal to possibly guilt-laden expatriates. A conflict exists between a right claimed by an individual to whom a host nation-state has no more than a universal moral obligation, compared with the interests of its citizens, to whom its government has a positive duty. Even this seemingly justifiable principle has been put in doubt by a recent immigration appeal decision [TM1 Aug. 00]. Two suspected Sikh terrorist asylum seekers won an appeal against deportation, even though the judge expressed disquiet about permitting terrorists proved to be a danger to national security to stay in Britain. This was because the European Convention on Human Rights would be breached, there being "substantial grounds" for believing that they would be tortured in India. Nonetheless Shah [1999:134] believes that "A whole battery of national security provisions, anti-terrorist laws, and extradition laws, are deployed with a view to suppressing any dissent from outside 'legitimate' political channels." Professor Said [133–4] also appears to sympathise with this view, in saying that "the terms 'fundamentalism' and 'terrorism' . . . derive from the concerns and intellectual factories in metropolitan centres like London and Washington . . . They are fearful images that lack discriminate contents or definition, but they signify moral power and approval for whomever uses them, moral defensiveness and criminalisation for whomever they designate."

It is contended that refugees should not exploit the privileges of Western culture when it suits them, and undermine it when it does not. Article 2 of the 1951 UN Convention says that "every refugee has duties to the country in which he finds himself etc." This should be strengthened to emphasise the obligation to respect its liberal ethos. Refugees should recognise that they have a reciprocal obligation not to abuse those norms of individual freedom that harm the interests of their hosts, nor should they expect to expect a culture of dutiless rights. The grant of asylum, or exceptional leave to remain, should not be a licence to abuse this privilege and to disappear while their claims to refugee status are being investigated. If refugees do this, it is breaking an implied contractual relationship that an immigrant enters into with the host society.

NOTES

Ellis, R. *Asylum Seekers and Immigration Act Prisoners—The Practice of Detention*. London: The Prison Reform Trust, 1998. 4.

Ibid. 8.

Humphries. S. and Taylor. J. *The Making of Modern London*. 1945–1985. London: Sidgwick and Jackson. 1986. 117.

Shah, P. "Taking The 'Political' Out Of Asylum. The Legal Containment Of Refugees 'Political Activism.'" In *Refugee Rights and Realities*. Nicholson, F and Twomey, P. (Eds.) Cambridge: Cambridge University Press, 1999. 133–4.

Trebilock, M.J. "The Case for a Liberal Imigration Policy." In *Justice in Immigration*. Cambridge: Cambridge University Press, 1995. 220.

BBC 2. *Correspondent—Desperately Seeking Asylum*. 22 April 2001.

17

Prejudice, Stereotyping, Victimhood, and the Culture of Complaint

A separatist multicultural society will invoke racial, cultural, and religious prejudices and stereotypes on both sides of the cultural divide. It can reinforce the perception of diversity and difference, whilst adversely affecting tolerance and acceptability. Human nature creates and perpetuates stereotypes and caricatures, and harbours prejudices, often as a substitute for actual knowledge. It is a convenient way of initially characterising the unfamiliar—perhaps mankind is instinctively territorial and racist. The Swann report [1985:199] recognised this: "By the late 1960s and early 1970s there was a growing realisation that the policies of assimilation and integration had failed to achieve their objectives . . . On the broader level ethnic minority groups as a whole had not 'disappeared,' as seems to have been hoped, by being absorbed by the majority community and the essential naivety of expecting the immigrant communities to be accepted by the indigenous majority as equal citizens of this country had been exposed by the rising tide of racial prejudice and hostility." This Committee favoured integration—not assimilation or separatism. Every society, social group, and culture has its prejudices, stereotypes, stigmas, and taboos, which support its self-definition with respect to its economic worth, lifestyle, race, gender, or age. These may change with time and trans-culturalisation under their own dynamism. Prejudice undermines trust, but like racism, may arise from a fear of difference, and cannot be legislated away. Tolerant and welcoming attitudes may be displayed towards immigrants because of their economic contribution. This can, however, be short-lived, and in a recession can turn into scapegoating, prejudice, feelings of resentment, and the accusation of "stealing jobs."

A stereotype can be manufactured by the selective exemplification of the abnormal, with the implication that it is the norm—it can be positive or negative, to be admired or condemned—serving to suppress individuality. If a false group stereotype has been created, legislation can unfairly compensate or unfairly victimise the group. An intolerant and aggressive ideology may feel the need to create a threat by a stereotyped out-group, which may be a minority. Beattie [1966: 273] observes that "[Some] stereotypes are due to ignorance, and sometimes ignorance affords moral or political advantage. It does so where it provides a ground for maintaining an elite, or justifies a system of economic exploitation." The Nazis dehumanised the Jews, the Slavs, homosexuals, Gypsies, and the mentally disabled, which facilitated the change from relative tolerance to the Holocaust. With television, stereotyping based on ignorance is now less likely than before. Before then, knowledge of the world had been limited, and cultural stereotypes more readily accepted. Geoffrey Parkins [1984:31] notes that "Stereotypes have been manufactured that have very little correspondence with the facts. Many members of ethnic minority groups who have greatly improved their circumstances since moving to Britain would be surprised to read the observations of many race-relations researchers and writers." In 1997, there were one hundred British Asian millionaires each worth an average of £40 million, with thirteen worth more than this average up to £1500 million [TM 19 Feb. 97]. In 2000, the top 250 Asian entrepreneurs were said to be worth £9 billion, an average of £36 million each [TM 27 March 01]. Nonetheless, the Indian, Chinese, and African communities tend to be more economically and educationally successful than African-Caribbeans, Pakistanis, Bangladeshis, and probably Albanians, who are below the national average.

A stigma is a condition, trait, or characteristic, which marks individual members of a stereotyped group as being socially unacceptable and inferior. A taboo is a prohibition or restriction imposed by custom or legislation, usually relating to race. Paradoxically, the humour of some 1970s/80s television comedy sitcoms in Britain provided an acceptable forum for airing the taboo subjects of race and class. Prejudice suggests intolerance and is considered to be a moral transgression if it is translated into discrimination. Like racism, knee-jerk accusations of prejudice, when used as a rhetorical moral weapon, can be almost as powerful as its manifestation. A genuine, well-considered but contrary opinion about an issue can be labelled as a prejudice. A prejudice is a pre-judgement, and not a considered view, which differs from its pejorative and incorrect interpretation. This pre-judgement may be the same as a well-considered opinion, but the prejudice label remains. Pre-judgements become prejudices only if they persist when exposed to contrary evidence. Although it may be seen as being wrong or eccentric, prejudice can be made more acceptable if it appears to be reasoned—provided that it is based on reflective thought, rather than subjective or emotive. Opposition to multiculturalism is prejudiced, but it can be an objectivised prejudice. Melanie Phillips, the journalist and broadcaster, observes [1994:38] "It seems to me to be a truism that we all harbour prejudices, just as we are all prone to selfishness, or jealousy, or any number of characteristics that make up every human being. But understanding the latent prejudices in human nature appeared to develop into the belief that everyone in majority groups exercised those prejudices, and that society was endemically oppressive as a result. The result seemed to me that, in some cases, people whose behaviour was blameless were attacked for behaving in a prejudiced manner, simply because they were part of the majority."

Berry [1986:71–2] highlights the socio-cultural role of prejudices which are "constituted by social practices established through time. These practices cohere into traditions. It is through such traditions that individuals participate in a whole greater than themselves. As conservatives have long emphasised, individuals only understand themselves, and they in their turn can only be understood, in supra-individualist terms." Gray [1992:44–5] takes the view that "the old fashioned ideal of toleration, with its insight into the imperfectibility of the human mind—would be one that accepts the inevitabilty of prejudice and acknowledges that it has uses and benefits, while at the same time being prepared to curb its expression when this has demonstrably harmful effects . . . A policy of toleration with regard to all but the most harmful prejudices makes sense for another reason: there is not much agreement among us as to what counts as a prejudice . . . The life of the mind can never be that of pure reason, since it always depends on much that has not been subject to critical scrutiny by our reason." Trust, better communication, and reciprocal toleration can serve to counteract prejudice and stereotyping between racial/cultural groups. However, some psychologists [Hayes and Orrell 1993: 310–1] believe that, although increased contact reduces prejudice between individuals, it does not against a group as a whole, unless there is a common interest such as their employment or a threat—to which loyalty is the prerequisite. People may accept a group stereotype, but exempt individuals of whom they have personal experience—an anti-semite might truthfully say that "some of my best friends are Jews."

According to Glover [1988:196–7] "People develop stereotyped pictures of other groups, seeing individuals in terms of the stereotype. We look for and notice differences that reflect well on our group, and so boost our self-esteem. And there is some evidence that, when groups compete against each other, this improves the self-esteem of their members." The public relations industry aims at creating positive acceptable stereotypes with instantly recognisable identities or rather images. Anti-racists use Enoch Powell, Nazis, fascists, and "right wingers" as racist stereotypes. Stereotypes are self-reinforcing and can be positive or negative. A negative group stereotype supports prejudice and intolerance, and leads to scapegoating and stigmatising. Nevertheless, high profile individuals do sometimes mirror and reinforce their group stereotype. Whenever a high visibility group, rather than its individual members remain separatist, it lends itself to both being stereotyped, such as the visibly different and ghettoised Hasidic Jews. This tends to marginalise any outliers of the group from the rest of society, and makes their assimilation difficult to accept. This is probably why the assimilated writer Bernard Levin [TMG 29 Mar. 97] complained that his friends will not allow him to forget his Jewish origins, and raises the question as to whether the totally assimilated Jews in Germany were self-deceiving adherents to a culture that actually never accepted them. The black activist MP Bernie Grant, who reportedly wanted to be the Minister for Minorities [TM 15 Aug. 98], contributed to a group stereotype, untypical of most blacks in Britain. He condemned the Gulf War as "racially motivated," and appealed to the Home Secretary [DM 30 June 98] to relax the ban on entry of Louis Farrakhan, the American black militant. He was branded by the Home Office Minister Douglas Hurd as the "high priest of racism." When the first black/Asian MPs were elected to Parliament, he tried, in 1987, to form a parliamentary black caucus.

It is no exaggeration to say that Britain and its public service institutions, particularly in the last three years, have been undergoing a veritable onslaught of high profile victimhood accusations, reinforced by claims of discrimination and racism by its ethnic minorities. It remains to be seen what effect this will have on the attitude of the general public to immigration and multiculturalism. There are genuine victims, but the West lives with victimhood, hyper-litigation, and legal appeals in a culture of blame, grievance, guilt, compensation and retrospective apologies—the most common qualification for which is to be a minority. The compensation culture has resulted in the number of practising barristers and solicitors rising from about 35,000 in 1976 to about 93,000 by the end of 2000 [TM 28 Feb.01]. There can be tyranny by a minority in a tolerant democracy, as well as by the majority in an intolerant democracy. A feature of a multicultural society is that its minorities will tend to claim discrimination whether real or imaginary as part of the politics of "minoritarianism."

Parkins [1984:31] notes that "It is almost a tradition in Britain for those seeking changes in legislation to exaggerate the extent of the evils they claim to be fighting. Under the sheer weight of literature and evidence highlighting the incidence of racial minority disadvantage, one is apt to forget there are far more in the white population who are in similar circumstances . . . in fact amongst those perceived to be suffering any particular disadvantage, our racial and ethnic minorities are always a minority." A Home Office report "The Attitudes of Ethnic Minorities" [Field 1984:Foreword], which was apparently not considered by the 1985 Swann Committee, examined the victimhood view that "Ethnic minorities lack self-respect because of their disadvantaged position, that young blacks are 'alienated,' and that young blacks and Asians have unrealistic job aspirations." It concluded that "Much of the evidence is negative; in many respects the attitudes of blacks and Asians living in Britain do not differ dramatically from those of whites. While there are exceptions to this rule, and further research is needed in some fields, these findings suggest that more caution is needed in future about accepting judgements made about black and Asian attitudes."

Victimhood can be claimed by most minorities—ethnic minorities, smokers, cyclists, animal right activists, environmentalists, fox hunters, the BNP. The Scots, the Welsh, and the Irish (but not the English) can claim that they are victimised, or discriminated against, or socially excluded. Any group or individual, not necessarily part of a minority, and be it by the accident of birth or otherwise, can perceive him/herself as being a victim or excluded. Eventually, if everyone is a victim, then no-one is. A genuinely disadvantaged group can attract sham claimants: university students have fraudulently claimed dyslexia to obtain disability awards and examination concessions. Victimhood is often accompanied by an assertive accusation of prejudice and/or discrimination, usually racial, gender or both. It can be reinforced by martyrdom, the ultimate example being hunger strikes, particularly if it attracts the attention of the media. This provides the claimant with an implied moral authority and political credentials due to the deprivation of rights, and calls for compensation. It removes any obligation by the victim to examine whether his own self-esteem and behaviour are contributory factors, which might contribute to the refusal of others to show "respect," and institutionalises a position which he may be inclined to exploit and is reluctant to surrender. A victimised group is effectively safe from ever being seen as victimisers—an anti-racist is unlikely to be accused of racism. The police, as well as other public service employees, can be perceived by the society they serve as inferior occupations, and their unique exposure to victimhood accusations results in their acting defensively with risk aversion before all their other priorities. Hughes [1993:9–10] notes that "Complaint gives you power—even when it's only the power of emotional bribery, of creating previously unnoticed levels of social guilt . . . we create an infantilized culture of complaint, in which Big Daddy is always to blame and the expansion of rights goes on without the other half of citizenship—attachment to duties and obligations." Sentiments of toleration and sympathy for the "underdog" can be particularly compelling if seen as virtuous, particularly if they are reinforced by emotional and moral blackmail, or a psychological guilt. But when victimhood is claimed by a group, it can be counter-productive to the merits of the claims of the individual if he is seen as being a stereotype of that group.

Victimhood, often self-designated, invites people to "aspect focus" in presenting an image that supposedly shows the whole story. It is susceptible to historicism, revisionism, and the distortions of reality with time. The picture presented depends on where the presenter is coming from, as does differing perceptions of whether the evidence is complete and factual. With it goes an aura of sufferring, relieving the victim from responsibility for his condition and enables him to blame others. Preferably it requires the identification of institutional perpetrators, or political or legal systems that allegedly create and perpetuate discrimination and inequality. It can be used as a tactic to create and sustain guilt and unequal obligations, which can undermine the confidence of the mainstream society in maintaining the traditional respect and confidence in their institutions and public services. Frequent, superficial and opportunist claims of victimhood erode toleration, obscuring the occasions where a person or group has been unjustly treated, and who may be provoked into responding in a militant way. The potentially litigious and/or politically exploitative claims of victimhood can corrupt what is unintended. Or they may encourage the search for stigmas, slights, or unfairness where none genuinely exist. Class and economic status is as much a social division as education, gender, religion, race, and culture, any or all of which may be founded on, and can be readily attributed to, victimisation. A former (black) Chairman of the CRE has accused [TM 23 April 01] the Prime Minister of neglecting the African-Caribbean community in favour of British Asians, because they are often wealthier and could give the Labour Party more money.

An American-Asian [DM 21 Sept. 95] in a Washington "think tank" questioned notions of white guilt and black injustice. As in Britain, blacks in the United States are the most likely to claim victimhood, and Asian-Pacifics the least. He found that black cabbies in New York, Washington, and Chicago would not pick up black passengers because of adverse experience. A theory underlying black victimhood which says that they have been "induced (by white society) to adopt a depreciatory image of themselves . . . they may be incapable of taking advantage of the new opportunities . . . they are condemned to suffer the pain of low self-esteem . . . which some of them have been unable to resist adopting. Their own self-depreciation in this view, becomes one of the most potent instruments of their own oppression. Their first task ought to be to purge themselves of this imposed and destructive identity." There is some truth in this—blacks were routinely portrayed as negative stereotypes in Hollywood films up to about fifty years ago.

The cluster of attitudes and objectives of different sociological victimhood groups may sometimes conflict within the same group, i.e. gay and lesbian rights versus the religiosity of Muslims, Africans, and Asians. In ethno-national conflicts, the neutral international peacekeepers are invariably seen by the victimized minority as the agents of the local majority or imperialism. In situations where there is no will for peace, they can become stereotyped as the victimizing peace enforcers. They present a common, and usually tolerant, target for complaints. Experience suggests that without the perceived common perpetrator or hate stereotype, the 'tribes' will once again conflict with one another.

Since WW2, and in particular since the 1967 Six Day War, Jews have reinforced an ongoing victimhood by films and documentaries on the Holocaust, which no doubt serves to reinforce international support for their conflict with the Palestinians. The 1961 Eichmann trial in Jerusalem was, according to the then Israeli Prime Minister,"'lessons' which he thought should be taught to Jews and Gentiles, to Israelis, and Arabs, in short, to the whole world" [Arendt 1994:9]. A Jewish academic has criticised what he calls the uniqueness of the Holocaust "industry" embraced by the American Jewish elite as being entirely self-serving, corrupt, and destructive. He says that it could be counter-productive by ultimately weakening the American victimhood support for Israel, and weaken the Jewish identity by accelerating "marrying out" [STM 12 June 00].

Recent inner city riots have exhibited not only a racial, but also a class identity. The second Brixton riot in 1995 may have been a protest not only predominantly of blacks, but also of a white underclass, for whom race may have provided a convenient vehicle for their protest. After the first Brixton riot in 1981, Lord Scarman focussed much of his balanced report and moderate conclusions on the disabilities and mistreatment of blacks by white society and its institutions. Nonetheless, in 1981 Scarman commented [1981:101] that "It is noticeable that large sums have been spent [on inner cities] to little apparent effect." After the second 1995 Brixton riot, he was said to be 'broken hearted' [TM 15 Dec.95], but it would have been instructive if he had revisited his earlier conclusions. Nevertheless, the solution to the problem of the ghettoised inner cities seemed at the time to be clear and is still repeated: spend money. Since 1981 more than £200 million had been spent in Brixton to combat urban dereliction and despair. Brixton Challenge, an independent company had £37.5 million of government money to spend between 1993 and 1998 to provide job training, set up businesses, refurbish buildings and improve estates. The Challenge attracted a further £69 million from other public bodies, plus £82 million from the private sector [TM 15 Dec. 95]. Peckham is another ghetto area in South London with a drug ridden crime culture. A regeneration project started five years ago to replace its "sink estates" and to replace them with 2,000 new homes about half of which have been built. The new facilities are often promptly smashed up by ghetto gangs. After the 1997 general election, the new [black] Home Office Minister visted the "sink estates" of Toxteth, Liverpool, the scene of the 1980/81 riots. He recently said [STM 7 Jan. 01] that "What struck me was that despite millions of pounds being poured into Liverpool under different councils of different political complexions, the reality was that life [on the streets] was as bad as ever, if not worse." His solution is to allow the locals, not government, to decide upon their spending priorities. Clearly money alone is not the answer.

The police, like the armed services, the civil service, and Parliament, are one of the institutions of the state, and in a democracy embody its more abstract national values. If the loyalty and respect of society for them is undermined and they become ineffective, then national identity becomes blurred and social coherence is threatened. The police are usually seen as the principal perpetrators of racial victimisation in most Western societies, including Britain—typified, following the racist murder in London in 1993 of a young black teenager, by the virtual persecution of individual policemen. Police are the target because they are the enforcers of the law, and they should not be made the scapegoat for society's problems—as they were in the Macpherson report on this murder. To overturn the law, one must first overturn its enforcers, or render them impotent to act. The public wants to live in an orderly, secure, and law-abiding society, but are shy to support the police in dealing with social ills, with which the police are often intimately involved. The police were the targets in the London Broadwater Farm riot of 1985, in which a policeman was set upon by up to thirty blacks, and stabbed forty times. A conviction was squashed on appeal. "White justice," including the verdicts of juries in coroners courts, is seen as unequal, or unfair, unless it gives the "right" result. In the year prior to August 1996, there were twenty murders of blacks in Britain, but with a lower-than-average proportion of prosecutions, which was perceived as being due to unequal British justice. The police were unable to make arrests because the eye witnesses, who were also black, would not come forward until after an arrest had been made. Witnesses kept silent due to mistrust of the police, but also by fear of reprisals by the black perpetrators [BBC 2 6 Aug. 96]. Nevertheless, the Home Office confirmed that thirty-five percent of police officer days had been devoted to solving the murders of black victims, and in 1997–8 the overall clear up rate for murders was 24.9 percent. If the victim was black, it was 41.4 percent [TM.16 March 99].

No witnesses came forward after a black-on-black murder of a security guard at a London reggae concert, even after an estimated 150 people witnessed the shooting. His brother declared [STMG 15 Aug. 99] "they've got every historical reason not to trust the police and they have a very real fear of violent repercussions from the gunmen . . . they [the police] are not even going to try." This perceived "victimization" is unavoidable if nobody will speak to the police. It took seven months after the murder in November 2000 of a second black teenager [STM 3 Dec. 00] in Peckham, a London ghetto estate, for a prosecution of four ethnic youths to materialize—after several public appeals for witnesses and a massive police effort. The residents were reluctant to cooperate with the police, although some must have known what happened. A former black social worker on this estate and a former Mayor of Wandsworth [STM 3 Dec. 00] said "The sad reality is that there is no black community. There are a number of communities of black people which are all too often violently prejudiced against each other, against ambitious Asians, and against the host community. We [Africans] are sneered at [by other blacks] because we make no attempt to conceal the fact that we opted to come to this country because of the positive experiences we had during the colonial period." The (black) Home Office Minister noted [STM 7 Jan. 01] that "The police are constantly battling against a culture of enforced silence." For some fatherless youths, the street gang provides the family, and they seem to have become their own victimizers. Although modest in comparison, "fake" racist incidents are not uncommon, sometimes to back up insurance claims [TM 29 May 00]. The accommodation of Muslim values in Bradford has gone quite far in Britain, but after three days of Asian riots in 1995 in which £1 million worth of damage was done, nineteen complaints were referred to the semi-independent PCA (Police Complaints Authority), who found them to be without foundation. The Muslim former Lord Mayor aptly observed [DM 11April 96] that "it's a question of perception. There is a belief that when the police deal with ethnic minorities they are not fair, and that perception has not changed." In the most recent riot, involving 1000 mainly Asian youths in Bradford (the worst riot since 1985), 260 policemen were injured, there were two stabbings, and thirty-six people were arrested—thirteen white and twenty-three Asian—and all but two were from Bradford. When the Commissioner of the MPS reported in 1996, after an anti-mugging campaign, that sixty percent of those arrested were black and that seventy percent of the victims described their attackers as black, the National Black Caucus labelled it "racist in design, intent and fact" [DM 1 March 96]. Perceptions can become as powerful as realities. The 1999 inquiry chaired by retired Judge Macpherson on the racial murder of teenager Stephen Lawrence addressed this issue. His appointment was initially challenged by the Lawrence family because of earlier allegedly "racist" immigration decisions which he had made [TM 25 Feb. 99/STel 28 Feb. 99]. The police failed to prosecute because they lacked a credible witness and were properly accused of an inept investigation. The accusations of corruption and collusion were disproved. The conclusions of this report, which accused the police of "institutional racism," were based on perceptions, and not on hard evidence, thereby stereotyping the whole police service.

The British legal system does not discriminate, and aims at "colour blind" justice. The system can be imperfect, and "colour blindness" can be criticized in that it is insensitive to the needs of ethnic groups, but it is as rigorous as anywhere in the world. Its rules of evidence protect the accused as well as the accuser—otherwise there can be no justice. Possibly its standard of proof is too high for justice to be served and needs rethinking, but the pros and cons of any change would be controversial. No judicial system yet devised is all things to all people, including a system that rightly gives the benefit of doubt and the presumption of innocence to the defendant. Unjustified accusations of racial victimhood, which exploit the basic tenet of fairness of the British culture of jurisprudence into which migrants have voluntarily entered, could be counter-productive. If ill-judged victimhood campaigns were to succeed, then the culture of "justice with fairness" would be undermined—today's victims could become tomorrow's victimisers. Moreover, could any system of law in a separatist multicultural society be synthesized to adjudicate between the claims of different cultures? Some judgements would continue to be labelled unjust and racist if they did not meet expectations of a particular ethnic group.

NOTES

Arendt, H. *Eichmann in Jerusalem*. London: Penguin Books, 1994. 9.

Beattie, J. *Other Cultures*. London: Routledge and Kegan Paul, 1966. 273.

Berry, C. J. *Human Nature*. London: Macmillan Education, 1986. 71–2.

Field, S. *The Attitudes of Ethnic Minorities*. London: Stationery Office, 1984. Foreword.

Glover, J. *The Philosophy and Psychology of Personal Identity*. London: Penguin Books, 1988. 196–7.

Gray, J. "Toleration and the Currently Offensive Implication of the Loss of Judgement." In *The Loss of Virtue*. (Ed.) Anderson, D. London: Social Affairs Unit, 1992. 44–5.

Jensen, A.R. "Race and Mental Ability." In *Heredity and Environment* . Halsey, A.H. (Ed.). London: Methuen and Co. 215–262.

Hayes, N. and Orrell S. *Psychology*. Harlow: Longmans, 1993. 310–11.

Hughes, R. *Culture of Complaint*. Oxford: Oxford University Press, 1993. 9.

Lynn, R. Letter In *The Spectator*. 20 May 1995. 30.

Macpherson, Sir, W. *Inquiry into Matters Arising from the Death of Stephen Lawrence. The Stephen Lawrence Inquiry: Report of an Inquiry by Sir William Macpherson of Cluny*. London, 1999.

Parkins, G. "Positive Racism in Britain." In *Reversing Racism—Lessons from America*. Holland, K.M. and Parkins, G. London: Social Affairs Unit, 1984. 31.

Phillips, M. "Illiberal Liberalism." In *The War of Words—The Political Correctness Debate*. Dunant, S (Ed.) London: Virago Press. 1994.

Scarman, Lord. *The Brixton Disorders 10–12 April 1981*. London: Stationery Office, 1981. 101.

Swann, Lord. *Education for All—The Report of the Committee of Inquiry Into the Education of Children from Ethnic Minority Groups*. London: Stationery Office, 1985. 199.

Ibid. 768.

BBC 2. *Black Britain*. 6 August 1996.

18

Racial Intolerance and Reverse Racism

Racial intolerance is a latent feature and a potential cause of conflict, particularly in a multiracial/cultural society. When pushed to the limit, it can descend into mob violence. Racism is a complex problem that has several underlying factors, both psychological and social, notably deprivation and "inequality." It appears that racism has become the ultimate Western "heresey." In a multicultural society, any of its contributory factors can become racialized and can be readily ascribed to racism. This can in fact become a self-fulfilling prophecy. Although cosmopolitans might wish to dismiss it, racial intolerance remains subliminally latent in human nature—and if this is so, it cannot be easily legislated or socially engineered away. An element of racism, particularly anti-black/anti-semitic, is endemic in most societies both white and non-white, with some black liberation movements being expressly anti-semitic. Robert Young [1994:119], a psychoanalyst, believes that racism "is a veneer of civilization we must attend to and not pretend that we can wish or liberalise the [racial] feelings away. They are part of what dwells in our inner worlds, inhabitants of our mental space—part of everyday human nature, just below the surface, awaiting the appropriate social and economic conditions to erupt again, with undimmed virulence. That is the lesson of the riot and of recent international relations . . . a pity, but I say again that it's best to know what we are up against." Visceral "racist" feelings can simply reflect a genuine albeit discriminatory preference, inasmuch that any race/ethnic group can be more comfortable with those in its own image. Even within the same racial phenotype, a physical disfigurement as a result of disease or accident can be viscerally rejected or discriminated against. A valid reponse to the pejorative accusation "are you racist?" might be, as Professor Joad the British philosopher and broadcaster used to say, "it all depends on what you mean by the term," or that in the theological sense at least, we are all sinners. Philosopher

Antony Skillen [1993:75] believes that "Racism is a belief-validated or 'ideological' disposition or attitude. As such, racism is not just a feature of this or that individual but a largely cultural matter, something that you learn or pick up as one more or less complex and virulent strand in the more or less conflicting fabric that constitutes your outlook . . . [86] To the extent that the dominant institutions hegemonise social life, relevant cultural differences will entail cultural marginalisation and the limitation of opportunity . . . [but] the issues of 'multiculturalism' are too large to stray into this [Skillen's] article. Suffice it to stress the obvious fact of the need both to keep the issues of cultural chauvinism and racism distinct and to see their potent interaction . . . [87] I [Skillen] do not regard racism as tied by definition to being an attribute of the dominant. Equi-potent neighbouring territories can be equally racist towards one another, and it is possible for the marginal and disadvantaged to put racist constructions on their predicament." This analysis emphasises the psychological influence of culture on racist attitudes. If all cultures qualify, then multiculturalism must be liable to multiple racisms, not exclusively between white and black, but between all ethnicities and all races.

Professor Flew [1993:275–6] notes that "the word 'racist,' like the word 'fascist,' has for many of those most eager to employ it, become a vehemently emotive term of abuse with precious little determinate descriptive meaning behind it . . . racism should be defined as advantaging or disadvantaging someone, as discriminating in their favour or discriminating against them, for no other or better reason than that they belong to one particular racial set and not another . . . manifestly, it is morally wrong precisely and only because it is unjust. The injustice consists not in treating people in different ways, and hence unequally, but in treating differently, and hence unequally, people who are themselves, in all relevant respects the same." Flew observes that no one complains that professional basketball is heavily over-represented by blacks, or that Jews are about nine times more likely to be American Nobel Prize winners. He criticised [1986:5] the Swann report inasmuch that "We are going to be asked to condemn [as racism] and abandon any and every institution or practice the actual effects of which are that the racial distribution in any social group is substantially different from that in the population as a whole." He ascribed differences of school performance "especially by Afro-Caribbeans, not to the racism of their white teachers and examiners, but to what are, in the broadest sense, cultural facts about the under-achievers themselves and about their families."

Honeyford [1998:299–300] reinforces these comments. "The CRE is involved in an unmistakable paradox—whilst existing to eliminate racism, it would cease to exist if it succeeded. Its discomfiture in this respect can be seen in a whole litany of intellectual contradictions which it feels it has to support. For instance, if it accepts that race relations are improving, it undermines its constant demand for increased powers. If it recognises the existence of ethnic minority success, it undercuts its claim that discrimination is preventing this. Whilst pointing out the absolute right to equal opportunities and free association for blacks and Asians, it attacks the same rights for whites by supporting notorious 'blacks only' employment, housing, and fostering and adoption policies. Whilst looking askance at any organisation where whites appear to be 'overrepresented,' it ignores the corresponding situation where blacks and Asians enjoy a statistical advantage—and that includes its very own organisation within which the ethnic minorities are 'overrepresented' by a factor of about ten."

Honeyford [1998: vii and 262] is critical of the CRE because it "possesses considerable legal powers, powers which seriously undermine our great civil liberties. Far too few British citizens are aware of the serious threat to freedom of speech, freedom of contract, and freedom of association the CRE, and the Act under which it functions, constitute. This is because the race relations lobby, at whose head stands the CRE, has been successful in labelling anyone who questions its orthodoxies 'racist' . . . There are three crucial and highly typical CRE messages beamed at the public. First Britain is a country rotten with endemic racism. Second, our ethnic minorities are victims of institutional racism. Third, personal and group failure is the inevitable lot of most blacks and Asians." In the lead up to the 2001 general election, the CRE reached new levels of assertiveness. In 1994 it had issued an "anti-racist" pledge to the political parties contesting a local election, which was again issued to the party leaders in the 1997 general election. In 2001 however, the CRE attempted to get individual candidates to personally sign this pledge and "named and shamed" on their website those who refused. These refusals were on the grounds of freedom of speech, "blackmail tactics," unconstitutional, politically intrusive, patronising, "guilt by association," and "what McCarthy did for communism" [TM 20–23 /DM 21April 01].

One of its former commissioners [STM 20 Dec. 98], backed by at least one other, has accused the CRE of perpetuating its own existence rather than doing anything useful. She revealed the destructive dislike and rivalry between its Asian and African-Caribbean commissioners, and questioned its introduction of litigious and aggressive attitude towards race relations. The CRE has itself been found guilty of discriminating against an Asian employee [TM 19 Nov 97/28 Feb. 99]. In a recent report, the CRE failed a "good management" audit because it allegedly denies its staff equality of opportunity [DM 28 April 01] because it is institutionally racist by discriminating in favour of African-Caribbeans, against Indians, Pakistanis and whites. The CRE has a budget of about £19.8 million and a staff of about 200 [STM 21 April 01], one third of which is white and two thirds ethnic. Its chairman normally changes every four years. Its last Chairman was criticised [TM 17

Oct. 98] by the Board of Deputies of British Jews for supporting a rally partly organised by the anti-Christian and anti-Semitic Nation of Islam. He was also a member of the Runnymede Trust Commission report *The Future of Multi-Ethnic Britain* [Parekh:2000], although reportedly he had [STM 20 Dec. 98] rejected the validity of a common culture on the premise that British society and English culture are racist. If so, this is at variance with an earlier remark, that "Britain is a fair and tolerant place, in many ways more so than most others" [STM 3 Jan. 99].

The Swann [1985], and later the Macpherson [2000], reports saw racism being, on the one hand, overt and intentional, and on the other hand, covert and unintentional, namely, indirect or subliminal, which is sometimes referred to as a "climate of racism." The label of *racist* has become so frequently and indiscriminately applied in Britain that it has begun to lose its impact, so much so, that it is now being used against the accusers. Institutionalised and collective racism, as distinct from individual racism, refers to established organisations, systems, practices and procedures. In Britain, these were originally conceived and developed to meet the needs of a relatively homogenous monocultural society. The term "institutional racism" was first used by the 1960s black activist Stokely Carmichael and it was referred to in Lord Scarman's 1981 report, but more properly should be applied to an institution which has racist rules and procedures. By that definition, the MPS is not institutionally racist as the Macpherson report would have it. Nevertheless, it is claimed that institutions such as the police/armed services reflect a racist ideology, which fails to take account of, ignores, or works against, the interests of ethnics. They are accused of racist attitudes or of subliminal racism, which is difficult to prove or to disprove satisfactorily. Whilst originally not racist in intent—with a homogeneous society they did not need to be—and not reflecting the attitudes of all the individuals in these institutions, they can be perceived as denying the ill-defined principles of equality and inclusiveness. It is claimed that they can have a pervasive climate and influence on institutional practices and procedures, which can reinforce, magnify, and perpetuate intolerance, even though individual attitudes may be open to change. Even if true, this is unsurprising. No society, be it racially white, black, brown, or yellow, will throw overboard lightly the institutions it has built up over centuries for its governance and security.

Psychologist Young [1994:96] observes that "a racist society will have a racist science." This may be true, but only as a generality. Otherwise, all racial science would be dismissed out of hand as being motivated by racism. Genetic research linking racial characteristics and evolutionary brain development is now becoming less of a taboo. It is now believed that mankind originated in Africa some 50,000 to 100,000 years ago, and that although there are no pure races, they now differ due to chance mutations and adaptations to different environments. Ultimately, genetics, together with mixed marriages, could render the differentiation of people by racial characteristcs less significant. Some recent genetic research suggests that one in every 100 "white" Britons has some African or Asian genes, possibly from soldiers and slaves brought to Britain by the Romans [STM 20 May 01]. Genetic research could help to target the special medical, educational, and social needs of all racial groups and help to explain why some racial groups are over-represented or under-represented in particular occupations. There are recognised genetic "medical" differences between European, black, and Asian racial groups, including the incidence of diabetes, cardiac disease, osteoporosis, schizophrenia, hypertension, and sickle cell anaemia. Genetics may also help identify the physical sporting/athletic activities in which particular races excel. Dr. Roger Bannister, the first four-minute miler, risked the wrath of the PC lobby some years ago when he speculated on the relationship between athletic performance and racial biology [DM 14/DT 17 Sept. 95]. It is no longer racist to claim that Ashkenazic Jews, due to intermarriage, have a higher propensity for Tay Sachs disease [TM 05 July 01]. There has been opposition to genetic research by some ethnic groups who potentially stand to benefit the most [Channel 4 00].

Scientific racism, or the linking of cognitive intelligence with genetics, is often seen as being racist. This ongoing nature/nurture controversy was initiated by Jensen in 1969 in an article in the Harvard Educational Review entitled "How Much Can We Boost IQ and Scholastic Achievement," with another article appearing in 1977 [Halsey: 215–62]. Jensen's later work on intelligence was refused by his publisher. Jensen's conclusions were reinforced by Professor Eysenck, and in 1994 by Herrnstein and Murray, co-authors of *The Bell Curve*. The ensuing "verbal vilification" of racism and eugenicism by the "ill-informed and politically correct minority" [Lynn 1995:30] was countered by quoting a 1988 survey of 661 experts. This claimed that "the mainstream experts accept that race differences in intelligence have a genetic basis"—they responded 46/15/39 respectively for the genetic/environmental/no opinion theories. However, based on what others claimed to be the "not compelling" evidence of two psychologists, the Swann Committee [1985:768] was "in no doubt that IQ is not a significant factor in [African-Caribbean] [educational] under-achievement."

A recent report [TM 27 Oct. 00] from OFSTED (Office for Standards in Education), the government education inspectorate, shows that, although set against a general improvement, the sixteen year old examination results [1986–97] of black, Pakistani and Bangladeshi children are falling further behind white and Indian children in their school performance. In 1997 there was a twenty-seven percent pass rate compared with forty-four percent. Under its "Excellence in Cities" programme, the government is spending £120 million in 2000 to provide extra support for inner city schools rising to £300 million by 2004. It is now generally argued in Britain that the educational under-performance and abnormal rate of permanent school exclusion of African-Caribbeans is due, at least in part, to the lack of male role models and family support. Dysfunctional families arise from widespread divorce and single parenthood. Arguably, in a single-parent family headed by a single mother, a son is more likely to be left feeling angry and alienated, and lacks the guidance and comradeship of a father figure. This makes him more likely to seek validation of his masculinity from his peers. OFSTED research [STM 30 Dec. 00] showed that African-Carbbean pupils were four times more likely to be excluded from school than their white counterparts, and that teachers were afraid of discussing black pupils behaviour for fear of being labelled racist. It was also found that only just over ten percent of black teenagers intend to go on to university, compared with twenty-five percent of whites and almost thirty percent of Asians. A significantly higher proportion of blacks intend to follow a vocational career than whites or Asians [TM 2 April 01].

It is noted by Alasdair Palmer [1995:10], that "Although it is widely accepted that intelligence has a genetic (racial) component," differences exist as to how large that component is, and the methods for "proving" it. It is also disputed whether or not IQ, or socio-economic factors such as culture or discrimination, influence scholastic under-achievement by ethnics. There is controversy as to whether intelligence is a single as opposed to a multiple talent, to include creativity, which is measurable solely by a pen and paper test, and whether differences between people in the same ethnic group are greater than the difference between groups. The psychologists Shackleton and Fletcher [1984:114–5] write that "The facts are not indispute. What is of concern to researchers in this field . . . is how these differences can be accounted for . . . why the difference in intelligence . . . The arguments and counter-arguments are often heated, bitter, and ideological. On both sides of the debate they are tinged with prejudice or charges of prejudice, racism or charges of racism, smear campaigns or charges of smear campaigns and careful selection of evidence to suit one's case . . . [some] of a more tender-minded disposition baulk at the subject, finding it unpalatable." It is ironic that the IQ test, whatever it actually measures, was originally devised in the late nineteenth century in France, and had nothing to do with race, but was to examine the effect of cultural and class prejudice in the assessment of children's academic performance.

Racial prejudice in the West can be manifest as a victimising and discriminatory attitude towards ethnic groups. They might be seen as being inferior, some may want them to be "kept in their place" to facilitate their economic exploitation (often as domestics), and assimilation is to be discouraged. Implicit in white racism is said to be the maintenance of the social institutions and practices that preserve the power relationship between the mainstream and its minorities, who usually are, or originally were, immigrants. It can simply be a dislike of "univited strangers." Racism in the West has largely changed from being "dominative" to being "aversive," i.e. socially exclusive. It can be manifested or perceived as discrimination in education, employment, and particularly in the public services (especially the police). The question is whether racial prejudices can be eradicated by postive discrimination and/or quotas, or will they slowly wither away due to intermarriage, generation gaps, and economic prosperity? Wistrich [1991:113] questions "Whether this latent anti-Jewish prejudice will stretch the limits of tolerance in Britain's liberal democracy should economic conditions deteriorate, political stability be threatened, religious fundamentalism grow, or racial tensions explode, must remain an open question."

All opinion surveys should be accepted with caution. Their results are sometimes not in accord with one's own personal experience. Yet, an unofficial 1995 survey [DE 8 Aug.95] indicated that one third of all Britons said that they were not racist at all. Two in three admitted to some some kind of racial prejudice, but only three percent labelled themselves as "extremely racist." Among non-white people forty-four percent admitted to some form of racism, and fewer than half felt British. Another survey [TM 20 Dec.97] also found that thirty-two percent of native born Britons admitted to racist views, but that Britain was the least prejudiced of the fifteen member states of the EU. Still, these surveys do not and cannot address the complex question as to what being "racist" actually means, let alone the validity of the responses. There is in Britain and other societies a racial divide that overlays and masks a schism of social class/status. In Britain, the socialist governments of the 1960/70s tried to promote an inclusive and classless society by the social engineering of comprehensive education. By the late 1990s, the socialist government (New Labour) recognised that this social engineering experiment had failed, and reverted to a more meritocratic system. All processes of selection from candidates having different qualifying features are multifactorial choices, which unavoidably discriminates. Whenever an ethnic minority perceives discrimination, the seemingly intractable reaction is to use the rhetorical moral weapon of racism, to which there often can be no convincing reponse. Accusations of racism of individuals, groups, and institutions are now everyday events. The Archbishop of Canterbury, the Church of England, the Home Secretary, the government, European Union judges, the wife of the Labour candidate for the mayoralty of London, pensioners, the Millennium Commission, the Chairman of the Stephen Lawrence inquiry, the Labour and Conservative parties, the armed services, the Home Office, the police, the probation and prison service, the CPS (Crown Prosecution Service), the Immigration Service, and virtually every other public service has been accused of racism. Even the 1999 Paddington rail crash produced an accusation of racism, because families of Muslims and Jewish victims were allegedly offerred bacon sandwiches for sustenance [STM 24 Oct. 99]. The Anglican diocese of Southwark commissioned a report, chaired by the head of the CRE [TM 18 March 00], that judged itself as not intentionally racist, but having an "imperial and colonial mentality." This was because the clergy were white where the congregations were mostly ethnic, and the remaining whites had moved to neighbouring parishes. However, an earlier Anglican report, "Faith in the City," had ascribed this not to white racism, but "reflect[ing] white, middle class attitudes, and concerns . . . the differences are not so much ones of colour, as of class and culture" [Bennett 1987:76].

The Macpherson report recommended (Items 12 and 13) an Orwellian or McCarthyian definition of a racist incident. This should be "any incident which is perceived to be racist by the victim or any other person," and must be understood to include "crimes and non-crimes in policing terms" and that (Item 6.4) racism consists of "conduct or words or practices which disadvantage or advantage people because of their colour, culture or ethnic origin." This implies that even if a person has no racist intent, they can still deemed as being racist or guilty of "unconscious racism" because someone makes this accusation. The practical problem is the level of objective proof necessary to support the accusation of racism beyond a reasonable doubt. The police and the CPS are then obliged to prove evidentially whether or not this is the case. In a statistical study of racial harassment, Mahood's [1997:267–8] comment on racially motivated incidents, as reported by victims, was that "An important methodological question . . . is whether research can really provide a precise measure of the 'true' scale of the problem. The data would seem to suggest that that in the absence of an account from the perpetrator, researchers are unlikely to achieve a completely accurate measure of the problem for a [number] of reasons . . . a victim of racial abuse, by definition, will be able to state categorically that the incident was racial in nature. On the other hand, in cases of property damage, the victim is often forced to make a subjective judgement as to whether an incident was racially motivated. This decision is likely to be influenced by a multitude of factors, each different for every individual." It might also be added that the outcome of any such research depends on the exact nature of the questions asked, and the pre-disposition of the rèsearchers. Until Macpherson, the policing definition (Item 45.16) of a racial incident was " . . . any incident in which it appears to the reporting or investigating officer that the complaint involves an element of racial motivation, or any incident which includes an allegation of racial motivation made by any person." Macpherson rejected (Item 45.16) this definition because "the emphasis on motivation was potentially confusing." Nevertheless since Macpherson noted (Item 1.11) that "Stephen Lawrence's murder was simply and solely and unequivocally motivated by racism:" hence the policing definition adequately covered the incident.

Macpherson himself inclined towards racial discrimination (Item 45.24) in saying that "Colour-blind policing must be outlawed. The police must deliver a service which recognises the different experiences, perceptions and needs of a diverse society." He employed multicultural rhetoric when he enjoined the police service on six occasions, not to simply recognise diversity, but to "value diversity." Nonetheless, he warned (Item 45.25) that "Racism either way must be treated with zero tolerance." Having said (Item 45.26) that "blanket criticism of the Police Service is both unfair and unproductive," he branded the police as being institutionally racist, thereby labelling the MPS with a collective guilt, and diminished the Commissioner of the MPS's apologies to the Lawrence family by calling them "abject" (Item 2.10). Nonetheless, the Crown Prosecution Service was sufficiently humbled by this thinking, that they prosecuted an eleven-year-old boy for racially aggravated assault for calling an Asian boy a "Paki bastard" and hitting him, in retaliation for being called a fat "Teletubby" [STM 13 May 01].

A (Jewish) columnist [STM 24 Sept. 00] observed that "In the style of the Stalinist show trials of 1936, the spirit of the proceedings was confessional with the quasi-religious insistence that the unbeliever must confess and if he did not this was merely further proof of his thought crime. Macpherson's [report] is the defining document of our times and the most shocking. The worst aspect of it is that almost the entire political and intellectual class is so cowed or enfeebled by the thought processes involved that hardly anyone dares to protest . . . Macpherson's evidence on racism was often as ridiculous as it was sinister." A former president of the Law Society has criticised the conduct of the Macpherson Inquiry, inasmuch that the police were not allowed to have the evidence against them properly cross-examined [TM 1 May 01]. Macpherson made a total of seventy recommendations—almost forty of these affecting the police should be in place within two years of the report [TM 7 Sept. 99]. Some of the most radical recommendations have not been accepted by the Home Secretary. These included a relaxation of the twelfth-century common law [and Fifth Amendment] double jeopardy rule, "giving the Court of Appeal the power to permit prosecution after acquittal where fresh and viable evidence is presented" (Item 38). This clearly impinges on a defendant's natural right to justice, and is not specific to race relations and is contrary to the principle of the presumption of innocence. If at all, this recommendation may be adopted in murder cases only, where there is compelling evidence that that guilt is highly probable [TM 6 March 01]—forensic genetic testing now makes this more practical. It was also recommended "to allow prosecution of offences involving racist language or behaviour, and of offences involving the possession of offensive weapons, where such conduct can be proved to have taken place otherwise than in a public place" (Item 39). This clearly impinges on the traditional rights of privacy and the freedom of speech, and may be contrary to the 1998 Human Rights Act. The philosopher Brenda Almond [1996:73–4] feels that "It would do more harm than good . . . [and] I think we should be very careful about policing thoughts." The anti-racist lobby would like to have special penalties for racially motivated crimes, which would result in a hierachy of punishments meted out according to the race of the victim. This would have the effect of polarising racism. And would it also apply to the white old lady mugged by blacks for money, and not because of her colour?

Ironically, some time before this Macpherson had argued that "racial discrimination should not be tackled by the law but by 'good will and common sense'" [TM 25 Feb. 99]. In his report (Item 46.29) he ingenuously admitted that "It may be thought that we have strayed outside our terms of reference." The whole of the police service was put on trial for racism. Note that his was an "Inquiry" and not an "Enquiry," meaning it was investigative and adversarial. Some of its conclusions, which were "reached upon the balance of probability" (Item 8.5), may be justified, but they were unsubstantiated. It remains to be seen what long term effect this wholesale condemnation of the MPS will have on recruitment, early retirement, and its morale and efficiency. Although no doubt, due to several reasons, in the year to April 2000, police recruitment in England and Wales fell by sixteen percent, with graduate recruitment falling by forty percent. From 1997 to 2000, more police left the service than were recruited [TM 29 Dec. 00]. The MPS need 5,662 extra officers to meet their target [TM 15 April 99]. The number of police has fallen from about 28,000 to 25,300, one of the lowest figures since the 1970s [TM 15 Dec. 00]. The number of black and Asian recruits into the MPS between March and September 2000 was only four, out of a total of 218 from all ethnic groups, which included other whites and mixed race groups from outside of Britain [TM 17 Jan. 01]. If police numbers continue to fall and violence escalates, as it did in Washington D.C., inner London may become the same. The republican Senate leader once described Washington as having a "third rate police department operating in what has become a Third World City. It's not safe here for citizens" [TM 10 Feb. 97]. Washington is one of America's most racially divided cities, and a report scathingly indicted the twenty-two-year experiment as running itself as the District of Columbia, independent of any of the states [TM 13 Dec. 96].

Throughout the Western world, the police are the prime target for their alleged institutionalised and collective racism and infringements of civil rights. In both the 1981 Scarman and 1999 Macpherson Inquiries, it was effectively the police who were on trial. Police statistics [DM 1 Mar. 96] on mugging arrests were labelled "racist in design, intent and fact," and a Home Office report showing that black people are far more likely than Asian and whites to become involved in crime was shelved [TM 25 Jan. 99]. London, which overall has an ethnic population of about twenty percent, has only 862 black or Asian police officers, or about three percent of its total—elsewhere it is about two percent [TM 20 Oct. 98]. This is in spite of the police targeting members of ethnic groups as recruits to eradicate racist attitudes in the street environment. With this under-representation, it is unavoidable that most arrests of ethnics will be made by white police officers, who are consequently disproportionately liable to accusations of racism. Consideration is being given by the Home Office for recruitment not only from within the EU, but also beyond [TM 21 Aug. 00]. This is not surprising in view of the public vilification to which the MPS and the police service have been subjected.

The Macpherson report (Item 60) did not recommend abandoning "stop and search" policing, but the Inquiry noted (Item 45.9) that "black people were five times more likely to be stopped by police than white people. The use of these powers for Asians and other ethnic groups varied widely"—the so-called "racial profiling." Nevertheless, after the Inquiry, a report by independent academics commissioned by the Home Office found that "overall, no general pattern of bias against people from minority ethnic groups either as a whole or particular groups takes place." In fact it found that officers appeared to be searching a disproportionately high number of white people [DM 21Sept. 00]. The explanation advanced was that the number of black and Asian people on the street was much higher than the numbers listed as living there, which distorted the earlier studies. The number of "stop and search" arrests made between mid–1998 and mid–1999, that is before and after the Macpherson Inquiry, fell by thirty percent [TM 12 Aug. 99]. Street crime in London in January 2000 rose by almost half compared with that of a year ago, the highest level for five years and mugging increased in thirty-one out of the thirty-two London boroughs [TM 29 Feb. 00]. The average monthly street crime rate in 1999–2000 was about thirty-five percent higher than in 1998–99. Nationwide, there has been a sharp increase in crimes of violence and robbery. These increases may in part have been due to a shortage of police as well as the backlash following this Inquiry.

Macpherson ingenuously remarked [TM 1 April 99] that "his report sparked off the most extraordinary debate and a reaction which he didn't expect in the beginning." He admitted that it had "hit police morale," which the new Commissioner of the MPS acknowledged as "a major problem and we have got to raise it" [TM 29 Dec. 99]. An independent report by a former Home Office expert concluded that "It reflects a general lack of morale . . . and the danger is that we have thrown the baby out with the bath water" [DM 16 Dec.99], and Macpherson had provoked a white backlash which has led to a hardening of racial attitudes [TM 2 June 01]. The earlier, more moderate Scarman report found that "the direction and policies of the MPS are not racist" [1981:127]. Macpherson's most controversial conclusion (Item 46.27) was "a finding of institutional racism within the police service." He qualified this by saying that "[this does not mean] that all officers are racist," and has since tried to play down this blanket condemnation. The then-commissioner of the MPS, although acknowledging the danger of institutionalisation of racism, would not accept this group stereotyping, saying (Item 6.25) that "labels can cause more problems than they solve." Its superficiality was illustrated by the fact that only eighteen months later the new commissioner was asserting that this accusation was no longer the case [STM. 23 July 00]. The MPS are to be issued with a "culture guide" to enable them to deal more sensitively with minority groups. London now has 340 spoken languages and thirty-three national groups of more than 10,000 people [CFX 29 Aug. 00].

The police are at the "sharp-end" of the inner-city ghettoes and have a difficult and sometimes dangerous task to carry out. Lord Scarman commented after the 1981 Brixton riot that "They stood between our society and a total collapse of law and order." The police can use physical force legitimately, but are expected to have standards higher than that of the hostile environment in which they operate. They reflect the attitudes of this environment in which their toleration may not be reciprocated, and in which claims of victimhood are the norm. They are liable to be pilloried by anti-racist or civil liberty groups or both, and confronted with provocation and intemperate remarks by "community leaders." This can result in alienation and bitterness, and their toleration and motivation has limits. Following the Macpherson report, persecution of the MPS bordering on reverse racism took place, apparently insensitive to its adverse consequences. The Lawrence parents sued forty-two police officers ranging from the Commissioner of the MPS, to the off-duty constable who placed a blanket over the murder victim before phoning for an ambulance [TM 22 April 99]. Their action was based on Section 20 of the 1976 Race Relations Act. This makes it unlawful to discriminate against a person who seeks to obtain or use the services of any local or public authority of the like quality, in the like manner, and on the like terms, as are normal in relation to other sections of the public. They had originally claimed £500,000 compensation, were offerred £175,000, and then a £250,000 out of court settlement which they refused, and finally accepted £320,000 [TM 19 Feb./DM 14 Oct. 00].

Race riots in Britain against black ex-servicemen, after years of modest immigration, first took place in 1919 after WW1 due to high unemployment, in the ports of Cardiff, Newport, Barry, and Liverpool. The government at that time offered assisted repatriation to the Caribbean to 2,000 immigrants. British society was then far more homogeneous—ethnic and racial diversity were generally of no concern. The deepest animosity was directed towards

Jews (who were not free of legal discrimination in Britain until 1846), particularly those arriving at the turn-of-the-century from the Eastern European pogroms. The largest immigrant group, the Irish, also sufferred intolerance and contempt, but they had declined to 1.6 percent of the English population by 1891 and were concentrated in Liverpool and the Midlands. Spencer [1997:20] observes that "at the end of the Second World War Britain was not, and never had been by any reasonable definition of the term, a multiracial society." But following the post-WW2 African-Caribbean immigration, serious race riots took place in Notting Hill and Nottingham in 1958; again in Notting Hill in 1976; in St. Paul's Bristol, Brixton, Moss Side Manchester, and Toxteth Liverpool in 1980/1981; in Broadwater Farm London in 1985; again in Brixton in 1995; and in Oldham, Bradford and Burnley in 2001. These focused on the police, but were essentially politicised. In Toxteth, CS gas was used for the first time in Britain, and at Broadwater Farm the police warned that they might have to use plastic bullets. Lord Scarman [1981:105 and 110], after the 1981 Brixton riot, warned against the "Danger of 'reverse racialism' in attributing all the ills of black people to exploitation by white people. A balanced approach, in this, as in much else, is needed . . . pride in being black is one thing, but black racialism is no more acceptable than white." This gives rise to the question—must racial pride, including white cultural pride, always be construed as racist?

Racism is not a uniquely white crime, as whites also belong to a race and experience reverse racism. Nevertheless, anti-racists deem that white racism is the only one that exists, presumably because (at least in the West), the white majority has supremacist power. One psychologist (Kovel 1988: xci) denies the existence of reverse racism: "But whatever black people may do in the way of a racist response, there is no such thing as black racism. The response is to white racism, and is part of its unfolding dialectic . . . Once instituted, white racism can infect all dominated groups promiscuously. But it remains white racism, and its primary object is the black, for the basic reason that it arose out of the enslavement of millions of Africans over three centuries." This pseudo-scientific opinion that racist incidents are exclusively between blacks and whites, or that black racism is not racism at all, might have had some historical validity in America prior to 1965. But this does not explain racism elsewhere and between non-whites, or the accusation made by some black women of white women "stealing a black man" in mixed relationships. Another psychologist [Richards 1997:310] aptly observed that "No psychologist is encountering the topics of 'race' and racism simply in the capacity of a 'pure scientist.' Every psychologist has to be some kind of psychologist, and which kind will seriously affect, if not totally determine, their approach."

Miles [1989:6] notes that "It is true, for example, that the experience of people of Caribbean and Asian origin in Britain is often different from that of the 'indigenous' population in so far as sections of the latter articulate racism and practice discrimination. It is also true that acceptance of racist and colonial imagery can lead to a closure of the space within which resistance to racism is formulated and practised by members of the 'indigenous' population. The mistake is to assume thereby that all Caribbean and Asian experience is different from that of the indigenous population and that all members of the indigenous population consistently engage in such acts of closure. It is a mistake because such assumptions inaccurately generalise about a socially constructed category on the basis of the experience of a sample in particular contexts, and because they deny a relative objectivity in order to advance an absolute subjectivity."

For racism to gradually disappear, other than "marrying out," one of the necessary requirements is for a society to have a permanently upward economic/class mobility that is in part dependent on its tolerance and its stability. Reverse racism and reverse intolerance may be understandable reactions and/ or compensation for white racism, perceived or otherwise, because intolerance begets reverse intolerance and can become politicized. The chair of the National Black Police Association asserted "Quite simply, the perpetuation of institutional racism is reliant upon the dominant ethnic group in any institution preserving their power base. Therefore, the dismantling of institutional racism is reliant upon the ethnic dominance group either voluntarily relinquishing some of that power, or being coerced or compelled to do so." [DT 10 May 00]. Racism and reverse racism are counter-productive—an attack on the pride, culture or history of any nation or race will produce resentment. However, as Mishan [1988:11] observes "Allowing that their [migrants'] numbers become stabilised in the near future, the unfeigned acceptance of members of minority groups by the white population of Britain may well be slow and grudging. But only if this acceptance is won—and won through the manifest patience, forbearance, and achievements of the minority groups— will it be genuine and enduring." A similar view is that, provided that the majority and minorities are not highlighted as being different and conflicting groups by separatist multiculturalism, then eventually racial prejudice will wither away. Mishan also [18] observes that "The future prospects for racial harmony will, of course, be influenced by prudent policies. But at a more basic level, they depend crucially upon the characteristics and the behaviour of the racial minorities themselves, on the one hand, and upon the circumstances of their entry into the country, on the other . . . nor does [the indigenous population] take easily to the implied presumption that, as a nation, it is directly responsible for the material welfare and the living conditions, for the grievances and frustrations, of the new races that have chosen to settle here since the Fifties." Tokenism and reverse tokenism can also give rise to accusations of racism (Uncle Toms) when a group has included, for example, a black employer with predominantly white employees, or less frequently when there is a white employer with predominantly Asian employees [TM 17 Nov. 99]. Moreover, the tendency to characterise all ethnics collectively as *black*, because *coloured* is politically incorrect, has the effect of rendering Africans as the unwitting tokens of every ethnicity.

It is a feature of reverse racism to deny the mainstream society a sense of national pride and history, and to promote a "cultural cringe'—a climate of guilt and shame about the nation's past. Most countries of the West, including the United States, have had in the past a period of colonialism, and are particularly susceptible to this treatment. It can be reinforced by rewriting its history and by a reductionism of its national culture, heroes, and achievements. Revisionists adversely stereotype colonial civil sevants, not acknowledging that, for example, in 1939, the twenty-six million people of West Africa were administered by only 1,250 British colonials. Even Schweitzer, the humanitarian doctor, has been a victim of reverse racism [STM 30 April 95/BBC 2 25 Sept. 94]. Although history has an influence on the present, it is misleading to be critical of the past by contrasting some situation in history unfavourably with a similar situation today. The objective comparison should be with the same situation elsewhere in the world at the same time. Professor Herbert Butterfield [1973:17 and 29] termed this the "Whig interpretation of history" or the historian's "pathetic fallacy:" "It studies the past with reference to the present . . . the practice of abstracting things from their historical context and judging them apart from their context—estimating them and organising the historical story by a system of direct reference to the present." An interesting comparison between the abject treatment of slaves in the United States in the eighteenth and nineteenth centuries might be with civilians cruelly conscripted into the Royal Navy by the Press Gangs; with minor criminals from Britain transported to the Americas and later to Australia until 1868; or to the harsh conditions of agricultural peasants in Britain, Ireland, and Spain at that time. Britain was the first to abolish slavery in 1834, and it paid former slave owners compensation. In Britain, as late as 1789, women were actually burned at the stake for counterfeiting coins [STM 30 Dec. 00].

Another tactic for engendering post-colonial guilt is to accuse Britain of exploiting colonial peoples, including their manpower contribution during WW2. Britain should refute continuing accusations of its colonial guilt and obligations. Other than in North Africa, where the Indian army made a substantial contribution, much of this was devoted to the defence of India and Burma. India shortly afterwards became independent, whilst Burma soon relapsed into despotism. In Malaysia, before its independence, British troops from 1948 to 1960 fought to suppress insurgency led by Chinese communist guerillas. The implication is that there is a debt to be repaid, which includes the unquestioning acceptance of multiculturalism and migration from the New Commonwealth. Contrast this with the regret of many Chinese at the handover in 1997 of the last British colony—Hong Kong. The British Empire of 400 million subjects was an institution that made a major contribution to the culture and civilisation of the world, in countries which were often primitive by Western standards, aspects of which they have come to emulate. The hasty independence of some of its colonies, promoted by a small Western educated elite, resulted in Britain disbanding its empire, albeit with some dignity. This resulted, and is still in evidence today some forty years later, in endemic civil wars, tribal rivalries, dictatorships, institutional corruption, and the misuse of international loans and natural resources in much of Africa and elsewhere. Some of their leaders indulge in reverse racism and acknowledge no benefits from the past.

The following illustrate the wide limits of institutional toleration in Britain towards reverse racism in the name of "good race relations:" the activities and outbursts of the late Kalim Siddiqui, the Iranian leader of the British Muslim Parliament; the late seditious Guyanan Rudy Narayan; the dissidents al-Massari, Abu Hamza and Omar Bakri Muhammed, and other Muslim extremists, and the late Bernie Grant. This toleration is apparently not equally and universally applied as an absolute principle, but is influenced by pragmatic politics. The Crown Prosecution Service did not prosecute Britain's first black woman MP who said that "I am surprised that they choose to bring in blonde, blue-eyed girls from Finland . . . Are Finnish girls, who may never have met a black person before, let alone touched one, best suited to nurse in multicultural Hackney?" [TM 28–30 Nov. 96] If so, presumably black nurses should not be employed in white communities. If BNP activists made similar racist remarks, no doubt the race relations industry would call for prosecutions under Section 70 of the 1976 Race Relations Act and/or the Public Order Act of 1986. A West Indian born British judge [TM 22 July 97], in imprisoning Nigerian fraudsters, said that "I am going to make an observation which other judges cannot make because they might be accused of being racist. This sort of offence is being committed by well-educated Nigerians."

The black activist Bernie Grant [1995:132–4] ascribed the adverse publicity given to his reverse racist comments to his words "meaning different things to different people:" "When I'm giving speeches I have to tailor my speech accordingly to the audience I'm dealing with [black or white]." Still, he thought that in Britain "you're able to act more out of the ordinary, and it will be accepted, than perhaps a number of other countries. I think on the continent it's vastly different . . . you can still have a measure of independence and go your own way and say a few things as long as you don't go too far. I think that there is a certain amount of tolerance in British society still that allows you basically [to] form your own path." He also thought that

"British colonisation was different from others. I think that they allowed a lot more development of the people themselves, politically and otherwise" [1995:158–162]. Grant sponsored victimhood campaigns, including compensation for slavery [DM 2 May 96] and West Indians wishing to return to Africa and the Caribbean [DM 30 Oct. 95]. No doubt the Caribbean states would only welcome those "returnees" who would add to their financial and human capital, and not those from the young black British underclass. An attack was made on the MPS by a black broadcaster, who was an unsuccessful candidate for deputy mayor of London and was a member of the Runnymede Trust Commission on the *Future of Multi Ethnic Britain* [Parekh: 2000]. If elected he would have headed its police authority [TM 9 Dec. 99]. He proposed the setting up of a South African apartheid-style Truth and Reconciliation Commission that would have given police officers an amnesty for admitting their supposedly past racist or corrupt misdeeds. He was seemingly unconcerned about the adverse effect on the morale, self-respect, and dignity of individual police officers of this provocative, insensitive, and self-flagellating proposal.

John Stuart Mill is regarded by Western culture as being an early proponent of individual liberalism and toleration both at his time and today. Lord Bhikhu Parekh is the Professor of Political Theory at the University of Hull. He is a former deputy-chairman of the CRE [1985–1990], and was the Chair of the Commission for the Future of Multi-Ethnic Britain set up by the Runnymede Trust in 1998, and which reported in 2000. In an article headed "Superior People," [TLS 25 Feb. 94], Parekh accused Mill, together with some contemporary Western liberals (Joseph Raz, Brian Barry, Ronald Dworkin, Michael Walzer and John Rawls), of not being truly liberal, and Mill for being a supporter of colonial rule and the pre-eminence of English culture in India. He said that "Mill maintained that even as a civilized society had a right to rule over a primitive or semi-civilized society, a more civilized group or nationality within a civilized society had a right to 'absorb' and dominate inferior groups . . . The cultural 'admixture' between the English and the Indians . . . was desirable only if the former group dominated the relationship." According to Parekh, "From time to time, Mill came pretty close to sharing the crude racism of his time, but by and large he managed to avoid it." Mill was an imperialist in the sense that he worked for thirty-five years in the East India Ofice in London, a trading company, from which he retired in 1858 when British imperial rule took over after the India mutiny of 1857. This was at a time when the British Empire was administering and developing primitive and semi-civilized societies in Africa and elsewhere. Parekh apparently does not allow that in the intervening century and a half, during which India has been free of Britain for more than fifty years, that things have moved on in India and elsewhere. This article did not go unchallenged by other academics [TLS Letters 11/25 March 1994]. It was noted that "In the black art of denunciation Parekh's article shows no small skill," and that "His general treatment of 'Millian liberalism' is bizarrely at odds with [Parekh's] constant pleas for cultural understanding." Parekh's revisionist criticism applied the universalism and values of today to Mill and India 150 years ago, when the Hindu custom of suttee, or the burning of widows (prohibited by the British), was practised until 1877, together with the illiberalism of the Hindu caste system that the imperialist hierachy actually reflected. According to a study published in the *Journal of the American Medical Association* [TM 25 Nov. 99], physical and sexual abuse of wives, female infanticide, child marriage, and bride burning are still prevalent today [TM 25 Nov. 99]. Note also that at that time, and until its independence in 1947, about one third of the Indian sub-continent comprised 562 princely states both large and small, which were not directly administered by the British, and upon independence, the Indian sub-continent immediately rejected Hindu/Muslim muticulturalism. Burma descended into despotism.

NOTES

Almond, B. "Climate of Hate." In *The Heart of the Matter*. (Ed.) Bakewell, J. London: BBC Books. 1996. 73–4.

Bennett, G. *Crockford's Clerical Dictionary*. (90th Ed) London: Church House Publishing, 1987–88. 76.

Butterfield, H. *The Whig Interpretation of History*. Harmondsworth. Middx: Penguin Books 1973. 17 and 29.

CARF. *Campaign Against Racism and Fascism*. Nos. 12–30. London, 1993/96.

Flew, A. "Three Concepts of Racism." In *Atheistic Humanism*. Buffalo, New York: Prometheus Books, 1993. 275–6.

_____ "Three Concepts of Racism." In *Salisbury Review*. October 1986. 5.

Grant, B. *In the Psychiatrist's Chair II*. Clare, A. London: Heinemann, 1995. 132–134.

Ibid. 158–162.

Honeyford, R. *The Commission for Racial Equality*. New Brunswick, NJ: Transaction Publishers. 1998. vii and 262.

Ibid. 299.

Kovel, J. *White Racism—A Psycho-History*. (Intro.) Ward, I. London: Free Association Books, 1988. Xci.

Mahood, T. Berthoud, R. et al. *Ethnic Minorities in Britain*. London: Policy Studies Institute, 1997. 267–8.

Miles, R. *Racism*. London: Routledge. 1989.

Mishan, E.J. "What Future for a Multicultural Britain?" In *The Salisbury Review*. Part 2. September 1988. 11.

Ibid. Part 1. June 1988. 18.

Palmer, A. "Does White Mean Right?" In *The Spectator*. 18 February 1995. 10.

Parekh, B. "Superior People." In *Times Literary Supplement*. 25 February 1994. 11–13.

Ibid. Letters. 11–25 March 1994.

Parekh, Lord. *The Future of Multi-Ethnic Britain.* London: Profile Books. 2000.

Richards, G. *'Race,' Racism and Psychology.* London: Routledge, 1997. 310 .

Scarman, Lord. *The Brixton Disorders 10–12 April 1981.* London: Stationery Office, 1981. 105 and 110.

Shackleton, V. and Fletcher, C. *Individual Differences.* London: Methuen.1984. 114–5.

Skillen, A. "Racism—Flew's Three Concepts of Racism." In *Journal Of Applied Philosophy.* vol. 10. no.1. 1993. 75.

Ibid. 86–7.

Spencer, I.R.G. *British Immigration Policy Since 1939.* London: Routledge, 1997. 20.

Swann, Lord. *Education for All—The Report of the Committee of Inquiry into the Education of Children from Ethnic Minority Groups.* London: Stationery Office, 1985. 25.

Wistrich, R.S. *Anti-Semiitism.* London: Methuen, 1991. 113.

Young, R.M. *Mental Space.* London: Process Press, 1994. 96 and 119.

19

Positive Discrimination
and the Equality Paradox

If there exists, or is believed to exist, a climate of discrimination in a multicultural society with ethnic groups believing that they do not have an equal influence in shaping its present and future, their willingness to assimilate will be affected. Positive discrimination (PD), or affirmative action—also known by the less forthright euphemisms of official targets and quotas—have been a feature of multiculturalism whenever ethnic groups are seen to be, or perceive themselves to be, disadvantaged. PD attempts to make good past discriminatory injustices and officially recognises victimhood. It is a well-intentioned social engineering policy for promoting and accelerating the inclusion of minorities, but it has clear drawbacks. It confers privileges to individuals solely by virtue of group membership, and it gives preference to some, but not all, racial or disadvantaged groups. This may be so even though their "deservedness" may seem to be no more than other groups. It can be counterproductive inasmuch that it acts counter to meritocracy, and can create a climate of reverse inequality and unfairness. This can, in turn, give rise to resentment and wider prejudice. Even so, governments may introduce the social engineering of PD in the belief that it will be tolerated, will improve social cohesion and stability, and will broaden their electoral support. Arguments both justifying and criticising PD are presented by Stephen Cahn [1995]. However, one contributor, Kekes [1995: 204], concluded that "affirmative action that calls for preferential treatment is an unjust and unjustified violation of impartial procedures" and argues that "it unjustifiably assumes that all members of some groups have been victims of injustice and its selection of the groups is arbitrary."

PD also raises the question: is it just for individual members of the majority to be penalised for past unequal treatment (whether actual or imagined), originating from before they were born, to some racial minorities? Dr. David Green, director of the Institute for the Study of Civil Society, notes that [TM 23 Feb. 01] "the government is in the process of imposing new laws on the assumption that statistical disparities between ethnic groups are proof of discrimination, when no such conclusion can logically be drawn . . . statistical differences in the representation of ethnic groups in certain jobs, can be based on many factors." He includes age, newcomer status, self-employment, and family structure. As Professor Brian Turner has observed [1986:129], "Whilst most democracies have successfully achieved some level of opportunity and of condition, it would appear sociologically problematic to establish a society in which equality of outcome could be achieved without the imposition of authoritarian rule." Some would say that it is not possible. The moral argument that individual members of a present group owe a penalising duty to compensate individual members of descendants of a past group is unconvincing. PD is essentially politically imposed social engineering. It can be judged consequentially, provided that it produces the intended macro sociological outcome, but then only so long as those directly penalised by it are prepared to tolerate it—as eventually occurred in the United States, notably multicultural California. A preferred solution to remedy today's discrimination and inequalities is equal opportunities legislation and its enforcement, based on merit. This is not the same as equality (of outcome) legislation and enforcement.

The terms *discrimination, inequality,* and *prejudice* have a pejorative interpretation, but are features of many aspects of everyday life, particularly social aspects, and could be seen as being inevitable and even justifiable. Otherwise, no hierarchies or social groups would exist. Most people unconsciously or otherwise discriminate against those whose physical appearance, dress, and manner they do not like. In spite of the political rhetoric, there can never be absolute equality of opportunity for everyone, let alone an equal outcome. Inequality of opportunity has always existed, and will probably continue, due to differences in wealth, class/status and education, but otherwise it should be independent of race/ethnicity, religion, gender or age. Equality of opportunity by itself cannot result in an equality of outcome, particularly in a competitive, meritocratic, and capitalist society. Tocqueville [1993:11–2] observed that "Men will never establish any equality with which they will be contented . . . when everything is nearly on the same level, the slightest [inequalities] are marked enough to hurt it. Hence the desire for equality always becomes more insatiable in proportion as equality is more complete."

Because a person's race/culture is often visually announced, and is sometimes intentionally proclaimed, by the received sensory perceptions of the physical features of facial appearance, colour, dress, language, and accent, the accusation of racial/ethnic discrimination always exists. Its real cause can also be interpreted incorrectly, and it is sometimes difficult to prove the assumed reason to be otherwise. Someone failing to get a job promotion may assert that this is due to race, whereas it could be due to any one of a number of unsatisfactory qualifications, including age. Hence, differentiated treatment may not always be racially/ethnically discriminatory, and not necessarily the result of prejudice. What is difficult to establish in practice is the real motive, and whether this justifies discrimination. The difficulty in distinguishing between discrimination because of race or culture is illustrated by a bizarre example [TM 2 Feb. 00]. The German Embassy in Tokyo complained to the mayor of a city in northern Japan about a racist ban on foreigners using two thermal bathhouses. The Japanese claimed that this ban was due to a grave breach of bathing etiquette by some foreigners, namely not first scrubbing their bodies, and using soap in shared bath water.

In the United States, the principle of the equality of individuals is the substance of the Fourteenth Amendment, which guarantee the rights of citizenship, including the right to vote and equal protection under its laws to anyone born or naturalised in the U.S. In practice, it did not universally apply to blacks until the Civil Rights Act of 1964, the Voting Rights Act of 1965, and the Fair Housing Act of 1968, all of which prohibited racial discrimination. And it was not until 1978 that the constitutional validity of PD in admission to universities was challenged by the seminal Bakke case. The Supreme Court ruled in a complex judgement that a white student denied admission to the University of California medical school was unlawful, and that he must be admitted. Nevertheless they also ruled that race could be one factor to be considered in admissions programmes. Ronald Dworkin's [1985:303] opinion was that "It is not Bakke's fault that racial justice is now a special need—but he [Bakke] has no right to prevent the most effective measures of securing that justice from being used." This opinion based on societal utility, rather than an individual's right, would be less likely to find much support today. Disagreements have centred around the Equal Protection Clause of the Fourteenth Amendment of 1868 and the Civil Rights Act of 1964. Since Bakke, the Supreme Court has given other rulings which have been well summarised up to 1989 by Grassian [1992:313–26]. There has been litigation to overturn the 1978 Supreme Court ruling, and two other universities in California and Texas abandoned PD. Cases have also been brought against academic institutions in Michigan and Boston [TM 6 Dec. 97/STM 3 Jan. 99]. In contrast to what, until recently, existed at some American universities, the recent political emphasis has been on ensuring a classless, rather than a non-racial, meritocratic selection policy, at least in the top British universities [TM 3 Jan. 97/27 May 00].

The United States is not alone in legislating PD. In multiracial South Africa, in spite of earlier claims to the contrary, PD is legal and whites in the public service are discriminated against [TM 28 June 97/7 Feb. 98/29 April

98]. Although the reasons are several, there is a brain drain leaving South Africa, mainly returning to Britain, said to be about 10,000 a year from originally nearly two million Britons. Migration to the white Commonwealth countries between 1989–97 was 233,600, almost three times the official figure [TM 11 Nov. 99]. In Israel, although Arab citizens enjoy the same voting rights as Israelis, they are nevertheless disadvantaged, inasmuch that they are unlikely to be appointed to senior government or civil service posts, or advance in the professions, academia, and business enterprises, and are not eligible for the benefits available to Israeli ex-servicemen [Galford and Fearman 1986: 105 and 111].

Government and institutional policies of PD are unlikely to completely satisfy minority claims. Equality of social acceptance can never be enforced: it can only be gained through voluntary gradualism. In contrast to the troubled black Americans, the Asian-Pacifics as a group are at the top of the American social strata, having the highest average incomes and the best educational performance, and are the largest group entering Yale and Harvard. Next are migrants from the Indian sub-continent, then the whites (Caucasians), the Hispanics, and finally the blacks. The American experience and educational performance is paralleled in Britain, where there are about 150,000 Chinese who are twice as likely to have degrees as the rest of the population. The ISER [TM 23 Nov. 98] published a study on the disadvantaging of ethnic minority groups in Britain. Chinese men had the highest average earnings and the lowest unemployment of any ethnic group including whites, with Pakistanis and Bangladeshis the reverse. When family income is taken into account, the Indian population overtakes the whites, but is still second to the Chinese. A British-Chinese [Barker 1997] offered an explanation of Chinese low profile assimilation and the low hostility towards them. They couldn't be seen as taking jobs, they were adding jobs, and they will continue to keep their heads down. "[We] haven't built big new churches, with crescents on top, shouting at everyone else to come and pray. The old [Chinese] saying is—Find what the customs of the new village are, and follow them." There are official statistics on "economic activity rates" [Social Trends 2001:77] which reports the percentage of the population, men and women, in the labour force, but which do not reflect earnings. The average, for all ages, is seventy-three percent, with whites at seventy-four percent, African-Caribbean seventy-five percent, Pakistanis at thirty percent, Bangladeshis at twenty-two percent, and Chinese at fifty-seven percent.

Whether officially or unofficially practised, PD, like any system of preference, gives rise to the paradox of inequality, given that a basic tenet of representative democracy is that all members of its society should have an equal right of opportunity. There is no equitable reason why PD should be limited to race and not to other underprivileged categories of society. The underclass can be characterised as people on the margins of society, not necessarily those who are merely poor, but young males who have dropped out of the labour force, chronic criminals, unmarried mothers, and pregnant teenagers (of which there is a very high incidence). It may have a high criminal element that resents the presence of police (which may result in more localised crime), or more probably, the presence in their territory of any authority other than their own. This description is clearly not applicable exclusively to blacks and other minorities.

In the United States, PD was introduced in 1961 to end federal employment discrimination. It was intended to promote a common national identity by eliminating the separatism of racial barriers, and creating a "level playing field." Initially it was seen as a transitional measure, and not one to be viewed by minorities as patronising a handicap. It recognised that some members of ethnic groups encountered special problems, but it is questionable whether the preferred solution might have been more prudential responses instead of compulsion. PD can generate resentment and create a belief that the advantaged could not have succeeded without it. It has not achieved its initial expectations, at least to the satisfaction of many, and has been judged to be counter-productive.

Although it can be seen as being consistent with the Rawlsian theory of "distributive justice," PD can appear to favour mediocrity and suggest tokenism. It is seen by some as being a negation of the ethos of "justice as fairness," and it contains the implication that all whites are a privileged group. It is divisive inasmuch that the majority perceive disproportionate resources being diverted to certain minorities, and it discourages toleration, particularly between adjoining white and ethnic urban neighborhoods. It assumes that because some minorities are underrepresented or underachieving, these problems should be recognised as being essentially racial. But whenever there are unequal winners, there will also be unequal losers, and the practice can be result in unintended consequences. In Washington D.C., Hispanics make up about five percent of the city's population, most of whom are illegal immigrants. After a three day riot and to prevent further violent outbreaks, an affirmative action programme to hire these immigrants for city jobs was proposed. This angered both legal Latino citizens and blacks because it extended privileges to illegal immigrants under the guise of civil rights [Chavez 1993:18 –9].

There are social and economic differences and barriers within all sections of society, including the whites, not the least of which is permanent unemployment, the loss of hope and self-esteem, and a disenchantment with a political/social system which seems to offer nothing. Even if PD was accepted by an older generation as a reparation for some past "colonial" injustice, this penance cannot continue indefinitely into future generations. Moreover, if any proposal is made by a commercial interest to remedy an alleged racially discriminatory practice, it should be treated at least a priori as self-serving, and not necessarily in the interests of equality or of the general public. Compensating for a perceived inequality between groups by official quotas and positive discrimination could make sense, provided that certain assumptions are made about human nature and toleration. An analogy can be drawn between different types of games. Some are played for social purposes and discriminatory handicaps are accepted, although they undermine the notion of equal treatment, irrespective of differential skills. In others, penalising different skills with handicaps is not appropriate or tolerated. Positive discrimination comes into this second category, and has become unfashionable in the United States because it does not apply meritocracy consistently. It is seen to be forced, artificial, and tampering with something basic in human nature, namely what is deserving and rewarding.

Discrimination in employment is more likely to be the concern of the competitive professional middle class, because a principal concern of the unskilled underclass is not competition, but poverty. The outcome of PD, including the recognition of genuine merit, can differ from what was expected and can result in some embarrassment for those appearing to be advantaged. "Quota blacks" may have to be better than "good" to counter suggestions that their promotion was due to an unfair advantage, or that they are diluting existing standards. Even so, middle class professional blacks can claim that they can encounter a "glass ceiling." It is particularly difficult in employment to counter accusations of discrimination and racism if the reasons could be due to other non-related factors. There were complaints by ethnic hospital doctors not reaching consultant grades and ending up in "unglamorous specialities" [Panday 1993:18–9]. This may be due to reservations about "foreign" qualifications. Nonetheless, everyday experience suggests that this does not apply to general practitioners, there being at present about twenty-two percent of "overseas " doctors working in the NHS, forecast to increase to about thirty percent by 2019 [TM 8 Nov. 99]. There may be cultural reasons for apparent disadvantaging. Some Muslims live in low-quality housing because strict Islamic law forbids the paying, or receiving, of interest on loans such as mortgages [TM 2 Feb. 97].

In Britain, race and gender, or sometimes both, have largely taken over the focus of inequality from social class, which is of course not readily amenable to legislation. Legislation in Britain began in the mid–1960s to protect minority groups against disadvantaging in certain fields of public life. The proposal by Lord Scarman [1981] after the Brixton riot, that wider directly-funded "resources should be devoted to either inner city or ethnic minority needs" was not adopted: he highlighted employment and education. The Sex Discrimination Act 1975, which is operated by the EOC (Equal Opportunities Commission), makes discrimination on the grounds of gender illegal. The

Race Relations Act 1976, which is operated by the CRE, makes discrimination on the grounds of race illegal, whether direct or indirect, in respect of employment, education, and in the provision of goods, facilities, services, and premises. If the discrimination is on the grounds of employment, a claim can be brought to an Employment Tribunal under either or both Acts. Due to a narrow interpretation by the House of Lords in 1983, the public facilities and services provision of the 1976 Race Relations Act was limited to a kind similar to those provided by a private person, and consequently did not apply to public services generally. The Race Relations (Amendment) Act, which came into force in April 2001, does not replace the 1976 Act, but basically extends its scope to include public authorities.

In Britain, official PD takes place under the euphemisms of monitoring "under-representation," "special needs," and the setting of targets, which are usually followed by quotas. In Britain, PD started in the London Borough of Brent in 1986, then by the Greater London Council, and then by the BBC (British Broadcasting Corporation), followed by a government drive to increase the number of blacks and Asians in the higher echelons of the Civil Service, which was later abandoned due to a legal challenge. The Home Office, the police, prison, immigration service, and armed forces have all had "targets" imposed after the publication of the Macpherson report. The BBC has said that it will increase its staff from minority backgrounds from the present eight percent to ten percent, and four percent in its management, by 2003 [TM 8 April 00/STM 14 Jan. 01]. Quotas depend on suitable applicants coming forward. If they do not, then standards have to be relaxed, and public respect, an emasculated operational efficiency, self-esteem, and the pride in belonging, tend to be undermined. Coercive egalitarianism can only put professionalism and elitism into disrepute and serve to undermine pride and dedication.

Predictably, racial discrimination and social inclusion were much of the substance of the recommendations of the report of the *Future of Multi-Ethnic Britain* [Parekh 2000]. These included "employment equity plans" and proposals for a new Equality Act, and for the Equality and Human Rights Commissions to enforce anti-discrimination and equality legislation. These coercive proposals serve to reinforce the sense of ethnic group victimhood, and imply that endemic racism exists in British society as a whole. The (black) Home Office Minister has said that local race equality councils "make absolutely no contribution to race relations and spend all their time feuding among themselves—I know, I speak as a former chairman of one" [TM 15 July 99].

If "race" is going to be used as the qualifying criterion, it could eventually require proof by genetic testing: how much, genetically speaking, must one be to be legally black, Asian, or of a mixed race? One might also ask what, and how much, "difference" constitutes a racial difference? The CRE [TM 28

Mar. 97] was said to be "delighted with" an Employment Tribunal ruling that Scots are a different race to the English because, since the Act of Union in 1707, they have retained their separate church, legal, and educational systems. If so, the CRE seems to be intent on creating more races rather than reducing racial grouping—a sure way of promoting diversity and separatism. Even Irish "travellers" (gypsies) won the legal right to be treated as a separate ethnic group protected by race laws [TM 29 Aug. 00]. There is a National Black Police Association which claims to be only a "self-interest" group, a Society of Black Lawyers, an Association of Black Probation Officers, an Asian Association in the Crown Prosecution Service, and a TUC Black Workers Conference—their objectives and qualifications for membership are presumably racial, and therefore discriminatory.

PD may be well-intentioned, but it is blunt, crude, and unfair. It also raises the question as to how many categories should there be to avoid other candidate groups being left out. Apart from eligible members of the underclass, one can think of a dozen racial or mixed race categories—not including the English, Scots, Welsh and Irish. Nevertheless, a recent advertising campaign by the CRE apologised (insincerely) for the fact that "thirteen percent of black people are burgled—twice the figure for whites," which is probably not discriminatory, but due to black-on-black crime. According to the Home Office [TM 19 July 01], the London Borough of Lambeth, which includes ghettoised Brixton, is the "robber hotspot" of England and Wales, having one of the lowest crime detection rates. In the year prior to March 2001, it had seventeen robberies for every 1,000 people, with five percent arrests and 49.3 domestic burglaries per 1,000 households. The CRE also had to defend itself against accusations of racism because of one of its advertising posters [TM 20 Sept. 98]. In the civil service, out of a total staff of 470,710 there are 20,060 ethnics, or about 4.3 percent, which compares with the national 1991 census figure of about six percent [TM 18 Sept. 00]. A survey [TM 25 Nov. 99] was carried out among the thirteen percent of ethnics out of a total of 8,021 employed in the Home Office—forty percent of the blacks and thirty percent of the Asians said that they "felt discriminated against" by their race. Asian women felt that they missed out on job promotion because they did not go to the pub (for cultural/religious reasons) to drink "with the boys." What was presumably not asked is what percentage of the whites and teetotallers felt "disadvantaged" in some way—if so, they could not ascribe this to race. In the Department of the Environment, Transport, and the Regions, there are fifteen to twenty percent ethnics (well above the national figure), but so far only one of its top 168 civil servants [TM 2 Nov. 99].

Compare these claims with that made by the Chief Executive (part black) on her resignation from the Lambeth Council in London [STM 12 Dec. 99]. She said that the staff were almost unmentionably sensitive; the over-promotion of staff, many of them black, was above their abilities, and a sop to the ethnic mix of the area. "I knew that if I dealt with certain people I'd be called a racist. It ought to have been harder for people to say that to me because of my colour, but actually it wasn't . . . When people started to fall out of the system, I got accused of ethnic cleansing, but it wasn't as if the white staff survived—they were all black. We had unqualified accountants, social workers, a director of law was not legally qualified, four legally qualified people in a legal department of sixty, and all that chaos done in the name of equal opportunities."

Criticisms of PD have been neatly summarised by Flew [1992:Preface]. He maintains that there are "People who are thoroughly opposed to individuals being discriminated against on the grounds of their race, but who have misgivings about some of the precise ways in which anti-racist campaigns have developed . . . they just feel that what is more or less officially presented as anti-racism is different from and even contradictory to their own decent rejection of racist discrimination . . . [He challenges the CRE] either to reject itself or repudiate in others [what he sees as being] the four main perversions of anti-racism, namely:

(a) To recommend the repeal of those clauses in the 1976 (Race Relations) Act which license the advantaging of categories of racial minority groups as such: clauses which are themselves racist.

(b) To abandon and repudiate the practice of taking the disproportionate under-representation of some racial minority in some enviable category of employment or achievement or its disproportionate over-representation in some unenviable category, as a warrant that someone has been guilty of hostile discrimination, and should reform or prove their innocence.

(c) To abandon and repudiate the misidentification of race with culture and the resulting confusions. For given that society is multiracial, it simply does not follow that it must necessarily be multicultural, nor that if it is, then the cultures must correspond with the races, nor that these cultures ought to be equally valued. To accept that our society is multiracial does not entail or justify a commitment to promoting all cultures equally or including them all in curricula.

(d) The last challenge is for the CRE to dedicate itself to the ideal of a colour blind society in which the colour of a person's skin is of no more interest or practical importance than the colour of his hair. This requires it to stop talking about and promoting good relationships between various racially defined 'communities.' Instead it ought to encourage everyone to think of himself and his neighbours as the individuals they are, not as representatives of some racially defined 'community.'"

NOTES

Barker, P. "Observations." In *New Statesman*. 31 January 1997.

Cahn, S. (Ed.) *The Affirmative Action Debate*. London: Routledge. 1995.

Chavez, L. "Just Say Latino." In *The New Republic*. 22 March 1993. 18–9.

Dworkin, R. *A Matter of Principle*. Oxford: Oxford University Press, 1985. 303.

Flew, A *A Future for Anti-Racism*. London: The Social Affairs Unit, 1992. Preface.

Galford, E. and Fearman, C. *Israel*. Amsterdam: Time-Life Books, 1986. 105 and 111.

Grassian. V. *Moral Reasoning*. New Jersey: Prentice Hall, 1992. 313–26.

Tocqueville Alexis de. "Democracy in America." (1835) In *Culture of Complaint*. Hughes, R. Oxford: Oxford University Press, 1993. 11–2.

Kekes, J. "The Injustice of Affirmative Action Involving Preferential Treatment." In *The Affirmative Action Debate*. (Ed.) Cahn, S.M. London: Routledge, 1995. 204.

Panday, K. "Colour Bar." In *B.M.A. News Review*. December 1993. 18–9.

Parekh, Lord. *The Future of Multi-Ethnic Britain*. London: Profile Books. 2000.

Scarman, Lord. *The Brixton Disorders 10–12 April 1981*. London: Stationery Office, 1981. 135.

Turner, B. *Equality*. Chichester: Ellis Horwood, 1986. 129.

20

Cultural Assimilation or Separatist Ghettoisation

Before WW2, distance and cost dissuaded migrants from abandoning their homelands, but if they did, assimilation was almost obligatory. Assimilation into the host culture was then the "price" the mainstream expected of migrants, otherwise their alien characteristics led to intolerance. With modern communication and ease of travel, settled immigrants can now more readily maintain a racial/ethnic separatism. Now, once immigrants have become domiciled, they may either become fully culturally assimilated into the mainstream society, which maintains society's cultural hegemony, or they may adopt a partial (liberal) or total (illiberal) cultural separatism, there being variants between these categories. Spencer [1997:1] observes that "The idea that Britain has for long been a multi-racial society is one that has been widely aired and is now widely believed, fostered principally by liberally minded people associated with spreading and reinforcing the multi-culturalist approach to education and race relations." The issues of multiculturalism are not as finite and as uncomplicated as that.

Flew writes [1995:2]: "Certainly it is possible for people professedly committed to aggressively incompatible religious beliefs to live together in friendly toleration. But this is achieved only by the more or less conscious and explicit abandonment of those of their pretended beliefs which would make such friendly and tolerant cohabitation impossible." It is said that there are three requirements necessary for a society to cohere: a shared history, a shared language, and a shared culture. Immigrants, in many cases, do not share a history or a culture, but they can be acquired with time. If the host society perceives that there is an unwillingness to assimilate, they may feel that their identity and cohesion are becoming undermined by "strangers," or as multiculturalists would have it, by xenophobia. As Jonathan Sacks, the

257

former chief rabbi of England, has observed [TM 28 March 01], "A state ought not to dismantle its history and culture, the things which give it strength and stability, to give full dignity to minority groups. It is fatal to believe that only by denying our identity can we make space for others." Paradoxically, the concern for many indigenous British is too much uniformity (Europeanization) and diversity (multiculturalism). The Swann Committee [1985:4] rejected both full assimilation and complete separatism, because "neither of these 'solutions' offers a just or indeed practicable basis for a multiracial society." On the fiftieth anniversary of African-Caribbean immigration, one immigrant triumphantly claimed [TMG 1998:34–8] that "Without them this country would be a poorer place . . . We, the second generation, had to change Britain with our intransigence—or what the police force called 'attitude'— because it certainly wasn't going to change of its own volition." In fact, the African-Caribbean influence has been largely in sports and pop music, and most have become as British as the British. Their assimilation is apparent when comparing the conformity of their appearance today with the unconformity of that of their parents fifty years ago. In their language, religion and other cultural characteristics, and in contrast to some other ethnic groups, African-Caribbeans hardly differ today from the indigenous British. The social aspect of assimilation is the most difficult to achieve. Because of their exclusion from the Yorkshire Cricket League, Bradford Asians formed their own Cricket League [BBC 2 4 July 1994]. Nevertheless, even a monocultural society has its own forms of social exclusion: class, status, family, wealth, education, and religion.

Complete cultural assimilation implies an overt acceptance of not only the external way of life, but also an habituation with the private way of life, values, practices, dress, and customs of the indigenous society. More than any other factor, the adoption of "sameness" eliminates discrimination, and it creates trust and removes doubts about loyalty, although convincing the mainstream society that one genuinely "belongs" is difficult. Complete assimilation involves discarding one's past and re-inventing oneself, and can be counter to human nature, at least over the short term. It requires the substitution of an inherited culture for another culture, and can give rise to an amorphous, plural split, or maybe resentful identity, if it is perceived as having been imposed. Partial assimilation involves examining what should be preserved from an inherited culture, and what can be discarded. Discarding inherited values, beliefs, and an identity can be difficult to accept without generation gaps, and at one time could lead to the accusation of being an "Uncle Tom." Role modelling by successful and assimilated immigrants such as athletes, performers, and professionals can be seen by separatists as their having "bought" their acceptance into the mainstream society. The retention by migrants of their inherited identity, or its delayed renewal, can reflect a belief about its continuity with time, and possibly an ambition to migrate later elsewhere in their diaspora. In general, assimilation into the mainstream society becomes easier for later generations, and as a result of mixed marriages/ miscegenation. If the expectations of migrants of unreserved social acceptance by the mainstream society are not realised, this marginalisation can be interpreted as racism, which punctures the myth of "belonging," promotes a retreat into ethnicity, and sometimes the formation of separatist ethnic political sections/parties. However, according to Gellner [1964:156], assimilation should not necessarily be assumed to be a right: "'Culture' is neither necessary nor sufficient: if incorporated by birth, the individual is of course likely to be 'of the same culture' as his fellows, having been reared with them; but if incorporated in other ways, he may or may not be culturally similar. His failure to be similar does not necessarily exclude him, if the group is nevertheless willing or constrained to incorporate him; his similarity, on the other hand, also confers no rights on him, and he cannot in virtue of it demand to be admitted."

Schlesinger believes that the earlier European immigrants to America voluntarily assimilated, and in that respect differed from the present-day ones. He says [1992:13] that "The United States had a brilliant solution for the inherent fragility of a multiethnic society: the creation of a brand-new national identity, carried forward by individuals who, in forsaking old loyalties and joining to make new lives, melted away ethnic differences . . . they expected to become Americans. Their goals were escape, deliverance, assimilation . . . the point of America was not to preserve old cultures, but to forge a new American culture . . . one reason why Canada, despite all its advantages, is so vulnerable to schism is that, as Canadians freely admit, their country lacks such a unique national identity." Zillah Eisenstein, a professor of politics [1993:70], is sceptical of this account: "There was little choice for most Eastern European immigrants but to adapt. The 'new' world they came to was a land of opportunity in comparison to what they had left. But the opportunities of Russian Jews, Italians, Poles, etc. were predicated on their willingness to assimilate and their capacity to conform. Schlesinger elicits a folk memory of immigration rather than an account of the limited options and constraints these people faced." What this suggests is that if immigrants have little or no opportunity or incentive to achieve relatively quickly the benefits of the indigenous host society, they will remain separate. In Australia, the demands for separatism became politicised [Jupp 1998:158]: "The major demands emerging from the largely hidden ethnic constituency were for an end to assimilationism and for a recognition that non-English-speaking immigrants needed special educational and welfare services . . . the growing opposition to assimilationism was taken up by the newly elected Labour government of Gough Whitlam, which pronounced itself committed to multiculturalism in 1973." Political separatism was proposed by black activists at the Labour Party Conference before the 1983 general election. This was rejected, but by 1987 the first three black, formerly separatist, and one Asian, Labour MPs were elected to parliament—the 1997 parliament had five Asians and four black MPs.

Even after two or three generations, some migrants resist the attrition of political, social and cultural assimilation and retain their inherited values, beliefs, and allegiances. This will be particularly the case if there is a strong religious and linguistic affiliation, and/or if their attempts to assimilate are met with hostility or discrimination. This will reinforce cultural fragmentation and ethnic assertiveness. Assimilation of another culture becomes more likely, and separatism less likely, it does not carry with it the inhibitory influence of either religious extremism, or a history of victimisation due to some perceived past injustice/discrimination.

Assimilation can follow a general pattern. The first generation is trapped in its cultural identity and makes few adjustments, and maybe does not speak the mainstream language. The second generation is educated, reacts both against their parents and the mainstream society, and is more assertive. The third generation often becomes more integrated into a Western identity. Some, however, may ask, "am I really the same as these people?" If they are susceptible to a cultural nostalgia or extremism and rejection, they can return to their roots. Practices which were forsaken twenty to thirty years ago by the earlier generations come to be revived as a badge of a separate identity. The internal contradictions and feelings of ambivalence will be articulated as: "I am an Indian living in Britain," "I am in this culture but not of it," or "I live in Britain and I am a Muslim, and I want to be both." This suggests that, depending on the circumstances, the minority member possesses a latent freedom and the privilege of choosing between two self-serving identities, as has been demonstrated in Ulster and Yugoslavia. The Ulster Protestant Unionists and the Bosnia/Kosovan Muslims are European in their attitudes and are visibly indistinguishable from the Ulster Catholic republicans and the Orthodox Bosnia/Kosovan Serbs respectively, but what counted in the end was the divide of culture, religion and national allegiance.

Sexual attraction/love can overcome racial/cultural barriers. Mixed marriages ("marrying out"), of which there are a very wide range of racial/religious combinations, will result in an increasing assimilation and deracination of an ethnic minority, or at least erosion of their racial/religious identity. Britain's rate of interracial relationships is ten times the European average [TM 9 April 00]. Mixed race black partners can be vilified as "black by day and white by night," and if their children are not completely accepted by white society, they can become embittered, or referred to as "coconuts" by blacks—black on the outside and white on the inside. The belief [Tizard and

Phoenix 1993:164–5] by children of mixed parentage that this gives them an advantage of bridging both cultures has been studied. The reality is more complex: "two thirds of the sample said that they felt equally comfortable with black and white people, and an even larger proportion said that they had no colour preference for a marriage partner . . . But these overall figures conceal the fact that some of the sample were strongly affiliated to white people and culture, whilst others were strongly affiliated to black people and cultures . . . It was a minority [about thirty percent] of young people who had a strong affiliation to both black and white people and cultures . . . This was partly because the boundaries between black and white people and cultures are to some extent also social class boundaries." In the days of Empire, the shortage of women created entire new communities of mixed race children (known then as *coloureds*), usually brought up by the mother in her tradition and language and/or in special schools or segregated into ghettoes. These children grew up culturally separate and discriminated against and not completely accepted by either culture. Intermarriage by British Jews, now fortyfour percent, has long been seen as the means by which the Jewish community preserved its identity, but this together with increasing secularisation and assimilation, is causing concern [Miller and Schmool 1996:1–3]. In Britain there are about 300,000 British Jews, but "The community has witnessed increasing secularization and assimilation, demographic shrinkage and ageing, the erosion of traditional values and beliefs." This is due to communal divisions, decreasing intermarriage, and Jews no longer formally associating themselves with a synagogue, or distancing themselves from Israel.

Clearly assimilation must be voluntary and cannot be socially engineered by the state. The Australian attempts at forced assimilation/de-racination did not work, quite apart from the moral objections to it. In 1954 the American Supreme Court declared school segregation unconstitutional, and bussing was introduced. It met with much resistance, and in 1974 the Supreme Court reacted by barring bussing across school district lines. Brown [1995:266–7], in his book on prejudice, contends that the use of interventionist programmes— be they assimilationist or pluralistic (multicultural)—is "the final and perhaps the thorniest issue of all, and one of special relevance to those working in any real multicultural setting." Interventionist assimilation policies in which linguistic or cultural identity is 'surrendered' can have deleterious consequences. "Such policies can be seen as attempts by the dominant group to impose an alien social order on less-powerful groups struggling for economic and psychological survival." Some educational multiculturalists [Saggar 1992:194] are also suspicious of apparently modest attempts to encourage assimilation: "The significance of the New Right in this area lies in its seemingly nonracial language and style, rendering charges of overt racism virtually meaningless. Nonetheless, the agenda of the New Right may constitute a new 'racism' by which cultural and social divisions are reinforced with a reformulated concept of [British] nationhood."

Although the English language is a uniquely integrating influence in the United States, a dispersed diversity is feature of its multiculturalism. After a move to find "an authentic black language and culture" was made in Oakland, California [TM 21 Dec. 96], President Clinton refused federal funds for bilingual schools teaching "black English," known as "ebonics" or "ghetto talk," on the grounds that it would only stigmatise and hinder those who speak it [TM 26 Dec. 96]. Federal funds continued to be available to bilingual schools to teach English to students who speak Spanish or other languages as their primary tongue. Until recently, the U.S. believed in the melting pot ethos, namely that immigrants and blacks would become assimilated and "Americanised," and that what was good would be taken from migrant cultures to forge a unique American identity. This ideal has been abandoned, arguably because it has been shown to be unattainable rather than undesirable, possibly as a result of the major change in American immigration policy in 1965. Some say that the melting pot was a myth which sprang out of the 1920s, when migrants were principally white and European. For instance, during the first half of this century, when many of its immigrants were of Jewish or Italian origin from Eastern and Southern Europe, it was necessary to Anglicise their names and origins in order to work the entertainment industry. But it has not worked well for many blacks and Hispanics: black entertainers, for example, had to conform to a black stereotype in the industry's earlier days. A British-Jewish journalist [Times 11 May 00], born in Russia and who spent almost half his life living in the United States, opines that "America is a melting pot in the literal sense. Foreigners are embraced, but only if they offer up their identities, for melting down into the great American collective unconscious . . . Britain does not expect the unquestioning patriotic allegiance and the cultural conformity of the American melting pot. This is one of the main reasons why London has become a more cosmopolitan city even than New York . . . [Foreigners] are accepted graciously and calmly, but are left to get on with their own way of life." The United States also offers a paradigm for those nation-states which have a native-born ethnic minority claiming special rights. Indigenous but racially/culturally different ethnic groups like American blacks, New Zealand Maoris, Australian/Canadian aborigines (and the Quebec French), seem to inherit an innate but understandable sense of victimhood, possibly validated by positive discrimination in their favour.

The probability of the large underclass of American blacks integrating into mainstream American society seems doubtful, and the racial tensions remain as problematic as ever. White fear of black violence is probably an obstacle to harmonious race relations in the United States. There is an alliance of its alienated minorities, and the divide is also one of economic class and not only that of race. Some blacks have created a different separatist identity by re-inventing themselves as black Muslims. The old-fashioned black liberals like Martin Luther King have been replaced by extremists who believe that American justice is a tool of white power. King supported non-violence and integration, but he was increasingly challenged by younger and militant black activists who believed that the only way to achieve freedom and equality was by militant separatism. Jesse Jackson and his Rainbow Coalition of all minorities, black and white, is a moderate black Democrat who was a presidential candidate in the 1984 and 1988 elections who believed that he could work within the American political structure. In the polarised political climate of the 1990s, he could no longer deliver to American blacks their expectations, or convincingly relate to black ghetto experience.

Glazer was involved in the early 1990s debate over multicultural education in New York State as a member of the curriculum committee. He says that he argued in 1974 [1997:123] that "Blacks would become residentially more integrated with whites as their economic circumstances improved, as their political power increased, and as they grew closer in all other respects to whites. And we could expect this to happen as a result of the powerful antidiscrimination legislation of 1964 and 1965 . . . there has [however] been little change in twenty years . . . separation, [136] as well as differences in interest, contributes to blacks and whites coming to see the world differently. The surprisingly large divergence that was shown in public opinion polls between blacks and non-blacks as to O.J. Simpson's guilt is only the most striking of these differences in how blacks and whites see the world . . . I [Glazer] believe [91] that the basic explanation is that in the late 1980s there was a build-up of frustration in the black population over the failure of civil rights reforms to deliver what was expected of them . . . whatever the causes, [120] the apartness of blacks is real. And it is this that feeds multiculturalism. For this one group, assimilation, by some key measures, has certainly failed." The 1995 O.J. Simpson trial Los Angeles took more than a year, and some 120 witnesses gave evidence. The jury reached a verdict in less than four hours [DM 4 Oct. 95]. Nine of the jurors were black, one Hispanic, and two were white. Before the trial, O.J. Simpson was believed to have transcended race, but after the not guilty verdict, a poll showed that seventy-seven percent of whites believed him to be guilty, and seventy-two percent of blacks believed him to be innocent. Before the verdict, President Clinton had said that "I hope that the American people will not let this become some symbol of a larger racial issue" [DM 30 Sept. 95].

Glazer [145–146] later believed that "government has been as ineffective in overcoming segregation at the elementary school level as it has been in overcoming the prevailing residential segregation, though government programmes have tried to do so. Government action can never match, in scale and impact, the crescive effects of individual, voluntary decision . . . the forces that will produce the changes we are looking for are individual and voluntaristic, rather than governmental and authoritative." He says [4] that "Multiculturalism in education has, in a word, won . . . and [6] if multiculturalism has established a powerful position in higher education, it is perhaps not so surprising." He concludes [47] that education should be culturally pluralistic and that "it would be better for young blacks to believe that there had been improvements in their situation, that opportunities are greater than ever before, rather than the reverse." His analysis is limited to the situation of a single indigenous ethnic group (black), and suggests that human nature can negate positive social engineering.

If ethnic minorities remain separate, then inevitably they will be perceived as being different, i.e. not "one of us." The "rejected" majority begins to perceive that the migrant has repudiated "our country, culture and values," and only wants to use them, but not be part of them. In other words, they are squatters rather than neighbours. They may also feel that migrants who have chosen to settle in their midst should make every effort to become part of it and to identify with it. Otherwise they remain minority groups rather than individual members of that society. Even the prime minister of India said [TM 29 Jan. 99] that "the task is to assimilate non-Hindus, like Muslims and Christians, in the mainstream. They must have a feeling of patriotism for this country." The "gastarbeiters" in Germany were suspected of having divided loyalties: "one cannot serve two masters, having one citizenship [Turkish] for the heart and another [German] for the money." Official resistance to separatism in small European countries is evidenced by regulations or incentives imposed by the Danish [SE 19 Feb. 95] and Dutch governments. A Dutch government spokesman, in announcing an assimilation programme, said [TM 30 Nov. 96] "We are saying to newcomers: We're glad you're here, but we also expect something from you in return"—there are penalties if they do not fulfil this condition. The leader of the anti-immigrant Freedom Party that entered Austria's ruling coalition said [TM 12 Feb. 00] "Turks do not integrate into society. They say 'We don't want to be Austrian, we want to stay Turkish.' So I say 'That's your problem, make up your mind.'" Austria's eight million inhabitants include about 170,000 Turks, or two percent. If migrants do not within two or three generations assimilate and remain residentially and/or culturally separate, then a potential fault line begins to develop.

Separatist groups are tolerated, but their long-term coexistence with the mainstream society is tenuous and fragile, and is largely contingent on their aspirations. Ultimately they are likely to become politicised, but this is likely to remain uncertain and quiescent unless and until they reach a position where they can exercise significant influence, as in Australia. A long-term permanent cultural separatism such as exists between the Quebec province and the rest of Canada, and between the Fleming and Walloon provinces and Belgium, is tolerated by means of a regional polity, but maybe only as long as the economic prosperity and security of the pluralist state are not threatened—the "hearts over minds" conflict. Hong Kong's reversion to China in 1997 may offer a special (non-racial) test of one version of "two domain" pluralism, namely for how long China can continue to exist as one country with two political, legal, and economic systems. Nevertheless, to build confidence in the run up to the handover, as it had done before with British passport holders for the Kenyan and 29,000 Ugandan Asians, Britain granted non-visa six months access to about two million Hong Kong Chinese, and its potentially stateless (mainly) 7,000 Pakistani and Indian minorities [TM 5 Mar. 96].

Some religious groups such as Moslems and non-secular Jews discourage assimilation, and promote a strong sense of independence. This separatism provides a shelter from the effects of any racism and discrimination and inroads into their religion and culture. Some establish patterns of visits "home" to their country of origin—their young people visit India/Pakistan for marriage, or perhaps visit or temporarily live on an Israeli kibbutz. Israel is funding visits "home" by young Jews in the diaspora [TM 18 Nov. 98]. This serves to reinforce their ethnic identity, and cushions them against the cultural influence of their adopted country. It provides an alternative view of themselves with an independent future. Sometimes the influence of parental attempts to reinforce this cultural divide does not work, particularly with young women forced into marriages who prefer the individualistic freedom of their adopted Western culture, and who may, as a result, go into hiding. Thousands of British Asian girls are said to lead double lives maybe resulting in emotional problems—a traditional cultural identity in the parental home, which metamorphoses outside. In fundamentalist Iran there are two parallel worlds for young women: a reverse "two domain" separatism—a secular Western behaviour in private and a fundamentalist religious behaviour in public [TM 8 April 97].

If ethnic groups remain fully or partially separatist, then that multicultural society will exhibit a greater degree of diversity, difference, and variety of lifestyles, which manifests itself in voluntary ghettoisation. Ghettoised separatism can lend itself to political "gerrymandering" and a direct route to political power. Ethnic politicians and businessmen might have a vested interest in maintaining ghettoes for electoral and/or commercial reasons. The Labour Party policy of "one man one vote" led to four local constituency parties in Birmingham (with similar disputes in ten other constituencies) being suspended by the National Executive Council after allegations of using local Council grants to buy votes and enrolling Asian voters en bloc as party members [Malik 1995:18–9]—reminiscent of the old Chicago "machine politics" controlled by the city boss. This "entryism," where an activist section of a political party (or a trade union) is more dominant than the majority of its members, can be defended on the grounds that it is democratic, but the nomination is that of fringe activists not representative of the silent majority, who only make their presence felt at general elections. During the 1997 General Election there were allegations of vote rigging in predominantly Asian constituencies [TM 23 Jan./17 Dec. 97]. In the 2001 general election, police and election officials were called upon to investigate allegations of postal vote-rigging in two inner city constituencies with large Asian electorates [TM 2 June 01]. In Britain, the number of ethnic candidates for parliament in the 2001 general election was sixty-three, compared with nineteen in 1997, and four in 1983. There were eight ethnic MP's in the 1997 parliament, all Labour [TM 2 May 01].

If migrants do not assimilate and/or this is resisted by the mainstream society, this lends itself to the formation of voluntary ghettoes. These expand because the latest immigrant arrivals will prefer self-segregation and separatism in voluntary and expanding inner-city ghettoes to avoid social isolation and loneliness. They also provide safe havens for illegal immigrants. Ghettoes satisfy a sociological and human need of minorities to maintain an ethnic/religious kinship, but usually also reflect differing economic and social circumstances. They compound separatism and virtually ensure that little assimilation takes place, or at least only in a limited range of non-social activities. This makes it unlikely that any common consensus will emerge, and increases the likelihood of future ethno-national instability, or in extreme cases, conflict. The inner-city ghettoisation of whites and blacks or Muslims, and long-term unemployment, leads to poverty, dependency, hopelessness, crime, alcoholism, and drug abuse. Its underclass can have an amoral culture with a different set of values. In Britain it has recently led to inter-ethnic, including anti-white, riots, and the setting up of unofficial "no-go" areas in the Muslim ghettoes of Oldham, near Manchester, and in Bradford [TM 20–21 April 01]. Before the recent riot in Bradford, the previous chairman of the CRE had found that racial tensions were being made worse by denominational schools and separatism in multiracial schools [TM 23 April 01], and communities are divided along racial and religious lines [TXT 10 July 01]. In Bradford, there are sixty-three Muslim, five Hindu, and six Sikh schools [STM 15 July 01]. The recent Bradford riots suggest that segregated schools clearly reinforce separatism. Although this was anticipated by the 1985 Swann report *Education for All*, its proposal of a multi-faith, nondenominational integrated approach did not prove to be acceptable. The universalised right to religious freedom gives rise to one of the insoluble problems of a multicultural society.

It is sometimes a victimhood claim of minorities that they are not allowed to escape the ghettoes—a claim that once had validity inasmuch as early migrants and American blacks were forced into ghettoes by racial discrimination in housing. In the United States these ghettos, barrios, and Chinatowns are well established in San Francisco, Los Angeles and Miami—"islands of homogeneity." At the turn of the century, New York already had more Italians than had Rome, more Jews than had Warsaw, more Irish than had Dublin, and more blacks than had any other city in the world. When a minority creates a ghetto by self-selected, as opposed to coercive, apartheid, it announces to the mainstream society its separatism and this can be used to legitimise opposition to multiculturalism. Inner cities, or districts thereof, can become the exclusive domain of a dominant ethnic group or groups, such as in Los Angeles, Washington (a black majority in 1960, now over seventy percent black), Oldham, Bradford, Burnley, Leicester or Brent. Any whites who live there, or return there, may feel like foreigners in their own land. The police in Manchester fear that some districts of the city could be turned into "no go" areas for whites [TM 20 April 01]. Leicester is expected to become the first city in Britain with a non-white majority by 2011 [TM 8 Dec. 00]. It may be seen as ironic that the police of the county of Leicestershire have only about five percent ethnic minority officers, but nearly thirty percent of its city councillors are Asian. Thirty years ago, most of its schools were predominantly white; now some schools are almost entirely Asian. Although inner city "sink estates' are often populated by blacks and immigrant minorities, this is not exclusively so. There are also economic and social ghettoes of an underclass in the post-industrial depressed areas of Britain, particularly in the North England. Those at the "sharp end" of ghettoisation may "vote with their feet," as evidenced in the London inner-city schools where white children have become the ethnic minority. There is a continuing problem in recruiting and retaining teachers in spite of salary incentives, and by the abnormal retirement of head teachers.

Voluntary ghettoes, which provide limited social interaction and mobility, are not confined to race and ethnicity, but also to religion and social class. Nor are they a feature of poverty, or necessarily the domain of an underclass. There are the long established Jewish ghettoes in London's Golders Green community and elsewhere, and a wealthy Arab ghetto around the Edgware Road. The Hindu Hare Krishna cult are the majority in the village of Letchmore Heath in Hertfordshire [BBC 1 2 Oct. 94]. Religious orders have their monasteries and convents, and the Mormons have Utah. Retired emigrant "Brits" live, socialise and celebrate British customs in their voluntary ghettoes, as in the days of Empire, knowing little about the local language, religion and customs. A study of older British expatriates in Spain who had lived there for ten years, found that fewer than fifteen percent could speak Spanish [TM 4

Sept. 00]. In a totally sociologically pluralist and separatist society, there is no reason why lesbians, prostitutes, gays, and feminist groups should not also construct their own socio-spatial boundaries. Housing in Britain is now being built for gays [STM 10 Aug. 97], and in Dublin for Gaelic speakers [TM 12 Aug. 97]. A gay village like Manchester in the centre of Newcastle has been proposed [TM 29 July 99/14 April 00]. Officially condoned prostitution and gay "tolerance zones" become ghettoes due to businesses and residents moving out [TM 6 Aug. 97]—this is known as physical distancing or "nimbyism" ("not in my back yard"). There are also university and residents' objections to the proposed architecture for the Centre for Islamic Studies at Oxford, which would have a 100 foot high minaret [STM 16 July 00].

In Greater London twenty to twenty-five percent of the population is ethnic, and London is home to fifty percent of the ethnic population of Britain. But in many rural areas the proportion of minorities is less than one percent. Two London Boroughs—Brent and Newham—are expected to have a non-white minority when the results of the 2001 census are published [TM 8 Dec. 00]. It is forecast that by the year 2010, almost thirty percent of London's total population will be ethnic minorities, with the Boroughs of Brent and Newham having more than fifty percent and Tottenham forty-five percent. In the twenty year period from 1991 to 2011, London's white population is expected to decline from 5.50 to 5.06 million due to "white flight." According to another prediction [TM 4 Sept. 00], white Britons will be outnumbered in the capital by 2010, and whites will be a minority in Britain by 2060, if the current trends in fertility rates and levels of immigration continue [TM 4 Sept. 00]. In Bradford, the council estimates that twenty-one percent of its population is now from ethnic minorities, compared with 15.6 percent in 1991, and the white population has declined from eighty-four percent to seventy-eight percent [TM 8 Dec. 00]. If so, the limits of toleration of the mainstream community may become increasingly at risk, and a previously tolerated but localised multicultural relationship could begin to disintegrate into intensified city ghettoisation and racial unrest. When a society turns a blind eye to "no go" areas, white, black or religious, then it becomes anarchic. Brixton is a largely black ghetto that has seen two major race riots within the last twenty years. The police in Brixton say that firearm incidents have recently doubled from an average of twenty per month. Darcus Howe [1996:17], a British Trinidadian and one-time anti-racist black broadcaster, says, after having lived in Britain for twenty-five years, that "black on black violence spreads and threatens . . . it's coming too close for the comfort of my family," and he was doubtful of remaining in this "fragile community." Of his old school in Trinidad, whose national anthem includes "every creed, every race, finds an equal place," he found that none of the children believes this to be true on a island where the Indian and African inhabitants barely coexist in an atmosphere of racial tension" [Channel 4 29 July/TM 31 July 00]. The government has recently recognised the problems inherent in ghettoisation, and asylum seekers will be dispersed around the country in an attempt to ease the burden on London and the South East. However, these asylum seekers are resisting this stratagem, and if moved, they may subsequently move back again.

It follows from demography that ghetto schools will not become secular or multi-faith, but will be all-black, all-Jewish, all-Asian or all-Muslim. Religious separatists oppose the teaching of Christianity in schools which are predominantly of their own faith, with their leaders noting that their children were being "bombarded with different ideologies" and were having difficulty in forming their beliefs. This response could offer a prognosis of the outcome of multiculturalism. In complete contrast to this, a white teacher with twenty-one years experience was suspended from his school where ninety-two percent of the pupils were Asian [TM 21 March 00]. This was because he said on television that he would not let his son be taught there, as "there's far too much bias towards the Asian community in that school . . . it is simply that we don't live in that community and are not part of it." An Asian parent complained that "It was bordering on racism for the teacher to make those remarks. It undermines the multicultural way of life." Personal distancing provides a practical test for supporters of multiculturalism, as it does for educationalists who publicly support state comprehensive education in Britain, but send their own children to private schools. Supposing that the nearest school to a white Christian multiculturalist's residence has the same academic performance as others in his area but the children at that school are, for example, predominantly Asian, would he send his children to that school, or somewhere further away? If so, would this decision be motivated by race, class, religion or culture?

Recent experience has shown that in the long run, some multiracial/cultural separatist societies do not continue to coexist harmoniously—the Israelis and the Palestinians, the Croats, Serbs and Bosnian Muslims/Kosovan Albanians, and the Czechs and Slovaks (to mention a few) have found coexistence unacceptable. The fragility of ghettoisation was exemplified by the failure by the UN to create and to protect isolated ethnic safe areas in Bosnia. In Western democracies, urban ghettoes remain separatist racial territories: when the blacks or ethnics move in, the whites and wealthy minorities move out, and its property values and its economic barriers to entry fall. When the professional and newly middle class minorities move out of the inner-city ghettoes, they are left to the most recently arrived and younger minorities whose ethnicity is reinforced thereby. In Southern California, separatism has been accelerated by whites moving out into new "edge cities"—euphemistically known as the "white flight" to "gated communities." The wealthy and mostly white inhabitants of San Fernando Valley commissioned a feasibility study to research secession from the Los Angeles metropolis (which incidentally has a museum of tolerance), which they saw as corrupt, burdened with racial tensions, and disproportionately resource-supported [TM 22 Oct. 98]. The last 2000 census in the USA showed that only fifty-two of the largest one hundred cities now have a white majority, compared with seventy a decade ago. This is largely due to white flight to the suburbs and the growth of the Hispanic population, with the percentage of blacks in these cities remaining virtually unchanged [TM 1 May 01].

When the Berlin Wall went up in 1961 the supply of labour from Eastern Europe ended, but when Germany unified in 1990, it no longer needed the Turkish *gastarbeiters* recruited in the prosperous era up to 1972, to whom it did not grant citizenship. Turkish economic migration continued because Germany had Article 16 of its 1949 Constitution: "persons persecuted on political grounds shall enjoy the right of asylum" and no anti-immigration laws. In 1993, Germany abolished its open-door policy and introduced immigration restrictions for immigrants from "persecution-free countries" and "secure third states." In 1960 there were about 100 Turks in Berlin; there are now in the Kreusburg ghetto about 140,000 who make up forty to fifty percent of its inhabitants. There is inter-ethnic violence between the Muslim Turks, and Christian Kurdish refugees.

Another example of the outcome of refugees forming separatist racial ghettoes was the case of the six-year-old Cuban boy refugee living with his relatives in Miami. Greater Miami has a Cuban population of about forty percent. The boy's relatives refused to allow him to be returned to Cuba to be reunited with his father, who exercised his parental right to have him returned. The American Immigration and Naturalization Service, in recognising the importance of the bond between parent and child, followed federal law, and insisted that the boy be returned. The mayors of Miami refused to allow the police force, many of whom are Cuban, to enforce the federal law, and threatened large-scale civil disobedience. A former president of the American Immigration Lawyers Association likened this dispute to the southern states during the 1960s that refused to enforce the civil rights laws that ended racial discrimination. He said that "Either Miami is a banana republic or it is part of the United States," i.e. is it a state within a state? This view was reportedly supported by Miami's non-Cuban residents—white, "Anglos," and African-American blacks [TM 30 March/1April 00]. Ultimately, the boy was forcibly seized by federal agents, reunited with his father, and both were returned to Cuba. Rioting subsequently broke out in Little Havana, with 200 fires started, and at least 290 arrests.

NOTES

Brown, R. *Prejudice—Its Social Psychology.* Oxford: Blackwell Publishers, 1995. 266–7.

Eisenstein, Z. *Hatreds—Racialized and Sexualiized Conflicts in the 21st Century.* London: Routledge. 1996. 70.

Flew, A. "The Menace of Islam." In *The New Humanist.* vol. 110. no. 3. August 1995. 2.

Gellner, E. *Thought and Change.* London: Weidenfeld and Nicolson, 1964. 156.

Glazer, N. *We Are All Multiculturalists Now.* Cambridge, Mass: Harvard University Press. 1997. 123 and 151.

Howe, D. *New Statesman.* 13 June 1996. 17.

Jupp, J. *Immigration.* Oxford: Oxford University Press, 1998. 158.

Malik, K. "Party Colours." In *New Stateman and Society.* 14 July 1995. 18.

Miller, S. Schmool, M. et al. *Social and Political Attitudes of British Jews.* London: The Institute for Jewish Policy Research. 1996. 1 and 3.

Purcell, H. *Fascism.* London: Hamish Hamilton, 1977. 62.

Saggar, S. *Race And Politics In Britain.* Hemel Hempstead: Harvester Wheatsheaf, 1992. 194.

Schlesinger, A.M. *The Disuniting of America—Reflections on a Multicultural Society.* New York and London: W.W. Norton, 1992. 13.

Spencer, I.R.G. *British Immigration Policy Since 1939—The Making of Multiracial Britain.* London: Routledge, 1997. 1.

Swann, Lord. *Education for All—The Report of the Committee of Inquiry Into the Education of Children from Ethnic Minority Groups.* London: Stationery Office, 1985. 4.

Tizard, B. and Phoenix, A. *Black, White or Mixed Race—Race and Racism in the Lives of Young People of Mixed Parentage.* London: Routledge, 1993. 164–5.

BBC 2. *In a League of their Own.* 4 July 1994.

BBC 1. *The Road to Hare Krishna—The Dispute Over the Hindu Temple.* 2 October, 1994.

BBC1. *Omnibus.* 7 July 97.

Channel 4. *Trouble in Paradise.* 29 July 2000.

21

Freedom of Speech, Social Censorship, and Political Correctness

Freedom of speech and a free press are intellectual liberties that are the bastions, and arguably, the ultimate foundation, of a democracy, a system that has the power to correct its electoral mistakes by changing the party in power peacefully, even though that party may leave behind its mistakes. A totalitarian state will restrict and/or manipulate the freedom of speech and information to avoid criticism of those in power and their ideology. Freedom of speech poses a dilemma, because a seemingly acceptable liberal principle must in the interests of justice and individual autonomy have limits and restrictions. In Britain, in the interests of toleration, all public debate about immigration and race has for decades been virtually a political and social taboo. Nonetheless, the principle laid down in Article 10 of the ECHR is that any interference with the freedom of expression must be deemed *necessary* in a democratic society, and *proportionate* [TM 20 April 99]. This has been legally argued successfully by both Farrakhan and the BNP [STM 5 Aug. 01]. Freedom of speech should not be abused by demeaning that which people cannot change, for example, their appearance, disability, race, or ethnicity.

Unlimited toleration would permit the public expression of views about issues that others might detest. Mill, though, argued that this should be tolerated because some desirable but independent consequences might result. This neutral position assumes that given a free market of ideas, the best view will triumph over competing ideas, and without it the best view may never be heard. Its validity depends on the dubious connection between unrestricted free speech and the promulgation and acceptance of the true, or best, ideas. Mill believed that the truth would emerge from competing arguments and not from censorship, although he recognised that censorship can be imposed by social, as well as by legal and institutional means. He said [1994:303] that "[protection] against the tyranny of the magistrate is not enough; there needs

273

protection also against the tyranny of the prevailing opinion and feeling; against the tendency of society to impose, by other means than civil penalties, its own ideas and practices as rules of conduct on those who dissent from them." Intellectual freedom can be defended not only on the grounds of utility and toleration, but on the Kantian principle that people should be treated as an end, and not as a means. This means that to restrict the intellectual freedom of expression of individuals denies respect for human beings as autonomous agents. This principled argument is unconvincing. If complete freedom of speech results in some direct, significant, and tangible harm to others, then this will also infringe upon their autonomy, even though this may have a utility by benefiting people in general. Neither has Mill's theory always been borne out by history, and this method of achieving the best outcome can be at a high cost. When democracy was abandoned in 1933 Germany, the adoption of what appeared at the time to be the most appropriate political ideology became irreversible.

Since at least the 1980s, freedom of speech in the English-speaking world has been eroded by the voluntary social censorship of political correctness (PC), or rather ethnic correctness, under the guise of anti-racism to promote multiculturalism and cultural relativism. This has served to undermine cultural hegemonies. This is a paradox, as proponents of multiculturalism who support a diversity of cultures are often reluctant to permit the expression of a diversity of opinions. In a multicultural society, there may have to be an additional level of voluntary censorship on the freedom to criticise the cultural beliefs, practices, and values of other cultures. Otherwise, these criticisms would either have to be tolerated or end up in litigation. There is nothing prima facie objectionable in voluntary social censorship, provided that it is based on unrestricted information and reflective thought, and is not merely an uncritical fashion. Orwell (1995) experienced voluntary social censorship in failing to get his book *Animal Farm* published until 1945 because of the intolerance of his then unfashionable anti-Stalinist views.

A Channel 4 television producer [1994:8–9] responding to criticism about a studio discussion on fascism which included the BNP said that "Television must uphold the freedom of speech—even for racists . . . how else can broadcasters coherently oppose the [then] broadcasting ban on Sinn Fein?" The anti-racist immigration lobby CARF argued that their "no platform" policy "does not mean a ban on reporting or investigating fascists and fascism . . . CARF is opposed to all state and media bans which only serve the interests of censorship . . . what we are saying is that journalists should be aware of the power the medium of television gives the fascists to propagandise and present their violent, anti-democratic creed in acceptable terms . . . the present vogue within TV is to debate fascism, rather than investigate the fascists." In effect, this means that fascists should not be allowed to express their own political views. Perversely, extremists may benefit from official censorship, or an unofficial "no platform for racists or fascists" policy, because this could indicate that their views are so appealing or popular that they must not be heard. Nevertheless, prior to the 1997 general election, the BNP (a minority party) were allowed to make a brief political broadcast, to which they were officially entitled, on the BBC and ITV, but were banned by Channel 4 [TM 26 April 97], the "minority interest" channel—which at that time was presumably available only to approved minorities. Brewer [1984:143] observed that "Racist attributes do not translate into support for fringe movements. When exploitation of race and immigration is left to these fringe movements, it cannot become a major political issue. It can be transformed into one very easily by the established parties . . . .disillusionment with the major political parties shows itself in abstention voting rather than support for fringe movements. The established parties are invariably seen as better channels for the expression of resentment over immigration." It is significant that in Britain it took until the year 2000 for immigration to become a publicly expressed and mutual concern for the two main political parties. In the 2001 general elections, the BNP obtain 16.4 and 11.2 percent of the vote in two constituencies in Oldham and 11.2 percent in Burnley—both towns having experienced serious race riots. This level of electoral support had the effect of allowing the leader of the BNP to be interviewed on two national television channels.

The United States has a greater freedom of speech than Britain, which is guaranteed by the First Amendment. This enshrines the principle of toleration in protecting the freedoms of religion, speech, and press, and the rights of peaceful assembly and to petition the government for redress of grievances. The pre-eminent status of freedom of speech in the hierarchy of constitutional rights was determined in 1969 by the Supreme Court, which made a "crucial distinction between advocacy of violent or unlawful conduct, which is protected, and intentional, imminent incitement of such conduct, which is not" [Strossen 1995:44]. Published material includes [TM 22 Oct. 98] racially provocative literature, programmes and manuals on how to, but not advocating, murder and torture. Whether published material that directly aids and abets murder should enjoy the protection of the First Amendment, however, has been taken to the Supreme Court [TM 22 Nov. 97]. The Supreme Court [TM 5 July 97] decided against banning indecent or offensive material on the estimated 500 American hate websites on the Internet [TM 13 Jan. 00]. Only five states out of fifty are said not to have active hate groups [STMG 8 Aug. 99].

Complete freedom of expression has been never lawful in Britain. Although this is guaranteed by Article 10 of the Human Rights Act 1998 that came into force in October 2000, there are legal restrictions on privacy, libel, slander, breach of confidentiality, official secrets, and incitement to racial hatred. Bizarrely, Britain still has an ancient religious (Christian) blasphemy law which has been upheld by the ECHR [TM 26 Nov. 96]. It is difficult to talk publicly or objectively about race because it will be labelled "opportunistic," "racist," and "playing the race card." The media will be accused of "negative reporting." Conversely, this could also be said about the views broadcast to national television audiences, as if representing substantial opinion, by small but impressively titled special interest pressure groups in the interests of "balance," which offer little opportunity for rebuttal. The terms *bogus* and *flood* (or *swamped*) in relation to numbers of asylum seekers, although they have been used by the prime minister and other politicians, were immediately labelled "inflammatory" by anti-racists, although acceptable PC alternatives have yet to be devised. The terms *coloured, immigrant, foreigner* and *ethnic minority* are objected to by some multiculturalists [DM 9 July 01]. It might be seen by some anti-racists as ironic that the Daily Mail, which is a prominent tabloid newspaper, has for years vigorously campaigned against the "flood of bogus asylum seekers and economic migrants," but at the same time puts anti-racism high in its political agenda. This newspaper was largely responsible for leading the public campaign into the Stephen Lawrence racist murder. Nevertheless, the British Broadcasting Standards Commission ruled that it was not offensive for a black comedian to call the Queen a 'bitch,' because in "rap" music the term is used to mean "woman" and not a term of abuse [TM 28 Feb. 01]. Social censorship is manifest in racist accusations about the publication of official statistics on differential crime rates and research into genetic determinism between races. This arises from the concern about its potential use for "scientific" racism or eugenics, whereas differences between pre-disposing genetic factors towards diseases (other than psychiatric) between races is acceptable. Glenn Tinder [1995:211–2] defends scientific racism inasmuch that "Arguments for the genetic inferiority of certain races, so far as these are made by geneticists, seem to me [Tinder] clearly to belong to the category of upsetting: they are offensive, but . . . may be tolerated without limit . . . Their methods, at least ostensibly, are scientific; their conclusions, as purportive science, invite reasonable dispute and refutation. To be intolerant toward them under these conditions compromises our relationship to the truth." The revisionist racist historian and Holocaust denier Irving, who is banned from entry into Germany, Canada, and Australia, lost a libel action [TM 10 Jan./12 April 2000]. Irving's critic did, however, advocate as much free speech as possible, defended the right of historians to reappraise the Holocaust, and opposed the laws in much of Europe that make Holocaust denial a criminal offence [TM 12 April 00].

This discussion contends that although the right to free speech should not be as near absolute as in the United States, it should be tolerated within wide legal limits. This would counteract the voluntary social censorship imposed by multicultural pressure groups often used in advancing their political agenda. This limited Millsean view is both democratic and pragmatic as the ideas, comments, and criticisms may have validity and/or merit, and if repressed, covert outlets will be found, particularly in this age of multiple and unregulated methods of communication.

The psychology of political correctness and its speech codes imply that "the words may not matter, but their meaning does." Political correctness—a term first used in 1984—has been satirised as political paralysis or heresy by thought. It has had damaging effects, not least to the freedom of speech, whereby it erodes the scope for a free and frank discussion. What seems to matter is the thought being "correct," irrespective of it being biased or contrary to the evidence. It has been influential for about the last ten years in providing intellectual respectability for the promotion of multicultural curricula in some American universities. PC has made an assault on traditional education, and has loosely united anti-racist, anti-capitalist, anti-sexist, and anti-homophobic groups. It has promoted revisionist history with its particular targets being the European culture and English literature. Under the social censorship of PC, the teaching of history and literature, and the pre-eminence of the English language, has come under attack, reinforcing the diversity and difference in a separatist society. Ferro [1984:viii-x] observed that "Independently of its scientific vocation, history effectively exercises a double function, both therapeutic [missionary] and militant [manipulative] . . . in the USA the evolution of history teaching is even more radical: it expresses an ideological transfer from 'melting pot' to mixed 'salad bowl.'"

PC asserts that there is no all-embracing, over-arching culture, and that it frees people to rethink their basic assumptions. It promotes cultural relativism, and is part of the ongoing ideological and politicised debate of the cultural upheaval which at present surrounds American and British identities. Given a liberal educational establishment, the influence of PC can be instrumental in the promotion of multiculturalism and multiethnic education. Opponents [Honeyford 1983:12-3] see this as "inverted McCarthyism" or intolerant "liberal fascism"—an assault on classical liberal education and Western culture, which imposes destructive social and political beliefs and stereotypes. Some perceive PC as a psychological tactic of those who want to undermine traditional society and its values: it reinforces separatism, undermines national identity, and reduces social cohesion by laying a disproportionate emphasis on past injustices. Unjustified and knee-jerk accusations of racism can create a climate of social fear rather than promoting toleration. The PC euphemisms of *guidance* and *positive image* are potentially insidious terms for social censorship. It gives rise to the concern that the suppression of free speech will lead to a personalised, customised anarchy, and a degradation of the truth, because the way to the truth is by free and open debate.

Fukuyama [1996:320] observes that "The ability of Americans to understand the nature of other cultures is harmed rather than helped by recent calls for multicultural studies. The purpose of multicultural curricula in American classrooms today is not to confront and understand cultural differences squarely. If that were all there was to it, no one could possibly object to this kind of broadening horizons. The problem with multiculturalism as it is practised in the American educational system is that its underlying objective is not to understand but to validate the non-Western cultures of the United States ethnic and racial minorities. Arriving at a positive evaluation of these cultures is far more important than being accurate about them. In some cases, the underlying message is an ecumenical but false one, that all cultures ultimately uphold the same decent, liberal values as the writers of the multicultural curriculum itself; in other cases, foreign cultures are held to be superior to that of the United States. This dogma serves to retard, not enhance, our understanding of them."

PC may have originated with the good intention, based on the norms of tolerant behaviour, of not causing offence, but it can degenerate into manipulative intolerance. It insists on conforming to a stereotype with regard to thoughts and opinions, outlaws "negative beliefs," and may require a "culture of denial." George Orwell once said that "Liberty is the right to tell people what they do not want to hear." The paradox of allegedly liberal PC is that although supporting pluralism depends on toleration, it nevertheless requires an intolerant conformity to a stereotyped thinking and the suppression of difference. The accusation of not being PC can itself be a potent threat. PC itself, though, is not wholly to blame—the public relations industry has created a semantic manipulation of the English language which is euphemistic, bland, oblique, circumlocutory, slippery, and opaque, used by politicians and spokespersons in official statements, press releases, photo calls and sound bites. In Kosovo, for example, there was no actual war, just a "moral war" and an "international armed conflict." As a former government spin doctor said, "a good spin doctor will not lie—but that is not the same as saying he would tell the truth," and he said that only in Britain is it the popular belief that NATO's campaign was a success; elsewhere in Europe, it is generally felt to be a failure [TM 26 May 00]. Government denials and the manipulation and falsification of statistics have almost become routine. The fog of language and speech codes can be used either to justify or to condemn almost any position on any issue. For example, government "spending" can become government "investment." Criticism of immigration controls can be labelled "the forces of conservatism," "socially exclusive," or populist, prejudiced, or xenophobic. PC can also soften the otherwise adverse emotional impact of words—i.e. the use of different words will cause something that is real to no longer exist. Thus, child abuse, pedophilia, and incest can become intergenerational sex. The S.S. never used the words *gassing, extermination*, or *liquidation* in their documents. Those who label their opponents propagandist or prejudiced are themselves safe from criticism, because they can only be opposed by those who sympathise with the alleged propaganda. The terms *moralist* and *propagandist* are not in ordinary usage emotively neutral. They are emotive antonyms: *propagandist* carries a stigma, whereas *moralist* carries respect. Moralists will be praised but propagandists will be condemned, and both terms endeavour to change attitudes [Stevenson 1944:243–4].

PC is a form of reverse or illiberal intolerance directed not simply against behaviour, but against the "wrong views" being expressed. Thought policing can ultimately involve the monitoring, informing, and anonymously denouncing that which is said in classrooms, lecture theatres, seminars, the media, as well as the revision of textbooks and history, and the purging and sanitising of libraries. Nationalism, culturalism, and multiculturalism cannot be discussed in any purposeful way without introducing the emotive and taboo topics of race, immigration, and religion. This voluntary social censorship is intentionally counterproductive to serious historical, political, and social studies, and negates any possibility that open-ended, truth-directed, critical discussion will have any effect on beliefs which, although sincerely held, may be irrational and prejudiced. In the ideology of multiculturalism, the teachings of DWEMs (dead white European males), namely their history, literature, and other representations of the past, have become a source of conflict between ethnic groups. In the United States, PC promotes the replacement of the white Euro-centric melting pot ethos with the adoption of separatist cultures. The chief judge of the United States Court of Appeals, Richard Posner [1997:41], has characterised the postmodern left as "radically multiculturalist." They oppose "the values, the beliefs, and the culture of the 'West;' the 'West' being conceived as the domain of the nondisabled heterosexual white males of European extraction and their east Asian and west Asian 'imitators,' such as the Japanese and the Jews."

The Western culture of tolerance has conditioned its society to believe that it ought to suppress its impulses and emotions and sublimate them into passive and tolerant language and behaviour. This may sometimes be cosmetic, because most people distinguish between what they are prepared to publicly express and their private feelings that they have no wish to publicise. What they claim publicly to think may differ from what they register in a secret ballot. Particularly in group discussions, people are reluctant to express their true feelings about moral and controversial issues such as sexuality, racism, and religiosity. Even in a multifaith conference specifically about toleration "there was a tendency to avoid hard questions" [Horton and Crabtree 1992:2].

Scepticism exists about the political motivation behind the rise of multiculturalist curricula in American universities. John Searle [1993:693 and

707] characterises (justifiably or otherwise) the multicultural opponents of traditional education, in spite of their diversity, to be of the "left-wing political persuasion, and they tend to write in terms of moral outrage—the outrage of those who are exposing vast and nameless oppressive conspiracies—that we have come to expect from the academic left since the 1960s . . . in such a situation of institutional loss of self-confidence, a determined minority can have an influence vastly out of proportion to its numbers or the strength of its arguments." Richard Rorty [1994] claims that "Its members [the academic left] total perhaps ten percent of university teachers of the humanities and social sciences, and perhaps two percent of all university teachers." David Sidorsky [1993:709–22] characterises the debate about the victimisation that underlies the multicultural interdisciplinary programmes in some American universities as a "confrontation about the politicization of the university, rather than as disagreement about the breadth of reading lists, [only then] can the polarization that it has generated be understood . . . the conceptual framework of many groups involved in multicultural curricular revision is that the university curriculum represents traditional Western culture as an expression of the historical domination and therefore an instrument of the illegitimate hegemony of the West . . . it enables politicized teaching to be sheltered in the University within groups which are generally perceived as having suffered deprivation or discrimination on grounds of race, sex or sexual orientation . . . [there is a] stress on the setting up of inter-disciplinary programmes of studies of deprived or victimised groups [as 'victimologies'] . . . on pain of violating the rule of never blaming the victim, the study of the culture of the victimised group will tend to the identification and indictment of the social forces which led to victimisation. Thus, the inclusion of the area in the curriculum becomes a kind of legitimation of claims of political and social deprivation. Further the texts of the legitimated authentic spokesmen of the victims emerge as sacred texts, immune from standards of criticism . . . their fundamental premises are not to be questioned."

Once the level of multiculturalism becomes influential, PC demands become more insistent for the submersion of aspects of the indigenous culture. Brigitte Berger [1993:517–8 and 524] adds to this concern: "at its hard, ultimate kernel the multiculturalist agenda is overwhelmingly a political agenda and has very little to do with the essential tasks and mission of a modern university. This is not to say that academic pursuits may not receive their inspiration from politics . . . but if the University is to remain true to its mission, if it is to continue to carry out its vital functions for individuals and modern society, it is essential to understand that politics cannot be made into the touchstone of any academic work . . . the implications of this reversal also spell grave dangers for the future of American society. For what is at issue here is a renunciation of the very premises that have provided the American experience with its unifying principle." The BBC, which is the public broadcasting corporation, has for more than sixty-five years had the motto "Nation shall speak peace unto Nation" [STM 4 April 99]. In a politically correct response to Scottish and Welsh devolution, it has instructed its staff not to use the word British to describe the generality of people living within the British Isles. In the place of *nation* it urges its presenters to use *United Kingdom*. This is ironic, because the UK, which at present includes Northern Ireland, is now less united than it has ever been.

NOTES

Berger, B. "Multiculturalism and the Modern University." In *Partisan Review*. vol. LX. no. 4 1993. 517–8 and 524.

Brewer, J.D. Mosley's Men—The British Union of Fascists in the West Midlands. Aldershot: Gower Publishing, 1984. 143.

Carf *Campaign Against Racism and Fascism*. No.18 London, January/February 1994. 8–9.

Ferro, M. *The Use and Abuse of History—Or How the Past is Taught*. London: Routledge and Kegan Paul, 1984. viii/ix.

Fukuyama, F. *Trust—The Social Virtues and the Creation of Prosperity*. London: Penguin Books, 1996. 320.

Honeyford, R. "Multiethnic Intolerance." In *The Salisbury Review*. Summer 1983. 12–13.

Horton, J. and Crabtree, H. (Eds.) *Toleration and Integrity in a Multifaith Society*. York: Dept. of Politics, University of York. 1992. 2

Mill, J.S. "On Lberty." In *A Dictionary of Philosophical Quotations*. A.J. Ayer and O'Grady, (Eds.) Oxford: Blackwell Publishers, 1994. 303.

Orwell, G. "The Freedom of the Press." In *New Statesman and Society*. 18 August 1995. 11–5.

Posner, R.A. "The Skin Trade." In *The New Republic*. 13 October 1997. 41.

Rorty, R. "A Leg-Up For Oliver North." (Book Review). *London Review of Books*. 20 October 1994.

Searle, J.R. "Is There a Crisis in American Higher Education?" In *Partisan Review*. vol. LX. 1993. 693 and 707.

Sidorsky, D. "Multiculturalism and the University." In *Partisan Review*. no. 4. 1993. 709–22.

Stevenson, C.L. *Ethics and Language*. New Haven and London: Yale University Press, 1944. 243–4.

Strossen. N. *Defending Pornography*. New York: Scribner. 1995. 44.

Tinder, G. *Toleration and Community*. Columbia, Missouri: University of Missouri Press. 1995. 211–2.

22

Freedom of Religion and its Misuse

Religion is an important component of most cultures and societies. It can reinforce social cohesion in a monocultural society, and separatism in a multicultural society. This raises the question as to the extent to which extremist religious expression should be tolerated. Religion can be politicised and appropriated to represent ethno-nationalism and social discrimination as happened in Ulster, i.e. it becomes the institutionalised focus of division. The religion of a minority can have a political dimension which is incompatible with a cultural hegemony. An indigenous society has a Lockean dilemma: what are the limits of toleration towards the religions of minorities, whose cultures do not subscribe to toleration, and whose primary loyalties are in doubt? Would this toleration be reciprocated or withdrawn if the balance of power was reversed?

There are nominally about seventy million Anglicans worldwide, with about twenty-six million in the Church of England (C-E), but the number of those actively practising is about one million. Some attribute the present national moral malaise to, at least in part, a loss of the compelling influence and authority of the traditional religion of the Anglican Church. But spirituality, with or without a church or a formal religion, still has a major but subtle influence on British culture and its values—including that of toleration. Religious belief in Britain was for many years a largely private matter, and was not used, at least overtly, secularly or politically other than in church school education. The balance of power between politics and the pulpit came into the public awareness in the 1980s, as the C-E became directly involved in secular social issues.

Religious freedom is a complex issue because of non-Christian and Western cult religions—some of which are of an alien culture and can have a political dimension. The division between religion and politics has become increasingly blurred, and raises the legal and philosophical questions: what qualifies as a religion (i.e. the worship of God)? and, if it does so qualify, of what beliefs and values is that religion's God? Furthermore, what if others do not consider this God to be the true God? In a multicultural society, non-Christian religions give rise to the problem of distinguishing between what is claimed to be solely a spiritual belief—which in the Western tradition merits toleration—and a religion that can embody an assertive political agenda with no secular and theological divide. Even the definition of a religion runs into difficulties: the Charity Commission in Britain has twice refused charitable status for Scientology [TM 10 Dec. 99], which was founded in 1954, and pagans, because their essential criterion of a religion is "a belief and public worship of a deity with commensurate public benefit." Neither does the Home Office regard Scientology as a religion in regard to immigration rules [TM 14 Jan. 97]. However, a French court [TM 30 July 97] has held that it is a religion. Should an intolerant religious sect qualify for a charitable tax-free status, effectively a British state subsidy? Does Buddhism, which has at least five versions and does not believe in a God, qualify? Some political sects use the title *Reverend* to suggest a spiritual dimension to their leader, as with Ulster Protestant fundamentalist Ian Paisley. In fascist Italy the Catholic religion flourished, as it did in Nazi Germany, in spite of Himmler's anti-Church programme—more than two thirds of the Allgemeine S.S. remained in the Church as Catholics or Evangelicals [Hohne 1969:144].

In Britain there are no restrictions on the practice of religion, but Christians have been persecuted by Hindus and Muslims for apostasy in India, Kuwait, and Pakistan. In the Islamic states of Iran, Saudi Arabia, and the Emirates, Christian activities are forbidden even for expatriates, and converts face persecution. In Saudi Arabia, the orthodox Sunni sharia law applies, based on the seventh century Qur'an and the sayings of the Prophet. This is strictly enforced by both the civil and religious (metawwah) police, and applies to the 30,000 Britons and others in Saudi who live mainly in ghettoes. In the more lenient secular Muslim countries such as Indonesia and Pakistan, Christian worship is tolerated, but no synagogues may not be built. There has, in the recent past, been a rise of Islamic fundamentalism in the heretofore largely secular states of Iran, Egypt, Algeria and Turkey. Intolerance is not, however, confined to Muslims. The Israeli Knesset [TM 9 June 98] passed an amendment to the penal code that would penalise evangelism or "missionary activity" by other faiths by fine or imprisonment. Russia has barred [TM 2 Jan. 01] certain Protestant, Catholic, and Muslim groups from preaching, as well as Scientologists and Salvation Army volunteers. This is seen as a move to re-establish the primacy of the Russian Orthodox Church and stamp out foreign missionary activities. Extremist non-Christian religious sects may condone assassinations and terrorism, and positively encourage confrontation with Western secular liberalism, which is seen as tolerating unacceptable standards of values.

Some argue that any special distinction today between the state and the Church, or between secular ethicists and moral theologians, is false. In the West, conflicts between secular and religious obligations are resolved by secular jurisprudence. Rorty [1994:2] neatly resolves the issue for a democracy: "I take religious toleration to mean the willingness of religious groups to take part in discussions as fellow citizens without dragging religion into it . . . to say it's against my religion isn't an argument." This is saying that it is undemocratic and not one's duty as a citizen to accept that certain behaviour or acts should be tolerated, at least insofar as they affect others, simply because they are claimed to be religious beliefs—the toleration of unacceptable religious and cultural practices and the authority of its clerics can be inappropriate in secular matters. Nevertheless, Western culture clings tenaciously to the liberal principle that almost any religious practice, Christian or otherwise, should be tolerated and given priority, whatever the objections.

The French government has recently decided to resolve a long-standing religious/cultural dilemma [BBC 2 1 April 01]. Paris has 10,000 West African men who were recruited during the labour shortage during the strikes of the late 1960s. They are culturally polygamists, and with their families, amount to about 140,000 people. Polygamy is illegal in France and the West, is often argued to be contrary to women's rights, and in the West is usually considered to be immoral. The French have demanded that these men divorce one wife, otherwise residency and work permits will be withdrawn. In Britain the case arose as to which of two Muslim widows was entitled to the widow's pension [TM 26 June 97]. This study contends that the French government was correct in insisting upon upholding its country's religious and cultural values, though arguably it should not have made the rule retroactive.

Huntington [1996] predicts that religious cleavages will constitute the next great international battle lines, replacing the political ideological split of the Cold War, and that global politics is being reconfigured along cultural lines. The conflict of nationalism in the Balkans was largely of cultural/religious origin. Evidence of this was the partisan support given to the factions in the Yugoslavian conflict by the Catholic West, the Orthodox Slavs, and Muslims. The Serbs, Croats, and Muslims are ethnically similar, but the Croats were supported by Germany and Austria, the Serbs by Russia, with some French sympathisers, and the Muslims with Middle Eastern money and arms. Allegedly, the American CIA covertly supported the Croats and Bosnian Muslims [BBC 2 24 June 01].

Huntington [1996:18–19] says that "Western belief in the universality of Western culture suffers from three problems: it is false; it is immoral; and it is dangerous." It is false because other civilisations have different ideals and norms; immoral because "imperialism is the necessary logical consequence of universalism;" and dangerous because "it could lead to a major intercivilizational war . . . A global war involving the core states of the world's major civilizations is highly improbable, but not impossible." To slow down this decline, the United States, he [Huntington] believes, should reaffirm its identity as a Western nation by repudiating multiculturalism at home.

This prognosis was challenged on the grounds that the trend towards global cosmopolitanism and exchanges make confrontation between different civilisations less likely. Huntington's book was described by the author of *Islam and the Myth of Confrontation* [Halliday 1997:42–3] as "fault-line babble" and "without doubt the worst and most pernicious [book]," because "Muslim states conduct their foreign policies like any other states, on the basis of national interests: and most of their wars have been with each other." Stephen Holmes [1997:6], in his review of the book, was equally dismissive: "why, for instance, does he allow the blanket category 'Islam' to obscure inner divisions between Arabs and non-Arabs, or between Shi'ites and Sunnis? Why does he lump together with a single homogeneous civilisation such disparate societies as, say, Indonesia, Pakistan, Iran, and Algeria? The answer is that he finds homogeneity, because he is looking for homogeneity." John Eposito [1992:211] also argues that "The many faces of contemporary Islamic revivalism tended to be subsumed under the monolith of 'Islamic fundamentalism,' which was equated with violence and fanaticism, with mullah-led theocracies or small radical guerrilla groups. The nineties have challenged these presumptions and expectations. There have been no other Iranian style Islamic revolutions, nor have any radical groups seized power . . . political Islam is itself challenged, challenged by its own rhetoric and message to be self-critical: to live up to the standards and principles it espouses and demands of others: to avoid and denounce the excesses that are committed by governments and movements that identify themselves as Islamic; and finally, to take or share responsibility, and not simply blame the West, for the failures of Muslim societies" [206]. Nevertheless, Archbishop Carey [Ind. 25 May 96] believed that Huntington's "beguiling hypothesis" had grasped "something essential to world peace." Yet, it is true that, at least at the present, the foreign policies of the world's cultural/religious blocs reflect their own national interests, and there is no evidence of pan-Muslim, pan-Arab, secular or theocratic collusion between them or an armed confrontation, apart from Iraq and the West, other than Middle East Arab support for the Palestinians in their conflict with Israel.

Apologists claim that Muslims have been demonised by Christians dating back to the Crusades, and the fear that Islam is the new enemy of the West is not credible and has been fostered by the media [Channel 4 20 Sept. 95]. Norman Daniel [1993:332] lends support to the sceptical view the Arab/

Muslim world takes towards the West: "Arab peoples believed that colonialism was the source of their miseries, but nominal independence from the colonial power did very little to help them; in its turn nationalism was successful in defying the West, but it still did not do enough; and the strength of extremists now is their desperate appeal for a total rejection of all Western culture, finally identified as having been the true culprit all along, and the vehicle of an alien corruption and infidelity, not only to Islam, but to the traditions of Islamic society . . . They seem unable to accept that the West is not Christian, or that European and American society and its politics are wholly secularised. To say that the West is no longer Christian, neither collectively nor in the majority of its citizens, is meaningless in the Arab world, where what we inherit determines our allegiance and collective identity, and what we think measures only our individual loyalty to that inheritance . . . [334] The extremists are alone in their use of violence, but not in their other sentiments . . . [335] Indifference and pragmatism are not a solution. The same basic relationship between the two religions subsists as always. The most irenic of observers must accept that there are irreducible differences between non-negotiable doctrines. Both sides deceive themselves if they think otherwise. The Christian creeds and the Qur'an are simply incompatible and there is no possibility of reconciling the content of the two faiths, each of which is exclusive, as long as they retain their identities. If either of them does not, the problem is not solved, it is obliterated." Nevertheless, the growth of religious fundamentalism could displace or reinforce secular Islamic national interests. Separatist Muslim multiculturalism could lend itself to an ethnic minority in the West invoking the support of a culturally/religiously related external state, who is called upon to "protect or liberate them from oppression," or alternatively provide it with support.

Religious toleration in Britain and the Act of Toleration in 1689 followed the deposition of the Catholic sympathiser James 2nd with the accession of the Protestant William of Orange and "The Glorious Revolution" of 1688. A limited representative parliamentary democracy and a constitutional monarchy were established, and the first formulation and justification of the political case for religious toleration was made by Locke in his *Letters Concerning Toleration* in 1685 (published anonymously in 1689), 1691 and 1692. Locke said that society should accept that if there was to be no encroachment on the rights of the individual, then society should not regiment the convictions of others. He argued that firstly, no man has such complete wisdom that he can dictate another man's religion. Secondly, each individual is a moral person before his own particular God, and this presupposes freedom of religious choice. Thirdly, compulsion cannot achieve an inner conviction, only an outward conformity. Susan Mendus [1989:37] observes that "Locke has no commitment to diversity, no belief in the inherent goodness of varieties of ways of life, and no argument for the preservation of religious sub-groups within the dominant culture of a society. Again, his point is simply that it would be irrational to suppress them, not that it would be morally wrong." Locke's pragmatic toleration had limits, inasmuch that he did not tolerate atheists whose loyalty would remain in doubt. They were not considered to be social beings—they were incapable of taking an oath and were not in fear of divine retribution. Neither would Catholics be tolerated because they were seen as tools of French aggrandisement. Locke [Horton and Mendus 1991:46–7] said that "what else do they mean, who teach that 'faith is not to be kept with heretics?' Their meaning, forsooth, is, that the privilege of breaking faith belongs unto themselves: for they declare all that are not of their communion to be heretics, or at least may declare them so whensoever they think fit . . . it is ridiculous for anyone to profess himself to be a Mahometan (Muslim) only in religion, but in everything else a faithful subject to a Christian magistrate, whilst at the same time he acknowledges himself bound to yield blind obedience to the Mufti of Constantinople, who himself is entirely obedient to the Ottoman emperor." Religious coexistence with but political exclusion of Catholics and Jews continued in Britain until these groups were allowed to become MPs in 1829 and 1858 respectively; the same occurred with atheists in 1886.

Locke was an economic mercantilist in that he believed that a large population was better than a small one, even it meant welcoming unskilled migrants to reduce the cost of labour. This theory prohibited emigration and was relaxed on immigration. This type of argument in favour of immigration continues to be advanced by some economists. Herbert Butterfield [1975:584] contends that (Lockean) religious toleration "the process making great advances in the latter half of the seventeenth century—owed much to purely secular motives: the inability to carry on war any longer, the economic interests that encouraged immigration, the need to reduce the status of religion itself, in order to establish public order and give the government better control over its territory . . . the general secularization that took place . . . gave a tremendous power to the cause of liberty." Locke was essentially a utilitarian pragmatist seeing limited religious toleration as bringing commercial advantages, for which political tranquillity and collective prosperity were supreme values. He contrasted the misery of the religiously intolerant Spain with the prosperity of the religiously tolerant [Dutch] United Provinces—this being a great persuasive influence in the eighteenth century. He recognised the importance of an expanding and prosperous economy to a stable and tolerant society, wanting to place only the minimum essential restrictions on its human resources. He tolerated the Dissenters (non-Conformists) because he did not want them to emigrate with their talents, and selectively accepted, mainly after 1685, under naturalisation, some 40,000 to 50,000 French Protestant

Huguenot refugees because of their industrial and commercial skills. Nevertheless, Locke's basic principle was not compromised thereby.

Locke looked upon a broadly based and established Church of England as an institution for national cohesion. At that time, the toleration of diversity and difference in Britain was limited to the religions of an essentially monoethnic/theist society whose affiliation was that of Christianity—Protestants, Catholics, and the Dissenters. His toleration was designed to protect the prevailing cultural hegemony and maintain political stability after years of bitter civil and religious strife between the monarchy and parliament, and between Catholicism and Protestantism. The distinction made by Locke, and is still relevant today, was between a "religion," meaning an apolitical belief system, and a "church," or an ecclesiastical institution having a political/secular affliliation. Locke's pragmatism was subsequently developed and extended by liberal thinkers in the nineteenth century in seeing religious toleration as an essential moral requirement of liberal individualism.

In France, Voltaire became increasingly hostile to the anti-Protestant religious fanaticism and dogmatism of Catholicism. The philosopher Maurice Cranston [1991:33] says that this "is not entirely unlike the fanaticism we observe in Islam today," although Voltaire's "work did nothing to correct another form of fanaticism which emerged during the French revolution in the 1790s—ideological fanaticism" [35]. Voltaire's treatise on religious toleration was also built upon "insignificant" mankind being unable to "know the mind of God," but unlike Locke, it did not have any connection with, or influence over, the governments and politicians of his time. Cranston believes [36] that "The messages of both Locke and Voltaire are very relevant to the condition of our times. We must cultivate the spirit of tolerance in our hearts; but we should not allow the policy of toleration to be exploited and abused by fanatical sectarian groups which are subversive political movements in ecclesiastical disguise."

There are alternative accounts of the commonly supposed virtue of the toleration of religious freedom. One says [Labrousse 1973:112] that "Lexicology tells us that up to the beginning of the eighteenth century the word tolerance had in French a pejorative meaning, a lax complacency towards evil. In 1691, in his admonition to Protestants, Bossuet [a French bishop] still proudly described Catholicism as the least tolerant of all religions and, as if to compete with this proud boast, the Walloon Synod of Leyden [mainly Huguenot refugees], firmly condemned religious toleration as a heresy . . . [subsequently] the meaning of the two words was reversed. Intolerance became a vice and tolerance a virtue; an opinion which had previously been held only by isolated and suspect theoreticians, was suddenly widespread and became part of the common language." In medieval times the coercive intolerance manifested by the persecution and torture of heretics by the Catholic Church, was rationalised by the belief that this was the only way of saving the unbeliever from purgatory. Butterfield [1975:574 and 578] also does not see a virtue-laden motive to religious toleration: "Martin Luther had not been provoked to his rebellion against the papacy by any desire for a greater freedom in religious matters. What had goaded him to action was rather an excess of liberty somewhere in the Church—the multitude of the evils which ecclesiastical authority was leaving uncorrected." He suggests other motives underlying religious toleration: "it became clear that toleration, as a working system, was subject to serious limitations. Its own upholders tended to regard it as only a temporary expedient . . . alternatively, there was an assumption that after a period of generous treatment, the heretics would voluntarily return to the fold." This Millian and missionary view would assume that re-conversion and re-assimilation would eventually follow from a recognition of the best (true) religion.

The Muslim religion, like the other monotheist religions of Judaism and Christianity, is a globally diverse and broad religion having differing "churches" and radical sects. In some countries these sects are extremist, intolerant, and operate their own cultural imperialism. The Shiite Hezbollah, Hamas, Taleban and other extremist groups are dedicated to waging an Islamic Jihad holy war against unbelievers—mainly Americans. Muslim political leaders and their Western apologists remain silent, and their ambivalence is interpreted as acquiescence. Muslim theologians also present in public a milder interpretation of the Qur'an. Nonetheless what is important, as with any religion, is not simply its theology, but how it is actually practised, namely the difference between its theocratic principles, and how these are interpreted and applied by its man-made Church and its followers.

There are now about 3.5 million Muslims in Germany, mainly Turks—the vast majority of whom are not fundamentalists. Nevertheless, Germany prosecuted the fundamentalist Muslim "Caliph" of Cologne, thought to have abundant funding from abroad, for incitement to murder following a fatwa against a rival German Muslim Caliph who was subsequently killed [BBC 2 3 June 00]. Jewish leaders in Britain called for the deportation of a fundamentalist Muslim cleric amid concern about the safety of their community following a stabbing, in which five men were arrested for allegedly inciting racial hatred [TM 20 Oct. 00]. These incidents highlight the dilemma of a Western secular democracy that guarantees religious freedom against an active, well-organised, and politicised sect for whom "God's will" counts for more than an indigenous democratic culture of toleration.

Akbar Ahmed [Hawkey 1995:16–7/Ind. 24 May 96], now a Washington but formerly a Cambridge academic, is a moderate Muslim spokesman. He says that "I believe . . . that the great global scenario of confrontation between Islam and the West that some scholars are already writing up [must be directed away]. If it doesn't happen, there will be a very ugly relationship developing into the next century. On both sides, awareness has to grow. Dialogue, harmony, communication, debate, are key issues. Now, this may be all right in rhetoric, but in the context of so much racial, cultural, and religious prejudice on both sides, it becomes a very difficult struggle. It can be uncomfortable, even dangerous, to stand in the middle . . . when they [Muslims in Britain] are surrounded by a society in which all [their] values are challenged, for whatever reason, Muslim families are under pressure." Ahmed also reportedly said [Ind. 24 May 96] that "A basic knowledge of Islam could be taught in Western schools so that children do not grow up in ignorance of it . . . conversely, Western values like democracy, need to be explained in Muslim schools." A letter writer aptly observed that "It is a basic knowledge of Christianity [as opposed to democracy] that should be taught in Muslim schools." Ahmed was later appointed the Pakistani High Commissioner to Britain by its military government, which overthrew the "democratically elected" government. He claimed that "It had the support of 90 percent of Pakistanis and was committed to social, economic and political reform" [TM 26 Nov. 99]. A British multicultural think tank report [TM 28 Feb. 97] concluded that 'Hatred of Islam and Muslims is prevalent in all sections of society and in the past twenty years has become more explicit, extreme and dangerous than ever—Islam is often seen as implacably hostile to the non-Islamic world." Britain has about 600,000 Pakistanis and this comment does not bode well for their toleration on the one hand, and their assimilation on the other. The Salman Rushdie affair in 1989 was a watershed in Britain, because it brought into sharp public focus the conflict between the Muslim religious and Western secular liberal values. This would have been even more so had Rushdie been murdered, and a Muslim "martyr" convicted. Parekh [Kymlicka 1995:310–11] notes on the Rushdie affair and Muslim immigration that "By not only admitting but positively recruiting them [immigrants] to help rebuild its post-war economy in full knowledge of who they were and what they stood for, Britain had consented to and incurred an obligation to respect at least the fundamentals of their way of life. It was true that British society might find some of their practices and values unacceptable, even as they might find some of its practices offensive . . . immigrants owed loyalty to the British state, but not to British values, customs and way of life." However, In the period referred to, namely the early 1960s, British society would not have had anything approaching a full knowledge of Muslim practices and values, and even if it did, this would not have extended to supporting the non-British custom of killing a religious dissident. Moreover, Parekh's argument is not relevant to the uninvited economic refugees and sham asylum seekers of the 1990s.

The controversy surrounding the freedom of religion manifests itself in the issue of religious education, particularly if used to reinforce racial/ethnic separatism and marginalise the Christian ethos. Education experts claim that multifaith, non-denominational religious education would lead to a more tolerant society. The Swann Committee [1985:772–3] was "In favour of a non-denominational [multifaith] and undogmatic approach to religious education . . . [so as] to appreciate the diverse and sometimes conflicting values involved and thus to determine and justify their own religious position. There should be no conflict between the role of the schools in providing religious education and the role of community institutions in providing religious instruction." This secular educational philosophy was rejected by the Muslim community [Hiskett 1989:25]. The 1988 Education Reform Act attempted an elliptical compromise in requiring that "religious education shall reflect the fact that the religious traditions of Great Britain are in the main Christian, whilst taking account of teaching and practices of the other principal religions represented in Great Britain." Muslims objected, claiming that this approach was nothing but a "confusing mish-mash" [TM 2 Oct. 97]. After a dispute lasting over several years that included school boycotts, the government has approved grant-maintained status to four Muslim primary schools, one in Brent London and another in Birmingham. This was seen by some, as a normalising "foot in the door." There are sixty independent Muslim schools [TM 10 Jan. 98], and to put this into perspective, there are 6,853 Christian schools and thirty-two Jewish schools in the state system. In Protestant/Catholic Ulster, only four percent of children attend mixed or integrated schools, and this segregation institutionalises its political sectarianism [TM 21 April 00].

State education, if legally completely secularised, can cause problems, as the French found with the symbolic head scarves of Muslim schoolgirls, although the Sunni Muslim sect's highest religious authority in Cairo ruled that Muslims in France have a duty to obey the laws of the country in which they live [TM 14 April 98]. The three largest Christian denominations in Britain, the Anglican, Roman Catholic, and Methodist, have accused the government [TM 2 Oct. 97] of promoting a secular morality by wrecking the "educational partnership between Church and state established in 1944." These churches are responsible for about a third of England's state schools, and the government proposed to reduce or remove the majority enjoyed by their nominees on their governing bodies, belatedly giving rise to fears for the future of their distinctive Christian ethos. Archbishop Carey later warned the government of a potential clash between state and the Church over proposals to weaken the Church's influence in the 5,000 or so Anglican schools [TM 18 Nov. 98]. Possibly prophetically, the Institute for Jewish Policy Research [TM 31 Jan. 00] opposed the House of Lords Reform Committee's multifaith proposal for official Jewish representation in the House of Lords: "this gesture will have the effect of increasing tensions within British Jewry. It could also lead to rivalries within and between other religious groups vying for seats in the House of Lords." Maybe the Jewish Institute foresaw the possible outcome if minority ethnic/religious groups compete for secular power.

One might suppose that in Britain's mainstream Christian culture, non-Christian faiths would be prepared to tolerate their children learning something about the religious tradition that has principally influenced the spiritual culture of the country in which they have settled. Moreover, ethnic children can find it difficult to pursue school friendships because, after the false environment of the secular school, they have to return to the real environment of separatist ghettos. The Nation of Islam, which is the black equivalent of the BNP (British National Party), has a mosque in Brixton, and operates three schools in which allegedly neither the teachers nor the curriculum have been state approved [STMG 17 Oct. 98]. It has about 100,000 members and 120 mosques in the U.S. [TM 30 June 98], and since its establishment in Britain in 1986, has gained 2,500 members. Since 1986, its racist and intolerant American leader, Louis Farrakhan, had been refused entry into the country [TM 1 Aug. 01]. The Anglican Church is proposing to establish twenty more secondary schools as the first phase of opening one hundred new church schools. The demand for these schools continues to rise [TM 15 June 01]. In a wholly Judaeo-Christian society, denominational church schools present few problems, but in a separatist multicultural society they can give rise to precedents and emphasise its divisions.

The British hereditary monarchy is an institution which is seen as being increasingly irrelevant, having lost much of its younger mainstream support. It is facing a demise in favour of some form of republicanism for the next generation. The hereditary principle has been abolished in the House of Lords, and the allegiance to the Crown has virtually been erased in Northern Ireland as a result of devolution, and as an implied feature of the "peace process." The monarchy is trying to restore its unifying image resulting from the separatism of Scottish and Welsh devolution [TM 20 May 00]. Prince Charles is heir apparent to the Crown and the next nominal head of the Church of England. He has become identified with ecumenical multiculturalism and the fading myth of the multiracial Commonwealth (which he will also head) although he may be replaced by a president [TM 26 April 99]. He would rather see himself as "Defender of Faith" than the "Faith" [Dimbleby 1994:528], and has said that "we could begin to have more Islamic teachers in British schools . . . [and] we need to be taught by Islamic teachers how to learn with our hearts, as well as our heads" [TM 14 Dec. 96]. He has since back-tracked, fearing that falling attendance may ruin the Anglican claim to be the national church [STM 31 May 98]. The monarchy, or at least Prince

Charles, is trying to be all things to all people, whilst assuming that its core mainstream support would remain undiminished, or alternatively, dependent on the institutional apathy of the general public.

A British Indian millionaire, later accused of an arms deal corruption in India, gave £1 million to the Faith Zone of the Millennium Dome. He did so on condition that all faiths should be treated equally, although 2000 years of Christianity could be "emphasised," effectively making it politically incorrect for the Faith Zone to be Christian. Perhaps the resulting diversity and difference is not unrelated to the fact that Dome attendance was just over half that estimated. Bankruptcy threatened, necessitating five government emergency fundings totalling £239 million [TM 6 Sept. 00], and a final cost of around £800 million.

NOTES

Butterfield, H. "Toleration in Early Modern Times." In *Fourth Conference of the International Society for the History of Ideas*. Venice. September/October 1975. 584.

Ibid. 574 and 578.

Cranston, M. "On Toleration and Tolerance." In *Quadrant*. March 1991. 33–6.

Daniel, N. *Islam and the West*. Oxford: One World Publications, 1993. 332.

Ibid. 334–5.

Dimbleby, R. *The Prince of Wales*. London: Little Brown and Co, 1994. 528.

Eposito, J.L. *The Islamic Threat—Myth or Reality?* Oxford: Oxford University Press. 1992. 206 and 211.

Halliday, F. "A New World Myth." In *New Statesman*. 4 April, 1997. 42–3.

Hawkey, I. "An Ambassador for Islam." In *Cambridge Alumni Magazine*. Easter Term, 1995. 16–7.

Hohne, H. *The Order of the Death's Head*. London: Martin Secker and Warburg, 1969. 144.

Holmes, S. "In Search of New Enemies." In *London Review of Books*. 24 April 1997. 6.

Horton, J. and Mendus, S. (Ed.) *A Letter Concerning Toleration*. London: Routledge, 1991. 46–7.

Hiskett, M. *Schooling for British Muslims—Integrated, Opted-Out or Denominational?* London: Social Affairs Unit. 1989. 25.

Huntington, S.P. *The Clash of Civilisations and the Remaking of World Order*. New York: Simon and Shuster, 1996, In *Decline of the West* (Book Review). McNeill, W.H. *New York Review*. 9 January 1997. 18–9.

Labrousse, E. "Religious Toleration." In *Dictionary of the History of Ideas*. vol. iv. USA: Charles Scribner's Sons. 1973. 112.

Mendus, S. *Toleration and the Limits of Liberalism*. London: Macmillan Education, 1989. 37.

Parekh, B. "The Rushdie Affair: Research Agenda for Political Philosophy." In *The Rights of Minority Cultures*. Kymlicka, W. Oxford: Oxford University Press, 1995. 310–1.

Rorty, R. "Towards a Liberal Utopia" In *Times Literary Supplement*. 24 June 1994. 2.

Swann, Lord. *Education for All—The Report of the Committee of Inquiry into the Education of Children from Ethnic Minority Groups*. London: Stationery Office, 1985. 772–3.
BBC 2. *Correspondent Europe*. 3 June 2000.
CHANNEL 4. *Images of Muslims*. 20 September 1995.
BBC 1. *Correspondent*. 1 April 2001.
BBC 2. *Correspondent*. 24 June 2001.

23

Toleration and the Demise
of the Anglican Church

The Church of England (C-E) has been the principal religion of England
and Wales since the Reformation. It is an institution of the state. But its
continuing toleration of internal theological differences and diversity, and its
tolerant multicultural equivocation towards non-Christian religions, are factors that could lead to its demise. The Anglican Church could be seen as a
paradigm of the eventual outcome of increasingly liberal toleration, within a
context of diversity and difference, across what may be unbridgeable cultural/
religious barriers: moral attrition and instability, and religious relativism.
Being a non-authoritarian institution and a broad church, ranging from
evangelicals to Anglo-Catholics, it is admittedly difficult for the C-E to counter
the perception of deep divisions both nationally and in the Anglican provinces worldwide. The Archbishop of Canterbury is only the "first among
equals" of its other 800 bishops. The resolutions passed at its ten yearly
Lambeth Conferences lack conviction because its global provinces exercise
their own autonomy. Conciliation and tolerance have been its watchwords,
but schisms have weakened the cohesiveness and integrity of Anglicanism.
The nature of its 1998 international Lambeth Conference (held at Canterbury,
Kent) was like its previous (1988) Conference. It had been characterised by
an academic cleric [Bennett 1987–8:59] who said that "The bishops would
seek to avoid or dispose of [the question about the nature and future of
Anglicanism itself] with the usual platitudes about 'unity-in-diversity' and
'mutual responsibility and inter-dependence.'" The Anglican religion has become marginalised, and if it loses its establishment by the British state, given
its continuing demise it could end up as being no more than a liberal sect,
shorn of its Anglo-Catholic and evangelical factions.
    It has to be said that the decline and problems faced by the Anglican

297

Church are certainly not unique, and are also faced by all other Christian religions. Nor do they solely arise from its liberal toleration. Even the evangelising Salvation Army has a membership of only one third of its peak in 1947, whilst it continues to expand abroad [TM 10 May 01]. The C-E faces the dilemma of how to reconcile its eucumenicism not only with other Christian, but also with non-Christian, religions, without it becoming relativist. The Christian churches—Protestant, Roman Catholic, Greek and Russian Orthodox—have been unable to accept a common doctrine, liturgy, or communion. The Catholic Church has recently refused to share Communion with Anglicans, and has said that it is not a "proper" church [TM 23 Feb. 01]. Since at least Locke and the seventeenth century, and unlike the United States, there has been no clear division in Britain between religion and politics, insofar that twenty-six Anglican bishops/archbishops sit in the House of Lords (facing a proposed reduction to sixteen), and the PM can and sometimes does veto the appointment of bishops. The present primate, Dr. George Carey, has said [STM 9 April 00] that he expects the Anglican Church to become disestablished "one day"—but a proposal to reduce the number of bishops in the House of Lords to make way for other religious leaders has been dropped. The Church has increasingly tried to directly involve itself publicly in domestic political and social issues, particularly during the 1980s, which some people felt took it beyond its remit, or was simply a distracting option. A recent example concerns a bishop who has only an increasingly theoretical constituency, and without an electoral remit, offering to form a convention with politicians and other interested parties to discuss ways of updating the asylum laws and procedures, because it "should not be left to the politicians" [TM 8 May 00]. Although the C-E is not alone in this respect, its situation highlights the problems and suggests a probable outcome of too liberal toleration, and of multicultural relativism in particular. It also has an influence on political toleration, since theological beliefs can extend to secular issues. When toleration eventually breaks down, religious diversity and difference are often essential features of ethno-national conflicts. And moralistic pleas for religious toleration confers on toleration in general the aura of being a theocratic virtue.

The influence of the Christian ethic prevailed in Britain until WW1, but it is now a Christian society in the sense that non-practising Christians are the largest spiritual group, and who still provide the moral structure of society, though few moral principles are unquestionably accepted as having a theocratic authority, and there is a diminished deference to theocratic authority in general. The Anglican church attendance has an average age of over seventy and in 1998 was between one and 1.1 million—its lowest ever—about the same as the Catholic Church, which has a nominal following in England and Wales of 4.2 million [TM 29 Nov. 99]. A measure of the decline of the

Protestant religion in Britain today, compared with the United States, is that there is now less than a total of one hour of religious broadcasting each Sunday on the five terrestial television channels, and this at an off-peak viewing time. For the past twenty years or so, the Anglican Church has been riven by accusations of racism, homophobia, and sexism, and arguably, as a result, has adopted an increasingly tolerant equivocation and liberal attitude towards non-Christian religions and towards secular morality generally. This supposedly "brings the Church in line with society"—for example, progresssively separating sexuality from a moral context. At the recent final vote of the House of Lords to lower the age of homosexual consent to sixteen, eighteen bishops abstained, four voted for, and four voted against. In the vote against the regulations allowing human fertilisation and embryology research, only two bishops were present [MoS 28 Jan. 01]. There may be a causality between the C-E's weakened authority and influence and its tolerant and indulgent attitude of being all things to all people in its lacking the moral certainty and conviction offerred by the evangelical version of Christianity.

Estimates vary as to the number of Muslims in Britain but it is said to be about two million, with about 500,000 Sikhs and as many Hindus. It is forecast that in addition to the present 385 registered mosques, another 100 were due to be built by the end of the millennium [TM 7 Feb. 97]. According to the UN there are about fourteen million Muslims in Europe, and it has been said that Islam is a "religion, a culture, a society and a way of life, thought and behaviour rolled into one." This concern has been echoed by a leading Italian contender for the Papacy. He warned that "Christian Europe" was in danger of being overwhelmed by a "Muslim invasion," saying that "Muslims do not integrate into Italian society," and that "We have to be concerned about saving the identity of the nation" [TM 15 Sept. 00].

The Anglican Church, which has in the past aspired to being a global community, is now facing its own cultural divide in theological/secular morality. Carey has spoken [DM 4 April 95] about the fragmentation and moral confusion afflicting British society, and some African and Asian bishops fear corruption by the liberalism of the West. The Anglican Archbishops of South East Asia and Rwanda ordained two bishops known for their opposition to homosexuality to work in the United States as missionaries in parishes disillusioned with the liberalism of their Episcopalian bishops in dealing with homosexuality [TM 17 Feb. 00]. They said that it was not their action, but the "violation of the faith" that caused disunity of the worldwide Anglican communion. The Archbishop issued an unprecedented rebuke for their acting "illegally." Archbishop Carey is in fact virtually powerless to take any action to resolve disputes, and this is one factor, together with his lack of resources that has led to the instigation of an internal review. This is supposed to enhance his authority and powers as head of the Anglican Church, although it has been denied that it would lead to a papal style of Anglican church government [TM 14 March 00].

Internal conflicts between Churchmen are unsurprising in view of their differing theological interpretations of the Bible in relation to contemporary controversies, such as women priests who are still not fully accepted, together with differing prioritisation of moral values. Occasionally a senior bishop will express views which some regard as a theological or moral heresy. Some of the views expressed by the head of the Anglican church in Scotland have been condemned by the Archbishop of Canterbury as "unacceptable" [TM 16 Sept. 99]. A leading C-E theologian [TM 27 Mar. 00] called for a revision of the Christian conservative moral stance on homosexuality, which he ascribed to a "false combination of prejudice and ignorance," and the decriminalisation of prostitution and soft drugs. Since presumably he thought, or accepted otherwise, for many years, it can only add to the conclusion that there are today no moral certainties, and if an authoritative theological opinion asserts them today, tomorrow they may be discarded by that same authority when the secular climate has safely provided a lead. Informed individuals are also more resistant to, and question, those received values which they are prepared to accept unreservedly. During what arguably was a most difficult and critical period of the Anglican Chuch's recent history, the former Primate Dr. Robert Runcie (1980–1991) was an exemplar of toleration. He ordained practising homosexuals on the Clintonian distancing principle of toleration—"don't ask-don't know"—because "it is ludicrous that practising homosexuals could be members of the Church but not ordained." His justification, which cannot rationally be faulted, was based on the cautious acceptance of artificial contraception by the 1930 Lambeth Conference [Carpenter 1996:104]. This indicates the way in which rational arguments can be progressively pyramided and inescapable anomalies created. Whenever Anglicanism has adopted a relativist view on secular moralistic (principally sexual/gender) issues, it has undermined its theological beliefs relative to the fundamentalist religions. Nevertheless, many find comfort and stability in a religion that provides some answers, and not the moral vacuum that can result from posing unanswered and unanswerable questions. There are however indications [DM 1 Dec. 95] that the C-E has begun to recognise that its apparently limitless toleration must end, or possibly be reversed. It rejected an internal report proposing that cohabitation should not be condemned.

In his 1991 Address on Toleration, the then newly appointed Archbishop Carey appealed for wide limits of toleration by the Church towards other cultures, religions, and secularism. He said that genuine toleration should reflect the "dynamics of tolerance . . . tolerance involves commitment not indifference . . . indifference is never a virtue . . . the indifferent exercise no self-restraint." Tolerance requires "sharing of their pain as well as one's own," by which we "gain in authority as a nation—not a loss of authority, but a gain." Without this, "strangeness, of course, can lead to alienation, something very dangerous . . . the scene is then set for conflict." He argued that "People who live in a monochrome culture need to be made aware of the exciting possibilities, as well as the disturbances, to their settled life-style, of a multicultural society. And that can only come about as we discover that 'strangeness' does not necessarily mean bad, but a different expression of good." Yet, Carey later made a theological affirmation of the primacy of Christianity in Britain saying "There has been a tendency to loosen the grip on the singularity of Christ who is the centre of the Christian faith. [It has been suggested that] it has no right to challenge Islam or any other religion. It is merely a Western face of God. This view is to be firmly rejected." He has demanded [TM 6 Dec. 97] that Christians in Pakistan, where they are a two percent minority and suffer persecution and discrimination, should be allowed to convert to Christianity, namely, that they should have the same rights Muslims expect in Britain. He has also expressed his fears of the danger of conflict with Islam [Ind. 25 May 96].

Carey's abstract thinking does not elaborate on how much pain the tolerant agent should suffer, nor how he should react to the intolerant, who will not share any pain. Nor does it indicate how much tolerance should be afforded to doctrines which include non-negotiable beliefs and values that are incompatible with those of the tolerator, whose dogma encompasses a secular political agenda. If the tolerator is not prepared to reject any alien beliefs, then his toleration becomes the acceptance of religious/moral relativism, which in a separatist multicultural society implies a "painful" co-existence. Exhortations to be excessively and unilaterally tolerant suggest that nothing merits caring about. Complete religious toleration could lead to a commitment to the universality of all faiths, and the abandonment of the missionary and evangelical activities of the Anglican Church. Carey recognised [1991:11–3] that Christianity faces challenges from multiculturalism. There is the concern that "the Christian message is being vitiated by inter-faith worship." Nevertheless he thought that "Evangelism is still a binding obligation on the Christian believer" . . . and that "as neighbours now, the cultural implications require the greatest sensitivity to those who are our fellow citizens . . . ultimately, the chief implication challenges all religious leaders who, passionate for the truth, are called not simply to an affable co-existence—a denial of true toleration— but an active partnership and deeper cooperation which means entering into and sharing each others 'pains.'" He did set an ultimate limit, inasmuch that "if adherence to religious principle threatens whole communities by the intensity of commitment, civilised society cannot and must not tolerate such an invasion of public order." Thus his toleration stopped somewhere short of civil disobedience, but by then the damage is irreversible.

Carey [1991:8] used the reaction to the 1989 Rushdie "fatwa"—partially removed by Iran in 1998—as ignorance exacerbating the problem of "strangeness." He noted that to the Muslim, Rushdie's book contained "an outrageous slur on the Prophet and so was damaging to the reputation of the faith," and that toleration "ought to help us better to enter the distress of the Muslim community." One might ask "since no Anglican would support the murder of Rushdie in Britain, what would a better understanding of the Islamic faith and wide limits of toleration lead to in practice, other than to pressure the government to impose [intolerant] censorship on Rushdie?" It would have been preferable had Carey admonished Rushdie, in that he had a special and moral obligation not to seriously offend his fellow Muslims in Britain, and that in his case, his legal right of free speech should not have been considered to be absolute. To confuse the issue further, the Pakistani-born Anglican Bishop of Rochester said [TM 18 May 98] that the Qur'an is the primary source of Islamic authority, but it contains no punishment for blasphemy or apostasy.

Archbishop Carey recognised [5] that "many ideological movements as well as religious groups have claimed a freedom when in a minority, which they have not been prepared to concede to others when in power," and that [9] "even today some fundamentalist groups repel thoughtful people by their language of intolerance." He noted [5] that in 1927, Monsignor Knox, the English theologian, said that "the very truth of the Catholic faith meant that in a country with a strong Catholic majority the Church must insist on Catholic education being universal, and would proscribe those who come with deviant teachings." Before the Second Vatican Council in 1962, the classical Catholic argument was that "When Catholicism was in power, error should be repressed. Only when Catholicism was not dominant should error be tolerated as a lesser evil." The Vatican Index of Forbidden Books, including those of Satre, was not closed until 1966 [Cornwell 1998:23], and it was not until 1997 that the Pope admitted [TM 30 Oct. 97] that Catholic prejudice had contributed to the persecution of the Jews, culminating in its failure to oppose the Holocaust after Roosevelt's request. It was only thirty years ago that the phrase "perfidious Jews" was removed from the Catholic liturgy. The Pope has also apologised for the Crusades, the Inquisition, and for ethnic and racial discrimination [TM 13 Mar. 00]. Nevertheless, the most recent declaration from Rome revives the 1896 Papal bull which declared Anglican orders to be "absolutely null and void on the grounds that they were defective in form, rite, and intention" [TM 7 Sept. 00]. And it is the objective of both Jewish and Muslim fundamentalists to end the influence of Western secularism in Israel and in the Muslim states. All this illustrates the contention that where any fundamentalist religion is involved, there is little scope for toleration and compromise.

It has been forecast [STM 11 May 97] that even with no further influx of

Muslim immigrants, by the year 2002 there will be more worshipping Muslims in Britain than Christians. The potential threat has been made clear [Hiskett1989:4–5]: "Islam is a total way of life that permits neither the individual nor the society any leeway. It has no time for pluralism. The most it is able to concede to other religious communities is a measure of toleration to those it regards as 'People of the Book,' for practical purposes Jews and Christians. But even they remain 'second class citizens.'.. [Islamic education] makes no concession to antecedent cultures and demands total commitment to literacy based on classical Arabic. It will not tolerate the translation of its sacred texts into any other language." (In fact, Muslim translations have been available since 1917.) Any expectation of reciprocal toleration from Muslim fundamentalists, at least if there were ever circumstances approaching political parity, has been dismissed by Flew [1995:2]. He notes that "To be properly accounted a Muslim, it is essential to be a fundamentalist with regard to the Koran . . . [therefore] one class of professedly Muslim movements cannot be distinguished from another as being, unlike that other, fundamentalist." Flew says that this differs from the Christian religion inasmuch that it is not necessary for a fully believing Christian to be fundamentalist, in the same sense that every proposition in the Bible must be accepted as being true. He continues, "Muslim theologians are unanimous in declaring that no religious toleration was extended to the idolators of Arabia in the time of Muhammed. The Koran (Qur'an) is full both of urgings to do battle with unbelievers and of promises of rewards for those who engage and die in such battles. And whereas Christianity in its first centuries, spread throughout the Roman Empire by means of peaceful missionary work and voluntary individual conversion, the explosive expansion of Islam in its first centuries was an achievement of military conquest and forced mass conversions."

One of the paradoxes of Protestantism is that it is generally tolerant towards almost any religion which could destroy that tolerance, if the processes of democracy were to bring them into power. In this sense it is fortunate for Christian Europe that Islam did not become a prominent religion in the West. It is true that the early Protestants were persecuted by the Catholics, but today the fear of Catholicism, which in Britain lasted until the middle of the nineteenth century, has been largely replaced by "Islamophobia." In a clash between religions and cultures, it is not simply intolerance that is the determining factor, nor does it depend on the number count of the areas of agreement, or the protestations of its moderate apologists. It is the intensity of the probably few, but major, disagreements, and their actual practice taken in the name of that religion.

The Anglican Church is increasingly seen as being out of touch with the nation it represents, and has lost much of its influence in the corridors of power. The decline in religiosity, at least in part, is due to its tolerant relativism. A report [TM 1 Mar. 00] commissioned by the Archbishops of Canterbury and York concluded that Church spokesmen were seen as "meek and weak" and the Church was criticised as "constantly trying to tear itself apart." The former Archbishop Runcie [Carpenter 1996:95] saw the Church as "dealing with the maintenance of tranquility," which may have amounted to no more than inactive procrastination. He had been described [Bennett 1987–8:68–9] as "[having] the disadvantage of the intelligent pragmatist: the desire to put off all questions until someone else makes a decision . . . it has become a Church which reflects the attitudes of the bourgeoisie, both in its constant propensity to guilt and in its highly selective forms of liberalism." During his term of office Runcie was accused of sitting on the fence, making effete responses, and avoided "rocking the boat" by delaying the resolution of the then pressing issues facing the Anglican Church: the ordination of female and openly gay priests, and homosexuality. After it voted in favour of women priests in 1992, 481 priests left the Church of England [TM 31 May 98]. An ad hominem view would be that Runcie's strategy was not one of genuine toleration, but the distancing of his decision-making with time whilst *appearing* to be tolerant.

NOTES

Bennett, G. *Crockford's Clerical Dictionary*. (90th Ed.) London: Church House Publishing, 1987–88. Preface, 59.

Ibid. Preface, 68–9.

Carey, G. *Archbishop of Canterbury's Morrell Address on Toleration*. York: University of York, 1991. 1–13.

Carpenter, H. *Robert Runcie—The Reluctant Archbisop*. London: Hodder and Stoughton, 1996. 95.

Ibid. 304.

Cornwell, J. "Burnt Offerings (The Vatican)." In *Sunday Times Magazine*. 23 Auguat 1998.

Flew, A. "The Menace of Islam." In *The New Humanist*. vol. 11. no. 3. August 1995. 2.

Hiskett, M. *Schooling for British Muslims—Integrated, Opted-Out or Denominational?* London: Social Affairs Unit. 1989. 4–5.

24

Toleration, Human Nature, and Distancing

The role of human nature and psychology are especially important when it involves a macro-social change such as multiculturalism. Psychology can explain human nature but it is unlikely to change it. Human nature has a major influence on public and private attitudes towards toleration, distancing, racism, prejudice, stereotyping, etc. Human nature invokes a person's innate behavioural characteristics, including the acceptance or rejection of diversity and difference; self-interest or altruism; fear or self-confidence; reason or emotion; beliefs or disbeliefs; conservatism and radicalism; guilt or conviction; voluntarianism or compulsion; and rigidity or flexibility. Theories of human nature include its being formed by societal culture, the Freudian notion of instincts, and the Existentialist denial that mankind has an innate nature. Berry [1986: xiii] observes that all "social and political organisation has to accommodate human nature and not vice versa." Although the human nature of groups, in terms of their race, culture, or ethnicity has to be discussed in generalised terms, individuals do not necessarily conform to the generalised behaviour of their group.

An important feature of human nature is attitude, propensity or disposition. The Swann and Macpherson reports made frequent references to attitudes of teachers, the police, and the perceptions of ethnic groups. Much of social engineering, including the recommendations of these reports, was directed towards changing group attitudes or a group culture in the hope of influencing the acceptance and toleration of other cultures, races, and religions. Increasingly, it is claimed—most recently in the Macpherson report—that while there may be little evidence of overt racism, there are, nevertheless, institutional and "unwitting, unconscious and unintentional" racist attitudes. A similar comment on "attitude change" appeared in the Swann report *Education for All* some fourteen years earlier. Attitude is a construct of reality that enhances an individual's psychological security, and is derived from a

305

number of sources, including one's social and working environment. Perception assists in the formation of attitudes, and is a complex process of interpreting the reality that is peculiar to each individual. Emotion, intuition, and inference may all play a role. Outside of the physical world, most human beings are conditioned by their perceptions, including their limits of toleration. Knowledge in itself is insufficient and may be used selectively—what may be an objective argument to one may not be accepted as such by another. Moreover, as Dewey [1963:10] observes "We are beginning to realize that emotions and imagination are more potent in shaping public sentiment and opinion than information and reason." Most studies on anti-racism and multiculturalism end up with recourse to changing attitudes, and calling for toleration.

The extent to which human nature is innate or malleable, and reflects an institutional or social culture, is important. It cannot be assumed to be controllable by outside influences, and can be unpredictable. If culture, identity, prejudice, racism, and toleration are deemed to be constructs, then it can be argued that they could be changed by education and/or social engineering. But human nature can neither be ignored nor made to completely conform to an imposed system. Hence the comment by the U.S. Joint Chief of Staff [STM 26 Oct. 97] on the prevalence of sexual harassment in the U.S. Army: "the system is working well. It's the people who have failed."

Adherents of multiculturalism and cosmopolitanism have a view of a social order which is often contrary to the human nature. Brian Crozier [1974:x] asserts that "There is absolutely no evidence to suggest that Man's nature is changing for the better, or at all . . . none of the social and political theories predicated on the perfectibility of Man has been validated by events . . . I should hesitate to conclude that social and political 'engineering' will never alter the nature of Man. But the proposition does seem to me highly improbable." This is echoed by Pfaff [1993:238]: "It is a great error to fail to understand [the] difference between this progress, that of civilization, and the progress of man . . . the crucial truth is that man as such does not grow better. He is free." Galbraith [1996:3–4] recognises that with "goals [that] are 'purely utopian.' The real world has constraints imposed by human nature, by history, and by deeply ingrained patterns of thought . . . Socially desirable change is regularly denied out of well-recognised self interest." This applies to the toleration of diversity and difference, which will be more forthcoming if it is reciprocated, and satisfies mutually compatible goals.

Fear (of water, heights, etc.) arising from a perceived threat, either real or imaginary, such as a loss of identity, is the most powerful emotion, and takes a great deal of "education" to overcome, if ever. Fear gives rise to anxiety, confusion, uncertainty, and irrationality, and a desire to avoid and preferably to get rid of the threat. It can give rise to a self-protective hatred, and abstract pleas for toleration will have little effect. The many massacres of the twentieth century have shown that civilisation is skin deep and does not advance cumulatively. Individuals and nominally civilised societies can be a mixture of both good and a latent evil, and can be aroused given certain circumstances. The notion of human nature was central to Hume's thinking. He believed [Norman 1983:92] that "Moral responses must be the product of sentiment rather than reason, because sentiment, unlike reason, has a necessary connection with action." He argued that human passions and instincts have more influence than reason, and this explains the way we relate to the physical world and with each other. Thomas Reid (1710–1796) also observed [1994:372] that "Reason, says the sceptic, is the only judge of truth, and you ought to throw off every opinion and every belief that is not grounded on reason . . . [then asks] Why, sir, should I believe the faculty of reason more than that of perception?—they both came out of the same shop, and were made by the same artist; and if he puts one piece of false ware into my hands, what should hinder him from putting another?" Rationalists can be dismissive or patronising towards the influence of feelings or emotion in contrast to that of reason. This is not to say that emotional reactions should not be interpreted and applied intelligently. Neither is rational analysis without its flaws, such as its dependence on the possession of all the relevant and authentic facts, rather than a selection and/or representations of incomplete or unreliable facts—some believe that nothing can be known rationally with total certainty. Political judgements can be both short-term and long-term, based not just on today's facts, but intuition.

A discussion of toleration should not be based exclusively on rationalistic or objective arguments, and should examine to what extent toleration is a moral "ought" done for its own sake, or a means to a good end and/or from a motive of self-interest. Peter Singer [1979:211] suggests that "Our notion of ethics has become misleading to the extent that moral worth is attributed only to action done because it is right, without any ulterior motive . . . morality is, on this view, no more rational an end than any other allegedly self-justifying practice, like etiquette or the kind of religious faith that comes only to those who first set aside all sceptical doubts . . . taken as a view of ethics as a whole, we should abandon this Kantian notion of ethics."

Recourse to arguments based on human nature and instinct or common sense tend to be seen as intellectually flawed. Emotion and feelings are not usually considered to be good characteristics, and intelligent "thinking" human beings should be amenable to rational, or what purports to be rational, arguments. Although human nature can provide a genuine explanation for actions, it can also have a questionable authenticity, inasmuch that it can be misused to provide an incomplete or insincere justification with feelings and beliefs outwardly expressed in rational terms. Stevenson [1987:17] says that

"If we are primarily concerned with the truth or falsity of what is said, and with whether there are any good reasons for believing it, then motivation is irrelevant . . . there is nothing to stop us discussing what he says purely on its own merits."

A closed belief may be no more than a value judgement, a belief in what ought to be rather than what is. Nietzsche noted that philosophers tended to insist on the truth of a belief, whereas psychologists are more interested in why one believes, rather than what one believes. He proposed the ad hominem theory of human nature that introduces the motives, interests, intentions and the circumstances of the agent and others who have a stake in the outcome of the argument—its focus is on persons as much as on their propositions. Some say [King 1976:201–2] that ad hominen criticisms should be excluded because "[they] address themselves to persons rather than to propositions, solely by reference to consideration of their relevance to propositions in debate . . . it is superfluous to the disagreement; and it is most important for this reason that it be excluded." Nevertheless, the agent and the argument are often inter-related, inasmuch that the outcome could be relevant to the motives and sincerity of the agent, as with politicians and judges having to declare an interest. It may also recognise that some individuals may not actually live according to their publicly expressed philosophy of living. The philosopher Berlin [1993:13] made a similar point to Nietzsche: "The ideas of every philosopher concerned with human affairs in the end rest on his conception of what man is and can be. To understand such thinkers, it is more important to grasp this central notion or image (which may be implicit, but determines their picture of the world) than even the most forceful arguments with which they defended their views, and refute actual and possible objections." Exactly which image of society the political rhetoric of "we should welcome diversity and difference" has in mind is unclear.

A democratic polity will reduce the risk of conflict within a society, provided that it does not require individuals to act in some way which is grossly contrary to their nature and self-interest, i.e. its legislation is generally supported or is unimportant to the individual. If the expression of a deeply felt psychological or social attitude is prohibited by law or inhibited by political correctness, then human nature will find ways to circumvent it, or there will be a contra-reaction. A danger inherent in socially engineered multiculturalism to what those in power see as a better society is that it can be counterproductive if its pace is artificially forced by imposing quotas or legalising positive discrimination. Once people perceive that they are being engineered or manipulated, they can rigorously oppose change. Changes in a free society evolve under their own dynamism—they cannot be compelled, and a government-supported policy of elective multiculturalism is one such case.

There often is a relationship between the toleration of an issue and the personal distancing from it. An early description of what Jonathan Glover later termed "moral [psychological] distancing" was called "psychical distance," albeit in connection with aesthetic appreciation. Edward Bullough [1912] said that "[Distancing] has a negative, inhibitory aspect—the cutting out of the practical sides of things and of our practical attitude to them—and a positive side—the elaboration of the experience on the new basis created by the inhibitory action of distance . . . consequently, this distanced view of things is not, and cannot be, our normal outlook. As a rule, experiences . . . [have] the strongest practical force of appeal. We are not ordinarily aware of those aspects of things which do not touch us immediately and practically, nor are we generally conscious of impressions apart from our own self which is impressed." It could be that idealists may never be "touched" by non-ideal experience. Distancing, or a "protective bubble," is a form of psychological denial, and is a characteristic of human nature. It is the mental process by which the individual detaches himself, or is detached from, the issue, and avoids expressing an opinion or being accused of being judgmental or exclusive. Multiculturalism and other forms of pluralism are premised not only on the extent of difference, but also on the physical and psychological proximity of the difference. There may be an ad hominen influence, and also the distinction that MacIntyre [1991:1 and 20] draws between "Genuine virtues . . . and mere counterfeits of those virtues, qualities which have the appearance of, but are not in fact genuine virtues . . . what the morality of the virtues articulated in, and defended by the moral rhetoric of our political culture provides, is, it turns out, not an education in the virtues, but rather an education in how to seem virtuous, without actually being so." If a threat is perceived as insufficiently distanced either in time and/or proximity, then the motive of self-protection may apply. Commitment and conviction are unlikely to be tested by opinion surveys on important issues that affect only others. There is a difference between merely being "generally in favour" and/or "supporting in principle," and being the person directly responsible/blamed for it, and having to act on the decision, and being accountable or directly affected by, and living with, its consequences. This is particularly so if there is an adverse outcome. Distancing can also be involved if the subjective perception and attitude differ from actual behaviour, inasmuch that they may be suppressed, at least to the extent that they outwardly conform to the sociological norms of toleration. Hence, most meat eaters have to distance themselves mentally from the abattoir. A form of distancing sometimes observed in public figures is the contradiction between their personal behaviour and their compensating or pseudo-macro-moral values. Politicians in particular should not allow themselves the luxury of distancing themselves, or becoming out of touch from, the consequences of any pseudo-virtuosity, and recognise their responsibilities and the effect on those whom they represent.

Looking at toleration in a completely objective manner would require it to be placed outside the context of personal needs and ends, whilst permitting those reactions that emphasise its objective features, and interpreting subjective affections not as modes of our personal being, but as the characteristics of the issue. Harrison [1975–6:131–2] distinguishes between the role of the participant and that of the role of the observer, which is a feature of distancing, although one which is not usually a matter of choice. The participant is the moral agent or moral critic who makes decisions, adopts attitudes, follows principles and acts tolerantly, or advocates toleration, from within the conventions of normative ethics. The observer sees morality from an extra-moral position. "There is nothing which the relativist, [as] a relativist, can say either for or against tolerance from a moral point of view. The moment he does this he ceases to be an observer of morality and becomes a user of a moral system . . . there is no such thing as a moral judgement made from a morally neutral or 'extra-moral' position."

If no threat or penalty is expected to ensue, toleration may be no more than a patronising or self-serving response. Arendt [1994:251] saw this in the "cheap sentimentality" of the guilt displayed by some young Germans, but not of their fathers' guilt, towards the Holocaust: "It is quite gratifying to feel guilty if you haven't done anything wrong—how noble." Students in the prosperous Britain and old socialism of the 1960–70s received free university tuition and maintenance grants, and usually did not have to compete for jobs. They were often demonstrably supportive of free tuition to overseas students. Arguably the resource-limited students of the 1990s/2000s belonging to a different generation might take a less distanced view of free grants to overseas students and to ethnic job quotas.

A research study [Koshechkina 1992:Preface] used an empirical statistical analysis based on the British Social Attitudes Survey 1990 of toleration in Britain towards political protest groups. It noted that "The difference [distancing] between the almost universal support for general political tolerance and the restricted application of the principle of political tolerance to concrete situations even on the level of bare attitudes. The difference between the universal agreement that there is a need of tolerance in society as far as democracy is concerned, and far less enthusiasm for the application of tolerant norms in concrete [actual] situations . . . almost nobody rejects the general principle, but the practical application has a very wide range of nuances" [5]. It also reached the interesting conclusion [129] that "The impact of education on tolerance when the respondent is concerned about general human rights is greater than in cases when a particular situation of people using such rights is under consideration . . . it must be recognised that the exercise of civil liberties generates a conflict of values. Democracy requires the right to express your views freely and the right to protect your views, but it also requires at least some social order. All these requirements must be balanced." It found [130] that "The difference involves understanding the contradiction between support for abstract democratic principles, and support for more decisive policy changes that benefit particular groups . . . also such abstract political judgements as 'whether society in Britain is an open one' or 'whether basic human rights in Britain are well protected' have a strong correlation with general tolerance showing no significant links with the applied one [133] . . . [and] with the approach of the threat, the level of tolerance dramatically decreases" [140]. This conclusion supports the view that the limits of toleration would narrow if increasing multiculturalism was perceived as a threat.

The passive toleration or indifference, albeit superficial and temporary, exhibited to the inroads of multiculturalism and immigration by those of the mainstream society who are distanced from it may be influenced by the extent to which they are directly or immediately affected by it. The influential patrician and privileged political and social classes—now dubbed, the "metropolitan liberal elite" or the "chattering classes"—have little social contact with the mainstream of society, let alone the underclass, and have not so far competed with ethnic minorities, and probably do not perceive multiculturalism as being a threat to their interests. In so doing, they may exhibit the myopia of the elite, sometimes articulated in terms of rights, because they feel that they ought to adopt the moral high ground and promote a liberal agenda. Contrast this prosperous and insulated class of society with the poor whites living in the ghettoised inner cities (such as the riot-torn Northern British former mill towns), who feel, whether justifiably or not, that the minorities around them are responsible for their unemployment, and unfairly compete for limited resources and benefits. This social underclass may see multiculturalism as a threat, and consequently their toleration will be narrow to intolerant, and their behaviour racist. They will be indifferent to accusations that it is irrational, unjustified, or immoral. A former deputy chairman of the CRE reported that the whites in Bradford "feared being swamped" [TM 2 Nov. 01]. Foot [1965:7], a 1960s anti-racist campaigner, "pleaded guilty" to "being completely inexperienced about the 'effects' of immigration from a working class angle." He ascribed [236] to class snobbery the courteous and helpful reaction to the wealthy Aga Khan compared with the reaction to the "class inferiority" of the Commonwealth immigrant. This difference in the "social distance scale" [Lambert and Lambert 1964:52] affects attitudes and behaviour towards strangers, both as individuals as well as towards groups, varying from "acceptance as a marriage partner to rejection even as visitors to one's country." An American columnist [STM 30 July 00] observed that "Multicultural elitists see alien cultures as a source of new exotic restaurants. Low wage workers see them as a source of strange cooking odours and neighbourhood disrupting life-styles." The Home Secretary also gave vent to his feelings on distancing when he called "well heeled" civil rights lawyers "hypocrites" for opposing social curfew orders and restraints on people who disturb their neighbours. He said [TM 15 Sept. 99] "These people will represent the perpetrators of crime and then get back into their BMW [cars] and drive to their homes in quiet and prosperous areas where they are immune from much of the crime."

Sociological research [Wolff 1972:29] was carried out on the effect of "distancing" towards the toleration of violence on the attitudes of different social classes in the United States—from the top social financial and political elite, to the affluent and educated middle class liberals, to the "blue collar" social group. Their limits of toleration progressively narrowed as their distancing from the violence decreased. For the social underclass however, violence meant the actions towards them from all forms of authority, and the institutions used by the upper social classes, such as the police, who were perceived as being intolerant and probably racist. Because they did not have and were never going to have access to power, this justified and legitimised their own (intolerant) use of violence—possibly reinforced by their own low self-esteem and sense of vulnerability.

Related to distancing is sentimentality or posturing—fake emotion done for affect rather than effect, or private avoidance with public sensitivity. Professor Fish [1997: 382–3] recognises distancing in distinguishing between what he calls "boutique" and "strong" multiculturalism: "Whereas the boutique multiculturalist will accord a superficial respect to cultures other than his own, a respect he will withdraw when he finds the practices irrational or inhumane, a strong multiculturalist will want to accord a deep respect to all cultures at their core, for he believes that each has the right to form its own identity and nourish its own sense of what is rational and humane. For the strong multiculturalist the first principle is not rationality or some other supra-cultural universal, but tolerance. But the trouble with stipulating tolerance as your first principle is that you cannot possibly be faithful to it, because sooner or later the culture whose core values you are tolerating, will reveal itself to be intolerant at that same core; that is the distinctiveness that marks it as unique and self-defining will resist the appeal of moderation or incorporation into a larger whole. Confronted with a demand that it surrender its viewpoint or enlarge it to include the practices of its natural enemies—other religions, other races, other genders, other classes—a beleaguered culture will fight back with everything from discriminatory legislation to violence. At this point the strong multiculturalist faces a dilemma; either he stretches his toleration so that it extends to the intolerance residing at the heart of a culture he would honour, in which case tolerance is no longer his guiding principle, or he condemns the core intolerance of that culture, in which case he is no longer according it respect at the point where its distinctiveness is most obviously at stake . . . Indeed it turns out that strong multiculturalism is not a distinct position but a somewhat deeper instance of the shallow category of boutique multiculturalism." Donald Pease [1997:402–3] says that "this answer discloses the motive for Fish's seemingly tireless rehearsal of liberals failure to reinvent themselves as multiculturalists . . . their failed intercultural encounters are reducible to one: liberal's inability to value what they find 'irrational' in another culture."

Rorty [1994:2] can see distancing in the support by the West for civil rights movements, and by implication, moral cosmopolitanism and universal claim rights. He says "What distinguishes the West is that as the rich part of the world it has a large comfortable class, which has lived in security for a long time and has become receptive to arguments . . . [and has] a susceptibility to those kinds of considerations, being persuaded that you should care about people far away who have no particular connection with you but who are suffering . . . the West is distinctive in having the leisure to do so." A possible prognosis of Rorty's analysis is that if the relative prosperity of the West declines, so will its multilateral concern about the rest of the world, together with its present unquestioning acceptance of universal claim rights for its non-citizens.

NOTES

Arendt, H. *Eichmann in Jerusalem*. London: Penguin Books, 1994. 251.
Berlin, I. In *Liberal Nationalism*. Tamir, Y. Princeton, NJ: Princeton University Press, 1993. 13.
Berry, C.J. *Human Nature*. London: Macmillan Education, 1986. Xiii.
Bullough, E. "Physical Distance." In *British Journal of Psychiatry*. London, 1912.
Crozier, B. *A Theory of Conflict*. London: Hamish Hamilton, 1974. x.
Dewey, J. *Freedom and Culture*. New York: Capricorn Books, 1963. 10.
Fish, S. "Boutique Multiculturalism, or Why Liberals are Incapable of Thinking about Hate Speech." In *Critical Enquiry*. Winter 1997. 382–3.
Foot, P. *Immigration and British Politics*. Harmondsworth, Middx: Penguin Books, 1965. 7.
Ibid. 236.
Galbraith, J. K. *The Good Society*. London: Sinclair Stevenson. 1996. 3–4.
Harrison, G. "Relativism and Tolerance." In *Ethics*. vol. 86 1975–76. 131–2.
King, P. *Toleration*. London: George Allen and Unwin. 1976. 201–2.
Koshechkina, TM. *Political Tolerance—From General Principles to Concrete Application*. M.A. Dissertation. Canterbury: University of Kent, 1992. Preface.
Ibid. 5.
Ibid. 129–130.
Ibid. 133.
Ibid. 140.
Lambert W.W. and Lambert, W.E. *Social Psychology*. New Jersey: Prentice Hall. 1964. 52.

MacIntyre, A. *How to Seem Virtuous without Actually Being So.* Occasional Papers Series No. 1. Lancaster, Lancaster University, Centre for the Study of Cultural Values, 1991. 1 and 20.

Norman, R. *The Moral Philosophers.* Oxford: Oxford University Press, 1983. 92.

Pease, D.E. "Regulating Multi-Adhocerists, Fish's Rules." In *Critical Enquiry.* Winter 1997. 402–3.

Pfaff, W. *The Wrath of Nations—Civilization and the Furies Of Nationalism.* New York: Simon and Schuster, 1993. 238.

Reid, T. "An Inquiry into the Human Mind." In *A Dictionary of Philosophical Quotations.* Ayer, A.J. and O'Grady, J. (Eds.) Oxford: Blackwell Publishers, 1994. 372.

Rorty, R. "Towards a Liberal Utopia." In *Times Literary Supplement.* 24 June 1994. 2.

Singer, P. *Practical Ethics.* Cambridge: Cambridge University Press, 1979. 211.

Stevenson, L. *Seven Theories of Human Nature.* Oxford: Oxford University Press, 1987. 17.

Wolff, R.P. "On Violence" In *Philosophical Issues.* Rachels, J. and Tillman, F. (Eds.), New York: Harper and Row, 1972. 329.

25

Toleration and its Features

It has become part of the everyday political and church rhetoric to urge toleration, wherever and whenever any contentious and divisive issue has arisen in society. The new Home Office logo proclaims its role as "Building a Safe, Just and Tolerant Society." The concept of toleration is complex. In this discussion it has been deemed essential to review its many facets, both in terms of its features and its limits, even though some of these may impinge only indirectly on the equally complex topic of culturalism. A response by Professor John Wisdom [1965:139] to the question "what is tolerance?" was that, although we all know what tolerance is, like other concepts such as justice, virtue and knowledge, "we have little to say in reply." The desire to have a firm definition and a set of principles may be an established and rationalized way of thinking, but toleration is not amenable to an inclusive definition. Nevertheless, Ludwig Wittgenstein emphasised the importance of clarifying principles before discussing their validity. A broad concept of toleration is that it is an attitude of liberal acceptance towards the beliefs, values and behaviour of others which facilitates social resilience, and is a necessary condition of a stable society. Those things of which we approve do not call for toleration. We only tolerate those things to which we object. An important question is "what motives underly toleration, and what are its limits?"

The inadequacy of definitions is borne out by the Oxford English Dictionary, which defines *tolerance, toleration* and *tolerant* in terms of the concept of *tolerate*, which is defined as (i) to allow the existence or occurrence without authoritative interference; (ii) to leave unmolested; (iii) to endure or permit (especially with forbearance); and (iv) to sustain or endure (suffering). None of these definitions is adequate for the complexity of the notion of toleration. The American Webster's Dictionary defines tolerance in general terms, and toleration principally in terms of its religious context. Some academics [Cranston 1991:33] [King 1976:13] [Tinder 1995:1–2] draw a distinc-

315

tion between toleration and tolerance—which is indicative of its complexity—but both are used in this discussion without distinction as does most of the literature. It is argued that any discussion of toleration should not be confined to what it is, but should recognise that it can subsume differing motives, not all of which are virtuous or praiseworthy. The appearance of being tolerant may be founded on no more than the hope that if the issue is ignored it will go away (looking the other way), or with young people, assuming that they will grow out of it.

Tolerance and intolerance are value-laden words. Toleration lends itself to comforting and flattering synonyms and near synonyms that can add to or disguise its underlying motives and can lend themselves to posturing—such as *charitable, magnanimous, broad-minded, non-judgemental, conciliatory, easy-going, uncomplaining, liberal, permissive, indulgent, condoning, flexible, forgiving, enlightened, moderate,* and *reasonable.* Other synonyms are to condone—allowing an offence or wrongdoing of which one consciously disapproves, but acquiesces— raising no objection. Particularly in a Western liberal individualistic society, there can be merit in being seen to have a tolerant disposition because it is unprejudiced and non-judgmental.

The morality of toleration derives from a respect for persons, namely, that everyone has the right to choose how to live in accordance with their being autonomous and rational agents, this principle being both universal and reciprocal. A immediate difficulty arises in establishing what justifies infringing the autonomy of others. The state has the authority to replace the voluntary toleration of a public act by individuals with legislation that prohibits it. Conversely, it can repeal legislation which has heretofore prohibited a public act, and leave it to individual toleration. Society and its legislation may tolerate acts which are generally regarded as immoral but permit them, provided that they are carried out in private so that they do not offend/influence the general public or minors—such as homosexuality or prostitution. The state always has to maximise the cost/benefit balance between the individual and society as a whole.

Indifference, such as bystander apathy, in avoiding helping someone being mugged, or ignoring a battered dog, is the abdication or the omission of an act. This could be seen as a parody of the acts and omissions doctrine, i.e. it is seen as less morally blameworthy if one tolerates inaction than to act to prevent it from happening. A philosophical question is asking whether a moral agent can justify his toleration of someone acting contrary to his genuinely held but opposing moral convictions, but disclaim any responsibility if there is a bad outcome. There are a range of acceptable maxims for neutral or passive toleration including "it is none of my business" or "I keep my thoughts to myself," but these usually apply to avoidable and distanced issues. Provided that it causes no harm to others, passive or neutral toleration may be genuinely no-one else's business, or show respect for the privacy of others, but there are differing concepts of what and to whom constitutes harm. Thus, one may passively or neutrally tolerate the behaviour of others to which one disapproves, such as defrauding the Inland Revenue, because the harm is distanced and diffuse, and it respects the individual's autonomy. For the sceptic however, passive or neutral toleration that merely "goes along with," or unnecessarily "puts up with," will not be seen as tolerance, but rather timidity or a pusillanimous lack of conviction or courage. Indifference, however, may reflect a genuine lack of interest or concern about an issue, although under sufficient personal stress, indifference may give way to intolerance. The passive toleration, official or individual, shown towards increasing multiculturalism may be no more than a pragmatic accommodation of it being seen as unavoidable or inevitable. Predictably, all minorities including members of ethnic groups, seek complete and unreserved acceptance and not mere toleration. Anthony Arblaster [1984:67–8] notes that "The pragmatic case for tolerance accepts that differences in belief and behaviour exist, and cannot be eliminated whether or not it is in principle desirable that they should be so eliminated . . . Generally a belief or movement or group can only be sure of being tolerated when its existence, is for most people, a matter of indifference." Neutral or passive toleration can, however, be a distancing posture designed to being all things to all people, without directly addressing the issue so as to avoid confrontation. Such was President Clinton's abandonment of his initiative against gays in the military for a neutral policy of "don't ask; don't tell." Toleration that is passive neutrality to avoid hostile comments or acts is not true toleration but indifference. In Nazi Germany most people were aware of, but became indifferent to, the fate of the Jews, because they were afraid to protest. This may have been due to being uninformed either by choice or by design, or the ability to psychologically distance themselves from the outcome. The rural British, whose knowledge of American society before WW2 was limited to Hollywood, objected to the colour bar practised by the American army in Britain [Ward 1988:107]— even black and white blood was segregated by the Red Cross [Brendon 1987:83]. Their toleration was ignorance—they had probably never seen a black person before. This was also apparent in the early days of Caribbean immigration into Britain, when the rare immigrant was seen as an interesting novelty, a sojourner, and not as a threat. The reaction was one of friendly curiosity, though often patronising. The first 492 Jamaicans to arrive in 1948 were invited to a civic tea by the Mayor of Brixton—the Evening Standard had the headline "Welcome Home" [Humphries and Taylor 1986:110].

Toleration differs from, but may overlap, condoning, indifference, permissiveness, appeasement and licence. It may be genuine or false, in which case its manifestation may be hypocritical and/or conceal an internalised intolerance. Toleration can give rise to the expectation that others should also conform, or at least feign indifference. Toleration or intolerance may not be based on a reflective conviction by an individual about an issue, but may be belief validated, received wisdom, or an acquired attitude, propensity or disposition, but if articulated publicly may be justified by moral and/or objective arguments. The Methodist John Wesley [Fitzhenry 1986: 291 said "Passion and prejudice govern the world; only under the name of reason." Hume [1994:197] said "Morals excite passions, and produce or prevent actions. Reason of itself is utterly impotent in this particular. The rules of morality, therefore, are not conclusions of our reason." Reason requires the discovery of truth or falsehood, the true relationship of ideas, or the real existence of matters of fact. Any analysis of toleration should allow for the belief that moral rules are not necessarily the outcome of reason, but are also intuitive and deterministic in nature and culturally dependent. Nor are they simply dependent on "education and understanding." This is not to say that feelings should not be queried to assess their rationality.

Professor Preston King [1976:63–64] considers tolerance in terms of its applicational fields rather than in terms of being descriptive of acts or activities. These are "ideational" in regard to ideas, such as religious, scientific, ethical or political; "organisational" in regard to organised groups, such as political, professional, religious, or trade union; and "identity" in regard to race, class, culture, or religion. The fields in which tolerance is exercised can also be personal, social, moral, religious, institutional, and political. This affects the relationship of the individual in differing, widening and sometimes overlapping areas of interest and concern, which range from one's family, other individuals and groups, up to and including the nation-state. Personal toleration can be towards noisy neighbours or to smoking in public; social toleration towards racists, feminists or gays; moral toleration towards capital punishment or abortion; religious toleration towards Jehovah's Witnesses or Mormons; institutional toleration towards the Church or Greenpeace; and political toleration towards communists or the BNP. Cultural toleration will subsume or overlap aspects of social, moral, racial, religious and sometimes political toleration. Toleration of the behaviour of others can be "learnt" by living in a tight social group and sharing its common objectives without proselytizing. Although similar communities rarely exist today, national service (conscription) was claimed to promote toleration and a sense of nationhood. One might hypothesise that if British culture is tolerant (as many would like to imagine) and has a sense of justice and fairness, this is because they have never lived under an alien totalitarian culture that might otherwise have normalised their intolerance.

Koshechkina [1992:51] notes that "To be tolerant in the new liberal context becomes a moral thing itself. It is very often considered 'immoral to be intolerant,' in the same way as it is considered to be immoral to be racist or sexist. This shows us that in spite of all liberal attempts to purify the concept of tolerance from all prejudices, it is still not free from one [pre-conceived] particular conviction." Tolerance is neither necessarily moral or immoral, nor can genuine toleration be created by legislation. Toleration raises questions: Firstly, what should be the role of the state be, if any, as distinct from the voluntarianism of the individual, in determining the scope and limits of toleration? Secondly, should there be differing limits towards different individuals or groups? Thirdly, what should these limits be? And fourthly, what are the acceptable end objectives of toleration if it is used as a means? As with the notion of equality, toleration can be exhibited in one field but not in others. Toleration of a person within the work environment may differ from his toleration socially, religiously, or politically, and will be reflected in differing levels of acceptance. Commercial research [Hofstede1980:11] has been done in the differing limits of toleration in the work related values of national cultures in forty different countries. The limits of toleration are influenced by factors including race, religion, political system, diversity, and ethnocentrism. This was measured in terms of their "Uncertainty [risk] Avoidance Index." According to some Japanese commentators, part of Japan's continuing economic malaise is attributable to the cultural "deference barrier" in their traditional management style, which inhibits innovation [TM 17 April 01].

Locke, and later Mill, were early exponents of toleration. The Enlightenment—the Age of Reason—began in Britain in the seventeenth century and continued into the eighteenth century. It was the belief that knowledge and rationality were the supreme guide to human behaviour and were contrasted with the irrationality and superstition of the Middle Ages. One of its doctrines was that toleration should be extended to other creeds and ways of life. The later Romantic movement of the "inner voice" and "feelings" began about 1760. Locke saw the limits of toleration by the state as those needed to protect it from threats and the civil interests of its citizens—their lives, liberties and property. Mill tolerated the freedom of individuals to choose, and valued the social utility of enhancing the autonomy of the individual. He tolerated self-regarding behaviour insofar as it promoted individual happiness up to the limit of it causing harm to others. This laid emphasis on the benefits to individuals, and seemed to marginalise its cost to the rest of society, or alternatively assumed that the summation of that which benefited individuals would benefit society overall. The broader principle of equal respect for persons states that every person is an end unto him/herself and is worthy of respect. It sees mankind as composed of rational and autonomous beings who are capable of making their own best judgements. This necessitates the toleration of individual behaviour, limited by the state only when it fails to show equal respect for others and does not therefore merit "respect worthiness." This could be because this individual behaviour is judged as irrational or immoral or a threat to the majority. A practical problem with this idealised principle arises when there are incompatible ways of living—then there can be a conflict of human rights. The state can justify its intervention by legislation and override individual autonomy to preserve the shared morality inherent in its culture. These abstract and overlapping principles of toleration are imperfect approximations, and leave practical questions unanswered. They form a complex philosophical composite that, in real-life, often has to be resolved by political means and the setting of social priorities, as well as by reference to competing moral principles including human rights. Herein lies the dilemma that a separatist multicultural society poses, because it makes a difficult issue even more complex. If a society is monocultural, then the state can more readily determine and maintain its shared culture and values. In a separatist multicultural society, the state will be obliged to accommodate its diverse cultural identities because it cannot impose the morality of one group on to other groups and undermine the respect for their autonomy and rights.

The scope in which toleration can be exercised lies somewhere between those issues that do not warrant legal proscription, and those of which society generally disapproves. Legalised prohibition or other forms of social exclusion can be perceived as being discriminatory against the rights of a particular social group, irrespective of the interests of the majority. It does not apply to matters society and the individual regard as being the norm, and occupies the area between licence and legal prohibition. It applies where whatever is being objected to is voluntarily endured but not endorsed by the tolerator (who exercises self-restraint). One cannot claim to be tolerant of something which one is powerless to alter, or because the law permits it, or because it is inevitable and cannot be removed. This is irrespective of whether or not the individual sees it as being acceptable, or because of the distancing effect of the length of time elapsing before he will feel its consequences. When the individual has no power to amend or to alter something, this is acquiescence, sufferance, or endurance. This may may be a pragmatic decision, but it is not toleration. Toleration is not an appropriate notion in respect of race, because race/colour cannot be altered. But cultural beliefs, including religion, practices, and values need not necessarily be tolerated, because conceivably they could be made private, modified or given up. Genuine toleration is unavoidably judgemental and not neutral, although a refusal to be judgemental can be seen as virtuous toleration. Professor Anthony O'Hear [1998:188–9] sees this as "emotional correctness:" "It is sentimental to avoid the roots of a problem, and it is sentimental to think that there is no problem which cannot be solved with a bit of good will on both sides, and dangerously sentimental to think that reason and compassion are a match for evil." Even if it may be perceived as being morally virtuous, with human nature as it is or can be, generous toleration can sometimes be used in the individual or group self-interest of the tolerator or abused by the tolerated. The generous toleration of liberalism may not be reciprocated by the intolerant, and may destroy that very liberalism. Extending the limits of toleration is easy—restricting them is not.

There is a spectrum of political and sociological philosophies related to toleration and to culturalism:

1. Conservative: An individual's identity is seen as historically given (inherited), and personal beliefs, values, and morals are neither chosen nor alterable. If so, there is no scope for the state promoting toleration, because the culture of ethnic groups is supposedly not malleable, and cannot be changed. If this theory is applicable, then multiculturalism would result in the separatism that underlay the "separate but equal" racial situation that existed in parts of the United States before Civil Rights.

2. Liberal: The state is seen as being neutral and tolerant so that individuals can be free to pursue their identity unhampered. This is sometimes articulated in terms of their autonomous rights. This is the policy towards the racial divide the United States has been trying to follow since the Civil Rights movement of the mid–1960s. The limits of toleration will be set at the level at which the autonomy of the individual is threatened, and if minorities value their autonomy, these limits will have to be generous. Nevertheless, minorities may expect more than just to be left alone. They may want to positively belong, be welcomed, and hope that their culture to attract esteem and respect.

3. Socialist: The individual is seen as belonging and having obligations to other members of the society. The state does not remain neutral, but actively promotes a tolerant and reciprocal ethos of a common society and citizenship. This reflects the assumption that although some aspects of people's lives are given and not a matter of choice, others are alterable and malleable.

Mendus [1989:154] notes that "There is no reason to believe that socialism, or conservativism, will be any more amenable to clear and uncontroversial definition than was liberalism. However, one important difference between socialism and liberalism lies in their differing conceptions of the relationship between individual and society. This much, at least, is true: socialists do not see the state as merely a neutral arena in which people may pursue their own interests and personal projects unhampered by others."

Liberal toleration can be misused. If a minority attains sufficient political power, there is no reason to suppose that it will be politically or morally liberal towards the previous dominant but tolerant culture. Also, if an individual believes that he has a right to be truly autonomous, then the community can appear as a threat because he will perceive it as limiting his freedom, and not as an agent for the exercise of that freedom.

The socialist theory of toleration can work in various ways. One way is where there are different Others who do not exhibit, or are suspected of not having, an undivided loyalty to the over-arching political/sociological culture. This can be seen as a threat to the mainstream culture and to the stability of the society, giving rise to tighter limits of toleration by the majority which could ultimately approach repression. Or the limits can be wide, because the morality of the mainstream society does not approve of coercion—maybe because it is not practicable. Socialist "solidarity" might alternatively be construed as being a construct of diverse cultures, which does not wholly reflect the values of the mainstream culture. This partial and undefined conflation is reflected in the incorporation or integrationist version of multiculturalism. It remains to be seen if the post-apartheid, post-Mandela, separatist and crime-ridden South Africa will be the exception. In Africa, post-independence political movements for the establishment of culturally hegemonic (tribal) nation-states have indicated that traditional tribal loyalties can be stronger than the continuing acceptance of the multiethnic/cultural states that were imposed by the former imperial powers. Neither does sociological toleration lend itself to a communitarianism, at least on a national scale, since this holds that human beings are constituted by the communal and contractual relationship in which they find themselves. If so, it is difficult to believe that those who are different will be readily accepted into their society by its founding members. Toleration exhibited towards an underclass, particularly one that includes immigrants who do not conform, will be influenced by the security and self-interests of the mainstream society. The political dilemma is where the balance should lie for it to be acceptable, and not be threatening. Galbraith [1992] calls this the "culture of contentment," and intolerance can arise whenever this social equilibrium ceases to exist.

There is a distinction between toleration and rights [King 1976:168]: "Tolerance consists in a negative view of an item conjoined with a socially conferred power to act against it, but a power which is not invoked. A right consists in a positive view of an item conjoined with a socially conferred power to act in support of it, whether or not that power is invoked. Tolerance and rights can be seen as being mutually exclusive." Tolerance and rights are symbiotic inasmuch that tolerance can be seen as pre-supposing the having of a right. Nevertheless, a right is agent-centred and can be insisted on, whereas tolerance can only be sought by the agent from society or be assumed to exist. The beneficiary of an absolute right should, though, enter into a moral self-discourse between exercising that right and the obligation of toleration not to insist on it. Prescriptive claims to rights not reinforced by law can put a stress on the limits of toleration because they imply that they should at least be tolerated irrespective of the objections individuals might have to them— the more claims to rights, the greater the tendency towards societal intolerance.

There is a theory that holds that a greater exposure to diversity will in fact reduce prejudice and improve tolerance. A nation-wide American sociological study [Allen Williams et al. 1976:394–408] replicated research which was first reported in 1955. It was designed to confirm that (political) tolerance arises from a recognition that a free society cannot exist unless one is willing to accept the civil liberties of others to think and behave differently, and that this is valuable, not only for self-protection, but for the preservation of a democratic society. The social and cultural diversity studied was not racial/ethnic/religious, but the willingness to practice "democratic restraint," namely, the toleration of political non-conformity, i.e. Communism, atheism, socialism, and someone whose loyalty had been questioned before a congressional committee but who had sworn under oath that he had never been a Communist. The effect of the exposure to diversity was measured in terms of "education" (meaning, different values to those learned at home), city size, region, mass media news, gender, and occupation. The original hypothesis in 1954–1955 was that contact with social and cultural diversity—other values, beliefs, life styles and the like—would result in Americans becoming more politically tolerant. It was recognised however, that "diversity [a high rate of social and geographic mobility] may sometimes foster intolerance . . . [and that] rapid social change could produce value conflicts within the mind of the individual," both of which might result in anxiety and individuals trying to prevent others from exercising their civil rights. With the exceptions of mass media exposure and female employment, the later research was said to confirm the earlier hypothesis, namely that increased exposure to diversity would result in more tolerance in the future.

This conclusion came under criticism [Harry Crockett 1976:409–12] as it "seriously distorted rather than illuminated understanding of political tolerance," because it had ignored the effect of the change in the political climate in the United States between 1954 and 1973, and that this was more important to tolerant attitudes than changes in "education." This meant the change in the extent of the perception of an internal danger, in this case, the fear of Communism. "A twofold conclusion seems prudent: at a given level of threat, a more highly educated population will be more politically tolerant than a less educated population; at the same time, increases in educational level of a population will not produce sharp increases in political tolerance, if the perception of internal danger among the population [as for example, from Communism] is widespread." The researchers [Williams et al. 1976:413–8] accepted that "The perceived threat from certain sources, for example from communists, may have declined, but fear of other sorts of non-conformists, for example from criminals, appears to have increased. The net result . . . is that the degree and distribution of feeling threatened remained constant."

In 1991, a later study [Koshechkina 1992:66–7], on broadly similar lines, asked more than 500 undergraduates at a mid-Western American university for their reactions to the activities of non-conformist political groups. "What the researchers expected [to find] was that greater thought and cognition [knowledge] will increase people's willingness to extend basic rights even to groups they dislike"—that in a democracy, people would be more tolerant if their reactions were objective rather than emotive. The results were unexpected. The "thinkers," who it was assumed would take into account the effect of intolerance on its long-term consequences, like maintaining democratic values and norms in society, were found to be less tolerant than the "non-thinkers," who responded on a visceral level to the nonconformity. One explanation proposed was that the thinkers "were in fact thinking about short-term, immediate, and practical consequences, leaving unconsidered the consequences of long-term significance, like those of maintaining the democratic values and norms in society in general," in which tolerance was not the only or the most important consideration. If nothing else, these studies illustrate the complexity and unpredictability of the objective/subjective psychology of toleration. The influences on it can be multi-factorial and selective, both direct and indirect, both short term and long term, and determined by a combination of experience and visceral reactions (particularly a threat), as well as by reflective thought.

Toleration is, therefore, usually a selective "pick and mix" in line with a personal prioritisation of beliefs and values, including those who urge wide toleration onto others. As early as 1965, the racially intolerant Enoch Powell was nevertheless in favour of legalising homosexuality and abolishing capital punishment [STM 15 Feb. 98]. Individuals within the same cultural group can have a plurality of issues to which they will be selectively tolerant which may not be mutually compatible. Cranston [1991:28] notes that "We find philosophers pleading for a general policy of toleration, and then, in a list of what should be denied toleration, including things that the ordinary reader might be quite willing to tolerate." There may for example, be toleration of abortion combined with an intolerance of racism. It is not convincingly credible, for politicians and clerics in particular, to maintain the rhetoric of toleration, and at the same time exhibit, in practice, a selective intolerance. Multiculturalism, which calls for the toleration of ethno-national diversity and difference, may be accompanied by absolutist intolerance of another diversity and difference, such as sexual orientation.

The principle of toleration was enshrined in the First Amendment of the American Constitution. Tinder [1995:5] observes that "It is easy for Americans to think of tolerance as altogether natural and logical and to assume that several fully adequate and self evident reasons for being tolerant could readily be brought to light by anyone who took the trouble to look for them. In this way we forget something that was widely realised three hundred years ago, before tolerance was established: tolerance is not only unnatural but also, given certain premises that are quite accordant with common sense, illogical." He [6] argues that "If tolerance were wholly natural and logical, presumably it would have prevailed in most places throughout history, and periods of intolerance would have been exceptional. But such, of course, is not the case . . . it is probably valid to say that intolerance has been normal and tolerance exceptional . . . to most of us they [the arguments for tolerance] still seem at first glance reasonable; when we reflect on them, however, their fragility becomes apparent" [7]. He warns [210] against the incursion of large numbers of Hispanics and Asians. He says that "Tolerance has been relatively easy. But circumstances have been changing. In coming decades American democracy may be tried more severely than at any other period, except, perhaps, that of the Civil War. We could lose our freedom not only by becoming hysterically and foolishly intolerant . . . but also by not having the wit to limit tolerance in order to preserve its social and spiritual grounds."

Still, the notion of toleration embodies a positive and sometimes virtuous connotation since it implies a recognition of and respect for the values of others, the worth of diversity, and a defence of the freedom and individuality of others. There is a saying attributed to Voltaire: "I disapprove of what you say, but I will defend to the death your right to say it." On the other hand toleration can be used in a vaguely negative sense—namely, a kind of restrained forbearance in "putting up with the behaviour, beliefs, and values of others." Toleration can in this situation be useful as a negotiating ploy with a prudential element of self-interest, inasmuch that "if I put up with your behaviour, then you will put up with mine." Galbraith [1992:26] sees this in the tolerance shown by the contented majority about great differences in wealth. He says that "A general and quite plausible convention is here observed—the price of prevention of any aggression against one's own income is tolerance of the greater amount of others."

Genuine toleration is not created between or within states by diplomatic, clerical, or political rhetoric. In the Preamble to the UN Charter in 1945, its fifty-one founder members promised "To practise tolerance and live together in peace with one another as good neighbours and to unite our strength to maintain international peace and security etc." Since then there has been considerable intolerance and little peace in the world—the estimated loss of life due to war and other conflicts between then and 1994 is eighteen million, of which more than fifteen million was in East Asia, Central and South Asia, and sub-Saharan Africa [TM 15 Oct. 97]. Pleas for (religious) toleration have been made in recent years, principally by the Church, but at the 1997 Conservative Party conference tolerance again entered into the political rhetoric of its leader William Hague. Three years later anti-racists claimed that Hague was intolerant when he described the numbers of asylum seekers as a "flood." However, Hague's "intolerance" was within the Millian tradition: "let's be tolerant of the way people wish to live when it doesn't damage the interests of other people."

Toleration has not always been considered a praiseworthy characteristic: religious intolerance was the norm, and thought to be justifiable. King [1976:73] observed that during the Middle Ages "Religious truth was assumed to be so self-evident that opposition to it was taken to imply evil, not error." Religious intolerance was rationalised by the conviction that men could be compelled to change their (false) beliefs, and no punishment was too severe to ensure their eternal salvation—hence the Inquisition. Elisabeth Labrousse [1973:112–3] says that the end of religious persecution (intolerance) in Western societies depended on secularisation, followed by the steady weakening of the once-intimate solidarity between Church and state—that is, when individual religious beliefs were relegated to the domain of private life and no longer appeared to be a menace to the loyalty, security, and prosperity of the state. Dworkin [1993:167–8] argues that "[Religious] tolerance is a cost we must pay for our adventure into liberty. We are committed, by our love of liberty and dignity, to live in communities in which no group is thought clever or spiritual or numerous enough to decide essentially religious matters for everyone else." This principled liberal view begs the question as to what are, and what should be, the limits of the "cost we must pay," and what are "essentially religious [as opposed to secular] matters."

NOTES

Arblaster, A. *The Rise and Decline of Western Liberalism*. Oxford: Basil Blackford, 1984. 67–8.

Brendon, P. *Ike*. London: Secker asnd Warburg, 1987. 83.

Cranston, M. "On Toleration and Tolerance—Locke and Voltaire Revisited." In *Quadrant*. March   1991. 28.

Dworkin, R. *Life's Dominion*. London: Harper Collins. 1993. 167–8.

Fitzhenry, R.I. (Ed.) *Book of Quotations*. Edinburgh: W & R. Chambers, 1986. 291.

Galbraith, J. K. *The Culture of Contentment*. London: Sinclair Stevenson, 1992. 26.

Hofstede, G. *Culture's Consequences*. California: Sage Publications, 1980. 11.

Hume, D. "A Treatise Of Human Nature." In *A Dictionary of Philosophical Quotations*. Ayer, A .J. and O'Grady, J. (Eds.). Oxford: Blackwell Publishers, 1994. 197.

Humphries, S. and Taylor, J. *The Making of Modern London*. 1945–1985. London: Sidgwicck and Jackson, 1986. 110.

King, P. *Toleration*. London: George Allen and Unwin, 1976. 13.
Ibid 63–4.
Ibid. 73.
Ibid. 168.
Koshechkina, TM. *Political Tolerance—From General Principles to Concrete Application*. M.A. Dissertation. Canterbury: University of Kent, 1992. 66–7.
Labrousse, E. *Religious Toleration—Dictionary of the History of Ideas*. vol. iv. USA: Charles Scribner's Sons, 1973. 112–3.
Mendus, S. *Toleration and the Limits of Liberalism*. London: Macmillan Education, 1989. 154.
O'Hear, A. In *Faking It—The Sentimentalism of Modern Society*. Anderson, D. and Mullen, P. (Eds). Altrinsham, Ches: The Social Affairs Unit, 1998. 188–9.
Tinder, G. *Toleration and Community*. Columbia, Missouri: University of Missouri Press, 1995. 5 –7.
Ibid. 210.
Ward, S. *War in the Countryside 1939–45*. London: Cameron Books. 1988. 107.
Weale, A. "Toleration, Individual Differences and Respect for Persons." In *Aspects of Toleration*. Horton, J and Mendus, S. (Eds). London: Methuen, 1985. 16–35.
Williams, J.A., Nunn, C, Z. et al. *"Origins of Tolerance*: Findings From A Replication Of Stouffer's Communism, Conformity And Civil Liberties." In *Social Forces*. vol. 55.(2). December 1976. 394–408. Crockett, H.J. "Comments on *Origins Of Tolerance*." 409–12. Williams, J.A, Nunn, C.Z., et al. *"Origins Of Tolerance—* Reply to Crockett." 413–8.
Wisdom, J. *Paradox and Discovery*. Oxford: Basil Blackford, 1965. 139.

26

Toleration as a Moral Virtue and its Limits

Toleration is an indeterminate and many-faceted concept, sometimes an aspirational ideal, aptly dubbed an "elusive virtue." Is it a praiseworthy moral principle or a second best tactical compromise, i.e. is toleration always an intrinsic "good," or is it only an instrumental "good," depending on its application? Toleration can be elevated from being a moral principle to which there can be exceptions, to being an absolute virtuous rule. Because of the fear of being labelled intolerant, toleration can become an absolutist obligation and its limits abused, eventually destroying toleration itself. Anyone having strong beliefs can be labelled as being (and may in fact be) intolerant by those who oppose them, but can be equally guilty of being intolerant themselves.

This discussion argues that the role of toleration in a separatist multicultural society should principally be one of an instrumental process for negotiation between the mainstream society and its separatist minorities. This should not be interpreted as being an unqualified imperative of acquiescing to every aspect of coexistence within such a pluralist society. Toleration can be virtuous, but only insofar as it is a prudential political mechanism for the avoidance or resolution of social conflict—cooperation and not confrontation— which is to say it should be a pragmatic but principled political and moral third way. Nevertheless, a cultural hegemonist could see toleration as being a misplaced virtue if its limits are so wide and incoherent that it acquiesces to the destruction of an indigenous culture.

Wisdom [1965:140–1] observed that "tolerance has been much praised" . . . [but] can be "false, or foolish, or unfair to others or unfair to oneself." The belief that toleration ought to qualify as a virtue merits examination—a virtue being a commendable disposition to follow an ethical ideal which contributes to "flourishing [fulfilment)] and happiness." Mary Warnock [1998:90] defines fundamental virtues as "Those which lead to co-operation; and for the sake of co-operation, my own wishes may have to go by the board," in which case toleration can qualify, if used instrumentally. Its virtuous foundation may be consequential, that is, producing good consequences for others rather than for the agent, such as the smooth running of a society. Or it may be ethical, that is, principally benefiting the agent's own self-fulfilment. Toleration, like justice, fairness, liberty, and equality, may be no more than self-indulgent licence, which can acquire a moralistic but seductive status, and can lead to a value-free society. The Chief Rabbi, in opposing the repeal of Section 28 on homosexual education in schools, put it well [TM 27 Jan. 00]. He said that it would lead to the "Promotion of a homosexual lifestyle as morally equivalent to marriage . . . if our society has become more tolerant, that is a good thing. However the current proposal is based on a fundamental confusion between tolerance and moral judgement. We are right to fight against prejudice, but quite wrong to suppose that this means abandoning a moral code shared by virtually all the world's great religions." In other words, toleration should not lead to moral blindness. Arblaster [1984:70] thinks that "In some ways tolerance can be a minimal and negative virtue. It means not interfering with people, leaving them alone. But leaving them alone can mean neglect." Although toleration can indeed be commendable, whether or not it is virtuous depends on its outcome and its underlying motive, which may be less than altruistic—namely, differentiating between the act and its motivation.

Peter Nicholson [1985:162 and 166] thinks that political toleration by governments and states should be a moral ideal. "Rather than being driven to toleration, we should deliberately seek it out. Toleration is not a second best, a necessary evil, a putting up with what we have to for the sake of peace and quiet, but a positive good, a virtue distinctive of the best people and the best societies . . . toleration is the virtue of refraining from exercising one's power to interfere with others' opinion or action, although that deviates from one's own over something important and although one morally disapproves of it." He distinguishes [169] "between the expression of opinions, which must always be tolerated, and the acting out of opinions, which need not always be tolerated." This is a distinction similar to that of the American judicial philosophy that distinguishes between expressions of *advocacy* and those of *incitement*. On the issue of censorship, Nicholson says [170] that "on this view of toleration, a government may not curb free expression of racialist opinions," and goes on to suggest other alternatives. "But the government may not proceed beyond persuasion; the final judge between opinions must be the individual." Mary Warnock [1987:125–6] takes issue with this view: "I simply do not believe that a distinction can be drawn as Nicholson seeks to draw it, between the moral and the non-moral, resting on the presumption that the moral is rational, or subject to argument, the non-moral a matter of feeling and sentiment . . . the concept of morality itself would wither away and become lost in the concept of expediency if strong feelings or sentiment were not involved in the judgement that something is morally right or wrong. This fact (for such, I [Warnock] take it to be) is of the greatest importance when we come to consider the question of the limits of toleration . . . we may simply feel, believe, conclude without reason, that something is unbearable, and must be stopped."

This is but one aspect of the debate about the role of government and the law on the issue of toleration. Because of its political and practical dimensions, it would seem to have been appropriate that the Morrell Trust on Toleration at the University of York was located in its Department of Politics. Another aspect of this debate arose in the 1960s with Devlin [1965] and Hart [1963], and the 1957 Wolfenden Report on homosexuality and prostitution. This debate reduced the principle as to whether the law should reinforce intolerance by enforcing a generally shared morality, or whether it should promote toleration by anticipating a shift in public morality, provided it did no harm by infringing liberty, invading privacy, or contempt for the law. If Britain is indeed a more tolerant society than it was, say, forty years ago, this reflects at least in part that its legislation has both anticipated and promoted toleration.

In Western culture, being tolerant is generally regarded as a personal characteristic that merits admiration, in contrast to being discriminatory and prejudiced, which are morally loaded transgressions. The Bible exhorts us to "love thy neighbour as thyself," and toleration has been encouraged by adages such as "turn a blind eye or the other cheek" and "live and let live." One of the four Platonic "natural" virtues is temperance, which the Thesaurus equates to moderation or restraint, and one of the three Christian virtues is charity, which the Thesaurus equates to indulgence. Hume saw a virtue in being that which is agreeable or useful to the possessor or to others. Toleration might thereby qualify as a virtue because of the agreeableness of its quality of magnanimity to the tolerator, and the usefulness of its quality of benevolence to the toleratee. Plato, in *The Republic*, saw that the virtue of a thing "is that state or condition which enables it to perform its proper function well." If this is so, it enabled Robert Wolff [1965:4] to see that "The virtue of the modern pluralist democracy which has emerged in contemporary America is tolerance . . . which enables a pluralist democracy to function well and to realize the ideal of pluralism." However [37–8], "The units of society between which tolerance and mutual acceptance are to be exercised are not isolated individuals but human groups, specifically religious, ethnic, and racial groups . . . we find a strange mixture of the greatest tolerance for what we might call established groups and an equally great intolerance for the deviant individual. The justification for this attitude, which would be straightforwardly contradictory on traditional liberal grounds, is the doctrine of pluralistic democracy. If it is good for each individual to conform to some social group and good as well that a diversity of social groups be welcomed in the community at large, then one can consistently urge group tolerance and individual intolerance." This he claims "eases the conflicts among antagonistic groups of immigrants, achieves a working harmony among several great religions, etc. . . . while at the same time encouraging the psychologically desirable forces of social integration which traditional liberalism tended to weaken." Some ethnic minorities perceive themselves as victims both as individuals and as a group, and that society as a whole is intolerant towards them. This reinforces their sense of grievance and separatism. Other ethnic minorities do not see themselves as victims, and opt to be left alone, often in two-domain separatism.

The incoherence of toleration as a moral ideal is that it could be seen as being contradictory, inasmuch that what is apparently accepted is actually rejected or is irreconcilable with a genuine conviction. The contradiction of toleration is that it is seen as being good, although it obliges us to put up with the bad, which cannot be good, or seeing value in an ideology or a religion which is not itself tolerant. This is not necessarily the paradox it might seem, because it may reflect a prioritisation of values including what counts as good, which to some extent is culturally dependent. Still, it cannot be virtuous to tolerate something which is clearly an evil. Hume said [1994:197] "t'is one thing to know a virtue and another to conform the will to it." Moreover, even if there is the will to be tolerant, it may not be able to survive unforeseen circumstances. In exploring the way in which contemporary democracies should deal with multiculturalism, Joseph Raz [1994:67] says that "The situation is analogous with that of a person who embarks on a journey to a distant destination. Ask him ahead of time to describe the route and he will be unable to do so"—namely, specifying the end without the means. "It is impossible to articulate comprehensively all the relevant moral considerations we are aware of, and impossible to state in general how much they weigh against each other in situations of conflict . . . not everything we know can we exhaustively state in the abstract. Moral knowledge escapes such formulation, and that means that moral theories are to be taken as mere approximations. Those who apply them inflexibly are fanatics heading for disaster."

Alasdair Macintyre [1991:1–20] is sceptical of false virtue. He says "what our contemporary political culture requires from those who claim public and political authority, is an appearance of virtue congruent with the rhetoric of shared values. And both that appearance and that rhetoric are well-served by the [vapid] indeterminacy of the virtue concepts of contemporary commonplace usage." He distinguishes between genuine virtues, and counterfeit virtues, which have the appearance of, but are not in fact, genuine virtues according to his criteria. These criteria include the act having not been performed for the "right" types of reasons or giving rise to the "right" kinds of responses in the virtuous agent. Self-righteousness (moral self-indulgence) is not seen as a virtuous response. MacIntyre argues that what the moral rhetoric of our political culture articulates and defends "is not an education in the virtues, but rather an education in how to seem virtuous without actually being so." If toleration is a temporary ploy, it may not be seen as a virtue, but as a self-serving moral condescension—an artificial virtue. It could be said that the psychology of the liberal view that toleration is a virtue is that it "feels good." Winston Churchill said that "Few facts are so encouraging . . . as the desire, which most men and all communities manifest at all times, to associate with their actions at least the appearance of moral right. However distorted may be their conceptions of virtue, however feeble their efforts to attain even to their own ideals, it is a pleasing feature and a hopeful augury that they should wish to be justified."

In some extreme circumstances, such as tolerating serious criminality, toleration is not commendable, although even this, given the virtue of forgiveness, is not without its advocates. Forgiveness might be seen as virtuous toleration, but provides the disconcerting precedent that future sins will also be tolerated. A former Chief Rabbi [DM 14 Dec. 95] gave the moral and pragmatic arguments against forgiveness for grievous crimes. He said "Forgiveness can be granted only by the individuals that have been wronged. It cannot be given at second hand. It is not something which can be dispensed by judges or politicians or by society at large. The [murder] victim is not in a position to forgive, and absolution can only be given by the Creator of life, God Himself. The rush to forgiveness can have a devastating impact on our society. It is under-mining justice, making a mockery of morality, and demoralising the decent law-abiding majority. If we are not prepared to mark our abhorrence of savagery, dishonesty and greed clearly and unambiguously, the core values of civilised society must be undermined. Forgiveness so easily translates into indulgence, and that kind of toleration has always been deeply damaging. Some kinds of behaviour are beyond the bounds of toleration. If we do not set limits to what is acceptable and what is not, if we forgive for the sake of it, we are collaborating in our own destruction." As well as Judaism, Islamic law and custom is said to hold that the blame for crime should be placed on the perpetrator. This contrasts with the late Cardinal Hume, the head of the Catholic Church in Britain, and Lord Longford, a prominent Catholic and prison reform campaigner, who have both urged forgiveness for convicted multiple killers. No doubt their admonitions reflect a generosity of Christian spirit, but neither were directly affected by these crimes, so they have little to forgive.

It is axiomatic that there is rarely genuinely complete and limitless toleration in human relationships. The English language has a discontinuity gap between tolerant and intolerant, and although there is eventually a firm limit or threshold, the process tends to be a continuum. A philosophy of liberal individualism and equality implies wide limits of toleration, but liberal individualism should not imply irresponsible tolerant egocentric hedonism, social atomisation, or neglect the relationship between individuals and society. Nor should equality imply an unlimited levelling of moral norms. At some point the collective interest takes precedence over individual claims. Limitless toleration would be anarchic, leading to the overturn of current norms and values, and would not be a virtue. In an idealistic and completely egalitarian society, all differential authority would be eliminated, and so the necessary condition for political, institutional, and social toleration would no longer exist.

Without limits or boundaries, both genuine and false toleration would be irresponsible because it may ultimately be harmful to others—the state, groups in society, or individuals. Wide limits of toleration may be interpreted as appeasement, which has the pejorative connotation of whetting the appetite for further concessions—appeasing the unappeasable. It also suggests a weakness or lack of conviction, or a non-evaluative acceptance of the unacceptable. The rhetoric of being "intolerant about intolerance" suggests that everything should be tolerated, as allegedly to do otherwise would be an infringement of the liberty of others. Hegel, amongst others, rejected this anarchic view—that man is free to the extent that he is guaranteed an (unlimited) sphere within which he can do anything he wishes without interference from others, who are guaranteed a like position. Lord Longford [Craig 1978:193], well-known for his advocacy of forgiveness said "[Freedom] can be abused and caricatured by those who treat it as a licence for unlimited selfishness and who show a total disregard of the community in the assertion of their own rights"—this would be a culture of "dutiless rights." On the other hand, dogmatic extremism, whether political or religious, undermines toleration, because it assumes that there is only one truth.

Given that toleration is normally accepted as a "good," there is a difference between this abstraction and what its limits should in practice be. The sceptic might see the benefit of toleration as one of making liberals "feel good," or a way of displaying a virtue, rather than as an objective, reflective, or responsible reaction to the issue. The arguments advanced to widen the existing limits of toleration, often in relation to moral standards, include (a) they already exist with a similar issue in our society; (b) although they do not yet exist in our society, they already exist in some other society; (c) although they do not exist at present in our society, they will in the longer term; and (d) although they are probably not acceptable now, they are an admirable ideal to which we should aspire.

It would be naive not to suppose that what may be presented as a moral case for wider limits of toleration may in fact have a different underlying motive. Once the limits have been widened and normalised, they then tend to be followed by further demands, preferably imposed by state legislation or promotion by a pressure group lobby, and a nibbling away can begin from the latest tolerated position. This is because, for a minority, toleration is not the same as acceptance. Nor is it nomalizing. It can be seen as patronising, or seen to hide a attitude of contemptuous superiority. History indicates that in a power struggle, too wide or imprecise limits of toleration can be seen as a weakness, appeasement, a lack of conviction, or an admission of guilt, and this precedent can become irreversible. On the other hand, the stronger the conviction about an issue, the limits become narrower and the scope for compromise less, and this conviction can be labelled judgmental or prejudiced. A compromise becomes possible only when the rational, emotional, or intuitive conviction of the other party becomes weakened, or a negotiated "quid pro quo" is found. As Butterfield [1975:573] observed, toleration is regarded not so much as an ideal, but a "retreat to the next best thing—a last resort." Toleration is rarely about "all or nothing" absolutes, and has limits which should be judged in relative terms. In a largely racially endemic world, the question "is Britain racially tolerant?" should be "how does the extent of racism in Britain compare with elsewhere in the West?" If Britain can in fact be credited with being a tolerant society, then its origin must at least in part be deterministic, nurtured by its indigenous culture.

If it seems appropriate that the limits of toleration should be widened, this should be done pragmatically and gradually, taking into account the actual experience and the reactions to it at each stage. This conservatism should ensure that the relaxation of limits does not create intolerance by the majority, which may be difficult to reverse. The acceptable limits can and normally do respond to a changing social/cultural environment, especially if they are not constrained by absolute principles or adverse experience of harm to society. For example, the legal and social toleration of homosexuality in Britain has altered significantly within the last forty years. The flexibility of the limits of toleration exercised by institutions and by individuals can differ. Toleration by individuals can allow for exceptions and excuses. Institutional toleration imposed by legislation applies to everyone without exception, but it will also be intolerant of individual exceptions. The administration of institutional toleration can also be "telescopic," inasmuch that an intolerant official can be distanced from the issue by its bureaucracy.

If all behaviour is tolerated, then there are no behavioural norms. Writing about 120 years ago when the rigid moral doctrines of Victorianism were threatened by the liberalism of Mill, the eminent Victorian judge James Fitzjames Stephen, a disciple of utilitarianism but a critic of Mill's toleration, wrote that "Complete moral tolerance is possible only when men have become completely indifferent to each other, that is to say when society is at an end." Even supposing that it is genuine and not harmful to others, open-ended toleration is not highly regarded. The tolerator is thought to have too little self-esteem, susceptible to manipulation, of being a martyr, or grossly unfair to himself. Nevertheless, Tinder [1995:211] advocates wide but selective limits of toleration: "We must distinguish among the upsetting, the dangerous, and the mortally threatening. The upsetting may not be dangerous, and the dangerous may not be mortally threatening. Even the dangerous, I [Tinder] am suggesting, should be tolerated in some measure. The upsetting should be tolerated even more fully." He [1–2] is however concerned with the "grey area" between toleration of expression and toleration of action which he argues can itself be a form of expression—which it may be, but more threatening and immediate. Limits of toleration tend to equilibrate around the importance of their consequences. For some types of behaviour they will be wide because of their substantial distancing, short duration, infrequency and reversibility. A burglar alarm will be tolerated because it is of temporary duration—a once-off occurrence, and a nuisance limited to a few neighbours. Outlandish clothes that are disliked or thought inappropriate will be accepted without comment or with indifference—their effect is localised, and does no harm to anyone else. There are no important consequences arising from radical views expressed in a university seminar because the audience is limited, there is no penalty, and it poses no threat. The difference in toleration displayed towards these relatively innocuous and limited day-to-day individual experiences differ from those in which a whole society feels its way of life to be under threat and sees as being permanent, irreversible, and harming the many, both born and as yet unborn. Fish [1994:217] calls this the "first law of tolerance-dynamics: Toleration is exercised in an inverse proportion to there being anything at stake." In Britain, the need to reduce teenage pregnancies (whose numbers are among the highest in Europe) has resulted from wide limits of sexual toleration. This need has taken priority over the morality of abortion, in that schoolgirls under the age of consent can now be given the "morning after" pill by the school nurse, without their parents knowledge [STM 7 Jan. 01].

Albeit from his position of political influence, Locke, and the Toleration Act 1689, proposed that the limits of toleration between the state and religion should be set by the principle that some groups forfeit their right to toleration by the rest of society. Mill later proposed a workable but generalised principle of the limits of toleration between individuals in general, and society and the state, and related these limits to the abstract notion of harm to others, which like his abstract criterion of "happiness and good" begs practical questions. Mill defended the autonomy of the individual against the unjustified interference of society and of the state, but the boundaries between private behaviour and public consequences can be diffuse. He claimed that freedom is essential to the originality and individuality of personal character. James Fitzjames Stephen [1967:80] parodied Mill's diversity by saying "Though goodness is various, variety in itself is not good. A nation in which everybody was sober would be a happier, better and more progressive, though a less diversified nation, than one of which half the members were sober and the other half habitual drunkards."

Mill's consequentialism supported those limits of toleration which maximised the "happiness" of the greatest number of people. A maximising utilitarian calculation taken together with one version of the "socialist" political theory of toleration would suggest that the limits of toleration by government and the institutions towards "harmful" cultural norms of minorities should be relatively narrow. This does not imply coercion or lack of respect. What it does suggest is that there are alternative criteria for the norms of toleration. If minorities do not accept and respect the cultural norms of the mainstream society, they should not expect theirs to be unreservedly accommodated, nor should they expect their public behaviour outside of these norms to be normalised by coercively widening the limits of toleration. Should not a reciprocal cost be expected from both the tolerated and the tolerator? The proverbs "love thy neighbour as thyself" and "do unto others as you would be done by" might be updated to: "the limits of toleration both received and given should be reciprocal."

Limits of toleration not only vary with distancing and with time, but between the individual, the group, and the society as a whole. Distancing from the issue can increase the limits, but proximity can sometimes also widen the limits due to direct experience increasing sympathy or empathy. Limits of toleration are not fixed or unidirectional, and they gradually change with the social, political, and economic environment in which the individual, the group and the society contemporaneously find themselves. They are generally wider whenever there is an environment of sustained economic prosperity and upward economic and social mobility. The limits of toleration towards different or non-conformist groups become tighter whenever a group is seen as having "too much influence," too many benefits, or becoming a threat. This can be the case when the critical mass of a minorities in a multicultural society is perceived by the majority as being too influential, or too wealthy in "their" society, or in certain businesses or key professions, such as law, finance and medicine. This has become particularly apparent with the Jewish, Asian and Chinese diaspora, and can be especially potent if this minority remains voluntarily segregated from the mainstream. Such was the case in Vienna pre-WW2, where Jews excelled in the arts, medicine and science, holding about seventy percent of the jobs in law, and about fifty percent in medicine. A similar concern is being voiced about the Chinese in Indonesia, as was the case in Uganda and Kenya regarding Asians who have concentrated in commerce and the professions [DT 18 June 96]. This is also happening against the white farmers in Zimbabwe and in Kenya [TM 10 May 00]. Racism, whenever combined with envy, results in hatred.

The response to the demands of articulate special or single interest pressure groups for more toleration should recognise that these lobbies have little or no obligation or interest in balancing other societal priorities and/or resources. They do not see it as their role or obligation to achieve a balanced or a stable outcome, they say that it is for others to argue their own case, or that it is for the politicians and the government to balance priorities and for society to bear the cost. Pressure groups that agitate for equality and against discrimination may harbour within themselves their own intolerant activists. Any improvement in legislation can be met with the complaint that "it does not go far enough," or "it should go the extra mile." The views broadcast to national television audiences by small but impressively titled special interest groups who might be assumed to represent a substantial opinion are tolerated in the interests of "balance," but often with little or no opportunity for substantial rebuttal. The "psychological violence" of mass demonstrations, sit-ins, or hunger strikes that are sometimes employed also trades on the fact that they will gain the attention of the media, thereby gaining a disproportionate share of publicity of a generally tolerant or apathetic public, and test the boundaries of tolerable behaviour. It was demonstrated with the tolerant policing of the anti-capitalism riots in London in 2000, and the defacing of the Cenotaph and other monuments, that public intolerance could for once be aroused—to the extent of the PM undertaking that "it would not be allowed to happen again." Zero tolerance tactics for policing petty and anti-social crime, which had been successful in New York, has also been tried in England and Wales.

The objective of most liberal pressure groups is for the limits of toleration to be replaced by a positive legal right, which removes the need for toleration. To be merely tolerated is something less than to be respected and positively welcomed as a member of society. A dilemma arises for a government whenever there is pressure for legislation that requires the legal normalisation of a departure from the behavioural norms. A responsibility of the government of a nation-state is to maintain and to protect the security and basic rights of its society as a whole, to maintain the norms of toleration, and to mediate between disputes, recognising that there are some issues that cannot be resolved solely by politicians. When a right has been granted, dissenting expressions or acts become ineffective and even prohibited, and they cease to be a matter of voluntary tolerant restraint. The practical problem arising with the drafting of legislation is that the limits and prioritization of rights cannot be defined linguistically with adequate specificity, and can only be expressed as general principles. They subsequently become prey to exploitation by legal activists experienced in appeal procedures, and who trade on the fact that once a claim has been allowed, a precedent is established. Legislation has to be "interpreted" by the judiciary, sometimes subjectively, as to "what was in the mind of parliament." The unintended consequences sometimes replaces toleration, and generally undermines respect for the law as a whole.

When wide limits of toleration become the norm, what was originally considered to be unacceptable but was condoned by apathy, lack of interest, indifference, or an attitude of virtuous tolerance, can be replaced by the accusation of the guilt-inducing sin of intolerance. Experience shows that in a liberal society, it is difficult to maintain stable limits of toleration, and there is always pressure to widen the established norms. The too ready acceptance of wider limits of toleration can lead to loss of guilt and responsibility by the tolerated. For the tolerator, this could result in the accusation of being patronising, or even in being viewed with contempt by the tolerated. Anti-abortionists may feel that the intention of the 1968 Abortion Act has since metamorphised into effectively tolerating abortion on demand. Anti-multiculturalists might feel that a similar unintended change might come about to their traditional way of life if some cultures succeeded in gradually normalising or legally imposing aspects of their political and cultural customs, values, and behaviour on the rest of society.

Although narrow limits of toleration may be seen as being judgmental of other lifestyles, a society is nevertheless entitled to be judgmental. If dissuaded from being so, its culture could become eroded. If the limits of its heretofore liberal toleration are finally breached, its resulting and now intolerant response can be abnormally severe or even violent. If this potential prognosis is recognised early on, then the toleration afforded should be conservative and tested before it is gradually relaxed. Moreover, limits of toleration should not be assumed to be founded on the premise of their being solely those of morality or claim rights, but also as having a political dimension. Using the Rushdie case as an example of the limits of toleration in Britain, compared with extremist Muslim intolerance, Gray [1995:24–5] suggests that "A policy of toleration must be willing to be repressive . . . toleration does not mandate turning a blind eye on those who flout the practices of freedom of expression that are among the central defining elements of liberal society in Britain: it mandates their suppression . . . the kind of diversity that is incompatible with civil society in Britain is that which rejects the constitutive practices that give it its identity . . . cultural traditions that repudiate these practices cannot be objects of toleration for liberal civil society in Britain or anywhere else." If the Iranians had displayed toleration in understanding the culture of the West, they might have said that, although neither Rushdie nor his book were acceptable in Muslim countries, and if he ventured there he would be executed, their fatwa (edict) would not be carried out as long as he was taking sanctuary in Britain, out of respect for its different culture.

NOTES

Arblaster, A. *The Rise and Decline of Western Liberalism.* Oxford: Basil Blackford. 1984. 69 and 70.

Butterfield, H. *Fourth Conference of the International Society for the History of Ideas.* Venice. September/October 1975. 573.

Craig, M. *Longford—A Biographical Portrait.* London: Hodder and Stoughton. 1978. 193.

Devlin, P. *The Enforcement of Morals.* Oxford: Oxford University Press, 1965.

Fish, S. *There's No Such Thing as Free Speech.* Oxford: Oxford University Press, 1994. 217.

Gray, J. *Enlightenment's Wake.* London: Routledge, 1995. 24–5.

Hart, H.L.R. *Law, Liberty and Morality.* Oxford: Oxford University Press, 1963.

Hume, D. "A Treatise of Human Nature." In *A Dictionary of Philosophical Quotations.* Ayer, A.J. and O'Grady, J. (Eds.) Oxford: Blackwell Publishers, 1994. 197.

MacIntyre, A. *How to Seem Virtuous Without Actually Being So.* Occasional Papers Series No. 1. Lancaster: Lancaster University, Centre for the Study of Cultural Values, 1991. 1–20.

Nicholson, P. "Toleration as a Moral Ideal." In *Aspects of Toleration.* Horton, J. and Mendus, S. (Eds.) London: Methuen, 1985. 162 and 166.

Ibid. 169 and 170.

Raz, J. "Multiculturalism—A Liberal Perspective." In *Dissent,* Winter 1994. 67.

Stephen, J. Fitzjames. *Liberty, Equality, Fraternity.* (Ed.) White, J.F. Cambridge: Cambridge University Press, 1967. 80.

Tinder, G. *Toleration and Community.* Columbia, Missouri: University of Missouri Press, 1995. 1–2.

Ibid. 211.

Warnock, M. *An Intelligent Person's Guide to Ethics.* London: Gerald Duckworth, 1998. 90.

Warnock, M. "The Limits of Toleration." In *On Toleration.* Mendus, S. and Edwards, D. (Eds.) Oxford: Clarendon Press, 1987. 125–6.

Wisdom, J. *Paradox and Discovery.* Oxford: Basil Blackwell, 1965. 140–1.

Wolff, R. P. "Beyond Tolerance." In *A Critique of Pure Tolerance.* Wolff, R.P. and Moore, B. et al. Boston: Beacon Press. 1965. 4 and 37–8.

27

Pragmatism and the Politics of Negotiation

This discussion contends that the limits of toleration towards alien cultures by a society that is committed to maintaining its traditional culture should not a priori be wide. Its toleration should not be deemed an idealistic moral ought, but should instead reflect a principled but conservative pragmatism: the political, social, and economic measures that are found to work and are generally tolerated and acceptable over the course of time. This implies the minimum intervention of government and the institutions of the nation-state in multiculturalism, either directly in its promotion, or indirectly in acquiescing to its furtherance. This policy recognises that although the indigenous majority has valid claims and concerns, these will not be advanced by coercive social engineering. In a democracy, authoritative social coercion is likely to be counter-productive, whereas gradual voluntarianism is more likely to work, albeit over a longer period of time.

Political pragmatism is neither "laissez faire," nor should it be short-term populism. Populism, which has a derogatory label, implies reponding to the feelings and views of the mass of "ordinary' people. It merits disapproval if it is knee jerk short-term opportunism. Political pragmatism has become fashionable in Britain in the post-ideological/post-modern age of managerial politics. The exponent of non-ideological political pragmatism is present Prime Minister Tony Blair. He believes that the realisation of his objectives is not in following the "Old Labour" (socialist) ideology, but one that incorporates the amorphous concepts of "modernising," "new," "embracing change," "inclusive" or "what works." Pragmatism can be seen as the philosophy of principled consequentialism. But it can also be unprincipled, lack direction, lead to apathy, cynicism, and a loss of political identity and conviction, and suggest that politics no longer works. This can be particularly so if what politicians publicly espouse as their principles they ignore in practice when convenient, or are seen to be mutually contradictory. Nor can one be sure that all change will work, for whom it will work, or if it will create unforseeable precedents. A feature of political pragmatism is the managing of extremes in which toleration has a part to play. It is the art of the possible and acceptable, rather than being driven by a purist ideology. It will involve a degree of sceptical realism that will modify ideals, and in some circumstances permit a utilitarian approach of the ends justifying the means. It can allow for *feelings*, whereas a strictly objective approach cannot. It can also allow a compromise between idealism and realism, and between the prudential and the moral. Reaching a negotiated compromise may require the prioritisation of some otherwise compelling principles and values.

Putnam [1995:22] takes such a view of morality. He says that "For [William] James, as for Socrates and his successors, the opposition between philosophy which is concerned with how to live and philosophy which is concerned with hard technical questions, is a false opposition. We want ideals and we want a world view, and we want our ideals and our world view to support one another . . . Today [1–2] we tend to take the ideas of tolerance and pluralism for granted . . . Few people realise that that [diversity of views and the clash of difference of opinions] is not how those societies [ancient Athenian or late Roman] themselves saw the matter. Classical thinkers saw diversity of opinions as a sign of decay and heresy; only since the Enlightenment have we been able to see it as a positive good . . . [while] the belief in tolerance is itself a 'shared moral belief,' and a most important one, it is true that modern societies are not held together by a single shared comprehensive world view. They are not held together by any one religion, and if there are still shared moral beliefs, there are no unchallenged moral beliefs . . . [3] pragmatism offers something far better than the unpalatable alternatives which too often seem to be the only possibilties today, both philosophically and politically."

Michael Oakeshott [1983:68–9] has drawn a realistic distinction between following moral rules (principles) and following moral ideals. He says "a morality which takes the form of the self-conscious pursuit of moral ideals is one which, at every moment, calls upon those who practise it to determine their behaviour by reference to a vision of perfection. This is not so much the case when the guide is a moral rule, because the rule is not represented as perfection and constitutes a mediation, a cushion, between the behaviour it demands on each occasion, and the complete moral response to the situation. But when the guide of conduct is a moral ideal, we are never suffered to escape from perfection . . . a morality of ideals has little power of self-modification; its stability springs from its inelasticity and its imperviousness to change . . . It has a great capacity to resist change, but when that resistance is broken down, what takes its place is not change but revolution—rejection and replacement; Moreover, every moral ideal is potentially an obsession . . . Too often the excessive pursuit of one ideal leads to the exclusion of others, perhaps all others . . . Every admirable ideal has its opposite, no less admirable." Oakeshott makes the pragmatic case for accepting the best possible, and not insisting on the perfect.

There are limits to moral pragmatism that cannot be defended. Such was the flawed prioritisation by Pope Pius XII towards the Holocaust, and the Vatican support of the Nazi Ustashe puppet regime in Croatia. Between 1941 and 1945, 487,000 Orthodox Serbs, 27,000 Gypsies, and 30,000 Jews were massacred, largely by the Ustashe, and although the Pope was aware of the fate of European Jewry, he failed to denounce this in 1942 [TM 05 Oct. 99]. Presumably, his overriding priorities were the German defeat of atheist Communist Russia, and the survival of the Catholic Church. Butterfield [1973:578] notes that Richelieu and the Catholics left the Huguenots with their religious privileges intact after he had taken from them their military and political privileges. His was a pragmatic policy of assimilation, because he thought that this generosity would win them over in the long run to what he considered to be the true religion. A similar approach to developing a religious belief that would be tolerable to all was a policy of "comprehension,' namely, "to see Christianity reduced to a restricted number of inescapable doctrines . . . finding a lowest common factor, and regarding the rest as nonesential."

Taylor [1974:253–4] argues the case for pragmatic conservatism in any changes to a traditional morality [or culture] between the extremes of all-out radicalism and all-out liberalism: [A traditional morality] "should not be lightly tossed aside in favour of new precepts, just because these are new and therefore exciting. Such change should be evolutionary—it should occur quietly by way of small specific steps, taken only after due consideration, and then tested over a sufficient period before being accepted as being successful. If deemed unsuccessful any step should be abandoned in favour of what existed before or of what can be proved to be more successful." This discussion believes that this should be the approach to the "novel and exciting precept" of the diversity and difference of cultural pluralism, and should follow the methodology constructed by Dewey: the instrumental use of philosophical knowledge (relating, in this case, to toleration) to assist in the resolution of a contemporary social/political problem. Toleration has a prudential and instrumental value as a negotiating tactic for resolving conflicts arising from difference when no other outcome is likely, other than continued division or conflict. So said the eminent Victorian lawyer James Fitzjames Stephen [1967:13]: "Toleration is in its proper sphere, so long as its object is to mitigate inevitable struggles." To be of practical value in a negotiation, toleration should be reciprocal and not seen as a uni-directional virtue. Reciprocal toleration can facilitate a compromise to find the right balance, or to arrive at a settlement between conflicting priorities and objectives. Questioning the virtue of toleration does not imply that it is devoid of "good"—its utility is that it can manifest a genuine desire to find the limits of acceptability at which the aspirations of two otherwise conflicting parties can be reconciled.

John Rawls [1973:220] has given his views as to whether justice requires the toleration of the intolerant, and if so, under what conditions. He concludes that "While an intolerant sect (or religion or culture) does not itself have title to complain of intolerance, its freedom should be restricted only when the tolerant sincerely and with reason believe that their own security and that of the institutions of liberty are in danger. The tolerant should curb intolerance only in this case . . . It is only the liberty of the intolerant which is to be limited, and this is done for the sake of equal liberty under a just constitution the principles of which the intolerant themselves would acknowledge in the 'original position.'" The practical questions here are: does Rawls' term "security and institutions of liberty" include the preservation of the majoritative culture, which they at least consider to be essential? and what should be the limits of tolerance before an intolerant minority becomes sufficiently politically empowered?

Labrousse [1973:120] characterises the appeal of Locke's religious toleration as one of "enlightened self-interest." In reflecting the individualism and utilitarianism of the seventeenth century, tranquility and prosperity are the supreme values—cooperation and not confrontation. Locke defined the limits between religion and the state, and Mill defined the limits between the individual and society. Federalists define the limits of authority centrally versus locally. Preston King points to the role of compromise in the context of multiculturalism, which he likens to contract theory [1976:212–3], and says that "What the full realisation of equal rights in this sphere would demand is not the creation of a strict homogeneity between all sections of a community, but the elimination or suppression of those aspects of a cultural tradition which negatively batten upon the differences between one tradition and another . . . where a cultural item of itself tends to generate hostility towards other peoples, then impliedly that item would require to be modified in such a way as to omit such hostility." In a separatist multicultural society, the practical difficulty arises as to how a mutually acceptable modification is be achieved, if at all. Whilst both parties might seek to retain their "unalienable rights," and although some of these might be modified for the benefit of both parties, others might be maintained as being non-negotiable. Each party cannot simply aim to maintain its original position, but should attempt to accommodate the other position. A problem with multiculturalism is how such a demarcation can be established that separates the legitimate claims of separatist minorities from the proper exercise of the political authority and will of the majority represented by the state. It may also be asked, what sanctions can and should the state impose for transgressions? Provided that an agreement can be reached, the individual, the group, or the institution would be left with those rights which have not been surrendered. Hiltrop and Udall [1995:9] recognise the influence of differing cultures on negotiating tactics, namely that "One of the biggest mistakes in any discussion of negotiation practices is to ignore differences between cultures. What makes someone a good negotiator in one culture may well not work in another . . . different social groups have different ideas of what is proper protocol and procedure. The emphasis on preliminaries varies, and the order and spirit in which different elements of negotiation are approached can be different among cultures." Different cultures can have different concepts of what constitutes "justice" and "fairness" and secular versus religious priorities.

The negotiating processes of compomise, bargaining, and accommodation (rather than control) in a deeply divided society in which the interests and desires of groups conflict is discussed by Ian Lustick [1978–9]. This consociational approach is a process whereby initial objectives are modified to a level of mutual acceptance by a process of prioritisation, which leads to a demarcation between the interested parties. He notes [334] that "All consociational models contain the assumption that sub-unit elites share an overarching commitment to the perpetuation of the political arena within which they operate." An attitude of mutual toleration (goodwill) is therefore the essential prerequisite and environment for any negotiation, without which it is unlikely to succeed—nor will it succeed if the objectives/principles are completely incompatible or incompatible with other factors or the cultures are antipathetic to the objectives. Not all differences can be resolved by the rhetoric of "getting round a table." There must be a genuine desire to establish a workable agreement by not "asking for the earth,'" and a climate of mutual trust must underwrite the belief that the agreement will be adhered to. In commerce, this is underwritten by the law of contract, but in settlements not enforceable by law, reliance on trust is essential. Both parties must be open to "reason," but where either or both parties dogmatically insist on absolute and/or religious principles, it is unlikely that a compromise will be reached. If these principles purport to identify fundamental interests, they cannot be prioritised for other interests in a maximising utility calculation. Exactly what form the negotiating process might take cannot be generalised, because its objectives and circumstances will differ. Negotiation will not always succeed on the international scale, as in the case of the United States making enormous efforts over the past decade to resolve the Israeli/Palestinian dispute.

If one party to the negotiation does not exhibit at the outset an attitude of bilateral toleration and trust, then as a sign of good faith, albeit for a limited period, the acceptance by the other party of a degree of a benign intolerant behaviour may encourage reciprocity. Belligerent intolerance should not be tolerated, and rewards and sanctions can be used by the state to demonstrate the limits of its toleration. The 1998 Good Friday Ulster Agreement was a pragmatically negotiated, but nevertheless fudged, accord. By the early 1990s, the IRA. had realised that their violence had been contained by the security forces, and that to further their aims they should now negotiate. The British government tolerated some breaches of the founding 1993 Downing Street Declaration, made possible by its ambiguity of language, to achieve the end objective of rule by democratic consent. However, because the vital issue of the decommissioning of IRA arms had been fudged in the 1998 Agreement—was it a pre-condition or was it only an objective?—after twenty-one months, the basic "no guns no government" principle resulted in devolution being suspended in February 2000 and twice in 2001, and the "peace process" put on hold. It was reconvened by a narrow vote of the majority Ulster Unionist Party after the IRA had first given an undertaking to "put its arms beyond use" as verified by two independent inspectors, and then finally the IRA actually decommissioned one arms dump. There now exists a semi-peace in Ulster, as there does in the Balkans.

Amy Gutmann [1993:172] discusses the controversy inherent in a multicultural society, which often arises because the standards of justice associated with different cultural groups conflict, as their different ethical standards yield opposing judgements on realising social justice. She rejects the "three important common responses to this challenge—cultural relativism, political relativism and comprehensive universalism—and [aims to] develop a more defensible response which [she] calls 'deliberative universalism.'" This seems to be a euphemism for a negotiated compromise having similar requirements and facing the same limitations, particularly when the differences are seemingly irreconcilable. She claims [206] that "Deliberative universalism offers an alternative to the cultural relativist view that social justice is what any particular culture deems to be just; the political relativist view that determines social justice by the outcome of legitimate procedures; and the comprehensive universalist [cosmopolitan] view that social justice consists of a comprehensive set of substantive moral prescriptions that apply to all human beings regardless of their particular culture." Warnock [1998:16] argues that "We must distinguish, though not absolutely, public from private morality . . . [50] as far as public morality goes, the concept of the acceptable is necessary, in that it may set the best goal possible in the circumstances." Public morality must be seen to be "reasonable" and for the common good, and people must be aware of long-term and unintended consequences; private morality is a mixture of individual principles, conscience, and sentiment.

On the global scale, nation-states having markedly differing ethno-national cultures manage to co-exist peacefully by recognising territorial boundaries along with a limited number of mutually accepted objectives, and usually have a tacit arms-length toleration of their differences. Within the confines of a multiracial/ ethnic/religious state such as was the case with Yugoslavia, endemic ethno-national and cultural conflicts are liable to break out, which experience has yet again shown that pre-emptive dialogue is unlikely to resolve. The lack of trust and the intensity of the intolerance across a major cultural faultline is too great for negotiation to initially succeed. Even if sponsored by a third party "honest broker," or mediator such as Senator Mitchell in Ulster, negotiation is only likely to succeed when the physical cost or emotional watershed in continuing the conflict has led to the emergence of a shift in attitude (albeit non-altruistic) to tolerant compromise and guarded trust between the opposing parties.

Any agreed demarcation/compromise between the conflicting rights of the mainstream and separatist ethnic groups in a nation-state must be firm, non-ambiguous, and not the basis for future creeping re-negotiation. A pluralist society can only co-exist stably if its limits of toleration are reciprocal, meaning, not only those expected and taken, but also those offerred and given up. The emphasis here is on all groups, not just the mainstream group. It is strongly argued that a minority cannot expect to claim the benefits of the rights and values associated with a democratic liberal and individualistic mainstream culture unless they are prepared to offer an equivalent communality and reciprocity of toleration. If this is not the case, then the ultimate sanction is that the "status quo" and priorities of the majority should prevail. This is justified by the responsibility of social stability together with a maximising utilitarian calculation, tempered by respect and fairness.

NOTES

Butterfield, H. "Toleration In Early Modern Times." In *Fourth Conference of the International Society for the History of Ideas*. Venice. September/October 1975. 578.

Gutmann, A. "The Challenge of Multiculturalism in Political Ethics." In *Philosophy and Public Affairs*. vol. 22. no. 3. Summer 1993. 172 and 206.

Hiltrop, J-M. and Udall, S. *The Essence of Negotiation*. London: Prentice Hall. 1995. 95.

Oakeshott, M. *On History and Other Essays*. Oxford: Basil Blackford, 1983. 68–9.

King, P. *Toleration*. London: George Allen and Unwin. 1976. 159.

Ibid. 212–3.

Labrousse, E. *Religious Toleration—Dictionary of the History of Ideas*. vol. iv. USA: Charles Scribner's Sons, 1973. 120.

Lustick, I. "Stability in Deeply Divided Societies—Consociationalism Versus Control." In *World Politics*. vol. 31. October/July 1978/79. 334.

Putnam, H. *Pragmatism*. Oxford: Blackwell Publishers, 1995. 1–2 and 22.

Ibid. 1–3

Rawls. J. *A Theory of Justice*. Oxford: Oxford University Press, 1973. 216–21.

Stephen, J. Fitzjames. *Liberty, Equality, Fraternity*. (Ed.) White, J.F. Cambridge: Cambridge University Press, 1967. 13.

Taylor, W. *Man and Nature*. London: Regency Press, 1974. 253–4.

Warnock, M. *An Intelligent Person's Guide to Ethics*. London: Gerald Duckworth, 1998. 16 and 50.

28

Cultural Nationalism and Multiculturalism Revisited

Difficult questions and difficult decisions face any culturally pluralist society, but particularly if it purports to positively welcome "diversity and difference." The outcome will either be some form of cultural and social separatism; or some undefineable eclectic culture will evolve; or, as this discussion argues, a stable society will survive the impact of ethnic and cultural diversity only if cultural assimilation with the indigenous society, at least in all its essential features, is in time gradually adopted by its minorities. Whatever the eventual outcome, it will naturally evolve, because although government can influence the outcome, it cannot proscribe it. This discussion argues that most indigenous societies have lived for too long in their historically constituted form for them to be prepared to readily forsake it for some form of cultural pluralism. The indigenous majority has this natural right, justified by a utilitarian calculation, and merited by their self-evident precedence. This natural right is conceived here as being the historical condition that a society would inherit if there had been no coercive intervention by a domestic government or an international agency. If so, this poses the question of "what should be the role and the limits of toleration towards multiculturalism in a nation-state committed to preserving its majoritative cultural hegemony?" There are three prima facie "givens." Firstly, that a nation-state has a natural right to preserve its cultural hegemony, assuming that this is its democratic will. Secondly, it is generally accepted that cultural homogeneity is a prerequisite for a stable society. Thirdly, that within a majoritative democracy, its government has a political mandate, if not a positive responsibilty, to prioritise this claim over any competing claims of its minorities. The issue reduces itself to the means by which this outcome can be properly achieved. Rex [1986:133] maintains that "Multiculturalism is only likely to be tolerated, if it does not threaten the shared civic culture, including of course the idea of equality of opportunity." This remark has to be considered from the standpoint of the government and the institutions of the state, and from the perception of its individual citizens, including those in both the mainstream and the minorities. A minimalist, or procedural version, sees the state as remaining essentially neutral between different interest groups who may be competing with one another. If so, they negotiate with each other, provided that they do not disturb the peace. A maximalist version sees the state as providing every group as far as practicable, with the support to pursue their particular concept of a good life. Taken literally, these two extremes are too simplistic to satisfy the complex issue of cultural pluralistic diversity and difference.

In his article "The New Right and the Politics of Nationhood," Professor Parekh says that the term "New Right" is of questionable value [1986:33]: "A careful examination of the history of conservatism would show that the allegedly new features [of the New Right] are not really all that new . . . [and that] some of these beliefs are shared by the Left as well and informed the policies pursued by successive Labour governments in the sixties and seventies." This is correct and has become even more true in the late 1990s under New Labour. He asserts that "It is suicidal and profoundly illiberal to suggest that Britain should give it [toleration] up and and resort to the crazy and inherently implausible schemes of repatriation and forced assimilation in order to attain the regressive and inherently impractical goal of nationhood." This is true insofar as the means proposed are unacceptable, but the goal of nationhood is not. At least when writing in 1986 [42], he seemed to accept that assimilation was feasible: "Customs and practices are never static. As people settle down to a new environment, they undergo a process of cultural adaptation and come closer to the host communities," and he also recognised that "What characterises Britain as a civilised society is its liberal tradition of tolerance and respect for individuals and groups holding different beliefs." In the Parekh Report [2000] issued fourteen years later, he seems to have distanced himself from assimilation and tolerance towards a policy of cultural/racial integration by legislation that enforces an equality of outcome for all ethnic groups.

The Runnymede Trust is a multicultural pressure group "dedicated to the development of a successful and equal and culturally diverse society." It sponsored in October 2000 a 400 page report of its twenty-four member commission—*The Future of Multiethnic Britain*—known by the name of its chairman as the Parekh Report. This report was on similar lines to the Swann Report published fifteen years earlier, which had proposed an integrationist educational solution to cultural pluralism. Its back cover proclaimed that "No other European country, nor even the United States, has produced such a report. All discussions of multiethnic Britain from now on will have to take this as their basis." This study was set up in January 1998 and was funded by more than £350,000 of public (National Lottery) money. In fact, this report served to highlight the concerns of many people in Britain about the end game of some multiculturalists.

The report [Parekh 2000] concluded with 124 recommendations, most of which were in line with its overriding political agenda, and proposed the setting up legislation, national commissions, committees, statutory duties, monitoring, targets, policies, programmes, structures, task forces, working parties, equity plans, forums, appeal panels/research/investigations/studies/ reviews/appraisals/reports/audits, grants, funding, and "guidance." These recommendations were directed at government departments and agencies, and non-government organisations, for intervention by the state in what it perceived as race-related issues. To achieve its objective, it proposed the imposition of a programme of social engineering with little concern as to its acceptabilty, substantive justification, or the views of the "silent majority" of the population. In so doing, it attempted to dissociate national identity with the unity of "stock and kind." One of its comments [224] for achieving this is that "Political leaders should shape, not pander to, public opinion on issues relating to race and diversity." This is a common plea of single-issue pressure groups, and says little for the legitimacy of public opinion. This multicultural pressure group represents no more than approximately eight percent of the population, with the largest ethnic group comprising about three percent. It recommended [313] that "The government should formally declare that the United Kingdom is a multicultural society, and should issue a draft declaration for consultation"—or social engineering by decree. Britishness was further demolished [38]: "Britishness, as much as Englishness, has systematic, largely unspoken, racial connotations. Whiteness nowhere features as an explicit condition of being British, but it is widely understood that Englishness, and therefore by extension Britishness, is racially coded . . . Race is deeply entwined with political culture and with the idea of nation and underpinned by a distinctively British kind of reticence—to take race and racism seriously, or even to talk about them at all . . . unless these deep-rooted antagonisms to racial and cultural difference can be defeated in practice, as well as symbolically written out of the national story, the idea of a multicultural post-nation remains an empty promise." The report accepted [56] that "Britain needs to be, certainly, 'One Nation'—but understood as a community of communities and a community of citizens, not a place of oppressive uniformity based on a single substantive culture. Cohesion in such a community derives from widespread commitment to certain core values, both between communities and within them: equality and fairness; dialogue and consultation; toleration, compromise and accommodation; recognition of and respect for diversity; and—by no means least—determination to confront and eliminate racism and xenophobia." Most people would recognise this as a fair description of British society and its culture as it exists today. The concept of civic nationalism was also seen as inadequate [19]. "Civic nationalisms are always embedded in particular cultural values and traditions. They involve not only a rational allegiance to the state, but also an intuitive, emotional 'ethnic' allegiance to the nation. It is these deeper cultural meanings that make a nation-state an imagined community."

The Runnymede Commission report rejected [45] assimilation because it asserts that "The essential problem with the nationalist and assimilationist model, is that it is based on a false premise of what Britain is and has been. Britain is not and never has been a homogeneous society . . . Assimilation is a fantasy, for there is no single culture into which all people can be incorporated." The multicultural "Vision for Britain" to which it aspires [42] is "pluralist" [termed in this discussion *integrationist*]: "There is both a unity and diversity in public life; communities and identities overlap and are interdependent, and develop common features . . . [43] it rejects the hard and fast distinction between public and private realms and envisages that the public realm should be continually revised to accommodate cultural diversity in society at large. Unlike the 'liberal' [two-domain] view, this model does not place the political culture beyond negotiation, and it maintains that recognition, as distinct from toleration, should be a central value. At the same time it envisages that there should be considerable interdependence and overlap within and between the various communities that constitute a society, and that these dynamic realities should be welcomed and protected." It added [x] "The term 'integration' is even more misleading, as it implies a one-way process in which 'minorities' are to be absorbed into the non-existent homogeneous cultural structure of the 'majority'" (note that this discussion sees this as being assimilation). Parekh argued [11] that "The essential task is to move [Britain] from the 'multicultural drift' to a purposeful process of change." Maybe the Commission felt that the natural "drift" of gradual voluntary transculturalisation and adaptation is resulting in *too* much assimilation. It claimed [44] that "This [Parekh's "pluralist"] model is to be found in acknowledged multicultural societies such as Canada, Australia, Malaysia and India"—note that the United States is not mentioned. No evidence is given for this claim, which could be disputed, and even if it were true, the history and nature of these societies differ from one another and from Britain, so their experience is not transferable. Schlesinger, in his book *The Disuniting of America* [1992:11], quotes Ignatieff (the English-resident son of a Russian-born Canadian diplomat, and thus presumably an example of the modern mixing of peoples) as saying "Here we have one of the five richest nations on earth, a country [Canada] so uniquely blessed with space and opportunity that the world's poor are beating at the door to get in, and it is tearing itself apart . . . If one of the top five developed nations on earth can't make a federal, multiethnic state work, who else can?"

The report acknowledged [53] that "Like any other society, Britain needs common values to hold it together and give it a sense of cohesion. At the same time it must acknowledge that its citizens belong to a variety of moral traditions and subscribe to and live by a range of values. Therefore common values cannot simply be the values of one community, even if it is the numerical 'majority,' but must emerge from democratic dialogue and be based on reasons individuals belonging to different moral and cultural traditions can agree on. They should not be so defined that they rule out legitimate moral differences or impose a particular rule of life on all."

Taken literally, this suggests that British society and its core values do not meet this criterion, and that British cultural values, which have been developed over centuries and are generally accepted and shown to work, have to be justified to a disparate group of minorities who may have fundamentally differing views on what they believe to be "legitimate moral differences." If each value cannot be satisfactorily justified to each ethnic group, then it has to be changed to something else, the nature of which is not clear. In turn, it will probably be no more likely to satisfy everyone. In any case, Parekh recognised that [52] "Disputes sometimes arise between a cultural community and a state institution, for example a school. Also there are disputes both between communities and within them in which the state cannot remain neutral." It rejects moral universalism and the "no-harm" principle, and discusses two ways of resolving such disputes: (1) reference to the majority's values and customs (i.e. assimilation, which it rejects), or (2) arriving at a consensus through intercultural deliberation, which it claims is frequently the only effective solution. The numerous ethno-national conflicts around the world indicate that some of the values and customs of differing ethnic cultures seriously conflict with one another, and are not resolvable by negotiation. Domestic cultural universalism is therefore hardly a option for a state. If irresolvable inter-ethnic conflicts arise in Britain, or cultural practices that seriously conflict with British values and customs, clearly the will of the majority must prevail. The report acknowledged [54] that "On the basis of such values [international human rights] it is legitimate to ban female circumcision; forced marriage; cruel punishment of children, and repressive and unequal treatment of women, even though these practices may enjoy cultural authority in certain communities." It attributed these prohibitions to international human rights standards rather than to the legislation, and more particularly the enforcement that already exists in Britain and is derived from its cultural values. The report continued "It should respect the custom in many cultures of basing marriages on introductions arranged by parents. It may also rightly insist that parents should not deny full-time education or opportunities for self-development to their daughters, but should respect their desire to withdraw them from certain kinds of sports." None of these are banned or otherwise prevented by British society. Although female circumcision was made illegal in 1985, not a single prosecution has been brought because of lack of the victims' evidence, although anecdotal evidence indicates that the practice is increasing [TM 1 April 99].

The report also contains anecdotal evidence of discrimination. Two such items focused on discrimination in the NHS, which is at present badly stretched for financial and other resources, and urgently appealing for organ transplant donors. One incident [176] was of a Somali interpreter complaining that the hospital had no budget to pay for his six hour interpreting session. He was upset because the hospital said that they would otherwise have asked relatives or a cleaner. Another alleged racist incident [176] was in the NHS conforming to the condition imposed by the relatives of an organ transplant donor—that the organ should only be given to a white recipient. This decision, we argue, respected the individual's autonomy. There was case reported in the press of "reverse racism," when an Asian donor laid down a similar condition for a Muslim recipient [TM 9 July 99]—though in this case the NHS declined the organs.

The recommendations of the Parekh report on immigration and asylum are largely confined to easing controls. However, its proposals [217] included a policy for the promotion of "public acceptance of and welcome for the diverse, multiethnic society that has been created as a consequence of immigration." Does this imply that the "consequence(s) of immigration" either are, or should be, unreservedly and universally accepted? It also recommended [309] that "The government should carry out and publicise research into the economic impact, and potential economic benefits, of immigration." This would be worthwhile, but the outcome might not be as this report expected. The report did not directly recommend employment quotas or positive discrimination, but it in effect did this by "equity plans," which would be enforced on all employers by regulation. Thus, it recommended [199] that "All public bodies and institutions, and all businesses in the private sector, should be required by legislation, to develop their own employment equity plans and to adjust these on the basis of regular monitoring ... [200] Such legislation should give the CRE power (a) to demand information about employment equity plans; (b) to obtain binding undertakings; and (c) to institute proceedings against businesses that have not introduced plans or have failed to implement them. Employment tribunals should have the power to order businesses to take appropriate action and, if they fail to observe such orders, to pay financial compensation."

This illiberal and tendentious report received a severely hostile reaction as shown by most of the articles and correspondence written to the national press. One British Indian wrote "Rarely has a study been so opposed by some of the very people whose interests it claimed to champion" [DM 21 Oct. 00]. Another former immigrant wrote "Racism can only be worsened by routinely using multiculturalism to beat the host community on the head. Common sense, prudence and justice require that immigrants treat the culture of their hosts with respect and learn to appreciate it, which most do" [TM 17 Oct. 00]. Another correspondent observed [TM 20 Oct. 00] "It is quite another matter to insist that 'multiculturalism' requires the cultural attributes and preferences and social divisions imported with migration to be permanently preserved by public policy in an ethnically corporate state. Justice and common sense lead to other conclusions. Migrants move at their own wish and for their own benefit. Their cultural preferences are a private matter. Migrants should in general accommodate themselves to local conditions, not oblige the customs and institutions of their new home to make way for them. The claims of their children born in the UK need a more complex response." Another wrote (unfairly) [TM 17 Oct. 00] that "The Runnymede Trust study might lead to a new Kosovo for future generations of this country."

Much of the hostile criticism was directed towards the assertion [38] that "It is evidently plain, however, that the word 'British' will never do on its own." This one comment overshadowed any serious media discussion about the many other substantial aspects of multiculturalism the report considers. The object of this assertion is to deconstruct and thereby demolish the belief that a distinct British national identity exists. Even the Home Secretary who, originally "launched" the report, said [TM 12 Oct. 00] "Unlike the Runnymede Trust, I firmly believe that there is a future for Britain and Britishness. I am proud to be British and what I believe to be the best of British values . . . redefining Britishness did not mean rejecting the idea of a single Britain or Britishness as a cultural force." A TV phone call poll was carried out immediately after the report was published. It asked "Do you think that 'British' carries a racist tag [overtone]?" Ninety-seven percent said "No" and three percent said "Yes" [ITV 11 Oct 00].

Yasmin Alibhai-Brown is a prominent multiculturalist who was a member of the Runnymede Trust Commission. In her review of race relations today in Britain, titled *Who Do We Think We Are?—Imagining a New Britain*, she describes her Indian, Ismaili, Ugandan, and British background, and is married to an Englishman. Mrs. Alibhai-Brown was generous enough to wish me well with the publication of this book. She is an admirer of Professor Parekh [2000:18]: "I have read every word Bhikhu Parekh has written in the past five years. He is arguably the most extraordinary commentator we have in this country." Alibhai-Brown is opposed to assimilation and separatism, and is an aspirational integrationist whose views are worth noting. Her book relies largely on individual interviews, and she comments intolerantly on those, past and present, who do not agree with her views. Typically [3–4], she states "Academics have, admittedly, been occupied with exploring these [multicultural] issues for some time, but they are largely people who recoil from any democratic obligations to make their work accessible or inclusive; their themes have been played out in ivory towers and their state-funded wisdom has not filtered into daily life. Educators, politicians, editors, even artists have not, on the whole, been able to answer the need to comprehend and engage with the massive transformations or interpret the complex realities within our nation. This is an unforgivable abdication of responsibility and opportunity which, if taken up by our leaders, would have enabled the distinct and changing communities of this country not simply to 'tolerate' one another but to interact in more robust ways and perhaps to create a country that is more optimistic and more at peace with itself. It is telling to realize that there is less optimism today about the future of a multicultural Britain than there was in 1968." Arguably, there are few in Britain, other than dedicated multiculturalists, who would recognise these reasons for this prognosis.

Alibhai-Brown believes [103] that "What all of us—black and white Britons—should be wanting is to participate in the creation of a new nation for the next century; to work with the various tribes of white Britain and black Britain to create something as dynamic, to embark on a project as revolutionary, as the one taken up by idealists in South Africa . . . a new country forged after melting down the best bits of the old." She continues [271–2] "We need a new future where we are better integrated society and better at managing our responsibilities in the world. In order to achieve these dreams, all Britons will need to be enlisted and involved. There can be no further talk about 'ethnic minorities' and the 'majority community' tolerating each other. We need our collective skills, wisdom, experiences, trust and faith to build a better nation, where we learn from each other and discard [even if it is painful] ways of seeing and acting which are damaging us or our country." Here, the term "integrated" differs with the term used in the Parekh report, where it is taken to refer to assimilation.

These generalised exhortations do not indicate which important, and maybe controversial, elements from which cultures would make up this integrated eclectic culture. However she does mention that [1] "It is more than half a century since the large-scale immigration of visible communities into this country, a movement which brought not only the excitement of new foods and music, but ideas, art, different social functions and formations and a sense of history." They are welcome indeed, but none of them are culturally fundamental or controversial. Support for her proposition is not encouraged when she makes a bizarre complaint about the British film *Four Weddings and a Funeral*. She comments [259]: "Was there a black wedding, or even a funeral for that matter? . . . The producers, writers and directors could not have tried harder to whiten the most famously Black area in London, Notting Hill Gate." Actually, Notting Hill has recently become a fashionable area in which to live. Moreover, the dust cover of her book blacks out the Union Jack and superimposes a black Asian face on a photograph of the Queen. The intolerant insensitivity of the multicultural lobby was the alleged comment [TXT 17 Oct. 00] by the white vice-chair of the Parekh Commission that "The Prince of Wales should have been told to marry a black woman . . . the Royal Family sent out the wrong message about Britain."

It is difficult to discern which cultural aspects of British society Parekh and Alibhai-Brown find lacking, and which public aspects of other cultures they believe should replace (be integrated with) them in order that they be acceptable to all ethnic cultures, including the mainstream. A preferred culture must be influenced by an individual's personal experience and background, and is contingent on the individual's particular conception of the good society—therein lies the practical dilemma. The principal criticism of the Parekh report is centred on the victimisation of ethnic groups in terms of exclusion and inequality of outcome. This also applies with equal validity to some groups in the white community, but in the case of ethnic groups this is unlikely to be completely eliminated in the absence of their assimilation.

This discussion argues that an approach towards multiculturalism, similar to that initially proposed by Professor Joseph Raz in 1986, is believed to be the most appropriate, at least in those societies like Britain which are not as yet predominantly multicultural. It is based on assimilation, together with the philosophy of toleration originally developed by Locke, and applied to cultural pluralism. The solution proposed by this author is that the majority, in the interests of maintaining a stable and secure society, should encourage gradual voluntary assimilation, while exercising appropriate limits of toleration towards separatism. An essential part of this policy is to control the pressure on cultural separatism by restricting immigration, by instituting selective quotas, and better control of asylum seekers. This approach is pragmatic, and attempts to recognise society and human nature as they are—in contrast to the aspirational approach favoured by some cosmopolitan and moral philosophers. As discussed, the role of toleration towards any unavoidable conflicts between cultural interest groups, including those of mainstream society, should be instrumental, which is to say, it should promote "negotiated positions." Nonetheless, toleration should not be seen as a rights-based claim or a patronising or unidirectional obligation towards minorities.

Locke was less idealistic and less liberal than Mill, being more concerned with the limits of rights. His priority was the state and its cohesion with social beings, who, with human nature as it is, have good and bad motives, and their own prioritisation of beliefs and values. He saw the commercial benefits of a stable hegemony and its inherent national and political loyalty. He knew, too, the benefits of tolerating the religious autonomy of individuals, albeit with restrictions. The overriding rationale for Locke's toleration was to preserve the sovereignty of the nation-state, founded on its natural right and duty to defend itself, and the interests of the majority of its citizens. Locke's approach to religious pluralism is analogous to the relationship today between separatist multiculturalism and the hegemonic nation-state. Locke recognised that real power lay with the state and not with the Church. One could opt out of the Church but not from the state, which commands considerable temporal resources. This is well-recognised by pressure groups claiming rights, whose objective is not to foster voluntary toleration, but to impose a "diktat" on society through legislation and coercive regulation. Toleration should be exercised both at government and individual levels, but it should not be a licence that could lead to the eventual disintegration of the state.

Mill believed that "good" would ensue from toleration due to the benefits arising from individual autonomy. This claim is too generalised and his principle is vague, and it is unable to discriminate between direct and indirect, physical and expressive, and psychological "harms." Mill's view of society and the world was limited to the Euro-centrism of the mid-nineteenth century, and could not be cognisant of the complexity of British society today. His liberal concept of toleration raises the question as to whether any major involuntary cultural change should be allowed to threaten the traditional morality, beliefs, and values of a society without causing it harm. Both separatist multiculturalism and an authoritarian/undemocratic cultural hegemony could both harm the autonomy of individuals. If multiculturalism would result in significantly harming the majority, then preserving the indigenous culture is the least harmful and maximising utilitarian option for the nation-state, subject to the basic rights of all of its citizens being maintained. It is contended that the validity of any sociological philosophy is ultimately contingent on its instrumental value. With almost any sociological policy and politicised decisions, what cannot be avoided are claims of some "harmful" consequences to some interest groups. Pragmatic and generalised, rather than particularised, political judgements have to be made.

The relationship between the issues of justice, toleration, immigration and cultural pluralism are of particular interest to liberal philosophers. A valuable analysis has been made by Chaplin [1993:32–49] of the alternatives underlying the role of toleration in a multicultural society, including those proposed by Nozick (a "pluralist utopian"), Kymlicka (a "cultural pluralist") and Raz (a "perfectionist pluralist"). It should be borne in mind that, when considering alternative proposals, including those advanced in this discussion, some are more appropriate to a particular multicultural society than to others. And as Chaplin aptly notes [49], "If these claims are valid, then the liberal project of devising a universally valid conception of justice which is endorsable by all irrespective of their particular conceptions of the good is unattainable . . . If it could be shown that all theories necessarily rest on 'perfectionist' assumptions of one kind or another, then the conclusion is that no theory will be able to succeed where liberalism fails. No conception of the acceptable limits of cultural and religious pluralism can be generated which is independent of particular [thick] conceptions of the good human life."

Nozick proposes a libertarian, neutral, voluntarianist, cosmopolitan, separatist, and minimal state vision of multiculturalism in which [33] "utopian experimentation can be tried, different styles of life can be lived, and alternative visions of the good can be individually or jointly pursued. Such a society would be a utopia in the sense of a 'utopia of utopias,' or 'meta-utopia.' . . . [34] No pattern is imposed on everyone, and the result will be one pattern if and only if everyone voluntarily chooses to live in accordance with that pattern of community . . . The fact that Nozick's neutrality is negative is consistent with his conception of the minimal state which is prohibited from any action having redistributed effects." Nozick's proposal leads one to ask: "How long would this unrestricted voluntarianism continue until it is seen that people can coexist peacefully?" "What would be the consequences if it did not work?" And, "who would have the authority to impose the necessary stability?" Suffice it to say that this has nowhere happened, at least on the national scale envisaged, and could not take place without at least the acquiescence of an extremely liberal or indifferent majority prepared to abandon its culture. Furthermore, such a plan would probably fragment into the conflicts of an unstable and insecure, and maybe even anarchic, society.

Chaplin concludes that Kymlicka rejects Nozick's proposal because of [39] "the neglect of the overwhelming reality of cultural plurality, of which, not only Nozick, but also other liberals such as Rawls and Dworkin, are guilty." He recognises that [40] "We become aware that we have been born into a certain form of life and that others exist which we are free to endorse . . . Being a member of a culture means that we tacitly endorse a way of living. If we have not endorsed it we are not a member of that culture, even though we may happen to be resident in it." He thus makes a distinction between an inherited cultural affinity and one in which we might happen to coexist, for example, as a non-assimilated immigrant. Kymlicka's argument [41] "Assumes the moral significance of the distinction between the different choices people make and [on the other hand] the different circumstances in which people find themselves. Since people are responsible for their choices they cannot expect special privileges to enable them to bear the cost of those choices." Liberal equality would require the latter—unequal circumstances—to be compensated, whereas the former would violate liberal equality because it resulted from free choice. This distinction is not clear cut, because the children of immigrants have made no such choice. Although the immigrant has an inherited culture which he may wish to retain, he has chosen to live in another culture, but claims a positive entitlement to the beneficial rights of that culture. The compensation argument does have a measure of validity for the claims of "native" indigenous groups (such as the American, Canadian, or Australian aborigines, or the New Zealand Maoris) to land and cultural rights, because they correct the unfair and relative disadvantage these groups initially face. This enables them to seek [42] "to secure by political action conditions of genuine equality of opportunity between different cultures," and argues that positive discrimination programmes are not enough, "because they benefit only individuals and not the minority culture as a whole." This argument, if applied to immigrant, as well as indigenous, minority groups, does not envisage the outcome whereby they could insist on their acquired liberal right not to give up their beliefs, values, and practices—some of which may be illiberal and intolerant, and some that could potentially be evangelistic and politicised. Or as Chaplin puts it [46]: "A striking feature of Kymlicka's discussion here is that he fails to recognise the fact that liberalism is itself a distinctive cultural community . . . Thus attempting to liberalise a minority culture by requiring that it adopt the range of liberal individual rights is not regarded by him as involving the transformation of one kind of cultural community into an entirely different kind."

Joseph Raz, at least in his 1986 book, reasserted the hegemony of the liberal culture of the West whilst accepting a selective and limited toleration of other cultures. According to Chaplin [1993], part of Raz's case posited [46] "the empirical claim that the central characteristic of modern Western society is the value which it attaches to the possibility for autonomous individual choice . . . [47] While such a position may allow considerable scope for diverse lifestyles based on autonomy, it does nothing to encourage and does much to discourage those lifestyles or practices [such as arranged marriages] based on heteronomy." Raz himself advocated [1986:423] that "a test of viability [is] the most important consideration in determining policy towards such groups . . . I am assuming that their own culture is morally worthy. That is, first, it does not lead them to harm others, nor to destroy the options available to those not members of these communities. Second, when their culture flourishes in any given society it enables members of that society to have an adequate and satisfying life. In that case their continued existence should be tolerated, despite its scant regard for autonomy. If those assumptions do not hold then the case for toleration is considerably weakened, or even disappears . . . The perfectionist principles [424] espoused . . . suggest that people are justified in taking action to assimilate the minority group, at the cost of letting its culture die or at least be considerably changed by absorption. But that is easier said than done . . . Toleration is therefore the conclusion one must often reach. Gradual transformation of these minority communities is one thing, their precipitate disintegration is another . . . Sometimes they survive as a dwindling community through the forceful stand of some of their members who sometimes combine with misguided liberals and conservatives to condemn many of the young in such communities to an impoverished, unrewarding life by denying them the education and the opportunities to thrive outside the community. In such cases assimilationist policies may well be the only humane course, even if implemented by force of law."

In a subsequent article [1994:69], Raz explains his later position on a qualified integrationist multiculturalism from a "liberal perspective," which he says [70] "is not one of utopian hope." He restates his objections and the risks in multiculturalism, in particular that it can undermine social solidarity [77]: "Civic solidarity is essential to the existence of a well-ordered political society . . . [78] a swift social change toward multiculturalism may severely test the existing bonds of solidarity in a society and threaten disintegration or a backlash of rabid nationalism." He notes [77] that " the perpetuation of several cultural groups in a single political society, also requires the existence of a common culture. First, coexistence calls for the cultivation of mutual toleration and respect . . . all [constituent groups] will be educated to understand and respect the traditions of other groups in the society . . . [Secondly] all communities will interact in the same economic environment . . . they will have to possess the same mathematical, literary, and other skills required for effective participation in the economy. Finally, members of all cultural groups will belong to the same political society. They will enjoying roughly equal access to the sources of political power and to decision-making positions . . . The emergence of such a common culture is still an aspiration . . . [and] whether the sort of common culture is capable of forming a basis for social solidarity sufficient to secure the cohesion and stability of modern political societies remains a moot point. But I [Raz] think that it may serve this purpose successfully, and should be given a chance to do so." He proposes [78-9] that "The more concrete policies which become appropriate gradually as developments justify them [include]—(1) The young of all cultural groups should be educated, if their parents so desire, in the culture of their own groups. But all of them should also be educated to be familiar with and cultivate an attitude of respect for the history and traditions of all the cultures in the country. (2) The customs and practices of the different groups should, within the limits of toleration we have explored earlier . . . be recognised in law and by all public bodies in society etc. (3) It is crucial to break the link between poverty, under-education, and ethnicity. (4) There should be generous public support for autonomous cultural institutions . . . [and] it also calls for disproportionate support for small groups that are strong enough to pass the viability test. (5) Public [media] space should accommodate all the cultural groups . . . [79] Of course, all such measures are designed to lead to relatively harmonious coexistence of non-oppressive and tolerant communities. They therefore have their limits . . . Toleration is limited only in denying communities the right to repress their own members, in discouraging intolerant attitudes to outsiders, in insisting on making exit from the community a viable option for its members. Beyond that, liberal multiculturalism will also require all groups to allow their members access to adequate opportunities for self-expression and full participation in the economic life and the political culture of the community. The combined effect of such policies is that liberal multiculturalism leads not to the abandonment of a common culture, but to the emergence of a new common culture that is respectful toward all the groups of the country, and hospitable to their prosperity." However, in proposing a more integrationist solution, Raz [78] recognises that "This doctrine has far-reaching ramifications. It calls on us to re-conceive society, changing its self-image. We should learn to think of our societies as consisting not of a majority and minorities, but of a plurality of cultural groups. Naturally such developments take a long period to come to fruition, and they cannot be secured through government action alone, as they require a widespread change in attitude."

Objections to this proposal are that it would require a nation-state to essentially accept, at least for an indefinite period, separatist multiculturalism, while being unsure about its assumed eventual integrationist outcome. It would have to promote an essentially aspirational agenda of social engineering, requiring the express support of the mainstream society, or assume that the society would remain acquiescent or apathetic during the transition period. The proposal assumes that its objective could be achieved without social disruption, the emergence of dominance by a new group, or its reassertion by the indigenous majority. It assumes that each and every ethnic group will be amenable to a policy meant to lead to mutual respect and transculturalisation, and in some way it will resolve the cultural differences that exist between minority ethnic groups, and between minorities and mainstream society. Such a proposal poses the question as to why this type of society should not continue in a separatist mode, and never develop and universally adopt an eclectic integrated common culture. The features of this new culture would remain undecided and perhaps contested—i.e. in what respect(s) would it be seen as an improvement on, and more generally acceptable than, the mainstream culture that already exists? It might be seen by some as containing the worst features and not the best. The changes that are to be brought about by Raz's proposal require what he denies—"not one of utopian hope." They would not be marginal and require simply changing attitudes or style, but would have to be equivalent to not accepting the "basic rules of the game"—namely, it would have to be an entirely new game. His proposal assumes that when this transformational social experiment has eroded the influence of the mainstream culture sufficiently, and/or the proportional political influence of ethnic groups has increased by further immigration and/or disparate birth rates, the unpredictable and probably unstable status quo which then existed would continue peacefully. This could instead eventuate into a society so different from the stability on which it had been currently founded that its cohesion would be in doubt. It is the duty of government to reflect the right of its electorate to resist unauthenticated change. The potential conflict is not only between deeply held private cultural values, beliefs, practices, and loyalties, but also those associated with unpredictable and open-ended political aspirations.

This discussion argues that government policy in Britain should adopt a qualified and detached approach towards further progression into acquired multiculturalism. This requires not promoting legislative, institutional, and financial preference or support to pressure groups dedicated to the furtherance of separatist social/political cultural objectives and other moves towards socially engineering this outcome. This policy should be non-interventionist and rely on voluntary cultural assimilation facilitated by the osmosis of intermarriage, transculturalisation, and individualism—as has taken place with the Jewish communities in the United States and Britain. At the same time, immigration from non-Western cultures should be recognised as being the main feeder for acquired, pervasive, and possibly separatist multiculturalism. Immigration controls should be made firmer, more selective, and quota—and visa-based. Nationality quotas should be gradually phased so as to be in line with the ongoing experience of assimilation in order to minimise separatism, avoid cultural disruption, and maintain continuity of the indigenous culture.

British immigration policy has to date been largely influenced by, and at the same time largely constrained by, the primacy of 1948 UN Declaration of Universal Human Rights and the 1951 (Geneva) UN Convention Relating to the Status of Refugees. Thus, the preamble to the 1993 Asylum and Immigration Appeals Act specifically acknowledges that "nothing in the immigration rules" shall be contrary to the 1951 Convention. Moreover, Sections 65 and 69 of the 1999 Immigration and Asylum Act allow for appeals under the new Human Rights Act 1998 and under the 1951 Refugee Convention. This Convention was formulated in vastly different circumstances over fifty years ago, largely with the small numbers of people fleeing Communist repression in mind. In Britain, it has since been subject to ever-widening legalistic and exploitative interpretations, to the extent that the government has today effectively little control over immigration and increasing multiculturalism, and these aspects are eroding its sovereignty and loyalty. In the forty years following WW2, Britain never received more than 4,500 asylum applications a year, but this was followed by a ten-fold increase in the following two years. According to UN figures [STM 13 Aug. 00], Britain has now become, with

Germany, one of Europe's two most popular destination for asylum seekers. Britain is ahead of the United States, Canada, and Australia in the international league table of twenty-four countries. In the first six months of the year 2000, there were 36,880 applications in Britain, compared with 36,006 in Germany, and 19,376 in France, which has approximately the same population as Britain, and much less-populated Portugal had eighty applications. Immigration officials say that "criminal gangs who abuse the system are keeping one step ahead of government controls." At the same time these UN figures were announced, the government had to defend its immigration policy before the UN Committee on the Elimination of Racial Discrimination [TM 23 Aug. 00]. Its report, which was published without a copy being sent to the government, expressed "deep concern" about the state of race relations in Britain [DM 24 Aug. 00] and condemned institutional racism, high unemployment, and social exclusion rates among ethnic minorities. It also claimed that more should be done for asylum seekers [TM 23 Aug. 00]. It has previously been noted [DM 28 Jan. 95] that some UN Committees include member states whose domestic standards are far inferior to the easy targets of the West. Their accusations do not reflect the UN's supposedly universal and impartial dimension. Maybe the UN Conventions are thought of as a Western cultural creation, to which only the West should be expected to conform.

Government policy should reflect that although there are 137 states party to the 1951 Convention and/or its 1967 Protocol, it is not materially relevant, strictly interpreted, or complied with in practice in some regions of the world, and that some of its provisions are outmoded and are exploited by economic migrants and sham asylum seekers—including those politically disruptive to the national interests of Britain and the West. No doubt being apprehensive of accusations of racism, the issue was swept under the carpet for decades, and immigration legislation was marginally tightened, particularly in the 1990s. The Home Secretary has now acknowledged that the UN Convention is applied in different ways in different EU countries, has been widely abused, is badly out of date, and needs a radical rethink [TM 2 March 00/DM 17 June 00]—a view recently publicly endorsed by the Prime Minister prior to the 2001 general election. The Home Secretary has proposed [TM 17 June 00] a list of safe countries, such as the United States, from which asylum claims would not even be considered. Other asylum seekers would have to prove their claim before entry into the EU states, except for a quota from the most repressive countries. It is, however, very unlikely that any changes to the Convention would be agreed to by the disparate "international community," some of whom like Portugal have virtually no asylum seekers. It would, though, be permissible under Article 44 to denounce the Convention with one year's notice, or to seek its revision under Article 45. A legal opinion [TM 23 Aug. 99] holds that it would also be lawful under the Convention for refugee status to be withdrawn if the circumstances of the persecution ceased to exist within, say, four years of the admission of a refugee. The conventional political mantra that "genuine asylum seekers will always be welcome" will no longer be tenable in the twenty-first century unless the Convention is modified. The number of people anywhere in the world potentially at risk, either individually or as a group, with a well-founded fear of each and every form of persecution—political or otherwise—could run into millions, which is clearly unsustainable. Although Britain has immigration visa regulations, it has no selective and quantified immigration policy. Canada, for example, assesses the suitability of immigrants on a points basis. This is based on the migrants age, occupation, education, work experience and training, language skills, resident family, and personal suitability. Germany is reportedly [TM 29 May 01] considering a similar selective scheme based on a points system. In 1997–98, Canada admitted immigrants equivalent to 0.6 percent of its population, Australia, 0.4 percent, and the United States in 1998 admitted 0.25 percent [DM 12 Sept. 00].

Arguably among the reasons why Britain is attractive to asylum seekers and economic migrants is because it is reputed to be a tolerant society. The role of toleration and its limits should be viewed instrumentally to promote a two-way obligation and responsibility between the mainstream society and ethnic minorities, founded on a climate of mutual trust, pragmatically-based, and not virtue driven. Otherwise, the risk is that the limits of toleration of the indigenous society will be breached, possibly at a stage before intolerance can be reversed. The Western ethos of true non-discriminatory equality of opportunity towards legally-domiciled minorities must in every respect be seen to be an ideal global model, both in respect of the openness of its practice and its enforcement. Because of its inequality, and the latent resentment it can engender, there should be no official policy of positive discrimination. Both racism and reverse racism, as well as being illegal, should be seen as being mutually destructive.

The toleration between individuals, whatever their culture, ethnicity, or race, and human nature being what it is, must remain a matter for personal and voluntary conviction, belief, and feelings. It is contended that the development of mutual trust between the mainstream society and minority groups would be reinforced by the absence of an increasing threat of acquired multiculturalism. Those separatist aspects of minority cultures that are in the public domain, such as language and education, should not be encouraged.

There should be no legal constraints, beyond the present safeguards that inhibit, prevent, or penalise citizens from the exercise of their freedom of expression. This is because, if such restrictions are not generally supported, they will be counterproductive. In particular, the institutional, educational, and media ethos of political correctness should be resisted. Political correctness is in effect an intolerant restriction on the freedom to dissent from received wisdom, official or otherwise, and on the validity and contribution of a plurality of opinion.

Revisionism of the cultural traditions and historical record of Britain, aimed at promoting an inflated and unjustified sense of national guilt and obligation towards immigrant universal claim rights, should be vigorously and directly countered by informed opinion. Exploitative claims by ex-colonial separatist ethnic groups of a perceived historical and continuing victimhood should not be validated by positive discrimination, quotas, or other forms of compensation.

NOTES

Alibhai-Brown, Y. *Mixed Feelings—The Complex Lives of Mixed-Race Britons.* London: The Women's Press, 2001.
Alibhai-Brown, Y. *Who Do We Think We Are?* London: Allen Lane, Penguin Press. 2000. 1.
Ibid. 3–4.
Ibid. 18.
Ibid. 103.
Ibid. 253.
Ibid. 271–2.
Chaplin, J. (Ed.) "How Much Cultural and Religious Pluralism Can Liberalism Tolerate?" In *Liberalism, Multiculturalism and Toleration.* Horton, J. (Ed.) London: Macmillan Press, 1993. 32–49.
Ibid. 33–4.
Ibid. 39–41.
Ibid. 42.
Ibid. 46–7.
Ibid. 49.
Ignatieff, M. In *The Disuniting of America—Reflections on a Multicultural Society.* Schlesinger, A.M. New York and London: W.W. Norton, 1992. 11.
Parekh, Lord. *The Future of Multi-Ethnic Britain.* London: Profile Books. 2000.
Parekh, Lord. "The New Right and the Politics of Nationhood." In *The New Right—Image and Reality.* London: Runnymede Trust. 1986. 33 and 42.
Raz, J. *The Morality of Freedom.* Oxford: Clarendon Press, 1986. 423–4.
Raz, J. "Multiculturalism—A Liberal Perspective." In *Dissent.* Winter, 1994. 70.
Ibid. 74–8.
Ibid. 78.
Ibid. 78–9.
Rex, J. *Race and Ethnicity.* Buckingham: Open University Press, 1986. 133.

Bibliography

Books

Alibhai-Brown,Y. *Who Do We Think We Are?* London: Allen Lane, Penguin Press, 2000.

Ahmed, A.S. *Post-Modernism and Islam—Predicament and Promise.* London: Routledge, 1992.

Alter, P. *Nationalism.* London: Edward Arnold, 1989.

Anderson, B. *Imagined Communities—Reflections on the Origin and Spread of Nationalism.* London: Verso, 1991.

Anderson, D. (Ed.) *The Loss of Virtue—Moral Confusion and Social Disorder in Britain and America.* London: The Social Affairs Unit, 1992.

Anderson, D. and Mullen, P. (Eds.) *Faking It—The Sentimentalisation of Modern Society.* London: The Social Affairs Unit, 1998.

Arblaster, A. *Democracy.* Buckingham: Open University Press, 1994.

Arblaster, A. *The Rise and Decline of Western Liberalism.* Oxford: Basil Blackford, 1984.

Archard, D. (Ed.) *Philosophy and Pluralism.* Cambridge: Cambridge University Press, 1996.

Arendt, H. *The Origins of Totalitarianism.* London: George Allen and Unwin, 1958.

Arendt, H. *Eichmann in Jerusalem.* London: Penguin Books 1994.

Arnold, G. *Britain Since 1945—Choice, Conflict, Change.* London: Blandford, 1989.

Bakewell, J. (Ed). *The Heart of the Matter—A Memoir—Climate of Hate.* London: B.B.C. Books, 1996.

Banton, M. *Discrimination.* Buckinhgham: Open University Press, 1994.

Barbalet, J.M. *Citizenship.* Milton Keynes: Open University Press, 1988.

Bassnett, S. (Ed.) *Studying British Cultures.* London: Routledge, 1997.

Baubock, R. *Immigration and the Boundaries of Citizenship.* Coventry: University of Warwick, Centre for Research in Ethnic Relations, 1992.

Beattie, J. *Other Cultures.* London: Routledge and Kegan Paul, 1966.

Beitz, C.R. et al. *International Ethics.* Princeton, NJ: Princeton University Press, 1985.

Beloff, M. *A Historian in the Twentieth Century.* London: Yale University Press, 1992.

Benedict, R. *Patterns of Culture.* London: Routledge and Kegan Paul, 1935.

Bernstein, R. *Dictatorship of Virtue—Multiculturalism and the Battle for America's Future.* New York, Alfred. A. Knopf, 1994.

Berry, C J. *Human Nature.* Basingstoke, Hants: Macmillan Education, 1986.

368   The Twilight of Britain

Bok, S. *Common Values*. Columbia, Missouri: University of Missouri Press, 1995.
Brewer, J.D. *Mosley's Men—The British Union of Fascists in the West Midlands*. Aldershot, Hants: Gower Publishing, 1984.
Brown, R. *Prejudice—Its Social Psychology*. Oxford: Blackwell Publishers, 1995.
Brown, S.C. (Ed.) *Objectivity And Cultural Divergence*. Cambridge: Cambridge University Press, 1984.
Brownlie, I. (Ed.) *Basic Documents on Human Rights*. (3rd Edn.) Oxford: Clarendon Press, 1992.
Butterfield, H. *The Whig Interpretation of History*. Harmondsworth, Middx: Penguin Books 1973.
_____ 'Toleration in Early Modern Times.' In *Fourth Conference of the International Society for the History of Ideas*. Venice. September/October 1975.
Cahn, S. (Ed.) *The Affirmative Action Debate*. London: Routledge. 1995.
Carpenter, H.—*Robert Runcie—The Reluctant Archbishop*. London: Hodder and Stoughton, 1996.
Carter, B., Harris, C. et al. *The 1951–55 Conservative Government and the Racialisation of Black Immigration*. University of Warwick, Centre for Research in Ethnic Relations, 1987.
Caws, P. 'Identity: Cultural, Transcultural, and Multicultural.' In *Multiculturalism*. Ed.Goldberg, D.T, Oxford: Blackwell Publishers, 1994.
Cohen, G., Bosanquet, N. et al. *The New Right—Image and Reality*. London: Runnymede Trust,1986.
Collings, R. *Reflections of a Statesman—The Writings and Speeches of Enoch Powell*. London: Bellew Publishing, 1991.
Connor, W. *Ethno-Nationalism—The Quest for Understanding*. Princeton, NJ: Princeton University Press, 1994.
Cranston, M. *John Stuart Mill*. London: Longmans Green, 1967.
_____ *John Locke*. Harlow: Longmans Green, 1969.
_____ *John Locke—A Biography*. Oxford: Oxford University Press, 1957.
_____ *What are Human Rights?* London: The Bodley Head. 1973.
Cross, C. *The Fascists in Britain*. London: Barrie and Rockliff, 1961.
Crisp, R. (Ed.) *How Should One Live? Essays on the Virtues*. Oxford: Clarendon Press, 1996.
Cross, C. *The Fascists in Britain*. London: Barrie and Rockcliff, 1961.
Daniel, N. *Islam and the West—The Making of an Image*. Oxford: OneWorld Publications, 1997.
Davis, M.C. (Ed.) *Human Rights and Chinese Values—Legal, Philosophical and Political Perspectives*. Oxford: Oxford University Press, 1995.
De Grand, A.J. *Fascist Italy and Nazi Germany—The "Fascist " Style of Rule*. London: Routledge, 1995.
Deutch, K. W. *Nationalism and Social Communication—An Enquiry into the Foundations of Nationality*. Cambridge, Mass: The M.I.T. Press, 1966.
Devlin, P. *The Enforcement of Morals*. Oxford: Oxford University Press, 1965.
Dewey, J. *Freedom and Culture*. New York: Capricorn Books, 1963.
Doob, L. *Patriotism and Nationalism—Their Psychological Foundations*. New Haven, Conn: Yale University Press, 1964.
Dunant, S. (Ed.) *The War of the Words—The Political Correctness Debate*. London: Virago Press, 1994.
Eisenstein, Z. *Hatreds—Racialized and Sexualized Conflicts in the 21st Century*. London: Routledge, 1996.
Ellis, R. *Asylum Seekers and Immigration Act Prisoners—The Practice of Detention*. London: The Prison Reform Trust, 1998.

Eposito, J.L. *The Islamic Threat—Myth or Reality?* Oxford: Oxford University Press, 1992.

Eysenck, H.J. *Race, Intelligence and Education.* London: Temple Smith, 1971.

Ferro, M. *The Use and Abuse of History—Or How the Past is Taught.* London: Routledge and Kegan Paul, 1984.

Fish, S. *There's No Such Thing as Free Speech.* Oxford: Oxford University Press, 1994.

Flew, A. *Atheistic Humanism.* Buffalo, New York, 1993.

_____ *Education, Race and Revolution.* London: Centre for Policy Studies, March, 1984.

_____ *A Future for Anti-Racism.* London: The Social Affairs Unit, 1992.

Foot, P. *Immigration and British Politics.* Harmondsworth, Middx: Penguin Books, 1965.

Frost, G. (Ed.) *Not Fit to Fight—The Cultural Subversion of the Armed Forces in Britain.* London: The Social Affairs Unit, 1998.

Fullinwider, R.K. (Ed.) *Public Education in a Multicultural Society—Policy, Theory, Critique.* Cambridge: Cambridge University Press, 1996.

Fukuyama, F. *Trust—The Social Virtues and the Creation of Prosperity.* London: Penguin Books, 1996.

Galbraith, J. K. *The Culture of Contentment.* London: Sinclair-Stevenson, 1992.

_____ *The Good Society.* London: Sinclair-Stevenson, 1996.

Galford, E. and Fearman, C. *Israel.* Amsterdam: Time—Life Books, 1986.

Garrard, J. A. *The English and Immigration 1880–1910.* Oxford: Oxford University Press, 1971.

Gellner, E. *Thought and Change.* London: Weidenfeld and Nicolson, 1964.

_____ *Nations and Nationalism.* Oxford: Blackwell Publishers, 1983.

_____ *Reason and Culture.* Oxford: Blackwell Publishers, 1992.

Gifford, Z. *The Golden Thread—Asian Experiences of Post-Raj Britain.* London: Pandora Press, 1990.

Ginsberg, M. *Nationalism—A Reappraisal.* Leeds: Leeds University Press, 1963.

Glazer, N. *We Are All Multiculturalists Now.* Cambridge, Mass: Harvard University Press, 1997.

Glover, J. *Causing Death And Saving Lives.* London: Penguin Books 1977.

Glover, J. *The Philosophy and Psychology of Personal Identity.* London: Penguin Books, 1988.

Goldberg, D.T. (Ed.) *Multiculturalism.* Oxford: Blackwell Publishers, 1994.

Gray, J. *Liberalism.* Buckingham: Open University Press, 1995.

_____ *Enlightenment's Wake—Politics and Culture at the Close of the Modern Age.* London: Routledge, 1995.

_____ *Post-Liberalism—Studies in Political Thought.* London: Routledge, 1996.

_____ 'Toleration and the Currently Offensive Implication of Judgement." In *The Loss of Virtue.* London: Social Affaifs Unit, 1992.

Greenfeld, L. *Nationalism—Five Roads to Modernity.* Cambridge, Mass: Harvard University Press, 1992.

Gregor, A.J. *The Ideology of Facism—The Rationale of Totalitarianism.* New York: The Free Press, 1969.

Griffiths, S. I. *Nationalism and Ethnic Conflict—Threats to European Security.* Oxford: Oxford University Press, 1993.

Hall, J.A. and Ikenberry, G.J. *The State.* Milton Keynes: Open University Press, 1989.

Hargreaves, A. G. *Immigration , Race and Ethnicity in Contemporary France.* London: Routledge, 1995.

Harris, C.C. *Kinship*. Buckingham: Open University Press, 1990.
Harris, R. *Prejudice and Tolerance in Ulster*. Manchester: Manchester University Press, 1972.
Hart, H.L.A. *Law, Liberty and Morality*. Oxford: Oxford University Press, 1963.
Heraclides, A. *The Self—Determination of Minorities in International Politics*. London: Frank Cass, 1991.
Heyd, D. (Ed.) *Toleration*. Princeton, NJ: Princeton University Press, 1996.
Hill, M. and Fee, L. K. *The Politics of Nation Building and Citizenship in Singapore*. London: Routledge, 1995.
Himmelfarb, G. *The De-Moralization of Society—From Victorian Virtues to Modern Values*. London: I.E.A Health and Welfare Unit, 1995.
Hiro, D. *Islamic Fundamentalism*. London: Paladin, Grafton Books, 1988.
Hiskett, M. *Schooling for British Muslims—Integrated, Opted-Out or Denominational?* London: Social Affairs Unit, 1989.
Hobsbawm, E.J. *Nations and Nationalism Since 1780—Programme, Myth, Reality*. Cambridge: Cambridge University Press, 1992.
Hockenos, P. *Free to Hate—The Rise of the Right in Post-Communist Eastern Europe*. London: Routledge. 1993.
Hofstede, G. *Culture's Consequences—International Differences in Work Related Values*. London: Sage Publications, 1980.
_____ *Writers on Organizations*. (Eds.). Pugh, D.S. and Hickson, D.J. London: Penguin Books.1989.
_____ *Cultures and Organisations*. London: Harper Collins, 1994.
Holland, K.M. and Parkins, G. *Reversing Racism—Lessons from America*. London: The Social Affairs Unit, 1984.
Honeyford, R. *The Commission for Racial Equality*. New Brunswick, NJ: Transaction Publishers, 1998.
Horton, J. *Political Obligation*. Basingstoke, Hants: Macmillan Press, 1992.
_____ (Ed.) *Liberalism, Multiculturalism, and Toleration*. Basingstoke, Hants: Macmillan Press, 1993.
Horton, J. and Mendus, S. (Eds.) *Aspects of Toleration—Philosophical Studies*. London: Methuen, 1985.
Horton, J. and Crabtree, H. (Eds.) *Toleration and Integrity in a Multi-Faith Society*. York: Dept. of Politics, University of York, 1992.
Horton, J. and Nicholson, P. (Eds.) *Toleration: Philosophy and Practice*. Aldershot, Hants: Avebury, 1992.
Hughes, R. *Culture of Complaint*. Oxford: Oxford University Press, 1993.
Huntington, S.P. *The Clash of Civilizations and the Remaking of World Order*. New York: Simon and Shuster, 1996.
Hutchinson, J. *The Dynamics of Cultural Nationalism—The Gaelic Revival and the Creation of the Irish Nation State*. London: Allen and Unwin, 1987.
_____ *Modern Nationalism*. London: Fontana Press, 1994.
Hutchinson, J. and Smith, A.D. (Eds.) *Nationalism*. Oxford: Oxford University Press, 1994.
_____ *Ethnicity*. Oxford: Oxford University Press, 1996.
Ignatieff, M. *Blood and Belonging—Journeys into the New Nationalism*. London: B.B.C. Books, Chatto and Windus, 1993.
Jenks, C. *Culture*. London: Routledge, 1993.
Johnson, H.G. (Ed.) *Economic Nationalism in Old and New States*. London: George Allen and Unwin, 1968.
Jones, P. *Rights*. London: Macmillan Press, 1994.

Jones, R.T. *The Desire of Nations*. Llandybie, Ammanford, Dyfed, Davies, C. 1974.

Jordan, G. and Weedon, C. *Cultural Politics*. Oxford: Blackwell Publishers, 1995.

Jupp, J. *Immigration*. (2nd Edn.) Australia: Oxford University Press, 1998.

Kamenka, E. *Nationalism—The Nature and Evolution of an Idea*. Canberra: Australian National University Press, 1973.

Kedourie, E. *Nationalism*. London: Hutchinson, 1966.

Kekes, J. 'The Injustice of Affirmative Action Involving Preferential Treatment.' In *The Affirmative Action Debate*. (Ed. Cahn, S.M.) London: Routledge, 1995.

King, P. *Toleration*. London: George Allen and Unwin, 1976.

King, P. *Toleration*. London: Frank Cass, 1998.

Koshechkina, T. *Political Tolerance—From General Principle To Concrete Application*. M.A. Dissertation. Canterbury: University of Kent, 1992.

Kovel, J. *White Racism—A Psycho-History*. London: Free Association Books, 1988.

Kymlicka, W. *Multicultural Citizenship—A Liberal Theory of Minority Rights*. Oxford: Clarendon Press, 1995.

_____ (Ed.) *The Rights of Minority Cultures*. Oxford: Oxford University Press, 1995.

Labrousse, E. 'Religious Toleration.' in *Dictionary of the History of Ideas*. vol. iv. USA: Charles Scribner's Sons, 1973.

Laszlo, E. (Ed.) *The Multicultural Planet—The Report of a Unes International Expert Group*. Oxford: One World Publications, 1993.

Leahy, M. and Dan Cohn-Sherbok. *The Liberation Debate—Rights at Issue*. London: Routledge. 1996.

Lee, S. *The Cost of Free Speech*. London: Faber, 1990.

Locke, J. *A Letter Concerning Toleration*. (Ed.) Tully, J.H. Indianapolis: Indiana Hackett Publishing, 1983.

_____ *A Letter Concerning Toleration—In Focus*. (Ed. Horton, J. and Mendus, S). London: Routledge, 1991.

_____ *An Essay Concerning Human Understanding*. London: J.M. Dent, 1988.

_____ *The Cambridge Companion to Locke*. (Ed. Chappell,V.) Cambridge: Cambridge University Press, 1994.

MacIntyre, A. *After Virtue—A Study in Moral Theory*. London: Gerald Duckworth, 1985.

_____ *How To Seem Virtuous Without Actually Being So*. Occasional Papers Series No. 1. Lancaster: Centre for the Study of Cultural Values, Lancaster University, 1991.

Maclean, C. (Ed.) *The Crown and the Thistle—The Nature of Nationhood*. Edinburgh: Scottish Academic Press, 1979.

Mackie, J.L. *Ethics—Inventing Right and Wrong*. London: Penguin Books, 1990.

Magee, B. *Popper*. London: Fontana Press, 1985.

Mahood, T. Berthoud, R. et al. *Ethnic Minorities in Britain*. London: Policy Studies Institute, 1997.

Malthus, T.R. (Ed. Winch, D.) *An Essay on the Principle of Population*. Cambridge: Cambridge University Press. 1992.

Mason, D. (Ed.) *From Where I Stand—Minority Experiences of Life in Britain*. London: Edward Arnold, 1986.

_____ *Race and Ethnicity in Modern Britain*. Oxford: Oxford University Press, 1996.

Mason, P. (Ed.) *India and Ceylon, Unity and Diversity*. Oxford: Oxford University Press, 1967.

Mauk, D. and Oakland, J. *American Civilisation*. London: Routledge, 1997.

Maccormick, N. *The Crown and the Thistle—The Nature of Nationhood*. Maclean, C. (Ed.) Edinburgh: Scottish Academic Press, 1979.

McGarry, J. and O'Leary, B. (Eds.) *The Politics of Ethnic Conflict Regulation.* London: Routledge, 1993.

_____ *Explaining Northern Ireland—Broken Images.* Oxford: Blackwell Publishers, 1995.

Mendus, S. and Edwards, D. (Eds.) *On Toleration.* Oxford: Clarendon Press, 1987.

Mendus, S. (Ed.) *Justifying Toleration—Conceptual and Historical Perspectives.* Cambridge: Cambridge University Press, 1988.

_____ *Toleration and the Limits of Liberalism.* London: Macmillan Education, 1989.

Mestrovic, S.G. *The Balkanisation of the West—The Confluence of Post Modernism And Post Communism.* London: Routledge, 1994.

Miles, R. *Racism.* London: Routledge. 1989.

Mill, J.S. *On Liberty.* London: Penguin Books, 1974.

Mill, J.S. and Bentham, J. *Utilitarianism and Other Essays.* (Ed.) Ryan, A. London: Penguin Books, 1987.

Mill, J.S. *Utilitarianism Incl. "On Liberty" And "Essay on Bentham."* Glasgow, Fontana Press, 1962.

Miller, D. *On Nationality.* Oxford: Clarendon Press, 1995.

Miller, S. Schmool, M. et al. *Social and Political Attitudes of British Jews: Some Key Findings of the J.P.R. Survey.* London: Institute for Jewish Policy Research, 1996.

Madood, T. et al. *Ethnic Minorities in Britain—Diversity and Disadvantage.* London: Policy Studies Institute, 1997.

Minogue, K. R. *Nationalism.* London: B.T. Batsford, 1967.

Mosley, N. *Beyond The Pale—Sir Oswald Mosley And Family. 1933–1980.* London: Secker and Warburg, 1983.

Mosley, O. *My Life—Sir Oswald Mosley.* London: Thomas Nelson, 1968.

Mounce, H. O. *The Two Pragmatisms—From Peirce to Rorty.* London: Routledge, 1997.

Nairn, T. *The Break Up of Britain—Crisis and Neo-Nationalism.* London: NLB, 1977.

Nairn, T. *After Britain.* London: Granta, 2000.

Neveu, C. *Ethnic Minorlties, Citizenship and Nationality—A Case Study for a Comparative Approach Between France and Britain.* Warwick: Centre for Research in Ethnic Relations, University of Warwick, 1989.

Newan, G. *The Rise of English Nationalism—A Cultural History. 1740–1830.* London: Weidenfeld and Nicolson, 1987.

Nicholson, F. and Twomey, P. (Eds.) *Refugee Rights and Realities.* Cambridge: Cambridge University Press, 1999.

Nisbet, R. *Twilight of Authority.* London: Heinemann, 1976.

Nussbaum, M.C. et al. *For Love of Country—Debating the Limits of Patriotism.* Boston, Mass: Beacon Press, 1996.

O'Day, A. (Ed.) *Reactions to Irish Nationalism.* London: Hambledon Press, 1987.

Owen, D. *Country of Birth—Settlement Patterns.* Warwick: University of Warwick, Centre for Research in Ethnic Relations, 1993.

Parekh, Lord. *The Future of Multi-Ethnic Britain.* London: Profile Books, 2000.

Parkes, J. *Anti-Semitism.* London: Valentine Mitchell, 1963.

Paul, E.F. Miller, F.D. et al. (Eds.) *Cultural Pluralism and Moral Knowledge.* Cambridge: Cambridge University Press, 1994.

Paxman, J. *The English—A Portrait of People.* London: Penguin Books, 1999.

Periwal, S. (Ed.) *Notions of Nationalism.* Budapest: Central European University Press, 1995.

Pfaff, W. *The Wrath of Nations—Civilisation and the Furies of Nationalism.* New York: Simon and Shuster, 1993.

Phillips, M. *The War of Words—The Political Correctness Debate*. Dunant, S. (Ed.) London: Virago Press, 1994.
Popper, K.R. *The Open Society and Its Enemies—Plato*. vol.1. (5th Edn.) London: Routledge, 1966.
_____ *The Poverty of Historicism*. London: Routledge, 1957.
Powell, E. *A Nation or No Nation*. London: Batsford. 1978.
Powell, E. *Reflections of a Statesman—The Writings and Speeches of Enoch Powell*. London: Bellew Publishing, 1991.
Putnam, H. *Pragmatism*. Oxford: Blackwell Publishers, 1995.
Rachels, J. (Ed.) *Moral Problems*. New York, Harper Collins, 1979.
Rawls, J. *Theory of Justice*. Oxford: Oxford University Press. 1973.
Raz, J. *The Morality of Freedom*. Oxford: Clarendon Press, 1986.
Rescher, N. *Pluralism—Against the Demand for Consensus*. Oxford: ClarendonPress, 1993.
Rex, J. *Race and Ethnicity*. Buckingham: Open University Press, 1992.
Richards, G. *Race, Racism and Psychology*. London: Routledge. 1997.
Rubio-Marin, R. *Immigration as a Democratic Challenge*. Cambridge: Cambridge University Press, 2000.
Runnymede Trust. *Multiethnic Britain—Facts and Trends*. London, 1994.
_____ *The Multiethnic Society Good Society—Vision And Reality*. London, March 1996.
_____ *The New Right—Image and Reality*. London, 1986.
_____ *Islamophobia—A Challenge to Us All*. London, 1997.
_____ *The Future of Multi-Ethnic Britain*. London: Profile Books, 2000.
Saggar, S. *Race and Politics in Britain*. Hemel Hempstead, Herts: Harvester Wheatsheaf, 1992.
Said, E. W. *Culture and Imperialism*. London: Chatto and Windus, 1993.
_____ *Orientalism*. London: Penguin Books, 1995.
Salins, P.D. *Assimilation American Style*. New York: Basic Books, 1997.
Scheffler, S. (Ed.) *Consequentialism and its Critics*. Oxford: Oxford University Press, 1988.
Schlesinger, A.M. *The Disuniting of America—Reflections on a Multicultural Society*. New York and London: W.W. Norton, 1992.
Schlesinger, R. *The Cycles of American History*. London: Andre Deutsch, 1987.
Shackletion, V. and Fletcher, C. *Individual Differences—Theories and Applications*. London: Routledge, 1984.
Schusterman, R. *Practicing Philosophy—Pragmatism and the Philosophical Life*. London: Routledge, 1997.
Schwartz, W.F. (Ed.) *Justice in Immigration*. Cambridge: Cambridge University Press, 1995.
Shaw, M.N. *International Law*. Cambridge: Cambridge University Press, 1997.
Shelley, M. and Winck, M. (Eds.) *Aspects of European Cultural Diversity*. London: Open University and Routledge, 1995.
Silber, L. and Little, A. *The Death of Yugoslavia*. London: B.B.C. Books and Penguin Books, 1995.
Skidelsky, R. *Oswald Mosley*. London: Macmillan, 1975.
Slote, M. *From Morality to Virtue*. Oxford: Oxford University Press, 1992.
Smith, A.D. *The Ethnic Revival*. Cambridge: Cambridge University Press, 1981.
_____ *National Identity*. London: Penguin Books, 1991.
Solomos, J. *Race and Racism in Britain*. (2nd Edn.) Basingstoke: Macmillan Press, 1993.

Spencer, I.R.G. *British Immigration Policy Since 1939—The Making of Multiracial Britain.* London: Routledge, 1997.

Szabo, I. *Cultural Rights.* Leiden: A.W.Sijthoff, 1974.

Tamir, Y. *Liberal Nationalism.* Princeton, NJ: Princeton University Press, 1993.

Taylor, C. *Multiculturalism—Examining the Politics of Recognition.* Princeton, NJ: Princeton University Press, 1994.

Terrill, R. *The Australians—In Search of an Identity.* London: Bantam Press, 1987.

Tinder, G. *Tolerance and Community.* Columbia, Missouri: University of Missouri Press, 1995.

Tizard, B. and Phoenix, A. *Black, White or Mixed Race—Race and Racism in the Lives of Young People of Mixed Parentage.* London: Routledge, 1993.

Trigg, R. *Ideas of Human Nature—An Historical Introduction.* Oxford: Blackwell Publishers, 1988.

Trusted, J. *Moral Principles and Social Values.* London: Routledge and Kegan Paul, 1987.

Tudjman, F. *Nationalism in Contemporary Europe.* New York: Columbia University Press, 1981.

Turner, B.S. *Equality.* Chichester, Sussex: Ellis Horwood, 1986.

Ullman, R. K. *Tolerance and the Intolerable.* London: George Allen and Unwin, 1961.

Viroli, M. *For Love of Country—An Essay on Patriotism and Nationalism.* Oxford: Clarendon Press, 1995.

Walzer, M. *On Toleration.* New Haven: Yale University Press, 1997.

Waters, M. *Globalisation.* London: Routledge, 1995.

Weiner, M. (Ed.) *Japan's Minorities—The Illusion of Homogeneity.* London: Routledge,1997.

Williams, R. *Culture and Society.* London: Hogarth Press, 1993.

Wistrich, R.S. *Anti-Semitism—The Longest Hatred.* London: Methuen, 1991.

Wolff, R.P. Moore, B. et al. *A Critique of Pure Tolerance.* Boston, Beacon Press, 1965.

Woolf, S. (Ed.) *Nationalism in Europe 1815 to the Present.* London: Routledge, 1996.

Yoshino, K. *Cultural Nationalism In Contemporary Japan.* London: Routledge. 1992.

Young, R.M. *Mental Space.* London: Process Press, 1994.

Journals and Periodicals

Appiah, K.A. "The Multiculturalist Understanding." (Book Review) *The New York Book Review.* 9 October 1997.

Appleyard, B. "The Battle of Wits (The Iq Debate)." *Sunday Times Magazine.* 13 June 1999.

Banton, M. "Modelling Ethnic and National Relations." *Ethnic and Racial Studies.* vol. 17. no. 1 Jan. 1994.

Barker, P. "Observations." *Times Literary Supplement.* 31 January 1997.

Berger, B. "Multiculturalism and the Modern University." *Partisan Review.* vol. LX. no. 4. 1993.

Berube, M. "Past Imperfect, Present Tense." (Book Review) *The Nation.* 12 May 1997.

Bhavnani, K.K. "Towards Multicultural Europe." *Feminist Review.* Autumn. no. 45. 1993.

Brah, A. "Re-Framing Europe—Engendered Racisms, Ethnicities and Nationalisms in Contemporary Western Europe." *Feminist Review.* Autumn. no. 45. 1993.

Brand, H.—"Inequality and Immigration." *Dissent*. Summer 1994.

Bromwich, D. "Culturalism, the Euthanasia of Liberalism." *Dissent*. Winter 1995.

Bullough, E. "Physical Distance." *British Journal of Psychiatry*. 1912.

Butterfield, H. "Toleration in Early Modern Times." *Fourth Conference of the International Society for the History of Ideas*. Venice, 1975.

Buruma, I. "Action Anglaise." (Book Review) *The New York Review*. 20 October 1994.

Carey, G. *Morrell Address on Toleration*. Nov. 22. York: University of York, 1991.

C.A.R.F. *Campaign Against Racism and Fascism*. Nos. 12—30. London, 1993/96.

Chowdhury, A. and Griffin, J. "U.N. Blues—50 Years of the United Nations." *The Guardian with Channel 4 TV*. 1994.

Connor, W. "Beyond Reason—The Nature of the Ethnonational Bond." *Ethnic and Racial Studies*. vol. 16. no. 3. July 1993.

Cornwell, J. "Burnt Offerings (The Vatican)." *Sunday Times Magazine*. 23 August 1998.

Cranston, M. "On Toleration and Tolerance—Locke and Voltaire Revisited." *Quadrant*. March 1991.

Curthoys, A. "Feminism, Citizenship and Identity." *Feminist Review*. no. 44. Summer 1993.

Eads, B. "Slavery's Shameful Return to Africa." *Reader's Digest*. vol. 148. April 1996.

Fish, S. "Boutique Multiculturalism, or Why Liberals are Incapable of Thinking about Hate Speech." *Critical Enquiry*. 23 Winter 1997.

Flew, A. "Three Concepts of Racism." *The Salisbury Review*. October 1986.

_____ "Three Concepts of Racism—Anti-Racism, Prejudice (and Worse)." *Encounter*. July/August. 1990

_____ "The Artificial Inflation of Natural Rights." *Vera Lex*. vol. 2. 1988.

_____ "The Menace of Islam." *The New Humanist*. vol. 11. no. 3. August 1995.

_____ "Education, Race and Revolution." *Centre For Policy Studies*. London, March 1984.

Fredrickson, G. M. "Demonising the American Dilemma." (Book Review) *The New York Review of Books*. 19 October 1995.

Gallagher, M. "How Many Nations are There in Ireland?" *Ethnic and Racial Studies*. vol. 18. no. 4. October 1995.

Glazer, N. "The Ethnic Factor." *Encounter*. July 1981.

_____ "The Universalisation of Ethnicity." *Encounter*. Vol. 44. February 1975.

Gray, J. "Free Thinkers." (Book Review) *Times Literary Supplement*. 24 January 1997.

Grosby, S. "The Verdict of History: The Inexpungeable Tie of Primordality." *Ethnic and Racial Studies*. vol. 17. No. 1. January 1994.

Gutmann, A. "The Challenge of Multiculturalism in Political Ethics." *Philosophy and Public Affairs*. vol. 22. no. 3. Summer 1993.

Hacker, A. "Good-Bye to Affirmative Action." (Book Review) *The New York Review*. 11 July 1996.

Halliday, F. "A New World Myth." (Book Review) *New Statesman*. 4 April 1997.

Hawkey, I. "An Ambassador for Islam." *Cambridge Alumni Magazine*. Easter Term, 1995.

Hoffman, S. "Dreams of a Just World." (Book Review) *The New York Review of Books*. 2 November 1995.

Holmes, S. "In Search of New Enemies." (Book Review) *London Review of Books*. 24 April 1997.

Honeyford, R. "Multiethnic Intolerance." *The Salisbury Review*. Summer 1983.
Hoppe, H. H. "Free Immigration or Forced Integration." *The Salisbury Review*. June 1995.
Huygen, M. "The Policy Challenge of Ethnic Diversity. Immigrant Politics in France and Switzerland." (Book Review). *New York Times Book Review*.October 1994.
Ignatieff, M. "Strange Attachments." (Book Reviews) *The New Republic*. 29 March 1993.
Jacques, M. "Tigers and Chameleons." *New Statesman*. 14 June, 1996.
Judt, T. "The New Old Nationalism." (Book Reviews) *The New York Review of Books*. vol. XLI. no. 10. 26 May 1994.
_____ "Europe: The Grand Illusion." *The New York Review*. 11 July 1996.
Kasfir, N. "Explaining Ethnic Political Participation." *World Politics*. vol. 31. October/July, 1978/79.
Kennedy, P. "Forecast: Global Gales Ahead." *New Statesman*. 31 May 1996.
King, C. "On Nationality." (Book Review). *Times Literary Supplement*. 10 May 1976.
Kymlicka, W. "Misunderstanding Nationalism." (Book Review) *Dissent*. Winter 1995.
Laczko, L.S. "Canada's Pluralism in Comparative Perspective." *Ethnic and Racial Studies*. vol. 17. no. 1. 1994.
Lewthwaite, G and Kane, G. "Slavery Sudan." *Sunday Times Magazine*. 23 June 1996.
Lustick, I. "Stability in Deeply Divided Societies—Consociationalism Versus Control." *World Politics*. vol. 31. October/July, 1978/79.
Luttwak, E.N. "Great Powerless Days." (Book Review) *Times Literary Supplement*. 16 June 1995.
Malik, K. "Party Colours." *New Statesman and Society*. 14 July 1995.
_____ "No Platform, or No Democracy?" *New Statesman*. 6 September 1996.
McGarry, J. and O'Leary, B. (Eds.) "Five Fallacies: Northern Ireland and the Liabilities of Liberalism." *Ethnic and Racial Studies*. vol. 18. no. 4   October 1995.
McNeill, W.H. "Decline of the West." Book Review of *The Clash of Civilizations and the Remaking of World Order*. Huntington, S.P. In *New York Review*. 9 January 1997.
Melvern, L. et al. "The Ultimate Crime—Who Betrayed the U.N. and Why?" *Sunday Times Magazine* 26 November 1995.
Melzer, A. M. "Tolerance 101." *The New Republic*. 1 July 1991.
Menand, L. "The Culture Wars." (Book Review) *The New York Review*. 6 October 1994.
Miller, J. "Europe's Badlands (Albania)." *Sunday Times Magazine*. 25 July 1999.
Mishan, E. J. "What Future for a Multiracial Britain." Pts 1 and 2. *The Salisbury Review*. June and September, 1988.
Newey, G. "Why Toleration Spells Trouble." (Book Review) *Times Literary Supplement*. 30 August 1996.
O'Duffy, B. "Violence in Northern Ireland 1969–1994: Sectarian or Ethno-National?" *Ethnic and Racial Studies*. vol. 18. no. 4. October 1995.
O'Sullivan, J. "Reaching the Right that Bill (Clinton) Can't." *New Statesman*. 9 August 1996.
Orwell, G. "The Freedom of the Press." *New Statesman* and Society. 18 August 1995.
Palmer, A. "Does White Mean Right?" *The Spectator*. 18 February 1995.
Panday, K. "Colour Bar." *B.M.A. News Review*. December 1993.
Parekh, B. "Superior People—The Narrowness of Liberalism from Mill to Rawls." *Times Literary Supplement*. 25 February 1994. See also "Letters." *Times Literary Supplement*. 11/25 March 1994.

Pease, D.E. "Regulating Multi-Adhoccerists—Fish('s) Rules." *Critical Enquiry.* no. 23. Winter 1997.

Posner, R.A. "The Skin Trade." (Book Review) *The New Republic.* 13 October 1997.

Raz, J. "Multiculturalism—A Liberal Perspective." *Dissent.* Winter 1994.

Rex, J.—"The Political Sociology of a Multicultural Society." *European Journal of Inter-Cultural Studies.* vol. 2. no. 1. 1991.

Rorty, R. "Towards a Liberal Utopia." *Times Literary Supplement.* 24 June 1994.

_____ "A Leg-Up for Oliver North." (Book Review). *London Review of Books.* 20 October 1994.

Ryan, A. "It Takes All Kinds." (Book Reviews*) The New York Review.* 5 November 1995.

Scheffler, S. "Family and Friends First?" (Book Review) *Times Literary Supplement.* 27 December 1996.

Schudson, M. "Culture and the Integration of National Societies." *International Social Science Journal.* 1994.

Scott-Clark, C. and Levy, A. "Little White Lies (Australian Aborigine Genocide)." *Sunday Times Magazine.* 31 October 1997.

Searle, J. "The Storm Over the University." *The New York Review.* 6 December 1990.

Searle, J. R. "Is There a Crisis in American Higher Education?" (Book Reviews) *Partisan Review.* Vol. LX. no. 4. 1993.

Sebastian, T. "United Nations—Rwanda." *Sunday Times Magazine.* 26 November 1995.

_____ "Why Justice Won't Be Done—Bosnia War Crimes." *Sunday Times Magazine.* 25 February 1996.

Sidorsky, D. "Multiculturalism and the University." *Partisan Review.* vol. LX. no. 4. 1993.

Silvester, C. "Britain's Least Wanted Man—Al Massari." *Sunday Times Magazine.* 10 March 1996.

Singh, A. I. "Is Ethnicity Enough?" (Book Reviews) *Times Literary Supplement.* 17 March 1995.

Skillen, A. "Racism: Flew's Three Concepts of Racism." (Discussion) *Journal of Applied Philosophy.* vol. 10. no. 1. 1993.

Smith, J.D. "Suburban Guerilla?" (In the Yemen) *Sunday Times Magazine.* 21 May 2000.

Smyth, G. "On Mohammed's Side." *New Statesman.* 21 June 1996.

Vines, G. "The Race Gallery: The Return of Racial Science." (Book Review) *New Statesman and Society.* 29 September 1995.

Weinstein, B. "Language Strategists: Redefining Political Frontiers On The Basis Of Linguistic Choices." *World Politics.* vol. 31. October/July 1978/79.

Wieseltier, L. "The Trouble with Multiculturalism." (Book Review) *The New York Times Book Review.* 1994

Walzer, M. "The New Tribalism." *Dissent.* vol. 39. Spring 1992.

_____ "Multiculturalism and Individualism." *Dissent.* Spring 1994.

_____ "Are There Limits to Liberalism?" (Book Review) *The New York Review of Books.* 19 October 1995.

Williams, J. A., Nunn, C. Z. et al. "Origins of Tolerance: Findings from a Replication of Stouffer's Communism, Conformity and Civil Liberties." *Social Forces.* vol. 55 (2). December 1976. Crockett, H. J. Comments on "Origins of Tolerance." Williams, J. A., Nunn, C. Z., et al. "Origins of Tolerance." Reply to Crockett.

Williams, P. "The Other National Front—Nation of Islam." *Times Magazine.* 17 October 1998.

Yoshino, K. *Cultural Nationalism in Contemporary Japan.* London: Routledge, 1992.

Official Documents

Central Statistical Office. *Social Trends 22 – 30*. London: Stationery Office, 1992—2000.

Commonwealth Secretariat. *The Commonwealth Year Book* . London: Stationery Office.

Field, S. *The Attitudes of Ethnic Minorities*. London: Stationery Office, 1984.

Peach, C. (Ed.) *Ethnicity in the 1991 Census*. vol. 2. London: Stationery Office, 1996.

Scarman, Lord. *The Brixton Disorders 10–12 April 1981*. London: Stationary Office, 1981.

Swann, Lord. *Education for All—The Report of the Committee of Inquiry into the Education of Children from Ethnic Minority Groups*. London: Stationery Office, 1985.

Stationery Office. *British Nationality Act*. London, 1948.

_____ *Commonwealth Immigrants Act*. London, 1962.

_____ *Commonwealth Immigrants Act*. London, 1968.

_____ *Immigration Appeals Act*. London, 1969.

_____ *Immigration Act*. London, 1971.

_____ *Race Relations Act*. London, 1976.

_____ *Supreme Court Act*. London, 1981.

_____ *British Nationality Act*. London, 1981.

_____ *British Nationality (Hong Kong) Act*. London, 1985.

_____ *Immigration (Carriers Liabilty) Act*. London, 1987.

_____ *Immigration Act*. London, 1988.

_____ *Education Reform Act*. London. 1988.

_____ *Britain 1994—An Official Handbook*. London, 1993.

_____ *Asylum and Immigration Appeals Act*. London, 1993.

_____ *Asylum and Immigration Act*. London, 1996.

_____ *The Special Immigration Appeals Commission Act*. London, 1997.

_____ *Human Rights Act*. London, 1998.

_____ *Criminal Justice (Terrorism And Conspiracy) Act*. London, 1998.

_____ *Immigration and Asylum Act*. London, 1999.

_____ *Inquiry into Matters Arising from the Death of Stephen Lawrence. The Stephen Lawrence Inquiry: Report of an Inquiry by Sir William Macpherson of Cluny*. London, 1999.

_____ *Terrorism Act*. London, 2000.

_____ *The Race Relations (Amendment) Act*. London, 2000.

Television and Radio Programmes

BBC 2. *Germany—Blood and Belonging*. 25 November 1993.

BBC 2. *Ukraine—Blood and Belonging*. 2 December 1993.

BBC 2. *Quebec—Blood and Belonging*. 9 December 1993.

BBC 2. *Ulster—Blood and Belonging*. 16 December 1993.

Channel 4. *Mixed Marriages—Audrey and Mark's Story*. 1994.

BBC 1. *Czech Racism—What Magdelena Said*. 2 January 1994.

BBC 1. *Racism In Britain. (Reportage)*. 12 January 1994.

BBC Radio 4. *U.S. Civil Rights (File On 4)*. 25 January 1994.

BBC 2. *Racism or Realism—Immigration (Timewatch)*. 5 April 1994.

BBC 2 . *Violent and Vicious—California (Black Bag Special)*. 14 April 1994.

BBC 2. *Stars, Tsars, Swastikas (Black Bag Special)*. 21 April 1994.

BBC 2. *Social Unrest in California (Assignment)*. 3 May 1994.

BBC Radio 4. *The Fate of Nations (Analysis)*. 5 May 1994.

BBC 1. *Hate Crime (Heart of The Matter)*. 19 June 1994.

BBC 2. *Scottish Nationalism*. July 1994.

BBC 2. *Moslem Cricket Club—In a League of their Own*. 4 July 1994.

Channel 4. *Jazzi B—Disillusioned Black Britons (Frontline)*. 6 July 1994.

BBC 2. *Questions of National Identity (Open University)*. 13 July 1994.

BBC 2. *Heretic—Hans Eysenck (Reputations)*. 26 July 1994.

BBC 2. *Young Turks in Germany*. 14 August 1994.

BBC 2. *Outsiders In (Open University)*. 21 August 1994.

BBC 2. *Albert Schweitzer—Darkness and Light (Reputations)*. 25 September 1994.

BBC 1. *The Road to Hare Krishna—The Dispute Over the Hindu Temple*. 2 October 1994.

BBC Radio 4. *Refugees and the Asylum Bill (File On 4)*. 18 October 1994.

BBC 2. *Border Disputes—Eastern Europe*. 5 November 1994.

BBC 2. *Fatwas—Publish and Be Damned (Everyman)*. 11 December 1994.

BBC 1. *Petrona's Honour—Black Lord Mayor of Liverpool (Everyman)*. 29 January 1995.

ITV. *Refugees (Network First)*. 14 February 1995.

Channel 4. *Alien Nations*. 2/9/16/23 March 1995.

BBC 2. *Japanese Americans (Open University)*. 4 March 1995.

BBC 2. *East Meets West (Open University)*. 17 March 1995.

BBC 2. *Immigration, Prejudice, Ethnicity (Open University)*. 1 April 1995.

BBC 2. *Ruling Passions—Sex, Race and Empire*. 27 March/3/10 April 1995.

BBC 2. *Britain's Survival as a Nation*. 23 April 1995.

BBC 2. *Reverse Racism—Taking Liberties*. 30 May 1995.

BBC 2. *Race and Education (Open University)*. 3 June 1995.

BBC Radio 4. *The Limits of Globalisation (Analysis)*. 25 June 1995.

BBC 2. *A Migrant's Heart (Open University)*. 1 July 1995.

BBC 2. *Reparations to Africa (The Radical Option)*. 19 July 1995.

BBC 2. *Islamic Groups in Britain (Public Eye)*. 25 July 1995.

Channel 4. *Bradford Riots (The Black Bag)*. 1995.

Channel 4 . *A Black Educational Psychologist (Frontline)*. 13 September 1995.

Channel 4. *Images of Muslims*. 20 September 1995.

BBC 2. *Knin Croatia—Ethnic Cleansing (Assignment)*. 21 October 1995.

Channel 4. *Mecca On Thames (Witness)*. 5 November 1995.

BBC 2. *Islamic Fundamentalism (Assignment)*. 11 November 1995.

BBC 2. *Divided We Stand—Is America Still Divided By Race?* 5 December 1995.

BBC 2. *Out of the Melting Pot*. 18 February /30 September 1995/6.

BBC 1. *Al-Massaria (Panorama)*. 1 April 1996.

BBC 2. *Racist Incidents (Modern Times)*. 1 May 1996.

BBC 2. *The End of the Western World*. 12/19 May 1996.

BBC Radio 4. *Diverging Dominions—Australia*. 22 May 1996.

BBC Radio 4. *Diverging Dominions—Canada*. 5 June 1996.

BBC 1. *Omnibus*. July 7 1997.

BBC 2. *National Identity (Arena)*. 14 July 1996.

BBC 2. *Black Britain*. 6 August 1996

Channel 4. *Alien Nations*. 2/9/16/23 March 1997.

BBC 2. *Planet Islam*. 3/10/17 August 1997.

Channel 4. *Illegal Immigrants*. 30 September/07 October 1997.

BBC 2. *The African Trade (Timewatch)*. 25 November 1997.
BBC 2. *Ugandan Asians (Timewatch)*. 9 December 1997.
Channel 4. *The Trouble with Omar Sheik (Witness)*. 8 April 1998.
Channel 4. *England My England*. 26 April 1998.
Channel 4. *In Search Of Palestine*. 17 May 1998.
BBC 2. *Windrush—Intolerance*. 6 June 1998.
_____ *Windrush—A New Generation*. 13 June 1998.
_____ *Windrush—A British Story*. 20 June 1998.
BBC 2. *Nation Of Islam (Everyman)*. 7 July 1998.
Channel 4. *The Reckoning—War Crimes in Bosnia*. 30 July 1998.
BBC 2. *The American Dream*. 9 August 1998.
BBC 2. *Love in Black and White*. 30 August 1998.
BBC 2. *The Nazis—A Warning from History*. 20 September 1998.
BBC 2. *Black Britain*. 23 September 1998.
Channel 4. *Hoping for a Miracle*. 17 January 1999.
BBC 2. *Against the War (Counter-Blast)*. 4 May 1999.
BBC 2. *Forced Marriages (Newsnight)*. 12 July 1999.
BBC 2. *78 Days—An Audit of War—Kosovo*. 17 October 2000.
BBC 2. *Playing the Race Card*. 24/31 October/7November 1999.
BBC 2. *Under Fire (Correspondent)*. December 1999.
Channel 4. *White Tribe*. 13/20/27 January 2000.
ITV. *A Kosovo Journey*. 16 January 2000.
BBC 1. *The Koran and the Kalashnikov*. 23 January 2000.
Channel 4. *Gypsies, Tramps and Thieves*. 30 January 2000.
BBC 2. *The Day Britain Died*. 31 January /1/2 February 2000.
BBC 1. *Panorama*. 7 February 2000.
Channel 4. *Girl Friends from Pristina*. 6 February 2000.
Channel 4. *The Colour of Love*. 17 February 2000.
BBC 2. *Future War*. 25 March /1 April 2000.
ITV. *Beware—Pickpockets About*. 8 May 2000.
BBC 1. *Brits Abroad—South Africa*. 9 May 2000.
BBC 2. *Black Britain Special—Bernie Grant*. 31 May 2000.
BBC 2. *Correspondent Europe*. 3 June 2000.
BBC 2. *Seoul Mates*. 17 June 2000.
Channel 4. *The Cricket Test—Darcus Howe*. 31 July/1/2 August 2000.
Channel 4. *Hitler's Search for the Holy Grail*. 5 October 2000.
Channel 4. *The Hunger Business*. 11/12 November 2000.
Channel 4. *The Difference*. 19/26 November/3 December 2000.
BBC 2. *R U E U ?—A Trip Around the European Union*. 10 December 2000.
BBC 2. *UK Confidential*. 1 January 2001.
Channel 4. *Kenyon Confronts—Bogus Marriages*. 26 February 2001.
BBC 2. *Hate Crime*. 15 March 2001.
BBC 1. *Correspondent*. 1 April 2001.
BBC 2. *Correspondent—Desperately Seeking Asylum*. 22 April 2001.
Channel 4. *Politics Isn't Working: Not Black on White*. 20 May 2001.
BBC 2 *Correspondent – Allies or Lies?* 24 June 2001.

Subject Index

acculturation, 50
Act of Toleration, 287
adoption, 35
advocacy, 330
affirmative action, 247
AFL-CIO (American Federation of
  Labor-Congress of Industrial
  Organisations), 86
Africa, 88–89, 141
Age of Reason, 319
Aliens Bill of 1905, 185
American Latino National Political
  Survey, 192
Americanisation, 87
Amsterdam Treaty, 184
Anglican Church, 293; attendance, 298;
  cultural divide, 299; internal conflicts,
  300; problems faced by, 298
Anglican Church, 41–42
anti-racism, four main perversions of, 255
anti-semitism, 122–123
assimilation, 257; complete cultural, 258;
  forced, 261; partial, 258; pattern of,
  260; and mixed marriages, 260; and
  religious groups, 265; social aspect
  of, 258
assimilation, 33, 50, 59, 357; cultural,
  88; voluntary, 72
Asylum Aid Organisation, 202
Asylum and Immigration Act, 1999, 209;
  proposals, 210
Asylum and Immigration Appeals Act of
  1993, 199
asylum seekers, 201–203, 209, 364–365;
  cost of, 204; educating, 213; and
  hijackers, 211; number of, 205;
  official figures, 211–212

attitude, 305
Australia, 75–76

Belgium, 77–78
belief, closed, 308
Blair, Tony, 5, 21, 104
Bosnia, 141
boundaries, national, 141
British Agencies of Fostering and
  Adoption, 35
British army, 132; recruitment by, 131–
  132
British Commonwealth, 149
British Union of Fascists (BUF), 122

camaraderie, 100
Canada, 76; ethno-national issues, 76
capitalism, 89
Catholicism, 302
censorship, 273, 276, 330
Children's Act, 1990, 35
Christianity, 41
Church of England (C-E), 283, 297
citizenship, 85
civil rights movements, 313
claim rights, See human rights
colonialism, 157; and guilt, 241
Committee of Inquiry, 55
Commonwealth, 85–86, 187
Commonwealth Immigration Act, 1962,
  198
Communism, collapse of, 136
communitarianism, 16
conservatism, moral, 18
consociational models, 345
cosmopolitan, 48, 146, 160; One World,
  161

Author Index